# CHINESE 今日汉语 FOR TODAY

# CHINESE

今日汉语

# FOR TODAY

## [BOOK 1]

Compiled and written by
Huang Zhengcheng, Ding Yongshou,
Liu Lanyun, Qiu Yanqing, Li Jiyu,
Lu Jianji, Hu Huainian and Xiong Wenhua
of The Beijing Languages Institute

THE COMMERCIAL PRESS

今日汉语（一）
**Chinese for Today — 1**

Compiled and written by
Huang Zhengcheng, Ding Yongshou, Liu Lanyun, Qiu Yanqing, Li Jiyu, Lu Jianji, Hu Huainian and Xiong Wenhua
of The Beijing Languages Institute

Publisher
Chan Man Hung
THE COMMERCIAL PRESS (HONG KONG) LTD.
Kiu Ying Bldg., 2D Finnie Street, Quarry Bay, Hong Kong.

Printer
C & C OFFSET PRINTING CO., LTD.
C & C Bldg., 36 Ting Lai Road, Tai Po, N.T., Hong Kong.

First Edition 1986
7th Printing March 1996

ISBN 962 07 4002 5
Printed in Hong Kong

# PREFACE

## I

*CHINESE FOR TODAY* is a series in two stages conceived and designed for people outside China who want to learn modern Chinese. It can be used as a textbook for regular classroom teaching, as well as for self-teaching purposes.

The textbook for Stage One contains 35 lessons preceded by a concise introduction to speech sounds and tones of modern Chinese. The texts of these lessons are all lively and true-to-life dialogues. They deal with situations a foreigner travelling or living in China is likely to find him or herself in. The major aim of this stage is to teach basic sentence patterns and ways of expression in modern spoken Chinese.

In the 35 lessons of the second stage, spoken and written Chinese are given equal attention, and a broader spectrum of life in modern Chinese society is presented through dialogues and stories. More complex sentence patterns and different ways of expression in a given situation are introduced and drilled, while what has been taught in the first stage is systematically revised. An integral part of each lesson in this stage is a Word Study section which illustrates, compares and summarizes the most frequently used expressions and phrases through examples and explanation.

In Stage One each text ranges from one to three hundred characters of which about 30 are new words. In Stage Two each text contains four to six hundred characters with some 40 of them being new words.

The learner, upon finishing the two stages, can expect to be able to recognize two thousand five hundred characters, at least half of which he should be able to write. These characters should be adequate for him or her to understand non-technical radio broadcasts, to carry on conversations on a variety of topics and to read newspapers and non-technical journals.

In compiling this series, conscious efforts were made to incorporate the finer features of other Chinese textbooks. The underlying objective of this series is to enable the learner to acquire a solid command of the Chinese language in aural comprehension, speaking, reading, and writing. This is achieved, among other ways, through careful grading of material, giving particular attention to what presents special difficulty to the foreign learner, and systematic presentation of ways of expression peculiar to the Chinese language. For the convenience of average users of this textbook linguistic terminology is cut down to the minimum.

To acquire facility in a language the learner needs to be familiar with the cultural and historical background of the nation where the language is spoken. This being the case, concise, clear annotations are provided where necessary. These will help the learner to understand what the Chinese would say in a given situation, how he or she would put it and why. The language taught in the series is consistantly standard modern Chinese, and gives due emphases to common set phrases, sayings and idioms.

To be used with Stage One is the companion book *EXERCISES IN READING AND WRITING CHINESE CHARACTERS*, in which exercises, notes, as well as interesting anecdotes serve to aid the user in recognizing, reading and writing characters. To meet the needs of some users, in the word lists, underneath all the simplified characters their originals in complex strokes are given. There is also a companion *READER* to go with the second volume. It is to help the learner revise what he or she has learned and obtain a broader and deeper understanding of Chinese history and culture.

In *CHINESE FOR TODAY* ample exercises of various types have been devised for those language points which the learner is expected to master. Answers to exercises marked by the sign " * " can be found at the end of the book. After every five lessons there is a special section for revision.

As a supplement, recordings of speech sounds and tones and the texts in standard spoken Chinese are available on cassette tapes.

## II

## HOW TO USE *CHINESE FOR TODAY*

Both the person wishing to learn Chinese on his own and the instructor teaching a course will find this series should serve their purposes admirably. Furthermore, the series is designed so that it may be used by learners with different specific goals. For example, the learner whose sole objective is mastery of basic spoken Chinese need only use the main textbooks of Stages One and Two, and the student equally interested in oral and written forms may use all materials simultaneously.

In using this series, the importance of practice should be emphasized. This is particularly so when a Chinese environment is lacking. The lessons are written and arranged in such a way as to facilitate the learner to do an ample amount of exercises.

The following are some hints the user of this textbook may find useful.

1 **Phonetics.** More time and effort should be given to the comparatively few difficult sounds and tones instead of directing equal attention to everything. The learner will find it rewarding to listen to the recordings and to compare his or her own voice with that on the tape and thus to correct errors in pronunciation and intonation. It is most stimulating to combine phonetic exercises with the study of the

texts.

2 **Dialogue/text and new words lists.** The student is encouraged to listen to the recordings first all the way through, then practise repeatedly reading aloud with the recordings afterwards. Difficult words and language points are numbered for quick reference. Extensive oral exercises on the new words and the text may be done in class to enable the learner to understand properly and to use correctly what is being taught in different situations.

3 **Study points.** The learner should bear in mind that not all that is annotated here is of the same importance. Some of the notes are just to provide background information.Those points which have exercises to go with them are the ones on which the student should concentrate.

4 **Exercises.** The exercises are designed to help the student to use in real situations the language they have just learnt. The phonetic exercises, oral exercises and listening exercises can be used for drills in class, while written exercises are recommended to be assigned as homework.

5 *EXERCISES IN READING AND WRITING CHINESE CHARACTERS* is a collection of exercises intended to improve the learner's ability to recognize, to read and to write characters, as well as to improve his or her reading comprehension. For those who are interested in Chinese characters, this supplement should prove invaluable. It is divided into two parts, one for reading and one for writing. As the two parts are independent, the learner who wishes to learn both reading and writing should use them simultaneously.

This textbook was written by Huang Zhengcheng(黄政澄), Ding Yongshou(丁永寿), Liu Lanyun (刘岚云), Qiu Yanqing(邱衍庆), Li Jiyu(李继禹) and Lu Jianji(鲁健骥).English translation is by Hu Huainian(胡怀年).Xiong Wen hua (熊文华) also took part in the translation of Book One. The compilers and translators are all teachers at the Beijing Languages Institute.

In the course of compiling this series, we have received generous assistance from Lo Chihong of the Commercial Press, Ltd. in Hong Kong and Linda Jaivin of Oxford University Press. For this we wish to express our appreciation and gratitude.

*The authors*

## FORMAT OF STAGE ONE OF *CHINESE FOR TODAY*

1 There are 35 lessons in this volume, with a section for revision between every five lessons. Preceding the lessons is an introduction to phonetics and coming after the lessons are a general word list in the Chinese alphabetic order and answers to the

exercises. Each lesson is composed of the following parts: the new words, the text, the notes, the supplementary words and the exercises.

2 *Pinyin* (Romanized spelling) is provided under each line of the text, which is translated into English on the right. Points in the text which are annotated are marked by small Arabic numerals.

3 New words, which are arranged in the order of their appearance in the text, are accompanied by their Romanized Chinese spellings (*pinyin*), English translation and indication of parts of speech. The student can also refer to the Word List in the appendix where the characters are listed in alphabetical order by *pinyin* spelling. English translations of the new words, as a rule, are of the same parts of speech as the Chinese originals. The relatively few words that don't correspond to standard English parts of speech are properly explained. Proper names are rendered into Romanized Chinese spellings. Accepted English spellings are also given for words such as Běijīng (Peking), and Guǎngzhōu (Canton). New words in the exercises are listed under Supplementary Words.

4 Some of the examples in the notes are taken from the text. Where necessary, extra examples have been added. These additional examples are accompanied by both Romanized Chinese spellings and English translations.

5 There are four types of exercises in this book. They are: phonetic exercises, oral exercises, written exercises and listening exercises.

6 All the simplified characters in this series follow the *LIST OF SIMPLIFIED CHARACTERS* published in January, 1956 by the State Council of the People's Republic of China. For the convenience of overseas learners, characters in complex strokes are provided underneath their simplified versions in the word lists of the *EXERCISES IN READING AND WRITING CHINESE CHARACTERS.*

# 目　　录

# PHONETICS

Traditionally a Chinese syllable is divided into two parts: the initial (*sheng*), which is the beginning consonant, and the final (*yun*). The syllable can be pronounced in different contours which are known as tones, e.g. in *sān* (三), *s* is the initial and *an* the final, and the syllable is in the high-level tone.

The initial is made up of only one consonant and the final might be made up of one, two or three vowels, or a combination of one or two vowels and a consonant (-n or -ng).

The following is a brief description of the initials (*sheng*), finals (*yun*) and tones.

## INITIALS

The 23 initials (*sheng*) in standard modern spoken Chinese are shown in the table below:

| Voiceless | | | | | Voiced | | | |
|---|---|---|---|---|---|---|---|---|
| unaspirated | aspirated | unaspirated | aspirated | | | | | |
| b | p | | | | | m | | w |
| | | | | f | | | | |
| | | z | c | s | | | | |
| d | t | | | | | n | l | |
| | | zh | ch | sh | r | | | |
| | | j | q | x | | | | y |
| g | k | | | h | | | | |

*b* is similar to "b" in the English word "bore" but is voiceless.

*p* is similar to "p" in "port" in English, but is invariably produced with a strong puff of air.

*m* is equivalent to "m" in "more".

*f* is equivalent to "f" in "four".

*d* is similar to "d" in "dirt" but is voiceless. It is pronounced with the tip of the tongue more to the front of the mouth than the "d" in English.

*t* is similar to "t" in the English word "term". It is produced with a stronger puff of air and with the tip of the tongue more to the front of the mouth than the "t" in English.

*n* is equivalent to "n" in "nurse" in English.

*l* is equivalent to "l" in "learn" in English.

*z* is similar to the cluster "ds" in "cards" in English but is voiceless and is produced with the tip of the tongue more to the front of the mouth.

*c* is the aspirated counterpart of *z*. It is similar to the cluster "ts" in "its" in English but is pronounced with a stronger puff of air and with the tip of the tongue more to the front of the mouth.

*s* is similar to "s" in the English word "air", but in pronouncing it, the tip of the tongue is more to the front of the mouth.

*zh* is a voiceless consonant produced with the tip of the tongue pressed against the hard palate and with the air puffed out from between the tongue and the hard palate. It is similar to the "dge" in the English word "judge", but is pronounced with the tip of the tongue drawn more to the back of the mouth.

*ch* is the aspirated counterpart of *zh*. In pronouncing it, the tip of the tongue is drawn more to the back of the mouth than when pronouncing "ch" in "church" in English.

*sh* is produced with the tip of the tongue raised toward the hard palate and air is squeezed out from the channel thus made. To pronounce it, the tip of the tongue is drawn more to the back of the mouth than when pronouncing "sh" of "shirt" in English.

*r* is the voiced counterpart of *sh*. It is different from "r" of "run" in English in that, to pronounce it, the tip of the tongue is drawn more to the back and the lips are not pursed.

*j* is produced by placing the tip of the tongue against the back of the lower teeth and pressing the blade against the hard palate. It is similar to the "d" and "y" combination in "and yet" in English, but is voiceless. When pronouncing it, the tip of the tongue is much lower than when pronouncing "j" of the English word "jeep".

*q* is the aspirated counterpart of *j*. It is similar to the "t" and "y" combination in "don't you", but is produced with a stronger puff of air. The tip of the tongue is much lower than when pronouncing "ch" in the English word "cheese".

*x* is produced by placing the tip of the tongue against the lower teeth and raising the blade toward the hard palate. It is similar to the "s" and "y" combination of "bless you" in English. The tip of the tongue is much lower than when pronouncing "sh" of the English "she".

*g* is similar to the English consonant "g" in "girl" but is voiceless.

*k* is similar to "k" in the English word "kerf", but is produced with a stronger aspiration.

*h* is produced by raising the back of the tongue toward the soft palate and releasing the air through the channel thus made. It is similar to the "ch" in the German word "ach", but is different from the "h" of English "hot" in that the former (Chinese *h*) is a velar fricative while the latter a glottal fricative.

*y* is similar to the English "y" of "yes", but it can be produced with slight friction.

*w* is similar to the English "w" in "woo", but it can be produced with slight friction.

In learning the Chinese initials, attention must be paid to the difference between the aspirated and unaspirated initials which differentiate words, e.g.

| Aspirated | Unaspirated |
|---|---|
| qīkān 期刊 (periodical) | jīgān 鸡肝 (chicken liver) |
| chū tǔ 出土 (unearthed) | zhūdǔ 猪肚 (pork tripe) |

When pronouncing the aspirated initials, the learner may hold a piece of thin paper close to the mouth. The paper would vibrate as the result of aspiration when the sound is properly pronounced.

If he has difficulty in producing *j, q, x,* the learner may press the tip of tongue with his finger to ensure that it doesn't move away from the back of the lower teeth.

To get the correct pronunciation of *zh, ch, sh, r,* the learner may push the tip of the tongue backward with his finger.

As a rule, we don't pronounce any initial alone. There must be a final after it, so that it sounds clear. Thus, for citation purpose,

*b, p, m, f* are followed by *o: bo, po, mo, fo.*

*d, t, n, l, g, k, h* are followed by *e: de, te, ne, le, ge, ke, he.*

*z, c, s* are followed by $i^2$: *zi, ci, si.*

*zh, ch, sh, r* are followed by $i^3$: *zhi, chi, shi, ri.*

*j, q, x, y* are followed by $i^1$: *ji, qi, xi* and *yi.*

*w* is followed by *u: wu.*

## FINALS

There are 29 finals in standard modern spoken Chinese:

| Simple finals | | | | | | | | | | | Diphthong and triphthong finals | | | | Finals ending with -n or -ng | | | | | | | |
|---|---|---|---|---|---|---|---|---|---|---|---|---|---|---|---|---|---|---|---|---|---|---|
| | | | | | a | | | | | | *a*i | | *a*o | | an | | | | | | | |
| | | | | | | | | | | | | | | | | | | | ang | | | |
| | | | | | | o | | | | | | | | *o*u | | | | | | | | |
| | | | | | | | | | | | | | | | | | | | | | | ong |
| | | | | | | | e$^1$ | | | | | | | | | | | | | | | |
| | | | | | | | | e$^2$ | er | | | | | | | | en | | | eng | | |
| | | | | | | | | | | e$^3$ | | | | | | | | | | | | |
| | | | | | | | | | | | | *e*i | | | | | | | | | | |
| i$^1$ | | | | | i*a* | | | | | i*e* | | | i*a*o | i*u* | | i*a*n | | in | i*a*ng | | ing | iong |
| | i$^2$ | | | | | | | | | | | | | | | | | | | | | |
| | | i$^3$ | | | | | | | | | | | | | | | | | | | | |
| | | | u | | u*a* | u*o* | | | | | u*a*i | u*i* | | | u*a*n | | un | | u*a*ng | | | |
| | | | | ü | | | | | | ü*e* | | | | | | ü*a*n | | ün | | | | |

In the Table, finals on the same line have the same beginning vowel and the italicized vowels of those in the same column, are roughly of the same value. The italicized vowel in a final represents one pronounced louder than the rest.

*a* is equivalent to the "a" in the English word "farm" as pronounced by Americans.

*ai* is roughly of the same value as "ai" in "aisle" in English, but the beginning *a* is pronounced shorter than that of English.

*ao* is roughly of the same value as "ou" in "out" in English, but the beginning *a* is shorter than the "o" (in "out") in pronunciation.

*an* is *a* with -n ending.

*ang* is equivalent to "a (as in "father")+ng" in English, or to "ang" in German.

*o* is similar to "or" in English in pronunciation. It is spelled only with *b, p, m, f, y, w*.

*ou* is equivalent to "oa" in "boat" in American English, but *o* is shorter than its counterpart in English.

*ong* is equivalent to "u (as in "put")-ng" in English or "ung" in German.

*e*$^1$ which occurs after *d, t, n, l, g, k, h, z, c, s, zh, ch, sh, r,* is produced with the same tongue position as that of *o*, but the lips are unrounded. It is similar to "er" in "herb" in English; only, the back of the tongue is raised a little.

*e*$^2$ which occurs in a neutral tone syllable, is equivalent to the unstressed "a" (the indefinite article) in English.

*$e^3$* is equivalent to "e" in "yes". It may stand alone or follow *y* or *ü* and may be written as *ê* to avoid confusion with *$e^1$*.

*er* is pronounced with the tongue in the same position as pronouncing *$e^2$* but the tip of the tongue turns up toward the hard palate. It is similar to "er" in "better" in American English.

*ei* is of the same value as "ei" in the English word "eight", but *e* in *ei* is very short.

*en* is the combination of "$e^2$ +n". It is pronounced as the unstressed indefinite article "an" in English.

*$i^1$* is equivalent to "ea" in the English word "eat" in pronunciation. Note that *$i^1$* is different from "i" of "it" in English.

*$i^2$* is vocalized *s*, i.e. when producing *s*, friction is released by a drawback of the tip of the tongue and the vocal cord is made vibrating at the same time. *$i^2$* occurs only after *z, c, s.*

*$i^3$* is vocalized *r*, i.e. when producing r, the tip of the tongue is lowered a bit, but there is no friction. It occurs only after *zh, ch, sh, r.*

*ia* is the combination of "*$i^1$ +a*", in which *a* is louder and clearer than *i* which serves only as a medial.

*iao* is the combination of "*$i^1$ +ao*".

*ian* is the combination of "*$i^1$ +$e^3$ +n*".

*iang* is the combination of "*$i^1$ +ang*".

*ie* is the combination of "*$i^1$ +$e^3$*" which is similar to "ye" in "yes" but without friction.

*iu* is the combination of "*$i^1$ +u*" and between the two vowels, there is a very weak *$e^2$*.

*iong* is the combination of "*$i^1$ +ong*".

*in* is the combination of "*$i^1$ +n*". This is different from the English "in" in that it is pronounced with a higher position of the tongue.

*ing* is the combination of "$i^1$ +ng".

*u* is similar to "u" in "rule" in English, but the lips are not so tightly pursed and is shorter than the English "u". It doesn't occur after *j, q, x, y.*

*ua* is the combination of "*u+a*".

*uai* is the combination of "*u+ai*".

*uan* is the combination of "*u+an*".

*uang* is the combination of "*u+ang*".

*uo* is the combination of "*u+o*".

*ui* is the combination of "*u*+*i*" with a very weak $e^2$ in between.

*un* is the combination of "*u*+*n*" with a very weak $e^2$ in between.

*ü* is similar to the French sound "u" or German sound "ü". It is produced with the same tongue position as when pronouncing $i^1$, but the lips are pursed as producing *u*. When spelled with *j, q, x, y,* the two dots in the letter *ü* are omitted, e.g. qūyù 区域 (region), but they will remain when spelled with the initials *n* and *l*.

*üan* is the combination of "*ü*+$e^3$+*n*". It is written *uan* (the two dots in the letter *ü* are omitted) when spelled with *j, q, x, y,* e.g. yuánquán 源泉 (source).

*üe* is the combination of "*ü*+$e^3$". It is written *ue* (the two dots in the letter *ü* are omitted), e.g. quèyuè 雀跃 (to jump for joy) and the dots remain when spelled with the initials *n* and *l*.

*ün* is the combination of "ü+n". It is only spelled with *j, q, x, y* and is written *un* (the two dots in *ü* are omitted), e.g. jūnyún 均匀 (homogeneous).

Note that all the beginning *i, u, ü* in the above finals are merely medials which are very short.

The Chinese initials and finals are very regularly combined with each other. Just read the following Table:

| Initials / Finals | b | p | m | f | w | d | t | n | l | g | k | h | z | c | s | zh | ch | sh | r | j | q | x | y |
|---|---|---|---|---|---|---|---|---|---|---|---|---|---|---|---|---|---|---|---|---|---|---|---|
| o | bo | po | mo | fo | wo | | | | | | | | | | | | | | | | | | yo |
| $e^1$ | | | | | | de | te | ne | le | ge | ke | he | ze | ce | se | zhe | che | she | re | | | | |
| $e^3$ | | | | | | | | | | | | | | | | | | | | | | | ye |
| $i^1$ | bi | pi | mi | | | di | ti | ni | li | | | | | | | | | | | ji | qi | xi | yi |
| $i^2$ | | | | | | | | | | | | | zi | ci | si | | | | | | | | |
| $i^3$ | | | | | | | | | | | | | | | | zhi | chi | shi | ri | | | | |
| u | bu | pu | mu | fu | wu | du | tu | nu | lu | gu | ku | hu | zu | cu | su | zhu | chu | shu | ru | | | | |
| ü | | | | | | | | nü | lü | | | | | | | | | | | ju | qu | xu | yu |

## TONES

There are, in standard modern spoken Chinese, 4 basic tones, commonly known as the 1st, 2nd, 3rd and 4th tones. The tones are represented respectively by the tone-graphs " ˉ ", " ˊ ", " ˇ " and " ˋ " which are written over the simple final or the main vowel in a compound final. The values of the four tones are shown in the five-degreed pitch-graph as follows:

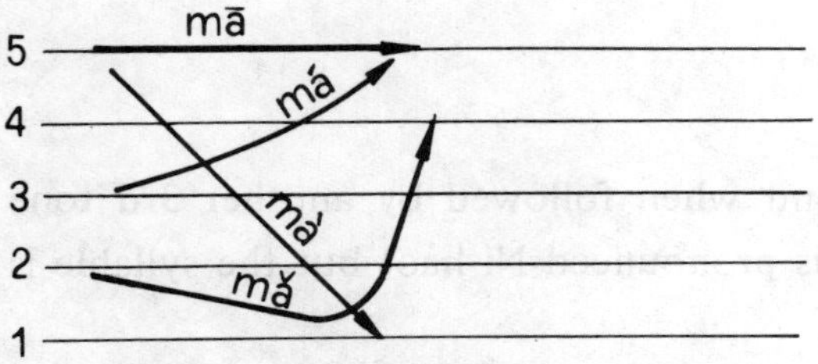


The first tone: 55, e.g. *mā* (mother)

The second tone: 35, e.g. *má* (hemp)

The third tone: 214, e.g. *mǎ* (horse)

The fourth tone: 51, e.g. *mà* (curse)

The 1st tone is a high level tone, the 2nd tone starts from the middle pitch and rises to the high pitch, the 3rd tone starts from the mid-low pitch, falls to the low pitch and then rises to the mid-high pitch, and the 4th tone is a complete falling tone, i.e. it falls from the high-pitch to the low-pitch.

The four tones can also be represented by musical notes as follows:

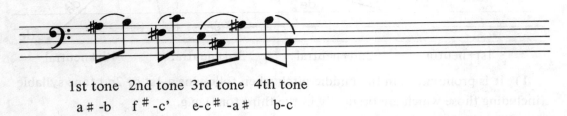

| 1st tone | 2nd tone | 3rd tone | 4th tone |
|---|---|---|---|
| a♯-b | f♯-c' | e-c♯-a♯ | b-c |

However, the pitch of a tone is not absolute. People speak in different pitch ranges, but the relative tone contours are the same.

Another point to be noted is that every tone contour, like the glide in music, is presented in a gradual glide rather than a sharp falling or rising.

The learner should not be satisfied with an approximately correct command of the tones, but should try to be perfect. When they have grasped the four tones in general, they have to learn which tone the syllable(s) of a word is (are) in, for tones can differentiate words. For example, *mǎi* 买 (to buy) is in the 3rd tone. If you fail to get it correct and pronounce it in the 4th tone, it becomes *mài* 卖 (to sell) which means completely differently. And if you read it in the 1st tone, the syllable carries no sense, for there is no such a syllable in Chinese.

Each of the four tones, when followed by another, will more or less undertake some changes, but the third tone changes most prominently. Here is a brief account of these changes:

1) The 3rd tone loses its final rise when followed by a 1st, 2nd, 4th or a neutral tone syllable, i.e. only the initial falling portion remains. This is called the half-third tone, e.g.

qǐng hē 請喝 (please drink)

(Note: The dot over *i* is replaced by the tone-graph where there is one.)

lǚyóu 旅游 (tour)
wǒ shì 我是 (I am)
nǐmen 你们 (you (pl.))

2) The 3rd tone changes to the second when followed by another 3rd tone syllable e.g. Nǐ hǎo! 你好 (How are you!) is pronounced Ní hǎo! but the syllable is still marked in the third tone.

Apart from the four basic tones, there is a special tone called the neutral tone which occurs always in syllables other than the beginning one. The neutral tone is pronounced short and soft and goes without any tone-graph in writing. The neutral tone has three values:

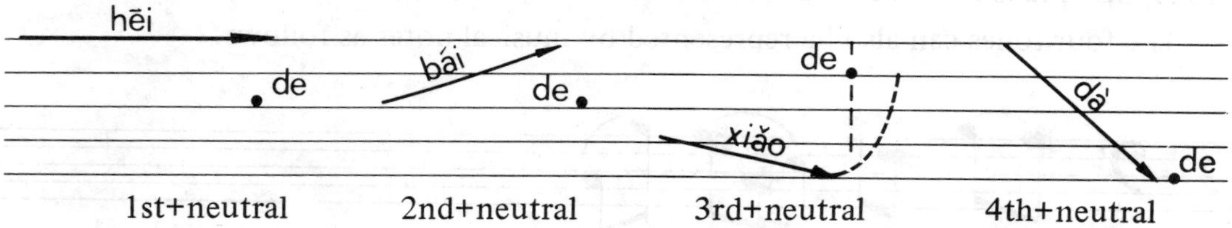


1) It is pronounced in the middle pitch when following a 1st or 2nd tone syllable (including those which are originally in the third tone), e.g.

hēide 黑的 (a black one)
báide 白的 (a white one)

2) It is pronounced in the mid-high pitch when following a 3rd tone syllable, e.g.

xiǎode 小的 (a small one)
jiějie 姐姐 (elder sister)

3) It is pronounced in the low pitch when following a 4th tone syllable, e.g.

dàde 大的 (a big one)

## EXERCISES

**1. Pronounce the following after the recording:**

1) Initials:

| | | | |
|---|---|---|---|
| b(o) | p(o) | m(o) | f(o) |
| d(e) | t(e) | n(e) | l(e) |
| z(i) | c(i) | s(i) | |
| zh(i) | ch(i) | sh(i) | r(i) |
| j(i) | q(i) | x(i) | |
| g(e) | k(e) | h(e) | |
| y(i) | w(u) | | |

2) Finals:

a ai ao an ang o ou ong e[1] e[2] e[3] er en eng
i[1] ia iao ian ìang ie iu iong in ing
u ua uai uan uang uo ui un
ü üan üe ün

3) Tones:

| | | | |
|---|---|---|---|
| ā | á | ǎ | à |
| lā | lá | lǎ | là |
| yī | yí | yǐ | yì |
| mī | mí | mǐ | mì |
| wū | wú | wǔ | wù |
| fū | fú | fǔ | fù |

**2. Discriminate the initials that are easily confused:**

1) Read the following in pairs:

| (1) b, p | (2) d, t | (3) g, k | (4) z, c |
|---|---|---|---|
| bō pō | dā tā | gē kē | zī cī |
| bāo pāo | dāi tāi | gāng kāng | zōng cōng |
| bēi pēi | dī tī | gū kū | zān cān |
| bēn pēn | duō tuō | guān kuān | zūn cūn |
| **(5) zh, ch** | **(6) j, q** | **(7) c, s** | **(8) ch, sh** |
| zhī chī | jīn qīn | cī sī | chē shē |
| zhuī chuī | jiē qiē | cāng sāng | chī shī |
| zhuāng chuāng | jiū qiū | cū sū | chuān shuān |
| zhōu chōu | jū qū | cā sā | chēn shēn |

(9) q, x
qī xī
qīng xīng
quē xuē
quān xuān

(10) zh, j
zhī jī
zhāng jiāng
zhōu jiū
zhūn jūn

(11) ch, q
chī qī
chōu qiū
chān qiān
chuān quān

(12) sh, x
shī xī
shā xiā
shēn xīn
shāo xiāo

(13) z, j
zī jī
zēng jīng
zāo jiāo
zuān juān

(14) c, q
cī qī
cā qiā
cāng qiāng
cāo qiāo

(15) s, x
sī xī
sōu xiū
sān xiān
sūn xūn

(16) z, zh
zī zhī
zā zhā
zū zhū
zōng zhōng

(17) c, ch
cī chī
cuō chuō
cāi chāi
cuī chuī

(18) s, sh
sī shī
sā shā
sōu shōu
suān shuān

* 2) Listen to the recording and cross out the wrong one from each pair of initials:

Example: b/p 八(eight)

(1) b/p 皮(skin)
(2) b/p 背(to carry on the back)
(3) d/t 太(too)
(4) d/t 对(right)
(5) zh/ch 吃(to eat)
(6) zh/ch 住(to live)
(7) j/q 去(to go)
(8) j/q 叫(to call)
(9) c/s 层(floor)
(10) c/s 扫(to sweep)
(11) ch/sh 上(upper)
(12) ch/sh 出(to come out)
(13) q/x 想(to think)
(14) q/x 晴(fine weather)
(15) zh/j 纸(paper)
(16) zh/j 几(several)
(17) ch/q 长(long)
(18) ch/q 墙(wall)
(19) g/k 关(to close)
(20) g/k 开(to open)
(21) z/c 次(time)
(22) z/c 坐(to sit)
(23) sh/x 深(deep)
(24) sh/x 新(new)
(25) z/j 见(to see)
(26) z/j 脏(dirty)
(27) c/q 层(floor)
(28) c/q 请(please)
(29) s/x 先(first)
(30) s/x 三(three)
(31) z/zh 租(to hire)
(32) z/zh 张(sheet)
(33) c/ch 村(village)
(34) c/ch 春(spring)
(35) s/sh 四(four)
(36) s/sh 市(city, municipality)

* 3) Listen to the recording and mark a "+" on the words in which the two syllables have the same initials:

Example: + 批评 (to criticise)
支持 (to support)

| | | | |
|---|---|---|---|
| (1) | 积极 (active) | (2) | 机器 (machine) |
| (3) | 刻苦 (industrious) | (4) | 赶快 (hurry up) |
| (5) | 普遍 (universal) | (6) | 宝贝 (treasure) |
| (7) | 态度 (attitude) | (8) | 探讨 (probe into) |
| (9) | 紫菜 (laver) | (10) | 自在 (at ease) |
| (11) | 支出 (pay) | (12) | 支柱 (pillar) |

* 4) Fill in the blanks with the initials according to the recording:

Example: zài jiàn 再见 (good-bye)

| | | | |
|---|---|---|---|
| (1) ___ì___ǐ | 自己 (self) | (2) ___á___ì | 杂志 (magazine) |
| (3) ___ié___àng | 结帐 (to settle account) | (4) ___ái___ǎn | 财产 (property) |
| (5) ___óng___ián | 从前 (before) | (6) ___īng___u | 清楚 (clear) |
| (7) ___iān___eng | 先生 (Mr.) | (8) ___uí___í | 随时 (any time) |
| (9) ___òng___íng | 送行 (to see off) | (10) ___iàn___ī | 电梯 (lift) |
| (11) ___ē___àn | 车站 (station) | (12) ___íng___ǐng | 情景 (situation) |

**3. Discriminate the finals which are easily confused:**

1) Read the following in pairs:

| | | | |
|---|---|---|---|
| (1) a, e | (2) an, en | (3) ang, eng | (4) ai, ei |
| dá dé | fān fēn | páng péng | bǎi běi |
| hā hē | gān gēn | dǎng děng | mǎi měi |
| zá zé | hǎn hěn | shāng shēng | lái léi |
| chā chē | zhān zhēn | zāng zēng | gǎi gěi |
| (5) ao, ou | (6) ou, uo | (7) ia, ie | (8) iao, iu |
| hǎo hǒu | gòu guò | jiā jiē | diāo diū |
| táo tóu | zǒu zuǒ | xià xiè | niǎo niǔ |
| zǎo zǒu | shōu shuō | liǎ liě | jiào jiù |
| shǎo shǒu | dōu duō | qiā qiē | xiǎo xiǔ |
| (9) ua, uo | (10) u, ü | (11) ü, iu | (12) uo, üe |
| huá huó | nǔ nǚ | jù jiù | luò lüè |
| guà guò | lǔ lǚ | xū xiū | chuō quē |
| zhuā zhuō | zhù jù | qū qiū | zhuó jué |
| shuā shuō | wǔ yǔ | lǜ liù | shuō xuē |
| (13) an, ang | (14) en eng | (15) in, ing | (16) ian, iang |
| fàn fàng | fēn fēng | xìn xìng | nián niáng |
| tán táng | shēn shēng | lín líng | liǎn liǎng |
| chǎn chǎng | zhēn zhēng | mín míng | jiàn jiàng |
| kàn kàng | rén réng | yín yíng | xiān xiāng |

(17) uan, uang
guǎn guǎng
huān huāng
chuán chuáng
zhuàn zhuàng

(18) un, ong
dūn dōng
hún hóng
chūn chōng
sūn sōng

* 2) Listen to the recording and cross out the wrong finals:

Example: ~~a~~ / e 和 (and)

(1) a / e 茶 (tea)
(2) a / e 这 (this)
(3) an / en 人 (person)
(4) an / en 山 (mountain)
(5) ang / eng 称 (to weigh)
(6) ang / eng 忙 (busy)
(7) ai / ei 给 (to give)
(8) ai / ei 开 (open)
(9) ao / ou 手 (hand)
(10) ao / ou 早 (early)
(11) ou / uo 过 (past)
(12) ou / uo 够 (enough)
(13) ia / ie 家 (family)
(14) ia / ie 写 (to write)
(15) iao / iu 小 (small)
(16) iao / iu 球 (ball)
(17) ua / uo 花 (flower)
(18) ua / uo 桌 (table)
(19) u / ü 女 (female)
(20) u / ü 路 (road)
(21) ü / iu 酒 (wine)
(22) ü / iu 局 (office)
(23) uo / üe 略 (omit)
(24) uo / üe 落 (to fall)
(25) an / ang 帮 (help)
(26) an / ang 谈 (to talk)
(27) en / eng 很 (very)
(28) en / eng 风 (wind)
(29) in / ing 请 (please)
(30) in / ing 新 (new)
(31) ian / iang 千 (thousand)
(32) ian / iang 讲 (to speak)
(33) uan / uang 逛 (to stroll)
(34) uan / uang 短 (short)
(35) un / ong 东 (the east)
(36) un / ong 准 (accuracy)

* 3) Listen to the recording and mark "+" on the expressions with same finals in both syllables:

Example: + 发达 (developed)
发射 (to launch)

(1) 卡车 (truck)
(2) 客车 (passenger train)
(3) 衬衫 (shirt)
(4) 谈判 (to negotiate)
(5) 长城 (the Great Wall)
(6) 帮忙 (to help)
(7) 配备 (to equip)
(8) 佩带 (to wear)
(9) 糟糕 (bad luck)
(10) 招手 (to beckon)
(11) 落后 (backward)
(12) 啰嗦 (verbose)

* 4) Give the finals and tone-graphs according to the recording:

Example: x*ue*sh*uo* 学说 (academic knowledge)

(1) f___n___ 妇女 (woman)
(2) l___q___ 录取 (to enroll)

(3) q___z___ 确凿 (established)  (4) y___l___ 约略 (about)
(5) f___m___ 繁忙 (busily)  (6) ch___zh___ 城镇 (city and town)
(7) x___q___ 心情 (state of mind)  (8) j___y___ 讲演 (lecture)
(9) g___g___ 观光 (to make a sightseeing trip)  (10) k___ch___ 昆虫 (insect)
(11) j___q___ 接洽 (to contact)  (12) j___l___ 交流 (to exchange)

***4. Tones discrimination:**

1) The 2nd and 3rd tones:

A. Read the following in pairs:

(1) bó bǒ (2) pó pǒ (3) mó mǒ (4) duó duǒ (5) tuó tuǒ
(6) luó luǒ (7) zhǒu zhóu (8) chǒu chóu (9) shǒu shóu (10) jiě jié
(11) qiě qié (12) xiě xié

B. Listen to the recording and cross out the wrong one from each pair of syllables:

Example: ~~bá~~ / bǎ 把 (a measure word)

(1) bái / bǎi 百 (hundred)  (2) cháng / chǎng 常 (often)
(3) qíng / qǐng 请 (please)  (4) jí / jǐ 极 (extreme)
(5) láo / lǎo 老 (old)  (6) méi / měi 没 (have not)
(7) liáng / liǎng 两 (two)  (8) guó / guǒ 国 (country)

C. Give the tone-graph to each syllable according to the recording:

Example: rén 人 (person)

(1) wan 完 (finish)  (2) wan 晚 (late)
(3) zuo 左 (left)  (4) zuo 昨 (yesterday)
(5) mai 买 (to buy)  (6) mai 埋 (to bury)
(7) lan 蓝 (blue)  (8) lan 懒 (lazy)

2) The 1st and the 4th tones

A. Read the following in pairs:

(1) gē gè (2) kē kè (3) hē hè (4) zāi zài (5) cāi cài
(6) sāi sài (7) bèi bēi (8) pèi pēi (9) fèi fēi (10) jiào jiāo
(11) qiào qiāo (12) xiào xiāo

B. Listen to the recording and cross out the wrong one from each pair of syllables:

Example: bā / ~~bà~~ 八 (eight)

(1) bāo / bào 报 (newspaper)  (2) fāng / fàng 放 (to put)
(3) qiān / qiàn 千 (thousand)  (4) jīn / jìn 斤 (a measure word)
(5) shū / shù 书 (book)  (6) wēn / wèn 问 (to ask)
(7) mō / mò 墨 (ink)  (8) yē / yè 夜 (night)

C. Give the tone-graph to each syllable according to the recording:

Example: shì 是 (to be)

(1) dai 带 (to bring)
(2) dai 呆 (to stay)
(3) shou 收 (to receive)
(4) shou 售 (to sell)
(5) ji 鸡 (chicken)
(6) ji 寄 (to send)
(7) jiang 姜 (ginger)
(8) jiang 酱 (sauce)

***5. Dictation**

1) Give the tone-graphs to the following words:

Example: xióngwěi 雄伟 (magnificent)

(1) youlan 游览 (to tour)
(2) youju 邮局 (post office)
(3) gongchang 工厂 (factory)
(4) gongyuan 公园 (park)
(5) maoyi 毛衣 (woolen jacket)
(6) maoyi 贸易 (to trade)
(7) laojia 劳驾 (excuse me)
(8) laojia 老家 (native place)

2) Write down the disyllabic words in the recording:

Example: mótuō 摩托 (motor)

(1) 收拾 (to put in order)
(2) 休息 (to rest)
(3) 香菜 (coriander)
(4) 现在 (now)
(5) 宽广 (wide)
(6) 请进 (come in, please)
(7) 球队 (team of ball games)
(8) 女婿 (son-in-law)

**6. Read the following:**

xiān xué shísì, zài xué sìshí;
xué sìshí bié shuō shísì, xué shísì bié shuō sìshí.
先学十四，再学四十；
学四十别说十四，学十四别说四十。
First learn fourteen, then learn forty;
When you learn forty, don't say fourteen,
When you learn fourteen, don't say forty.

# 词 类 简 称 表

## Abbreviations of Parts of Speech

| | | | |
|---|---|---|---|
| (名) | míng | 名 词 | noun |
| (代) | dài | 代 词 | pronoun |
| (动) | dòng | 动 词 | verb |
| (助动) | zhùdòng | 助动词 | aux. verb |
| (形) | xíng | 形容词 | adjective |
| (数) | shù | 数 词 | numeral |
| (量) | liàng | 量 词 | measure word |
| (副) | fù | 副 词 | adverb |
| (介) | jiè | 介 词 | preposition |
| (连) | lián | 连 词 | conjunction |
| (助) | zhù | 助 词 | particle |
| (叹) | tàn | 叹 词 | interjection |
| (象声) | xiàngshēng | 象声词 | onomatopoeia |
| | | | |
| (头) | tóu | 词 头 | prefix |
| (尾) | wěi | 词 尾 | suffix |

# 1 Welcome
## 欢迎 huānyíng

(Wang Fang, a staff member of the Tourist Bureau, goes to the Beijing International Airport to meet Mr. Chen Mingshan, an overseas Chinese, and his family.)

(一) I

王　芳①:　　　您　好！②　　　　Hello!
Wáng Fāng:　　Nín hǎo!

| | | |
|---|---|---|
| 华侨：<br>huáqiáo: | 您好！<br>Nín hǎo! | Hello! |
| 王：<br>Wáng: | 请问，您是陈明山先生吗？③<br>Qǐng wèn, nín shì Chén Míngshān xiānsheng ma? | Excuse me, are you Mr. Chen Mingshan? |
| 华：<br>huá: | 我不是陈明山。④<br>Wǒ bú shì Chén Míngshān. | No, I'm not. |
| 王：<br>Wáng: | 对不起。<br>Duì bu qǐ. | I'm sorry. |
| 华：<br>huá: | 没关系。<br>Méi guānxi. | It's all right. |
| 王：<br>Wáng: | 再见。<br>Zàijiàn. | Good-bye. |
| 华：<br>huá: | 再见。<br>Zàijiàn. | Good-bye. |

## （二） II

| | | |
|---|---|---|
| 王：<br>Wáng: | 您好！<br>Nín hǎo! | Hello! |
| 陈明山：<br>Chén Míngshān: | 您好！<br>Nín hǎo! | Hello! |
| 王：<br>Wáng: | 请问，您是陈明山先生吗？<br>Qǐng wèn, nín shì Chén Míngshān xiānsheng ma? | Excuse me, are you Mr. Chen Mingshan? |
| 陈：<br>Chén: | 对，我是陈明山。<br>Duì, wǒ shì Chén Míngshān. | Yes, I am. |
| 王：<br>Wáng: | 我是旅游局的，⑤我叫王芳。欢迎您，陈明山先生。<br>Wǒ shì Lǚyóujú de, wǒ jiào Wáng Fāng. Huānyíng nín, Chén Míngshān xiānsheng. | I'm from the Tourist Bureau. My name is Wang Fang. Welcome, Mr. Chen. |
| 陈：<br>Chén: | 谢谢您，王小姐。<br>Xièxie nín, Wáng xiǎojie. | Thank you, Miss Wang. |

## • new words • 生词 • shēngcí

| | | | | |
|---|---|---|---|---|
| 1 | 欢迎 | （动） | huānyíng | to welcome, to meet |
| 2 | 您 | （代） | nín | you (respectful form of address for the second person singular ) |
| 3 | 好 | （形） | hǎo | good, all right |
| | 您好 | | nín hǎo | Hello, How are you? |
| 4 | 华侨 | （名） | huáqiáo | overseas Chinese |
| 5 | 请问 | | qǐng wèn | Excuse me, but ... ?, May I ask ... ? |
| 6 | 是 | （动） | shì | to be (is, are ... ) |
| 7 | 先生 | （名） | xiānsheng | Mr., sir, gentleman (as in 'who is that gentleman?') |
| 8 | 吗 | （助） | ma | a particle used at the end of a sentence to turn it into a question |
| 9 | 我 | （代） | wǒ | I, me |
| 10 | 不 | （副） | bù | no, not |
| 11 | 对不起 | | duì bu qǐ | I am sorry. Excuse me. |
| 12 | 没关系 | | méi guānxi | That is all right. It does not matter. |
| 13 | 再见 | （动） | zàijiàn | good-bye, see you again. |
| 14 | 对 | （形） | duì | yes, right, correct |
| 15 | 的 | （助） | de | (See 5 under Study Points.) |
| 16 | 叫 | （动） | jiào | to call, to be called, one's name is ... |
| 17 | 谢谢 | （动） | xièxie | to thank |
| 18 | 小姐 | （名） | xiǎojie | miss |

| 专名 | Zhuānmíng | Proper Names |
|---|---|---|
| 王芳 | Wáng Fāng | a woman's name |

| | | |
|---|---|---|
| 王 | Wáng | a common Chinese family name |
| 陈明山 | Chén Míngshān | a name |
| 陈 | Chén | a common Chinese family name |
| 旅游局 | Lǚyóujú | The Tourist Bureau |

## study points • 注释 • zhùshì

1 王芳 (Wáng Fāng)

With Chinese names, the family name comes before the given one. The given name can be one character or two characters:

| family name | given name |
|---|---|
| 陈 (Chén) | 明山 (Míngshān) |
| 王 (Wáng) | 芳 (Fāng) |

2 您好！(Nín hǎo!)

This is a common greeting that may be used any time of the day.

3 您是陈明山先生吗？(Nín shì Chén Míngshān xiānsheng ma?)

1) In modern Chinese a sentence is made up of two parts, the subject and the predicate, with the subject placed before the predicate:

| subject | predicate |
|---|---|
| 您 | 是陈明山。(Nín shì Chén Míngshān.) |
| 我 | 叫王芳。(Wǒ jiào Wáng Fāng.) |

2) The pattern for the verb "是" (shì) used as the predicate is:

a) subject＋"是"(shì)＋object 我是陈明山。(Wǒ shì Chén Míngshān.)

In negative sentences the adverb "不"(bù) must precede the verb.

b) subject＋"不"(bú)＋"是"(shì)＋object 我不是陈明山 (Wǒ bú shì Chén Míngshān.)

3) Chinese verbs are not conjugated. Thus:

a) 我是华侨。(Wǒ shì huáqiáo.)
(I am an overseas Chinese.)

b) 您是华侨。(Nín shì huáqiáo.)
(You are an overseas Chinese.)

c) 他是华侨。(Tā shì huáqiáo.)
(He is an overseas Chinese.)

d) 我们是华侨。(Wǒmen shì huáqiáo.)
(We are overseas Chinese.)

4) Questions are commonly formed by adding "吗"(ma) at the end of a statement:
您是王芳小姐吗？(Nín shì Wáng Fāng xiǎojie ma?)
(Are you Miss Wáng Fāng?)

5) In Chinese, forms of address and titles always follow the family name or the whole name:
陈明山先生 (Chén Míngshān xiānsheng)
王小姐 (Wáng xiǎojie)

4 我不是陈明山。(Wǒ bú shì Chén Míngshān.)
When preceding a word of the fourth tone, "不"(bù) changes to the second tone marked by "ˊ", e.g. "不是"(bú shì); while in some phrases, such as "对不起"(duì bu qǐ), it is in the neutral tone, and consequently unmarked.

5 我是旅游局的。(Wǒ shì Lǚyóujú de.)
The sentence means "I am from the Tourist Bureau".
的(de) approximates 'of' in meaning, but is used differently from its English equivalent.

## supplementary words • 补充生词 • bǔchōng shēngcí

| | | | | |
|---|---|---|---|---|
| 1 | 同志 | (名) | tóngzhì | comrade |
| 2 | 那么 | (连) | nàme | then |
| 3 | 一定 | (形、副) | yídìng | definite, definitely, must |

| | | |
|---|---|---|
| 张大中 | Zhāng Dàzhōng | name of a man |
| 张 | Zhāng | a common Chinese family name |
| 李 | Lǐ | a common Chinese family name |
| 赵 | Zhào | a common Chinese family name |
| 张文汉 | Zhāng Wénhàn | name of a man |

## • exercises • 练习 • liànxí

**1. Phonetic Exercises:**

1) Tones

(1) Changes of the 3rd tone

| (3) + | (4) | |
|---|---|---|
| qǐng | wèn | |
| nǐ | shì | |
| wǒ | jiào | |
| Wǒ | jiào | Wáng Fāng. |
| Wǒ | shì | Míngshān. |

(2) Changes of the tone of "不"(bù)

| 不(bù) + | (4) |
|---|---|
| bú | shì |
| bú | jiào |
| bú | duì |
| bú | xiè |

(3) Neutral tone

xiānsheng
xièxie
duì bu qǐ
méi guānxi
lǚyóujú de

2) Sound discrimination

| | | | |
|---|---|---|---|
| sh | x | shēng | xing |
| shì | xì | shǎo | xiǎo |
| shān | xiān | | |

***2. What to say when you are not sure if you are speaking to the right person.**

Model: 请问，您是陈明山先生吗？
Qǐng wèn, nín shì Chén Míngshān xiānsheng ma?
(陈明山先生)
(Chén Míngshān xiānsheng)

1) ________，您是________吗？(张大中先生)
________, nín shì ________ ma? (Zhāng Dàzhōng xiānsheng)

2) ________，您是________吗？(王同志)
________, nín shì ________ ma? (Wáng tóngzhì)

3) 请问，________？(李小姐)
Qǐng wèn, ________? (Lǐ xiǎojie)

4) 请问，________？(赵先生)
Qǐng wèn, ________? (Zhào xiānsheng)

**3. I'm not..., I'm...**

Make a dialogue after the model.

Model: A: 您 是 陈 明山 先生 吗?
Nín shì Chén Míngshān xiānsheng ma?

B: 我 不是 陈 明山。
Wǒ bú shì Chén Míngshān.

A: 对不起,您 是 ________?
Duì bu qǐ, nín shì ________?

B: 我 是 张 文汉。
Wǒ shì Zhāng Wénhàn.

1) 您 是 张 大中 同志 吗?
Nín shì Zhāng Dàzhōng tóngzhì ma?

2) 您 是 陈 同志 吗?
Nín shì Chén tóngzhì ma?

3) 您 是 赵 小姐 吗?
Nín shì Zhào xiǎojie ma?

4) 您 是 王 先生 吗?
Nín shì Wáng xiānsheng ma?

**4. What to say when welcoming someone.**

Fill in the blanks with "您好"(nín hǎo) and "欢迎您"(huānyíng nín)

Model: A. 您 好, 陈 明山 先生! 欢迎 您!
Nín hǎo, Chén Míngshān xiānsheng! Huānyíng nín!

B. 陈 明山 先生, 您 好! 欢迎 您!
Chén Míngshān xiānsheng, nín hǎo! Huānyíng nín!

C. 您 好! 欢迎 您, 陈 明山 先生!
Nín hǎo! Huānyíng nín, Chén Míngshān xiānsheng!

1) A. ______, 陈 小姐! ______!
______, Chén xiǎojie! ______!

B. 陈 小姐, ______! ______!
Chén xiǎojie, ______! ______!

C. ______! ______, 陈 小姐!
______! ______, Chén xiǎojie!

2) A. 赵 先生, ______! ______!
Zhào xiānsheng, ______! ______!

B. ______! ______, 赵 先生!
______! ______, Zhào xiānsheng!

C. ______, 赵 先生! ______!
______, Zhào xiānsheng! ______!

3) A. ＿＿＿！＿＿＿＿，李 同志！
＿＿＿！＿＿＿＿，Lǐ tóngzhì!

B. ＿＿＿，李 同志！＿＿＿＿！
＿＿＿，Lǐ tóngzhì! ＿＿＿＿！

C. 李 同志，＿＿＿！＿＿＿＿！
Lǐ tóngzhì, ＿＿＿！＿＿＿＿！

**5. Listen to the dialogues:**

1) 王 芳： 陈 明山 先生！
Wáng Fāng: Chén Míngshān xiānsheng!
陈 明山： 王 芳 同志。
Chén Míngshān: Wáng Fāng tóngzhì.
王： 您 好！
Wáng: Nín hǎo!
陈： 您 好！
Chén: Nín hǎo!

2) 陈 明山： 张 先生！
Chén Míngshān: Zhāng xiānsheng!
张 大中：
Zhāng Dàzhōng: 您 好！
张 文汉： Nín hǎo！
Zhāng Wénhàn:
陈： 您 是 张 先生 吗？
Chén: Nín shì Zhāng xiānsheng ma?
张 大中： 对。
Zhāng Dàzhōng: Duì.
陈： 您 是 张 文汉 先生？
Chén: Nín shì Zhāng Wénhàn xiānsheng？
张 大中： 我 不是 张 文汉，我 叫 张 大中。
Zhāng Dàzhōng: Wǒ bú shì Zhāng Wénhàn, wǒ jiào Zhāng Dàzhōng.
陈： 对 不 起。
Chén: Duì bu qǐ.
张 大中： 没 关系。
Zhāng Dàzhōng: Méi guānxi.
陈： 那么，您 一定 是……
Chén: Nàme, nín yídìng shì...

张 文汉： 对，我是张 文汉。
Zhāng Wénhàn: Duì, wǒ shì Zhāng Wénhàn.
陈： 欢迎，欢迎！张 先生！
Chén: Huānyíng, huānyíng! Zhāng xiānsheng!

***6. Translate the following sentences into Chinese:**

1) How do you do!
2) Excuse me, but are you Miss Zhao?
3) Welcome, Comrade Zhang!
4) I am not Wang Fang.
5) My name is Zhang Dazhong.

# 2 Introduction 介绍 jièshào

(Li Wenhan, a friend of Chen Mingshan's, visits the Chens at the Beijing Hotel.)

(A knock at the door)

| | | |
|---|---|---|
| 陈 ： | 请 进！啊，老 李，①你 好！ | Come in, please. Ah, |
| Chén: | Qǐng jìn! À, Lǎo Lǐ, nǐ hǎo! | Lao Li. How are you? |
| 李 文汉： | 你 好，老 陈 。 | Fine, and you, Lao Chen? |
| Lǐ Wénhàn: | Nǐ hǎo, Lǎo Chén. | |
| 陈 ： | 请 坐。 | Have a seat. |
| Chén: | Qǐng zuò. | |

| | | |
|---|---|---|
| 李：<br>Lǐ: | 谢谢。<br>Xièxie. | Thank you. |
| 陈：<br>Chén: | 请抽烟。<br>Qǐng chōu yān. | Have a cigarette. |
| 李：<br>Lǐ: | 谢谢，我不会。②<br>Xièxie, wǒ bú huì. | No, thanks. I don't smoke. |
| 陈：<br>Chén: | 我来介绍一下儿，③<br>Wǒ lái jièshào yíxiàr,<br>这是李文汉先生，<br>zhè shì Lǐ Wénhàn xiānsheng,<br>这是我太太艾琳。④<br>zhè shì wǒ tàitai Àilín. | Let me introduce everyone. This is Mr. Li Wenhan. This is my wife, Irene. |
| 李：<br>Lǐ: | 您好，陈太太。⑤<br>Nín hǎo, Chén tàitai. | How do you do, Mrs. Chen. |
| 艾琳：<br>Àilín: | 您好，李先生。<br>Nín hǎo, Lǐ xiānsheng. | How do you do, Mr. Li. |
| 陈：<br>Chén: | 这是李伯伯。<br>Zhè shì Lǐ bóbo.<br>这是我女儿莉莉，⑥<br>Zhè shì wǒ nǚ'ér Lìli,<br>那是我儿子大伟。<br>nà shì wǒ érzi Dàwěi. | This is Uncle Li. This is my daughter Lily, and that's my son David. |
| 莉莉：<br>Lìli:<br>大伟：<br>Dàwěi: | 李伯伯好！⑦<br>Lǐ bóbo hǎo! | How do you do, Uncle Li? |
| 李：<br>Lǐ: | 你们好！<br>Nǐmen hǎo! | How do you do? |
| 艾琳：<br>Àilín: | 李先生，请喝茶。<br>Lǐ xiānsheng, qǐng hē chá. | Please have some tea, Mr. Li. |
| 李：<br>Lǐ: | 谢谢。<br>Xièxie. | Thank you. |

## • new words • 生词 • shēngcí

| | | | | |
|---|---|---|---|---|
| 1 | 介绍 | （动、名） | jièshào | to introduce |
| 2 | 请 | （动） | qǐng | please, to invite |
| 3 | 进 | （动） | jìn | to come in, to enter |
| | 请进 | | qǐng jìn | Please come in. |
| 4 | 啊 | （叹） | à | an interjection like "ah" |
| 5 | 老 | （头、形） | lǎo | old, elderly (see study Point 1) |
| 6 | 你 | （代） | nǐ | you (sing.) |
| 7 | 坐 | （动） | zuò | to sit |
| 8 | 抽烟 | | chōu yān | to smoke a cigarette (or a pipe or cigar) |
| 9 | 会 | （助动、动） | huì | can, will, to know how to (see study Point 2) |
| 10 | 来 | （动） | lái | to come (here used to indicate intention) |
| 11 | 一下儿 | （量） | yíxiàr | a measure word for verbs, also used to indicate the action as being short or informal |
| 12 | 这 | （代） | zhè | this |
| 13 | 太太 | （名） | tàitai | wife, Mrs, madam |
| 14 | 伯伯 | （名） | bóbo | uncle (father's elder brother), also a respectful form of addressing men of about the age of one's father |
| 15 | 女儿 | （名） | nǚ'ér | daughter |
| 16 | 那 | （代） | nà | that |
| 17 | 儿子 | （名） | érzi | son |
| 18 | 们 | （尾） | men | a suffix added to nouns or pronouns |

| | | | |
|---|---|---|---|
| | | | (such as comrades, students etc.) to make them plural. |
| 19 你们 | (代) | nǐmen | you (pl.) |
| 20 喝 | (动) | hē | to drink |
| 21 茶 | (名) | chá | tea |

| 专名 | Zhuānmíng | Proper names |
|---|---|---|
| 李 | Lǐ | a common family name |
| 李文汉 | Lǐ Wénhàn | name of Chen Mingshan's friend |
| 艾琳 | Àilín | name of Chen Mingshan's wife-Irene |
| 莉莉 | Lìli | name of Mr. Chen's daughter-Lily |
| 大伟 | Dàwěi | name of Mr. Chen's son-David |

## study points • 注释 • zhùshì

1 老李 (Lǎo Lǐ)

老 (lǎo) + the family name is a form of address often used for friends or colleagues of similar age as the speaker. This usage is most common among middle-aged and elderly people. (See text of Lesson 25)

2 我不会。(Wǒ bú huì.)

"不会" is a common way of refusing tobacco or liquor. It is equivalent to 'I don't smoke' in English.

N. B. When used with an auxiliary verb, "不" (bù) must be put before the auxiliary verb to give the main verb a negative meaning.

3 我来介绍一下儿。(Wǒ lái jièshào yíxiàr.)

When followed by a verb, "来" (lái) indicates intention. However, it can be left out without changing the meaning of the sentence.

4 这是我太太艾琳。(Zhè shì wǒ tàitai Àilín.)

In Chinese, attributives always go before the words they describe. Personal pronouns can be placed directly before nouns that indicate family relations:

我女儿 (wǒ nǚ'ér)

my daughter

我儿子 (wǒ érzi)
my son
你太太 (nǐ tàitai)
your wife
你伯伯 (nǐ bóbo)
your uncle

5 陈太太 (Chén tàitai)
In modern China, women do not take their husbands' names after marriage. However, they are sometimes addressed by their husbands's family names＋太太 (tàitai).

6 这是我女儿莉莉。(Zhè shì wǒ nǚ'ér Lìli.)
In phonetic transcription the symbol " ' " is employed to separate a syllable beginning with a vowel (like a, o or e) from the preceding syllable: nǚ'ér(女儿)。

7 李伯伯好！(Lǐ bóbo hǎo!)
When greeting someone with a form of address, we usually use the form of address (name)＋好 (hǎo).

## supplementary words · 补充生词 · bǔchōng shēngcí

| | | | |
|---|---|---|---|
| 1 | 爷爷 | (名) yéye | grandpa |
| 2 | 奶奶 | (名) nǎinai | grandma |
| 3 | 叔叔 | (名) shūshu | uncle |
| 4 | 啤酒 | (名) píjiǔ | beer |
| 5 | 咖啡 | (名) kāfēi | coffee |
| 6 | 啊 | (助) a | ah, oh |
| 7 | 啊 | (叹) á | exclamation of doubt |
| 8 | 哈 | (象声) hā | ha (laughing sound) |

## · exercises · 练习 · liànxí

**1. Phonetic exercises:**

1) Tones

(1) Changes of the 3rd tone

| (3) + (1) | (3) + (2) | (3) + (3) | (3) + (4) |
|---|---|---|---|
| qǐng hē | Lǎo Chén | Lǎo Lǐ | Qǐng jìn! |
| qǐng chōu | nǚ'ér | Nǐ hǎo! | Qǐng zuò! |
| | | Xiǎojie, nǐ hǎo! | |
| | | Nǐ hǎo, lǎo Lǐ! | |

(2) The neutral tone

érzi
bóbo
nǐmen
tàitai
Lìli

2) Sound discrimination

| | |
|---|---|
| in | ing |
| nín | níng |
| lín | líng |
| jìn | qǐng |
| mín | míng |

**2. Practice with the greeting "……好" (…hǎo):**

你 好！（您， 你们）
Nǐ hǎo！ (nín, nǐmen)
爷爷 好！（奶奶， 莉莉，大伟， 叔叔）
Yéye hǎo! (nǎinai, Lìli, Dàwěi, shūshu)
李伯伯 好！（张 先生， 陈 太太， 王 叔叔， 老 赵）
Lǐ bóbo hǎo! (Zhāng xiānsheng, Chén tàitai, Wáng shūshu, Lǎo Zhào)

***3. Polite requests.**

Say what you should in each of the following situations.

1) ____________ 2) ____________ 3) ____________

4) ______________ 5) ______________ 6) ______________

## *4. How to introduce people:

Fill in the blanks with "是" (shì) and "介绍" (jièshào):

1) 我 来________一下儿,我 太太艾琳, 女儿莉莉,儿子大伟。
Wǒ lái________ yíxiàr ,wǒ tàitai Àilín, nǚ'ér Lìli, érzi Dàwěi.

2) 我 来________一下儿, 这____ 老 赵, 这____ 张 先生 。
Wǒ lái________ yíxiàr , zhè____Lǎo Zhào, zhè____ Zhāng xiānsheng.

3) 太太们, 先生 们, 我____ 陈 明山, 我 来 ____ 一下儿,这____ 王 先生 , 这 ____王 太太, 这____艾琳。
Tàitai men, xiānsheng men, wǒ____ Chén Míngshān, wǒ lái ____ yíxiàr, zhè____ Wáng xiānsheng, zhè____ Wáng tàitai, zhè____ Àilín.

## 5. Listen to the dialogues:

1) A: 请 您 介绍 一下儿。
Qǐng nín jièshào yíxiàr.

B: 啊,我 来 介绍。这 是 王 先生 , 王 太太, 那 是 张 先生 , 张 太太。
À, wǒ lái jièshào. Zhè shì Wáng xiānsheng, Wáng tàitai, nà shì Zhāng xiānsheng, Zhāng tàitai.

A, C: 欢迎 , 欢迎 你们。
Huānyíng, huānyíng nǐmen.

2) (A knock at the door)

A: 请 进!
Qǐng jìn!

B: 老 陈, 你好!
Lǎo Chén, nǐ hǎo!

A: 老 张 啊, 请 坐! 抽 烟 吗?
Lǎo Zhāng a , qǐng zuò! Chōu yān ma?

B: 抽 烟。
Chōu yān.

A: 请 。
Qǐng.

B: 谢谢。
Xièxie.
(A knock at the door)

A: 请 进!
Qǐng jìn!

C: 您 好!
Nín hǎo!

A: 您 好!您 是……
Nín hǎo! Nín shì…

B: 老 陈, 我来 介绍 一下儿,这 是我太太。
Lǎo Chén, wǒ lái jièshào yíxiàr, zhè shì wǒ tàitai.

A: 啊, 张 太太, 欢迎 , 欢迎 。您 请 坐! 您 请 喝 茶!
A, Zhāng tàitai, huānyíng, huānyíng. Nín qǐng zuò! Nín qǐng hē chá!

C: 谢谢。
Xièxie.

A: 老 张 , 抽 烟啊。
Lǎo Zhāng, chōu yān a.

C: 你 抽 烟?
Nǐ chōu yān?

B: 不,我, 我不 抽 烟, 我 不 抽 烟,我 不 抽 烟。
Bù, wǒ, wǒ bù chōu yān, wǒ bù chōu yān, wǒ bù chōu yān.

A: 老 张 ,你不 抽 烟?
Lǎo Zhāng, nǐ bù chōu yān?

C: 他 不 抽 烟。
Tā bù chōu yān.

B: 对, 我不 抽 烟, 不会 抽 烟。
Duì, wǒ bù chōu yān, bú huì chōu yān.

A: 啊?啊,对,对,你不 会 抽 烟,哈哈哈……
Á ? À , duì, duì , nǐ bú huì chōu yān. Hāhāhā…

# 3 Looking For Someone 找人 zhǎo rén

(Mr. Chen Mingshan goes to the Hotel of Nationalities to look up his friend, Mr. John Smith, interpreter for a U. S. trade delegation.)

| | | |
|---|---|---|
| 陈 ： | 同志，① 我 找 一个人。② | Hello comrade, I'm looking for someone. |
| Chén: | Tóngzhì, wǒ zhǎo yíge rén. | |
| 服务员： | 您 找 谁？③ | Who is it you want to see? |
| fúwùyuán: | Nín zhǎo shuí? | |
| 陈 ： | 我 找 约翰·史密斯 先 | John Smith. Can you tell me his room number? |
| Chén: | Wǒ zhǎo Yuēhàn Shǐmìsī xiān- | |

| | | |
|---|---|---|
| | 生 。请 问，他住 哪个<br>sheng. Qǐng wèn, tā zhù nǎge<br>房间 ？<br>fángjiān? | |
| 服：<br>fú： | 他 是 哪国 人？<br>Tā shì nǎguó rén? | What country is he from? |
| 陈 ：<br>Chén: | 美国人 。<br>Měiguórén. | He's an American. |
| 服：<br>fú： | 他 住 三一二八 ④ 房间 。<br>Tā zhù sānyāo' èrbā fángjiān. | He's staying in Room 3128. |
| 陈 ：<br>Chén: | 三一二八 在哪儿？⑤<br>Sānyāo'èrbā zài nǎr? | Where is Room 3128? |
| 服：<br>fú： | 在 三层。⑥<br>Zài sāncéng. | On the third floor. |
| 陈 ：<br>Chén: | 谢 谢。<br>Xièxie. | Thank you. |
| 服：<br>fú： | 不 谢。<br>Bú xiè. | You're welcome. |

## • new words • 生词 • shēngcí

| | | | |
|---|---|---|---|
| 1 | 找 | （动）zhǎo | to look for, to look up |
| 2 | 人 | （名）rén | person, people |
| 3 | 同志 | （名）tóngzhì | comrade |
| 4 | 一 | （数）yī | one |
| 5 | 个 | （量）gè | a measure word |
| 6 | 服务员 | （名）fúwùyuán | receptionist, waiter, etc. (any service personnel) |
| 7 | 谁 | （代）shuí, shéi | who, whom |
| 8 | 他 | （代）tā | he, him |
| 9 | 住 | （动）zhù | to live, to stay |
| 10 | 哪 | （代）nǎ | which |

| | | | |
|---|---|---|---|
| 11 房间 | (名) | fángjiān | room |
| 12 国 | (名) | guó | country, nation |
| 13 三 | (数) | sān | three |
| 14 二 | (数) | èr | two |
| 15 八 | (数) | bā | eight |
| 16 在 | (动) | zài | to be (is, are...), to be situated |
| 17 哪儿 | (代) | nǎr | where |
| 18 层 | (量) | céng | floor, storey, layer |
| 19 不谢 | | bú xiè | You are welcome. Don't mention it. |

| 专名 | Zhuānmíng | Proper names |
|---|---|---|
| 约翰·史密斯 | Yuēhàn Shǐmìsī | John Smith |
| 美国 | Měiguó | the United States |

## study points • 注释 • zhùshì

1 同志 (tóngzhì)

This is a common form of address in the PRC, particularly among people who meet for the first time or do not know each other well.

2 我找一个人。(Wǒ zhǎo yíge rén.)

1) In modern Chinese, a numeral cannot be placed immediately before a noun. There must be a measure word in between. "个" (ge) is one of the most frequently used measure words:

一个同志 (yíge tóngzhì)
一个儿子 (yíge érzi)
一个美国人 (yíge Měiguórén)
一个房间 (yíge fángjiān)

Note that "个" is in the neutral tone.

2) "一" (yī), which is usually in the first tone, changes to the second tone when coming before a syllable in the fourth tone (even if that word is in the neu-

tral form), and is marked by "ˊ": "一下儿" (yíxiàr) "一个" (yíge)

3 您找谁? (Nín zhǎo shuí?)

When using interrogative pronouns like "谁" (shuí), "哪" (nǎ), "哪儿" (nǎr), etc. to form questions, the word order is the same as that of statements:

| statement | question |
|---|---|
| 你找他。 (Nǐ zhǎo tā.) | 你找谁? (Nǐ zhǎo shuí?) |
| 他是美国人。(Tā shì Měiguórén.) | 他是哪国人?(Tā shì nǎguó rén?) |
| 他住三一二八。 (Tā zhù 3128.) | 他住哪儿?(Tā zhù nǎr?) |

4 他住三一二八房间。(Tā zhù sānyāo'èrbā fángjiān.)

In spoken Chinese, "一" (yī) in a number containing more than three numerals can be pronounced "yāo".

5 三一二八在哪儿?(Sānyāo'èrbā zài nǎr?)

In Beijing dialect, in addition to "er", there is a number of syllables ending with "r". These syllables are written in two characters "×儿", for example: nǎr-哪儿 (where).

6 三层 (Sāncéng)

The Chinese count the ground floor (of a building) as the first floor.

## supplementary words • 补充生词 • bǔchōng shēngcí

| | | | |
|---|---|---|---|
| 饭店 | (名) | fàndiàn | restaurant, hotel |
| 中国 | (名) | Zhōngguó | China |
| 英国 | (名) | Yīngguó | England, Britain |
| 日本 | (名) | Rìběn | Japan |
| 加拿大 | (名) | Jiānádà | Canada |
| 北京 | (名) | Běijīng | Beijing |
| 北京饭店 | (名) | Běijīng Fàndiàn | Beijing Hotel |

## • exercises • 练习 • liànxí

**1. Phonetic exercises:**

1) Tones

| (1) Changes of the tone of "yī (一)" | (2) The neutral tone | |
|---|---|---|
| yíxiàr | yíge | one |
| yíge | nǎge | which |
| sānyī (yāo) 'èrbā | nàge | that |
| èryī (yāo) bāsān | zhège | this |

2) Sound discrimination

| (1) The retroflex final | (2) a | e | (3) zh | j |
|---|---|---|---|---|
| nǎr | chá | zhè | zhè | jiè |
| zài nǎr | dà | de | zhù | jú |
| zhù nǎr | nǎ | ne | zhì | jì |
| qù nǎr | hā | hē | zhǎo | jiào |

**2. Practice questions and answers according to the table:**

A: 他是 哪国 人?
Tā shì nǎguó rén?

B: 他是 美国人。请 问,他住 哪个 房间?
Tā shì Měiguórén. Qǐng wèn, tā zhù nǎge fángjiān?

A: 三二一八。
Sān'èryāobā.

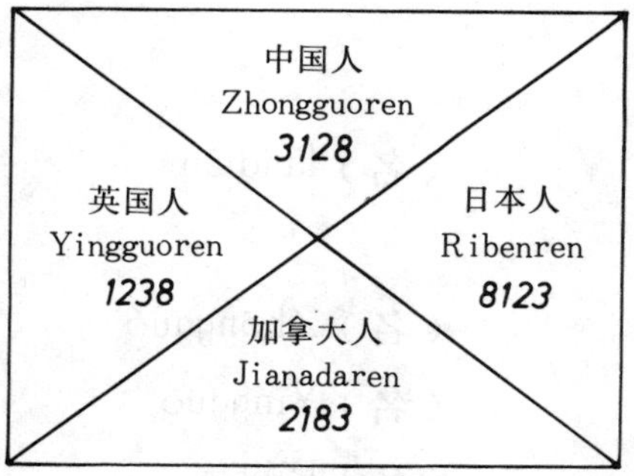


***3. Complete the dialogues with the right word showing family relations:**

1) 大伟 找 谁?
Dàwěi zhǎo shéi?
他找 他______。(爷爷)
Tā zhǎo tā______. (yéye)
大伟 找 谁?
Dàwěi zhǎo shéi?

他 找 他______。(奶奶)
Tā zhǎo tā______. (nǎinai)
大伟 找 谁?
Dàwěi zhǎo shéi?
他 找 他______ (叔叔)
Tā zhǎo tā______. (shūshu)

2) 陈 先生 找 谁?
Chén xiānsheng zhǎo shéi?
他 找______。(艾琳)
Tā zhǎo______. (Àilín)
陈 先生 找 谁?
Chén xiānsheng zhǎo shéi?
他 找______。(莉莉)
Tā zhǎo______. (Lìli)
陈 先生 找 谁?
Chén xiānsheng zhǎo shéi?
他 找______。(大伟)
Tā zhǎo______. (Dàwěi)

***4. Ask questions on the underlined parts using the correct interrogative pronouns:**

1) 这 是 张 大中 同志。
Zhè shì Zhāng Dàzhōng tóngzhì.
2) 他 叫 张 大中。
Tā jiào Zhāng Dàzhōng.
3) 他们 是 中国人。
Tāmen shì Zhōngguórén.
4) 他们 住 北京 饭店。
Tāmen zhù Běijīng Fàndiàn.
5) 张 文汉 找 陈 明山 先生。
Zhāng Wénhàn zhǎo Chén Míngshān xiānsheng.
6) 他 爷爷 住 3128 房间。
Tā yéye zhù 3128 fángjiān.
7) 老 赵 找 他 儿子。
Lǎo Zhào zhǎo tā érzi.
8) 8132 房间 在 八层。
8132 fángjiān zài bācéng.
9) 他 爷爷 住 北京 饭店。
Tā yéye zhù Běijīng Fàndiàn.

***5. Ask three questions on each sentence with "谁" (shuí).**

1) 他 是 我儿子。
Tā shì wǒ érzi.

2) 李 叔叔 找 我爷爷。
Lǐ shūshu zhǎo wǒ yéye.

**6. Listen to the dialogues:**

1) A: 他们 找 谁?
Tāmen zhǎo shéi?

B: 找 莉莉。
Zhǎo Lìli.

A: 莉莉住哪儿?
Lìli zhù nǎr?

B: 8321。
bāsān'èryāo.

2) A: 王 先 生 住哪儿?
Wáng xiānsheng zhù nǎr?

B: 他 住 北京 饭 店。
Tā zhù Běijīng Fàndiàn.

A: 哪个 饭店?
Nǎge fàndiàn?

B: 北 京 饭 店 。 王 先 生 住 北 京 饭 店
Běijīng Fàndiàn. Wáng xiānsheng zhù Běijīng Fàndiàn
3812。
sānbā yāoèr.

A: 哪个 房间?
Nǎge fángjiān?

B: 3812。
Sānbāyāoèr.

A: 谢谢 您。
Xièxie nín.

B: 不 谢。
Bú xiè.

***7. Translate the following sentences into Chinese:**

1) Who is he?
2) Where's he from?
3) Where does he live?
4) In which room is he staying?
5) Whom do you want to see?

# 4 Where Are You Going?
# 你去哪儿? nǐ qù nǎr?

(Mr. Chen Mingshan comes across Henry, a friend of his.)

| | | | |
|---|---|---|---|
| 陈： Chén: | 哦， 亨利， 你去哪儿？① Ò， Hēnglì， nǐ qù nǎr？ | | Hello, Henry. Where are you going? |
| 亨利： Hēnglì: | 我 去 大使馆 看 一个 Wǒ qù dàshǐguǎn kàn yíge 朋友 。②你呢？③ péngyou. Nǐ ne？ | | I'm going to the Embassy to see a friend of mine. And you? |

| | | |
|---|---|---|
| 陈：<br>Chén: | 我去买一点儿东西。④<br>Wǒ qù mǎi yìdiǎnr dōngxi. | I'm going to do some shopping. |
| 亨：<br>Hēng: | 晚上你有活动吗？⑤<br>Wǎnshang nǐ yǒu huódòng ma? | Are you doing anything tonight? |
| 陈：<br>Chén: | 没有。<br>Méi yǒu. | No. |
| 亨：<br>Hēng: | 有杂技，你看吗？<br>Yǒu zájì, nǐ kàn ma? | There's an acrobatics performance. Are you going to see it? |
| 陈：<br>Chén: | 对不起，我不看。你明天干什么？⑥<br>Duì bu qǐ, wǒ bú kàn. Nǐ míngtiān gàn shénme? | No, thanks. What are you doing tomorrow? |
| 亨：<br>Hēng: | 我明天去长城。你呢？<br>Wǒ míngtiān qù Chángchéng. Nǐ ne? | I'm going to the Great Wall tomorrow. What about you? |
| 陈：<br>Chén: | 我去参观故宫。<br>Wǒ qù cānguān Gùgōng. | I'm going to visit the Palace Museum. |
| 亨：<br>Hēng: | 你太太也去吗？<br>Nǐ tàitai yě qù ma? | Is your wife going too? |
| 陈：<br>Chén: | 不，她有别的事儿。⑦<br>Bù, tā yǒu biéde shìr. | No, she has something else to do. |

## • new words • 生词 • shēngcí

| | | | |
|---|---|---|---|
| 1 | 去 | （动）qù | to go |
| 2 | 哦 | （叹）ó | an interjection indicating surprise or doubt |
| 3 | 大使馆 | （名）dàshǐguǎn | embassy |
| 4 | 看 | （动）kàn | to see, to look at |
| 5 | 朋友 | （名）péngyou | friend |
| 6 | 呢 | （助）ne | a particle (see study point 3) |
| 7 | 买 | （动）mǎi | to buy, to purchase |

| | | | |
|---|---|---|---|
| 8 | 一点儿 | （量）yìdiǎnr | a bit, a little |
| 9 | 东西 | （名）dōngxi | thing, things |
| 10 | 晚上 | （名）wǎnshang | evening, night |
| 11 | 有 | （动）yǒu | to have, there is (are) |
| 12 | 活动 | （名、动）huódòng | activity, to move |
| 13 | 没（有） | （副）méi(yǒu) | (to have) not, (there is (are)) not, no |
| 14 | 杂技 | （名）zájì | acrobatics |
| 15 | 明天 | （名）míngtiān | tomorrow |
| 16 | 干 | （动）gàn | to do, to be engaged in |
| 17 | 什么 | （代）shénme | what |
| 18 | 参观 | （动）cānguān | to visit (usually a place) |
| 19 | 也 | （副）yě | too, also |
| 20 | 她 | （代）tā | she, her |
| 21 | 别的 | （代）biéde | other, else |
| 22 | 事儿 | （名）shìr | business, work, engagement |

| 专名 | Zhuānmíng | Proper names |
|---|---|---|
| 亨利 | Hēnglì | Henry |
| 长城 | Chángchéng | the Great Wall |
| 故宫 | Gùgōng | the Imperial Palace (the Forbidden City or the Palace Museum) |

## study points • 注释 • zhùshì

1 你去哪儿？(Nǐ qù nǎr?)

This is more a casual greeting than a real question. It is said by people who know each other fairly well. Depending on the circumstances, the answer could be general as well as concrete.

2 我去大使馆看一个朋友。(Wǒ qù dàshǐguǎn kàn yíge péngyou.)

In Chinese, the predicate in a sentence may include two or more than two verbs or verbal structures:

他去买东西。 (Tā qù mǎi dōngxi.) go + to buy

你去参观故宫吗？ (Nǐ qù cānguān Gùgōng ma?) go + to visit

3 你呢？(Nǐ ne?)

In certain situations, questions can be formed by placing "呢" (ne) after nouns, pronouns or phrases. What is being asked refers to what was being discussed immediately beforehand:

明天你去长城。陈先生呢？(Míngtiān nǐ qù Chángchéng. Chén xiānsheng ne?)

Tomorrow you're going to the Great Wall. How about Mr. Chen?

他晚上看杂技。你呢？(Tā wǎnshang kàn zájì. Nǐ ne?)

He's going to see the acrobatic show this evening. Are you going too?

4 我去买一点儿东西。(Wǒ qù mǎi yìdiǎnr dōngxi.)

1) "一点儿" (yìdiǎnr) is used before nouns to indicate small quantity.

2) If an "r" appears after an "n", the "n" becomes mute. If it appears after "ai" or "ei", "i" in them is dropped.

diǎnr → d + iǎ + r
wánr → w + á + r
páir → p + á + r
wèir → w + è + r

The 'r' ending most often appears in the Beijing dialect, on which standard Chinese is based.

5 晚上你有活动吗？(Wǎnshang nǐ yǒu huódòng ma?)

1) In Chinese, phrases indicating time can be placed at the beginning of a sentence or between the subject and predicate:

明天我去长城。(Míngtiān wǒ qù Chángchéng.)

他晚上有活动。(Tā wǎnshang yǒu huódòng.)

2) The verb "有" (yǒu) forms its negative by adding "没" (méi) in front:

晚上我没有活动。(Wǎnshang wǒ méi yǒu huódòng.)

6 你明天干什么？ (Nǐ míngtiān gàn shénme?)

Here "干什么" (gàn shénme) is a colloquial way of saying "做什么" (zuò shénme) which means "what are (you) doing?"

7 不，她有别的事儿。 (Bù, tā yǒu biéde shìr.)

In Chinese, there are two ways of giving negative answers to questions, for example:

你明天去长城吗？(Nǐ míngtiān qù Chángcheng ma?)

我明天不去长城。 (Wǒ míngtiān bú qù Chángchéng.)

or

不，我明天去故宫。(Bù, wǒ míngtiān qù Gùgōng.)

## supplementary words • 补充生词 • bǔchōng shēngcí

| | | | |
|---|---|---|---|
| 1 | 那儿 | （代）nàr | there |
| 2 | 文化宫 | （名）wénhuàgōng | cultural palace |
| 3 | 画展 | （名）huàzhǎn | exhibition of paintings |
| 4 | 下午 | （名）xiàwǔ | afternoon |
| 5 | 安排 | （动）ānpái | to arrange |
| | 西单 | Xīdān | name of a commercial centre in the west of Beijing |

## • exercises • 练习 • liànxí

**1. Phonetic exercises:**

1) Tones

(1) The neutral tone

| (1) +neutral | (2) +neutral | (3) +neutral | (4) +neutral |
|---|---|---|---|
| dōngxi | péngyou | wǎnshang | sìge |
| sānge | biéde | Nǐ ne? | qù ma |

(2) Changes of "一 (yī)"

"yī (一)" + (3)

yìdiǎnr

yìběn

yìbǎi

(3) Changes of the 3rd tone

dàshǐguǎn→ dàshíguǎn

zhǎnlǎnguǎn→ zhánlánguǎn

Wángfǔjǐng→ Wángfújǐng

2) Sound discrimination

| (1) The retroflex final | (2) d | t |
|---|---|---|
| nǎr | dà | tā |
| diǎnr | dōng | tóng |
| páir | diǎn | tiān |
| huìr | duì | tuì |
| shìr | | |

**2. Complete the dialogues:**

Model: A: 你去哪儿？
Nǐ qù nǎr?
B: 我 去 北京 饭店 。
Wǒ qù Běijīng Fàndiàn.
A: 去那儿干 什 么？
Qù nàr gàn shénme?
B: 找 一个 人。
Zhǎo yíge rén.

1) A: ________?
________?
B: 我 去 英 国 大 使馆。
Wǒ qù Yīngguó Dàshǐguǎn.
A: ________?
________?
B: 看 朋 友。
Kàn péngyou.

2) A: ________?
________?
B: 我 去西单。
Wǒ qù Xīdān.
A: ________?
________?
B: ________。（东 西）
________。(dōngxi)

3) A: ________?
________?
B: ________。（文 化 宫）
________。（wénhuàgōng)
A: ________?
________?
B: 参 观 画 展。
Cānguān huàzhǎn.

***3. Practice with negative answers:**

1) Answer according to the pictures.

Model: A: 明天 你去 故宫 吗?

Míngtiān nǐ qù Gùgōng ma?

B: 我 不去。我 去 文化宫 。

Wǒ bú qù. Wǒ qù wénhuàgōng.

(1) 明天 你去 长城 吗?

Míngtiān nǐ qù Chángchéng ma?

(2) 晚上 你去看杂技吗?

Wǎnshang nǐ qù kàn zájì ma?

(3) 下午 你去大使馆 吗?

Xiàwǔ nǐ qù dàshǐguǎn ma?

(4) 你们 明天 去 故宫 参观 吗?
Nǐmen míngtiān qù Gùgōng cānguān ma?

2) Model: A: 你们 晚上 有 活动 吗?
Nǐmen wǎnshang yǒu huódòng ma?
B: 没 有，你 呢?
Méi yǒu, nǐ ne?

(1) 下午， 活动
xiàwǔ, huódòng

(2) 晚上 ，事儿
wǎnshang, shìr

(3) 明天 ， 安排
míngtiān, ānpai

***4. Select the correct form of each question from the three choices given:**

1) a. 哪儿他住?
Nǎr tā zhù?
b. 他住哪儿?
Tā zhù nǎr?
c. 哪儿住他?
Nǎr zhù tā?

2) a. 什么 看 你?
Shénme kàn nǐ?
b. 什么 你看?
Shénme nǐ kàn?
c. 你 看 什么?
Nǐ kàn shénme?

3) a. 什么 活动 他有?
Shénme huódòng tā yǒu?
b. 他 什么 活动 有?
Tā shénme huódòng yǒu?
c. 他 有 什么 活动?
Tā yǒu shénme huódòng?

4) a. 哪国 人 是他?
Nǎguó rén shì tā?
b. 他 是 哪国 人?
Tā shì nǎguó rén?
c. 他 哪国 人 是?
Tā nǎguó rén shì?

5) a. 谁 他 找?
Shéi tā zhǎo?
b. 找 他谁?
Zhǎo tā shéi?
c. 他 找 谁?
Tā zhǎo shéi?

6) a. 什么 事儿你们 有?
Shénme shìr nǐmen yǒu?
b. 你们 有 什么事儿?
Nǐmen yǒu shénme shìr?
c. 你们 什么 事儿有?
Nǐmen shénme shìr yǒu?

**5. Listen to the dialogues:**

1) A: 赵 先 生， 明天 你去 长城 吗？
Zhào xiānsheng, míngtiān nǐ qù Chángchéng ma?

B: 我 有 点儿 事儿， 我 不去。
Wǒ yǒu diǎnr shìr, wǒ bú qù.

A: 你 太太他们呢？
Nǐ tàitai tāmen ne?

B: 他们 也不去。
Tāmen yě bú qù.

A: 那么，你们 干 什么 呢？
Nàme, nǐmen gàn shénme ne?

B: 我 去 北京 饭店 看 李 先 生，我太太、我女儿 去 买 东西。
Wǒ qù Běijīng Fàndiàn kàn Lǐ xiānsheng, wǒ tàitai、wǒ nǚ'ér qù mǎi dōngxi.

A: 你儿子呢？
Nǐ érzi ne?

B: 啊， 他去看 画展。
À, tā qù kàn huàzhǎn.

2) A: 晚上 您 不 看杂技？
Wǎnshang nín bú kàn zájì?

B: 我 不去， 我 有 点儿 事儿。
Wǒ bú qù, wǒ yǒu diǎnr shìr.

A: 明天 晚上 呢？
Míngtiān wǎnshang ne?

B: 明天 晚上 也 有 杂技？
Míngtiān wǎnshang yě yǒu zájì?

A: 有 啊。
Yǒu a.

B: 明天 我 一定 去 看。
Míngtiān wǒ yídìng qù kàn.

# 5 Going To The Post Office
## 去邮局 qù yóujú

(Before going to the post office, David asks his parents and his sister if they want him to get anything for them.)

| | | |
|---|---|---|
| 伟：<br>Wěi: | 爸爸，我 去 邮局 寄 一封 信。①<br>Bàba, wǒ qù yóujú jì yìfēng xìn.<br>您 买 什么 吗？<br>Nín mǎi shénme ma? | Dad, I'm going to the post office to mail a letter. Do you need anything? |
| 陈：<br>Chén: | 给 我 买 几张 八分 邮票。②<br>Gěi wǒ mǎi jǐzhāng bāfēn yóupiào. | Please get me some eight-cent stamps. |

| | | |
|---|---|---|
| 伟：<br>Wěi: | 买 几张？③<br>Mǎi jǐzhāng? | How many do you want? |
| 陈 ：<br>Chén: | 五 张 。<br>Wǔzhāng. | Five. |
| 莉：<br>Lì: | 大伟，你给 我 买几个信封 。<br>Dàwěi, nǐ gěi wǒ mǎi jǐge xìnfēng. | David, will you get me some envelopes? |
| 伟：<br>Wěi: | 买 多少？<br>Mǎi duōshao? | How many? |
| 莉：<br>Lì: | 十个。<br>Shíge. | Ten. |
| 伟：<br>Wěi: | 妈妈，您 买 点儿 什么 吗？④<br>Māma,nín mǎi diǎnr shénme ma? | Mom, is there anything you want? |
| 艾：<br>Ài: | 不 买。<br>Bù mǎi. | No, thank you. |
| 莉：<br>Lì: | 大伟， 再 给我 买一本<br>Dàwěi, zài gěi wǒ mǎi yìběn<br>《中国 画报》吧。⑤<br>《Zhōngguó Huàbào》ba. | David, get me a copy of *China Pictorial* as well, will you? |
| 伟：<br>Wěi: | 好 。<br>Hǎo. | Sure. |

## • new words • 生词 • shēngcí

| | | | |
|---|---|---|---|
| 1 | 邮局 | （名）yóujú | post office |
| 2 | 爸爸 | （名）bàba | father, dad |
| 3 | 寄 | （动）jì | to post, to mail |
| 4 | 封 | （量）fēng | a measure word for letters |
| 5 | 信 | （名）xìn | letter |
| 6 | 给 | （介）gěi | for, to |
| 7 | 几 | （代）jǐ | some, several |
| 8 | 张 | （量）zhāng | a measure word (piece, sheet) |
| 9 | 分 | （量）fēn | the lowest denomination of Chinese |

| | | | |
|---|---|---|---|
| | | | currency |
| 10 | 邮票 | (名) yóupiào | stamp |
| 11 | 五 | (数) wǔ | five |
| 12 | 信封 | (名) xìnfēng | envelope |
| 13 | 多少 | (代) duōshao | how many, how much |
| 14 | 十 | (数) shí | ten |
| 15 | 妈妈 | (名) māma | mother, mom |
| 16 | 再 | (副) zài | too, also, in addition to |
| 17 | 本 | (量) běn | a measure word (copy) |
| 18 | 吧 | (助) ba | a modal particle |

**专名　　Zhuānmíng　　Proper name**

《中国画报》《Zhōngguó Huàbào》　*China Pictorial*

## study points • 注释 • zhùshì

1　我去邮局寄一封信。(Wǒ qù yóujú jì yìfēng xìn.)

In Chinese, many nouns have special measure words:

一封信 (yìfēng xìn)

五张邮票 (wǔzhāng yóupiào)

N. B. 张 is often used for things that are flat, such as tables, paper and postage stamps.

八个信封 (bāge xìnfēng)

四个朋友 (sìge péngyou)

十本《中国画报》(shíběn《Zhōngguó Huàbào》)

N. B. 本 is usually used as the measure word for things in the form of book such as magazines, books, catalogues, etc.

2　给我买几张八分邮票。(Gěi wǒ mǎi jǐzhāng bāfēn yóupiào.)

"给我" (gěi wǒ) means "for me". In Chinese, it and other adverbials go before the verb they modify. It would be wrong to say "买几张邮票给我。" (Mǎi jǐzhāng yóupiào gěi wǒ.)

3 买几张？(Mǎi jǐzhāng? )

Although both “几”(jǐ) and “多少”(duōshao) mean “how many”, “几”(jǐ) is only used to ask for figures under ten. “多少”(duōshao) can be used for any amount. Another difference is that a measure word is necessary between “几”and the noun, while for “多少”the measure word can be omitted:

| | |
|---|---|
| 几封信 (jǐfēng xìn) | 多少（封）信 (duōshao (fēng) xìn) |
| 几张邮票 (jǐzhāng yóupiào) | 多少（张）邮票 (duōshao (zhāng) yóupiào) |
| 几个朋友 (jǐge péngyou) | 多少（个）朋友 (duōshao (ge) péngyou) |

4 您买点儿什么吗？(Nín mǎi diǎnr shénme ma?)

“什么”(shénme) here does not mean “what” as in a question. It is used as an indefinite pronoun, corresponding to “something” in English.

5 再给我买一本《中国画报》吧。(Zài gěi wǒ mǎi yìběn《Zhōngguó Huàbào》ba.)

1) In China, the post office is the main agent for newspapers and magazines. People can buy and subscribe to newspapers and magazines there.

2) “吧”(ba) can be used at the end of sentences to indicate that the statement is a suggestion, a request, an order, etc. Here it is used as a request.

## supplementary words • 补充生词 • bǔchōng shēngcí

| | | | | |
|---|---|---|---|---|
| 1 | 报 | （名）| bào | newspaper |
| 2 | 杯 | （量）| bēi | cup, glass |
| 3 | 瓶 | （量）| píng | bottle |
| 4 | 学校 | （名）| xuéxiào | school |
| 5 | 椅子 | （名）| yǐzi | chair |
| 6 | 把 | （量）| bǎ | a measure word |
| 7 | 桌子 | （名）| zhuōzi | table |
| 8 | 床 | （名）| chuáng | bed |

## • exercises • 练习 • liànxí

**1. Phonetic exercises:**

1) Tones

(1) Changes of the tone of "一 (yī)"

"一 (yī)" + (1)

yìfēn

yìfēng

yìzhāng

(2) Neutral tone

duōshao

māma

bàba

(3) 2nd tone

| (2) + (1) | (2) + (2) | (2) + (3) | (2) + (4) |
|---|---|---|---|
| fángjiān | huáqiáo | méi yǒu | huódòng |
| míngtiān | yóujú | Nín hǎo! | yóupiào |

2) Sound discrimination

| (1) an | en | (2) en | eng | (3) j | q |
|---|---|---|---|---|---|
| wǎn | wèn | chén | chéng | jǐ | qǐ |
| cān | chén | fēn | fēng | jú | qù |
| shān | shén | shén | shēng | jiào | qiáo |
| | | běn | péng | jiàn | qián |

**2. Questions and answers:**

Use "干什么" (gàn shénme) and "买几张" (mǎi jǐzhāng) to make questions and answers as in the model.

1) Model: A: 你去邮局干什么?

Nǐ qù yóujú gàn shénme?

B: 买几张八分邮票。

Mǎi jǐzhāng bāfēn yóupiào.

A: 买几张?

Mǎi jǐzhāng?

B: 买三张。

Mǎi sānzhāng.

(1) 《中国画报》，八本

《Zhōngguó Huàbào》, bāběn

(2) 信，三封

xìn, sānfēng

(3) 报，五张

bào, wǔzhāng

(4) 信封，十个

xìnfēng, shíge

(5) 寄，《中国　画报》，五本
jì, 《Zhōngguó Huàbào》, wǔběn

2) Ask questions using "买什么" (mǎi shénme) and "买多少" (mǎi duōshao) and answer them following the models.

A: 你买　什么？
Nǐ mǎi shénme?

B: 买　信封。
Mǎi xìnfēng.

A: 买　多少？
Mǎi duōshao?

B: 买　五个。
Mǎi wǔge.

(1) 买，报，三张
mǎi, bào, sānzhāng

(2) 喝，茶，一杯
hē, chá, yìbēi

(3) 买，啤酒，五瓶
mǎi, píjiǔ, wǔpíng

(4) 喝，咖啡，一杯
hē, kāfēi, yìbēi

(5) 买，椅子，三把
mǎi, yǐzi, sānbǎ

(6) 买，桌子，一张
mǎi, zhuōzi, yìzhāng

(7) 买，床，一张
mǎi, chuáng, yìzhāng

***3. Fill in the blanks with "几" (jǐ) or "多少" (duōshao):**

1) 你们　住_____个　房间？
Nǐmen zhù_____ge fángjiān?

2) 你　买_____信封？
Nǐ mǎi_____xìnfēng?

3) 你们　学校　有_____个人？
Nǐmen xuéxiào yǒu_____ge rén?

4) 这个　房间　住_____个人？
Zhège fángjiān zhù_____ge rén?

5) 陈　先生　有_____个女儿？
Chén xiānsheng yǒu_____ge nǚ'ér?

**4. Listen to the dialogues:**

1) A: 同志，我买八分的邮票。
Tóngzhì, wǒ mǎi bāfēn de yóupiào.

B: 您　买　几张？
Nín mǎi jǐzhāng?

A: 三张。同志，那是《中国　画报》吧？
Sānzhāng. Tóngzhì, nà shì《Zhōngguó Huàbào》ba?

B: 是。
Shì.

A: 请 给我看一下儿。
Qǐng gěi wǒ kàn yíxiàr.

B: 请 看吧。
Qǐng kàn ba.

A: 好。我买一本。
Hǎo. Wǒ mǎi yìběn.

2) A: 爷爷, 您喝点儿什么?
Yéye, nín hē diǎnr shénme?

B: 我 喝啤酒。
Wǒ hē píjiǔ.

A: 好, 给您一杯啤酒。奶奶, 您呢?
Hǎo, gěi nín yìbēi píjiǔ. Nǎinai, nín ne?

B: 我 不喝啤酒。给我一杯茶吧。
Wǒ bù hē píjiǔ. Gěi wǒ yìbēi chá ba.

A: 好。大伟, 你喝什么?
Hǎo. Dàwěi, nǐ hē shénme?

D: 我 喝咖啡。
Wǒ hē kāfēi.

A: 好。
Hǎo.

D: 再 给 我 一杯啤酒。
Zài gěi wǒ yìbēi píjiǔ.

A: 啊?
Á?

***5. Translate the following into Chinese:**

1) a friend
2) a letter
3) several stamps
4) a "China Pictorial"
5) five envelopes
6) eight chairs
7) ten tables
8) three beds

# 复习 (1) Revision (1) fùxí (1)

1. **Read aloud:**

我们，你们，他们。
wǒmen, nǐmen, tāmen.
同志们，朋友们，服务员们
tóngzhìmen, péngyoumen, fúwùyuánmen
先生们，小姐们，太太们，伯伯们，叔叔们
xiānshengmen, xiǎojiemen, tàitaimen, bóbomen, shūshumen
饭店 服务员们，美国 朋友们
fàndiàn fúwùyuánmen, Měiguó péngyoumen

*2. **Fill in the blanks using "不" (bù) or "没" (méi):**

1) 他是中国人，______是日本人。
Tā shì Zhōngguórén, ______shì Rìběnrén.

2) 我住八一二五房间，______住八一二三房间。
Wǒ zhù bāyāo'èrwǔ fángjiān, ______zhù bāyāo'èrsān fángjiān.

3) 明天她______有什么事儿。
Míngtiān tā______yǒu shénme shìr.

4) 妈妈买信封，姐姐______买信封。
Māma mǎi xìnfēng, jiějie______mǎi xìnfēng.

5) 他们______去长城，我去长城。
Tāmen______qù Chángchéng, wǒ qù Chángchéng.

6) 他______叫王小明，他叫王小山。
Tā______jiào Wáng Xiǎomíng, tā jiào Wáng Xiǎoshān.

7) 他们有一个女儿，______有儿子。
Tāmen yǒu yíge nǚ'ér, ______yǒu érzi.

8) 我喝啤酒，______喝咖啡。
Wǒ hē píjiǔ, ______hē kāfēi.

9) 我们几个人______会抽烟。
Wǒmen jǐge rén______huì chōu yān.

10) 我 有信封，______有 邮票 。
Wǒ yǒu xìnfēng, ______yǒu yóupiào.

3 . **Ask 3 questions for each sentence using “吗” (ma) and interrogative pronouns “谁” (shuí), “哪” (nǎ), “哪儿” (nǎr), “什么” (shénme):**

Model: 他是 赵 明。 他是 赵 明 吗？
Tā shì Zhào Míng.——Tā shì Zhào Míng ma?
谁 是 赵 明？
Shuí shì Zhào Míng?
他 叫 什么？
Tā jiào shénme?

1) 他 买《 中国 画报 》。
Tā mǎi《Zhōngguó Huàbào》.

2) 赵 明 住一五二三 房间 。
Zhào Míng zhù yīwǔ'èrsān fángjiān.

3) 张 先生 去故宫 。
Zhāng xiānsheng qù Gùgōng.

4) 他们 住 北京 饭店 。
Tāmen zhù Běijīng Fàndiàn.

5) 她 是 英国人 。
Tā shì Yīngguórén.

6) 他们 找 赵 先生 。
Tāmen zhǎo Zhào xiānsheng.

# 6 Mailing A Letter
## 寄信 jì xìn

(David is in a post office posting a letter and buying stamps.)

| | | |
|---|---|---|
| 伟： | 同志 ，我寄信。 | I'd like to send a letter, comrade. |
| Wěi: | Tóngzhì, wǒ jì xìn. | |
| 营业员： | 寄哪儿? | Where to? |
| yíngyèyuán: | Jì nǎr? | |
| 伟： | 美国 。 | The United States. |
| Wěi: | Měiguó. | |

| | | |
|---|---|---|
| 营：<br>yíng: | 挂 号吗？<br>Guà hào ma? | Registered? |
| 伟：<br>Wěi: | 挂 号。多少 钱？<br>Guà hào. Duōshao qián? | Registered. How much is it? |
| 营：<br>yíng: | 一块 二（毛）。①<br>Yíkuài èr (máo). | One yuan and twenty fen. |
| 伟：<br>Wěi: | 同志，你 看，这封 信<br>Tóngzhì, nǐ kàn, zhèfēng xìn<br>超 重 吗？<br>chāo zhòng ma? | Comrade, would you see if it is overweight? |
| 营：<br>yíng: | 我 称一下儿。不 超 重。<br>Wǒ chēng yíxiàr. Bù chāo zhòng. | Let me weigh it. No, it isn't. |
| 伟：<br>Wěi: | 我 还 要 五张 八分 邮票<br>Wǒ hái yào wǔzhāng bāfēn yóupiào<br>和 五张 明信片。<br>hé wǔzhāng míngxìnpiàn. | Thanks. I also want five eight-fen stamps and five post-cards. |
| 营：<br>yíng: | 一共 一块 八毛 五（分）。<br>Yígòng yíkuài bāmáo wǔ (fēn). | The total is one yuan and eighty-five fen. |
| 伟：<br>Wěi: | 给 你 钱。②<br>Gěi nǐ qián. | Here's your money. |
| 营：<br>yíng: | 你 这 是 两 块。③ 这 是<br>Nǐ zhè shì liǎngkuài. Zhè shì<br>邮 票，这 是 明 信 片。<br>yóupiào, zhè shì míngxìnpiàn.<br>找 你一毛 五（分）。④<br>Zhǎo nǐ yìmáo wǔ (fēn). | This is two yuan you are giving me. Here are your stamps and post-cards. Your change is fifteen fen. |

## • new words • 生词 • shēngcí

| | | | | |
|---|---|---|---|---|
| 1 | 营业员 | （名） | yíngyèyuán | clerk |
| 2 | 挂号 | | guà hào | register, registered |
| 3 | 钱 | （名） | qián | money |
| 4 | 块〔元〕 | （量） | kuài (yuán) | colloquial form for "*yuan*" |
| 5 | 毛〔角〕 | （量） | máo (jiǎo) | colloquial form for "*jiao*" |

| | | | |
|---|---|---|---|
| 6 | 超重 | chāo zhòng | overweight |
| 7 | 称 | （动）chēng | to weigh |
| 8 | 还 | （副）hái | also, as well, in addition, still |
| 9 | 要 | （动）yào | to want, to need, to ask |
| 10 | 和 | （连、介）hé | and, with |
| 11 | 明信片 | （名）míngxìnpiàn | post-card |
| 12 | 一共 | （副）yígòng | altogether, in all |
| 13 | 给 | （动）gěi | to give |
| 14 | 两 | （数）liǎng | two |
| 15 | 找 | （动）zhǎo | to give change |

## study points • 注释 • zhùshì

1 一块二（毛）(yíkuài èr(máo))

The three denominations of Chinese currency (Renminbi) are "元" (yuán), "角" (jiǎo) and "分" (fēn). In colloquial Chinese, they are called "块" (kuài), "毛" (máo) and "分" (fēn).

1 fen × 10 = 1 jiǎo (or máo)    1 分 × 10 = 1 角（毛）

1 jiǎo × 10 = 1 yuán (or kuài)    1 角 × 10 = 1 元（块）

In ordinary conversation, the last denomination "分" (fēn) can be left out:

| | In conversation | In writing |
|---|---|---|
| 0.58 元 | 五毛八（分） | 五角八分 |
| 18.34 元 | 十八块三毛四（分） | 十八元三角四分 |

2 给你钱。(Gěi nǐ qián.)

The Chinese verb "给" (gěi), functioning like the English verb "give", can take two objects. In the above sentence, the two objects are "你" (nǐ) and "钱" (qián). In English we can either say "Give you money" or "Give money to you", but in Chinese the object indicating a person always comes first, therefore we put "你" (nǐ) in front of "钱" (qián).

3 你这是两块。(Nǐ zhè shì liǎngkuài.)

1) This is the kind of expression a Chinese shopkeeper usually uses when s/he takes the customer's money. It is an acknowledgement of the amount of money received.

2) Both "二" (èr) and "两" (liǎng) mean "two", but usually they are not interchangeable. "两" (liǎng) is used with a measure word:

两本书 (liǎngběn shū)
两个朋友 (liǎngge péngyou)
两封信 (liǎngfēng xìn)

When the figure exceeds ten, such as 12, 20, 32, etc., the word "二"(èr) must be used instead of "两" (liǎng):

十二本书 (shí'èrběn shū)
二十个朋友 (èrshíge péngyou)
三十二封信 (sānshí'èrfēng xìn)

4 找你一毛五(分)。(zhǎo nǐ yìmáo wǔ (fēn).)
Notice the change of tone of the word "一" (yī). It changes from the first tone to the fourth tone (yì) and is marked by "丶". This always happens when the word appears before a syllable of the first, second or third tone: "一分" (yìfēn), "一元" (yìyuán) and "一点儿" (yìdiǎnr).
However the tone of the word "一" remains unchanged before the following numerals: "一" (yī), "三" (sān), "五" (wǔ), "七" (qī), "八" (bā) and "九" (jiǔ).

## supplementary words • 补充生词 • bǔchōng shēngcí

| | | | |
|---|---|---|---|
| 1 | 怎么 | (代) zěnme | how |
| 2 | 卖 | (动) mài | to sell |
| 3 | 顾客 | (名) gùkè | customer |
| 4 | 大概 | (副) dàgài | about |
| 5 | 包裹单 | (名) bāoguǒdān | parcel invoice |

## • exercises • 练习 • liànxí

**1. Phonetic exercises:**

1) Tones

(1) Changes of the tone of "一 (yī)"

| "一 (yī)" + (1) | "一 (yī)" + (2) |
|---|---|
| yìfēn | yìmáo |
| yìzhāng | yìyuán |
| **"一 (yī)" + (3)** | **"一 (yī)" + (4)** |
| yìdiǎnr | yíkuài |
| yìběn | yígòng |

(2) Changes of the tone of "不 (bù)"

| | |
|---|---|
| bú huì | bù mǎi |
| bú kàn | bù chāo zhòng |

(3) The 4th tone

| (4)+(1) | (4)+(2) | (4)+(3) | (4)+(4) |
|---|---|---|---|
| xìnfēng | sìmáo | yìdiǎnr | jièshào |
| Gùgōng | Àilín | Jì nǎr? | guà hào |

2) Sound discrimination

| (1) ch | sh | (2) ua | uo | (3) ang | eng |
|---|---|---|---|---|---|
| chēng | shēng | huá | huó | cháng | chéng |
| chāo | shào | guà | guó | fāng | fēng |
| cháng | shàng | shuā | shuō | shāng | shēng |

**2. Practice after the model:**

Model: 1.32 元　　一块 三毛 二(分)
1.32 yuán　　yíkuài sānmáo èr(fēn)

2.30 (yuán)　10.00 (yuán)　3.58 (yuán)　2.22 (yuán)　0.13 (yuán)
0.80 (yuán)　0.53 (yuán)　0.22 (yuán)　0.08 (yuán)　0.02 (yuán)

***3. Answer the questions:**

1) 明信片 几分 一张？(0.05 元/张)
Míngxìnpiàn jǐfēn yìzhāng? (0.05 yuán/zhāng)

2) 信封 几分 一个？(0.01 元/个)
Xìnfēng jǐfēn yíge? (0.01 yuán/ge)

3) 《中国 画报》 多少 钱 一本？(1.30 元/本)
《Zhōngguó Huàbào》 duōshao qián yìběn? (1.30 yuán/běn)

4) 桌子 多少 钱 一张？(15.00 元/张)
Zhuōzi duōshao qián yìzhāng? (15.00 yuán/zhāng)

5) 信封 怎么 卖？(0.10 元/10 个)
Xìnfēng zěnme mài? (0.10 yuán/10 ge)

6) 椅子怎么卖？(8.50 元/把)
Yǐzi zěnme mài? (8.50 yuán/bǎ)

***4. Complete the dialogues using the words given in the brackets:**

1) 营 业 员: 同 志, 您 买 什么?
Yíngyèyuán: Tóngzhì, nín mǎi shénme?
顾客: ________。(八分 邮 票, 一张)
Gùkè: ________. (bāfēn yóupiào, yìzhāng)
营 : 还 要 什 么?
Yíng: Hái yào shénme?
顾 : ________。(五分 明信片 , 三 张)
Gù: ________. (wǔfēn míngxìnpiàn, sānzhāng)
营 : 一共________。
Yíng: Yígòng________.
顾: 给 您 钱。
Gù: Gěi nín qián.

2) 顾客: 同 志, 有 信封 吗?
Gùkè: Tóngzhì, yǒu xìnfēng ma?
营 业 员: 有。 您 要________?
Yíngyèyuán: Yǒu. Nín yào________?
顾: 我 要 二十个。________?
Gù: Wǒ yào èrshíge. ________?
营 : 一分一个, 二十个, ________。
Yíng: Yìfēn yíge, èrshíge, ________.
顾:《中 国 画 报》________?
Gù:《Zhōngguó Huàbào》________?
营 : 一块 三。
Yíng: Yíkuài sān.
顾: 我 要 两本 。
Gù: Wǒ yào liǎngběn.
营 : 一共________。
Yíng: Yígòng________.
顾: 给 您 钱 。
Gù: Gěi nín qián.
营 : 您 这 是 三块, 找 您________。
Yíng: Nín zhè shì sānkuài, zhǎo nín________.

**5. Listen to the dialogues:**

1) 顾客: 同志, 我寄 挂号信。
Gùkè: Tóngzhì, wǒ jì guàhàoxìn.
营 业 员 : 您 这 两封 信 大概 超 重。
Yíngyèyuán: Nín zhè liǎngfēng xìn dàgài chāo zhòng.

顾：是 吗？
Gù: Shì ma?

营：我 称 一下儿。您 看，超 重 。
Yíng: Wǒ chēng yíxiàr. Nín kàn, chāo zhòng.

顾：是 啊。
Gù: Shì a.

2) 顾客：同 志，请 给 我 一 张 包 裹 单。
Gùkè: Tóngzhì, qǐng gěi wǒ yìzhāng bāoguǒdān.

营 业 员：好。寄 哪 儿？
Yíngyèyuán: Hǎo. Jì nǎr?

顾：英 国。 多少 钱？
Gù: Yīngguó. Duōshao qián?

营： 我 称 一下儿。啊， 五块 二毛 三。
Yíng: Wǒ chēng yíxiàr. À, wǔkuài èrmáo sān.

# 7 Exchanging Foreign Money For Renminbi
# 兑换外币 duìhuàn wàibì

(Mr. Chen Mingshan is exchanging foreign money for Renminbi in a bank.)

| | | |
|---|---|---|
| 陈 :<br>Chén: | 同志，我兑换外币。<br>Tóngzhì, wǒ duìhuàn wàibì. | Comrade, I'd like to have some foreign currencies exchanged. |
| 工作人员：<br>gōngzuò rényuán: | 什么外币？<br>Shénme wàibì? | What currencies? |
| 陈 :<br>Chén: | 美元和英镑。今天<br>Měiyuán hé Yīngbàng. Jīntiān | American dollars and English pounds. What are |

| | | |
|---|---|---|
| | 牌价是 多少？<br>páijià shì duōshao? | today's exchange rates? |
| 工：<br>gōng: | 一百 美元 兑换 人民币<br>Yìbǎi Měiyuán duìhuàn Rénmínbì<br>一百五十三块 三毛 八<br>yìbǎiwǔshísānkuài sānmáo bā<br>(分)，①一百 英镑 兑换<br>(fēn)， yìbǎi Yīngbàng duìhuàn<br>人民币 三百二十八块 四毛<br>Rénmínbì sānbǎi'èrshíbākuài sìmáo<br>三（分）。<br>sān (fēn) . | One hundred American dollars to one hundred and fifty three yuan, thirty-eight fen of Renminbi, one hundred pounds to three hundred and twenty-eight yuan, forty-three fen. |
| 陈：<br>Chén: | 我兑换 一千 美元，<br>Wǒ duìhuàn yìqiān Měiyuán,<br>一百三十 英镑。<br>yìbǎisānshí Yīngbàng. | I want to have one thousand dollars and one hundred and thirty pounds exchanged. |
| 工：<br>gōng: | 请 你填 一张 单子。<br>Qǐng nǐ tián yìzhāng dānzi. | Fill in this form, please. |
| 陈：<br>Chén: | 好。<br>Hǎo. | O. K. |
| 工：<br>gōng: | 一千 美元 兑换 一千<br>Yìqiān Měiyuán duìhuàn yìqiān-<br>五百三十三块 八(毛)，<br>wǔbǎisānshísānkuài bā (máo) ,<br>一百三十 英 镑 兑换<br>yìbǎisānshí Yīngbàng duìhuàn<br>四百二十六块 九毛 六（分），<br>sìbǎi'èrshíliùkuài jiǔmáo liù (fēn) ,<br>一共 一千九百六十块<br>yígòng yìqiānjiǔbǎiliùshíkuài<br>七毛六（分）。请 点<br>qīmáo liù (fēn) . Qǐng diǎn<br>一下儿。<br>yíxiàr . | One thousand five hundred and thirty-three yuan and eighty fen for one thousand dollars, four hundred and twenty-six yuan and ninety-six fen for one hundred and thirty pounds. The total is one thousand nine hundred and sixty yuan and seventy fen. Please count it. |
| 陈：<br>Chén: | 好。谢谢。<br>Hǎo. Xièxie. | Good. Thank you. |
| 工：<br>gōng: | 不用 谢。②<br>Bú yòng xiè. | You're welcome. |

## • new words • 生词 • shēngcí

| | | | | |
|---|---|---|---|---|
| 1 | 兑换 | (动) | duìhuàn | to exchange (currencies) |
| 2 | 外币 | (名) | wàibì | foreign currency |
| 3 | 工作 | (动、名) | gōngzuò | to work, work, job |
| 4 | 人员 | (名) | rényuán | personnel, staff |
| 5 | 美元 | (名) | Měiyuán | American dollar |
| 6 | 英镑 | (名) | Yīngbàng | English pound |
| 7 | 今天 | (名) | jīntiān | today |
| 8 | 牌价 | (名) | páijià | exchange rate |
| 9 | 百 | (数) | bǎi | hundred |
| 10 | 人民币 | (名) | Rénmínbì | Renminbi (Chinese currency) |
| 11 | 四 | (数) | sì | four |
| 12 | 千 | (数) | qiān | thousand |
| 13 | 填 | (动) | tián | to fill (in) |
| 14 | 单子 | (名) | dānzi | form, list |
| 15 | 六 | (数) | liù | six |
| 16 | 九 | (数) | jiǔ | nine |
| 17 | 零 | (数) | líng | zero, nil |
| 18 | 七 | (数) | qī | seven |
| 19 | 点 | (动) | diǎn | to count |
| 20 | 不用 | | bú yòng | not necessary |
| | 不用谢 | | bú yòng xiè | don't mention it, you're welcome, not at all |

## study points • 注释 • zhùshì

1 一百美元兑换人民币一百五十三块三毛八（分）。(Yìbǎi Měiyuán duìhuàn Rénmínbì yìbǎiwǔshísānkuài sānmáo bā (fēn).).

The decimal system is being used in China:

| | | | | | | | | | |
|---|---|---|---|---|---|---|---|---|---|
| 1 | 2 | 3 | 4 | 5 | 6 | 7 | 8 | 9 | 10 |
| 一 | 二 | 三 | 四 | 五 | 六 | 七 | 八 | 九 | 十 |
| 11 | 12 | | | | | | | 19 | 20 |
| 十一 | 十二 | | | | | | | 十九 | 二十 |
| 21 | 22 | | | | | | | 29 | 30 |
| 二十一 | 二十二 | | | | | | | 二十九 | 三十 |
| 91 | 92 | | | | | | | 99 | 100 |
| 九十一 | 九十二 | | | | | | | 九十九 | 一百 |
| 101 | 102 | | | | | | | | 110 |
| 一百零一 | 一百零二 | | | | | | | | 一百一十 |
| 111 | 112 | | | | | | | | 200 |
| 一百一十一 | 一百一十二 | | | | | | | | 二百 |
| 1001 | 1002 | | | | | | | | 1100 |
| 一千零一 | 一千零二 | | | | | | | | 一千一百 |
| 1101 | 1102 | | | | | | | | 2000 |
| 一千一百零一 | 一千一百零二 | | | | | | | | 二千 |
| 2010 | | | | | | | | 9999 | |
| 二千零一十 | | | | | | | | 九千九百九十九 | |

2 不用谢 (bú yòng xiè)

As a reply to “谢谢” (xièxie)，“不谢” (bú xiè) and “不用谢” (bú yòng xiè) are interchangeable.

## supplementary words • 补充生词 • bǔchōng shēngcí

| | | | | |
|---|---|---|---|---|
| 1 | 没错儿 | | méi cuòr | exactly |
| 2 | 法郎 | （名） | Fǎláng | franc |
| 3 | 日元 | （名） | Rìyuán | (Japanese) Yen |

| | | | |
|---|---|---|---|
| 4 | 万 | （数）wàn | ten thousand |
| 5 | 马克 | （名）Mǎkè | Mark |
| 6 | 存 | （动）cún | to deposit |
| 7 | 款 | （名）kuǎn | deposit |
| 8 | 定期 | （名）dìngqī | time (deposit), fixed (deposit) |
| 9 | 活期 | （名）huóqī | demand (deposit), current (deposit) |
| 10 | 正好 | （形、副）zhènghǎo | precise, precisely; no more, no less |
| 11 | 取（款） | （动）qǔ(kuǎn) | to draw (money) |
| 12 | 凭 | （动）píng | to use (as evidence) |
| 13 | 存折 | （名）cúnzhé | bank-book |
| 14 | 没什么 | méi shénme | you're welcome: don't mention it |
| | 中国银行 | Zhōngguó Yínháng | China Bank |
| | 西德 | Xī Dé | West Germany |

## • exercises • 练习 • liànxí

**1. Phonetic exercises:**

1) Tones

(1) Changes of the tone of "一(yī)"

yìqiān
yìshí
yìbǎi
yíbàng

(2) Changes of the 3rd tone

liǎngqiān
Měiyuán
jiǔbǎi
wǔkuài

(3) The 1st tone

| (1)+(1) | (1)+(2) | (1)+(3) | (1)+(4) |
|---|---|---|---|
| jīntiān | huānyíng | tā yǒu | Yīngbàng |
| cānguān | Zhōngguó | qībǎi | gōngzuò |

2) Sound discrimination

| | | | | | | | | |
|---|---|---|---|---|---|---|---|---|
| (1) | ia | ie | (2) | iao | iu | (3) | c | q |
| | jià | jiè | | jiào | jiǔ | | cān | qiān |
| | xià | xiè | | qiáo | qiú | | céng | qǐng |
| | qià | qiè | | xiǎo | xiū | | cù | qù |
| | | | | liǎo | liù | | | |

**2. Fill in the blanks with Chinese numerals:**

1) A: 同志，请问张 先生 住哪儿?
Tóngzhì, qǐng wèn Zhāng xiānsheng zhù nǎr?

B: 他住_______。(3087 房间)
Tā zhù_______. (3087 fángjiān)

2) A: 老 赵 在吗?
Lǎo Zhào zài ma?

B: 他不住这个 房间，他住_____。(4069)
Tā bú zhù zhège fángjiān, tā zhù_____. (4069)

3) A: 他们 学校 有_______? (6000 人)
Tāmen xuéxiào yǒu_______? (6000 rén)

B: 没错儿。
Méi cuòr.

4) A: 找 你_______? (4.67 元)
Zhǎo nǐ_______? (4.67 yuán)

B: 是 啊，没错儿。
Shì a, méi cuòr.

5) A: _____ 英镑 兑换 _______? (100 英镑，328.43 元)
_____ Yīngbàng duìhuàn_______? (100 Yīngbàng, 328.43 yuán)

B: 没错儿。
Méi cuòr.

6) A: 他们 给你 多少 钱?
Tāmen gěi nǐ duōshao qián?

B: _______。(764 元)
_______. (764 yuán)

***3. Practice conversation about exchanging foreign currencies:**

1) A: 你去哪儿?
Nǐ qù nǎr?

B: 去 中国 银行 兑换 外币。
Qù Zhōngguó Yínháng duìhuàn wàibì.

A: ________?
________?

B: 法 郎。
Fǎláng.

2) 顾客: 同 志, 这儿________?
Gùkè: Tóngzhì, zhèr________?
营 业 员: 兑换。
Yíngyèyuán: Duìhuàn.
顾: 请 问, 今天 日元 牌价________?
Gù: Qǐng wèn, jīntiān Rìyuán páijià________?
营: 十万 日元 ________。
Yíng: Shíwàn Rìyuán________.

3) 顾: 同志, 我 兑换 英 镑。
Gù: Tóngzhì, wǒ duìhuàn Yīngbàng.
营: 兑换________。
Yíng: Duìhuàn________?
顾: ________。(500 英 镑)
Gù: ________. (500 Yīngbàng)
营: ________兑换 人民币 ________。
Yíng: ________duìhuàn Rénmínbì ________.

4) 顾: 请 问, ________ 马克 兑换 多少 人民币?
Gù: Qǐng wèn, ________ Mǎkè duìhuàn duōshao Rénmínbì?
(1200 马克)
(1200 Mǎkè)
营: 西德 马克 吗?
Yíng: Xī Dé Mǎkè ma?
顾: 对。
Gù: Duì.
营: ________兑换________。
Yíng: ________duìhuàn________.

Exchange Rates between Renminbi and Foreign Currencies:
人民币对外币汇价表

| 外币名称 Foreign currency | 外币单位 Counting unit | 买价 buy | 卖价 sell |
|---|---|---|---|
| | | yuan | yuan |
| 美 元 | 100 | 153.38元 | 154.14元 |
| 英 镑 | 100 | 328.43元 | 330.47元 |
| 马 克 | 100 | 84.68元 | 85.10元 |
| 法 郎 | 100 | 36.06元 | 36.24元 |
| 日 元 | 100,000 | 685.23元 | 688.67元 |

**4. Listen to the dialogue:**

顾：同志，我存款。
Gù: Tóngzhì, wǒ cún kuǎn.

营：存多少？
Yíng: Cún duōshao?

顾：三百。
Gù: Sānbǎi.

营：存定期吗？
Yíng: Cún dìngqī ma?

顾：不，存活期。
Gù: Bù, cún huóqī.

营：请填一下儿存款单。
Yíng: Qǐng tián yíxiàr cúnkuǎndān.
(The customer hands his money and the form to the clerk.)

营：(Having counted the money) 正好三百。
Yíng: Zhènghǎo sānbǎi.

顾：请问怎么取款？
Gù: Qǐng wèn zěnme qǔ kuǎn?

营：凭存折取款。
Yíng: Píng cúnzhé qǔ kuǎn.

顾：谢谢。
Gù: Xièxie.

营：没什么。
Yíng: Méi shénme.

# 8 What's The Date Today?
# 今天几号？ jīntiān jǐhào?

(David and Lily ask their parents when they are leaving for Xian and when they are going to the Great Wall.)

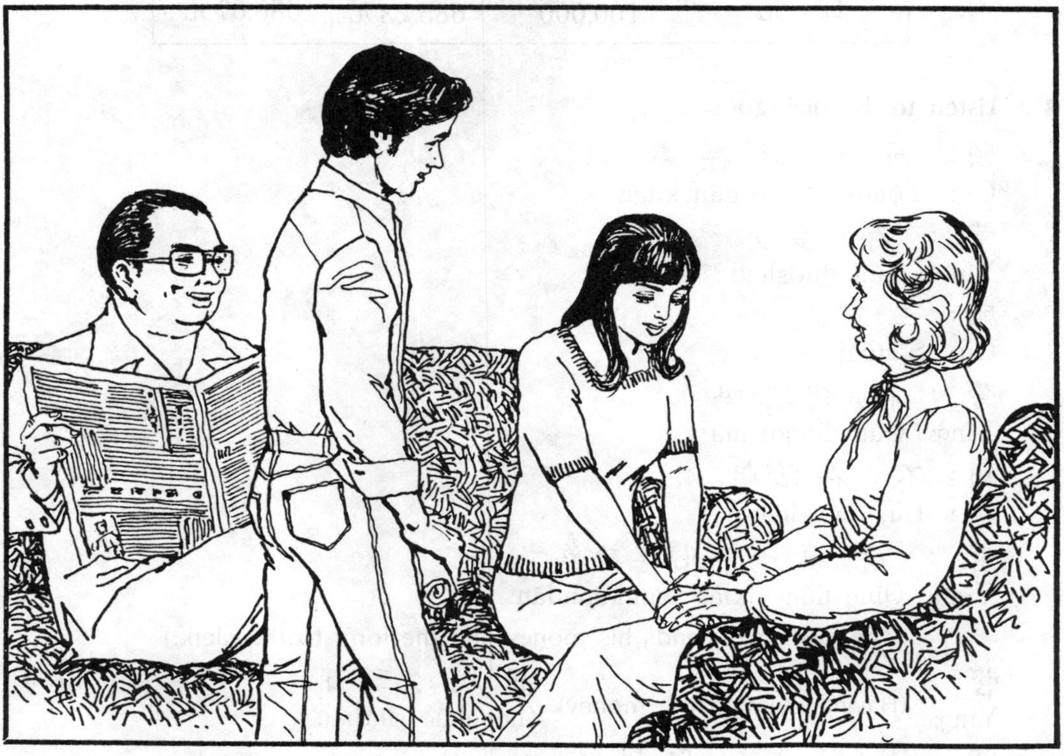

(一) I

| | | |
|---|---|---|
| 莉： | 妈妈，今天 几号？① | Mother, what date is today? |
| Lì： | Māma, jīntiān jǐhào? | |
| 艾： | 二十八号。② | The twenty-eighth. |
| Ài： | Èrshíbāhào. | |

| | | |
|---|---|---|
| 莉：<br>Lì： | 我们 什么 时候 去西安？<br>Wǒmen shénme shíhour qù Xī'ān? | When are we going to Xian? |
| 艾：<br>Ài： | 十月 六号。③莉莉，明天是你弟弟的生日，④今天下午 我们 去买礼物和生日 蛋糕。<br>Shíyuè liùhào. Lìli, míngtiān shì nǐ dìdi de shēngrì, jīntiān xiàwǔ wǒmen qù mǎi lǐwù hé shēngrì dàngāo. | On the sixth of October. Lily, tomorrow's your brother's birthday, we'll buy him a present and a birthday cake this afternoon. |
| 莉：<br>Lì： | 爸爸去吗？<br>Bàba qù ma? | Is dad going? |
| 艾：<br>Ài： | 不去，他要 给西安的张伯伯写信。⑤<br>Bú qù, tā yào gěi Xī'ān de Zhāng bóbo xiě xìn. | No, he has to write a letter to Uncle Zhang of Xian. |

## （二） II

| | | |
|---|---|---|
| 伟：<br>Wěi: | 爸爸，今天 星期几？<br>Bàba, jīntiān xīngqījǐ? | Dad, what day is today? |
| 陈：<br>Chén: | 星期三。⑥<br>Xīngqīsān. | Wednesday. |
| 伟：<br>Wěi: | 星期天 咱们 去 长城吗？⑦<br>Xīngqītiān zánmen qù Chángchéng ma? | Are we going to the Great Wall this Sunday? |
| 陈：<br>Chén: | 不去。<br>Bú qù. | No, we're not. |
| 伟：<br>Wěi: | 哪天 去？<br>Nǎtiān qù? | Which day are we going then? |
| 陈：<br>Chén: | 下 星期二。<br>Xià xīngqī'èr. | Next Tuesday. |

## • new words • 生词 • shēngcí

| | | | | |
|---|---|---|---|---|
| 1 | 号〔日〕 | （名） | hào (rì) | colloquial form for date |
| 2 | 时候 | （名） | shíhour | time |
| 3 | 月 | （名） | yuè | month |
| 4 | 弟弟 | （名） | dìdi | younger brother |
| 5 | 生日 | （名） | shēngrì | birthday |
| 6 | 下午 | （名） | xiàwǔ | afternoon |
| 7 | 我们 | （代） | wǒmen | we, us |
| 8 | 礼物 | （名） | lǐwù | present, gift. |
| 9 | 蛋糕 | （名） | dàngāo | cake |
| 10 | 要 | （助动） | yào | will, would |
| 11 | 写 | （动） | xiě | to write |
| 12 | 星期 | （名） | xīngqī | week |
| | 星期一 | | xīngqīyī | Monday |
| | 星期二 | | xīngqī'èr | Tuesday |
| | 星期三 | | xīngqīsān | Wednesday |
| | 星期四 | | xīngqīsì | Thursday |
| | 星期五 | | xīngqīwǔ | Friday |
| | 星期六 | | xīngqīliù | Saturday |
| | 星期几 | | xīngqījǐ | what day (of the week) |
| 13 | 星期天〔星期日〕 | （名） | xīngqītiān (xīngqīrì) | Sunday |
| 14 | 咱们 | （代） | zánmen | we, us (inclusive first person) |
| 15 | 天 | （名） | tiān | day, sky |
| 16 | 下 | （名） | xià | next, lower, below, under |

| 专名 | Zhuānmíng | Proper name |
|---|---|---|
| 西安 | Xī'ān | Xian, capital of Shaanxi Province in |

the north-west of China.

## study points • 注释 • zhùshì

1 今天几号？(Jīntiān jǐhào？)
This is the usual way of asking today's date.
A positive reply is:
今天十七号。(Jīntiān shíqīhào.)
If you want to ask the day of the week, you can say:
明天星期几？(Míngtiān xīngqījǐ?)
The answer is:
明天星期三。(Míngtiān xīngqīsān.)

2 The days of the month are expressed in the following way:

| | | | |
|---|---|---|---|
| 一号（日） | 二号（日） | 三号（日） | ……十号（日） |
| 十一号 | 二十一号 | | 三十一号 |

"日" (rì) is usually used in writing while "号" (hào) is common in spoken Chinese.

3 The months of the year 月 (yuè)

| | |
|---|---|
| 一月 (yīyuè) | 七月 (qīyuè) |
| 二月 (èryuè) | 八月 (bāyuè) |
| 三月 (sānyuè) | 九月 (jiǔyuè) |
| 四月 (sìyuè) | 十月 (shíyuè) |
| 五月 (wǔyuè) | 十一月 (shíyīyuè) |
| 六月 (liùyuè) | 十二月 (shí'èryuè) |

e. g. 十月六号 (shíyuè liùhào) October 6th.

4 明天是你弟弟的生日。(Míngtiān shì nǐ dìdi de shēngrì.)
When the particle "的" (de) comes after a noun, it indicates what follows belongs to the noun. In the above example, "生日" (shēngrì), belongs to "弟弟" (dìdì).
弟弟的生日 (dìdi de shēngrì) brother's birthday.
爸爸的信 (bàba de xìn) father's letter
老李的礼物 (Lǎo Lǐ de lǐwù) Old Li's gift.

5 他要给西安的张伯伯写信。
(Tā yào gěi Xī'ān de Zhāng bóbo xiě xìn.)
In the above sentence, the word "给" (gěi) functions as an auxiliary verb. The direct object is "信" (xìn) and it comes after the main verb "写" (xiě). The

indirect object, “西安的张伯伯” (Xī'ān de Zhāng bóbo), is placed between the auxiliary verb “给” (gěi) and the main verb “写” (xiě).

6 Wednesday 星期三 (Xīngqīsān)

The seven days of the week are:

| | | |
|---|---|---|
| Sunday | 星期日（天） | xīngqīrì (tiān) |
| Monday | 星期一 | xīngqīyī |
| Tuesday | 星期二 | xīngqī'èr |
| Wednesday | 星期三 | xīngqīsān |
| Thursday | 星期四 | xīngqīsì |
| Friday | 星期五 | xīngqīwǔ |
| Saturday | 星期六 | xīngqīliù |

7 星期天咱们去长城吗？(Xìngqītiān zánmen qù Chángchéng ma?)

“咱们” (zánmen), is different from “我们” (wǒmen), although both are translated into English as “we”. The phrase 咱们 (zánmen) refers to both the addresser and the addressee. But 我们 (wǒmen) may or may not include the addressee.

## supplementary words • 补充生词 • bǔchōng shēngcí

| | | | |
|---|---|---|---|
| 1 | 昨天 | （名）zuótiān | yesterday |
| 2 | 后天 | （名）hòutiān | day after tomorrow |
| 3 | 前天 | （名）qiántiān | day before yesterday |
| 4 | 回 | （动）huí | to come back, to return |
| | 颐和园 | Yíhéyuán | the Summer Palace |

## • exercises • 练习 • liànxí

**1. Phonetic exercises:**

1) Tones

(1) The neutral tone
tāmen
zánmen
nǐmen
wǒmen

(2) (3)+(4)
lǐwù
xiě xìn
Jīntiān jǐhào?
Xīngqījǐ qù?

2) Sound discrimination

(1) z j
zán jiàn
zá jià
zào jiào

(2) q x
qiáo xiǎo
qián xiān
qǐng xīng

**2. Answer the following questions:**

1) 今天 几号?
Jīntiān jǐhào?

2) 昨天 几号?
Zuótiān jǐhào?

3) 明天 多少号 ?
Míngtiān duōshaohào?

4) 星期天 几号?
Xīngqītiān jǐhào?

5) 下 星期三 多少号 ?
Xià xīngqīsān duōshaohào?

6) 今天 星期几?
Jīntiān xīngqījǐ?

7) 后天 几号?
Hòutiān jǐhào?

8) 前天 星期几?
Qiántiān xīngqījǐ?

9) 二十八号星期几?
Èrshíbāhào xīngqījǐ?

***3. Fill in the blanks with the right time expressions:**

什么 时候, 几号, 星期几,
shénme shíhour, jǐhào, xīngqījǐ,

1) 我们 ________去 故宫 ?
Wǒmen ________ qù Gùgōng?
六号。
Liùhào.

2) 他们 ________去 颐和园?
Tāmen ________ qù Yíhéyuán?
星期四。
Xīngqīsì.

3) 咱 们________去西安?
Zánmen ________ qù Xī'ān?
十 月 五号。
Shíyuè wǔhào.

4) 你们 ________去 长城 ?
Nǐmen ________ qù Chángchéng?

下 星期二。
Xià xīngqī'èr.

5) 他大概________回国？
Tā dàgài________huí guó?

十一月十二号 。
Shíyīyuè shí'èrhào.

**4. How to say your birthday and their birthdays:**

1) 你的 生 日
Nǐ de shēngrì

2) 你爸爸的 生日
Nǐ bàba de shēngrì

3) 你妈妈 的生日
Nǐ māma de shēngrì

4) 你爷爷的 生日
Nǐ yéye de shēngrì

5) 你弟弟的生日
Nǐ dìdi de shēngrì

**5. Listen to the dialogues:**

1) 艾琳：大伟，今天几号？
Àilín: Dàwěi, jīntiān jǐhào?

大伟： 二十七号。有 什么 事儿吗？
Dàwěi: Èrshíqīhào. Yǒu shénme shìr ma?

艾： 明天 要 去看 李伯伯， 咱们 去买 点儿礼物吧。
Ài: Míngtiān yào qù kàn Lǐ bóbo, zánmen qù mǎi diǎnr lǐwù ba.

伟：好 。
wěi: Hǎo.

2) 女儿：妈， 咱们 什么 时候 去颐和园？
Nǚ'ér: Mā, zánmen shénme shíhour qù Yíhéyuán?

妈妈： 星期天 。
Māma: Xīngqītiān.

女儿：星期六吧。星期天 我 和弟弟要 去 看 杂技。
Nǚ'ér: Xīngqīliù ba. Xīngqītiān wǒ hé dìdi yào qù kàn zájì.

妈妈： 星期六 张 先生 和 张 太太要 来。
Māma: Xīngqīliù Zhāng xiānsheng hé Zhāng tàitai yào lái.

女儿：下星期一呢？
Nǚ'ér: Xià xīngqīyī ne?

妈妈： 下 星期一、二、四你爸爸有事儿，下星期三吧 。
Māma: Xià xīngqīyī、èr、sì nǐ bàba yǒu shìr , xià xīngqīsān ba.

女儿：好吧 。
Nǚ'ér: Hǎo ba.

# 9 What Time Is It?
# 现在几点? xiànzài jǐdiǎn?

(David suggests to Lily that they go and see a film together.)

| | | |
|---|---|---|
| 伟：<br>Wěi: | 姐姐，你 今天 干 什么？<br>Jiějie, nǐ jīntiān gàn shénme? | Lily, what are your plans for today? |
| 莉：<br>Lì: | 上午 九点 我 要 去 看 (一)个 朋友。①<br>Shàngwǔ jiǔdiǎn wǒ yào qù kàn (yí) ge péngyou. | I'm going to see a friend at nine in the morning. |

| | | |
|---|---|---|
| 伟：<br>Wěi: | 几点 回来？<br>Jǐdiǎn huí lai? | When will you be back? |
| 莉：<br>Lì: | 下午 两点。②<br>Xiàwǔ liǎngdiǎn. | Two o'clock in the afternoon. |
| 伟：<br>Wěi: | 下午 咱们 去 看 电影，<br>Xiàwǔ zánmen qù kàn diànyǐng,<br>好 吗？ ③<br>hǎo ma? | How about going to a movie with me in the afternoon? |
| 莉：<br>Lì: | 什么 电影？<br>Shénme diànyǐng? | What movie? |
| 伟：<br>Wěi: | 中国 电影 《李 时珍》。<br>Zhōngguó diànyǐng "Lǐ Shízhēn". | A Chinese movie called Li Shizhen. |
| 莉：<br>Lì: | 几点 的？④<br>Jǐdiǎn de? | When is it? |
| 伟：<br>Wěi: | 下午 有 三 场： 两点<br>Xiàwǔ yǒu sānchǎng: liǎngdiǎn<br>零 五（分）的，四点 三刻<br>líng wǔ (fēn) de, sìdiǎn sānkè<br>的，六点半 的。<br>de, liùdiǎnbàn de. | There are three showings in the afternoon: 2:05, 4:45 and 6:30. |
| 莉：<br>Lì: | 看 四点 三刻 的吧。⑤<br>Kàn sìdian sānkè de ba. | Let's go to the 4:45 show then. |
| 伟：<br>Wěi: | 我 去 买 票。<br>Wǒ qù mǎi piào. | I'm going to get the tickets. |
| 莉：<br>Lì: | 现在 差 十分 九点 了，我<br>Xiànzài chà shífēn jiǔdiǎn le, wǒ<br>该 走 了。⑥<br>gāi zǒu le. | It's ten to nine now. I must be going. |
| 伟：<br>Wěi: | 你的 表 停 了吧？⑦<br>Nǐ de biǎo tíng le ba? | Your watch must have gone wrong. |
| 莉：<br>Lì: | 哎呀！ 停 了！⑧ 现在<br>Āiyā! Tíng le! Xiànzài<br>几点？<br>jǐdiǎn? | Oh dear! It sure has. What's the time now? |
| 伟：<br>Wěi: | 九点 五分 了。<br>Jiǔdiǎn wǔfēn le. | Five after nine. |
| 莉：<br>Lì: | 糟糕！⑨ 晚 了。<br>Zāogāo! Wǎn le. | My goodness! I'm late. |

## • new words • 生词 • shēngcí

| | | | | |
|---|---|---|---|---|
| 1 | 现在 | (名) | xiànzài | present, now |
| 2 | 点 | (量) | diǎn | o'clock |
| 3 | 姐姐 | (名) | jiějie | elder sister |
| 4 | 上午 | (名) | shàngwǔ | morning |
| 5 | 回来 | | huí lai | to come back, to return |
| 6 | 电影 | (名) | diànyǐng | motion pictures, movie, film |
| 7 | 场 | (量) | chǎng | show |
| 8 | 分 | (量) | fēn | minute |
| 9 | 刻 | (量) | kè | quarter (of an hour) |
| 10 | 半 | (数) | bàn | half |
| 11 | 票 | (名) | piào | ticket, coupon |
| 12 | 差 | (动) | chà | to be short of, to differ from; not up to the standard |
| 13 | 了 | (助) | le | a particle |
| 14 | 该 | (助动) | gāi | should, ought to |
| 15 | 走 | (动) | zǒu | to go, to leave, to walk |
| | 我该走了 | | Wǒ gāi zǒu le | I must be leaving |
| 16 | 表 | (名) | biǎo | watch |
| 17 | 停 | (动) | tíng | to stop |
| 18 | 哎呀 | (叹) | āiyā | Oh dear! (surprise or annoyance) |
| 19 | 糟糕 | (形) | zāogāo | awful, too bad |
| 20 | 晚 | (形) | wǎn | late |

**专名　　Zhuānmíng　　Proper names**

| | | |
|---|---|---|
| 中国 | Zhōngguó | China |
| 《李时珍》 | 《Lǐ Shízhēn》 | title of a film after the name of an ancient Chinese pharmacist |

## study points • 注释 • zhùshì

1 上午九点我要去看(一)个朋友。(Shàngwǔ jiǔdiǎn wǒ yào qù kàn (yí)ge péngyou.)
The word "一" (yī), when used with a measure word and a noun to form the object of a sentence, can often be omitted.

2 下午两点 (xiàwǔ liǎngdiǎn)
The Chinese way of telling time is as follows:
1:00——一点 (yìdiǎn)
1:05——一点(零)五分 (yìdiǎn (líng) wǔfēn)
1:15——一点十五分 or 一点一刻
(yìdiǎn shíwǔfēn or yìdiǎn yíkè)
1:30——一点三十分 or 一点半
(yìdiǎn sānshífēn or yìdiǎnbàn)
1:45——一点四十五分 or 一点三刻
(yìdiǎn sìshíwǔfēn or yìdiǎn sānkè)
1:55——一点五十五分 or 差五分两点
(yìdiǎn wǔshíwǔfēn or chà wǔfēn liǎngdiǎn)
The usual sentence patterns of asking and telling time are:
现在几点? (Xiànzài jǐdiǎn?)
现在____点____分。(Xiànzài____diǎn____fēn.)
The verb "是" (shì) which is functionally similar to the English verb 'to be' is not necessary in these sentences.

3 下午咱们去看电影，好吗? (Xiàwǔ zánmen qù kàn diànyǐng, hǎo ma?)
This is a common form of question to ask for opinion in conversation. The first part of the question reveals the content on which opinion is being sought. The second part "好吗?" (hǎo ma?) is similar to 'O. K. ?' in English.

4 几点的? (Jǐdiǎn de?)
This is a short, colloquial form of asking what time is the show. The full sentence should be "几点的电影?" (Jǐ diǎn de diànyǐng) 'The show of what time?' (See Point 1 under Study Points of Lesson 11)

5 看四点三刻的吧。(Kàn sìdiǎn sānkè de ba.)
Without the particle "吧" (ba) at the end, the sentence sounds like a command. "吧" here indicates a suggestion.

6 我该走了。(Wǒ gāi zǒu le.)
In this sentence, the particle "了" (le) indicates a certain sense of degree,

meaning the time has come for me to go. (See Point 3 under Study Points of Lesson 17)

7 你的表停了吧？ (Nǐ de biǎo tíng le ba?)

"吧" (ba) here expresses uncertainty as well as conjecture.

8 停了 (tíng le)

"了" (le) in this sentence is used in the same way as that in "晚了" (wǎn le). (See 1 under Study Points of Lesson 16.)

9 糟糕 (zāogāo)

This is a colloquial exclamation showing dismay over something undesirable or unfortunate.

## supplementary words • 补充生词 • bǔchōng shēngcí

| | | | | |
|---|---|---|---|---|
| 1 | 起床 | | qǐ chuáng | to get up, to get out of bed |
| 2 | 吃 | (动) | chī | to eat |
| 3 | 早饭 | (名) | zǎofàn | breakfast |
| 4 | 午饭 | (名) | wǔfàn | lunch |
| 5 | 晚饭 | (名) | wǎnfàn | supper, dinner |
| 6 | 睡觉 | | shuì jiào | to sleep |
| 7 | 打球 | | dǎ qiú | to play ball games |
| 8 | 散步 | | sàn bù | to go for a walk |

## • exercises • 练习 • liànxí

**1. Phonetic exercises:**

1) Tones

(1) The neutral tone

māma
bóbo
jiějie
dìdi

(2) (3)+(3)

jǐdiǎn
Xiànzài jǐdiǎn?
Shàngwǔ jiǔdiǎn.
Xiàwǔ liǎngdiǎn.

2) Sound discrimination

| | | | | |
|---|---|---|---|---|
| (1) zh | ch | | (2) ai | ei |
| zhāng | chǎng | | gāi | gěi |
| zhēn | chén | | bǎi | běi |
| zhǎo | chāo | | wài | wěi |
| | | | mǎi | měi |

***2. Look at the pictures and then answer the questions accordingly:**

1) 现在 几点？
Xiànzài jǐdiǎn?

2) 现在几点了？
Xiànzài jǐdiǎn le?

3) 几点了？
Jǐdiǎn le?

4) 你的表 几点了？
Nǐ de biǎo jǐdiǎn le?

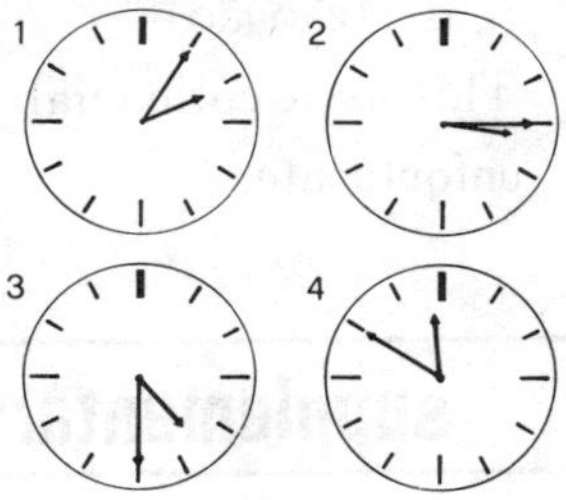

**3. Answer the questions according to the text:**

1) 莉莉和大伟要 看 几点 的 电影？
Lìli hé Dàwěi yào kàn jǐdiǎn de diànyǐng?

2) 莉莉几点去看 朋友？
Lìli jǐdiǎn qù kàn péngyou?

3) 莉莉几点回来？
Lìli jǐdiǎn huí lai?

4) 大伟 的表 几点了？
Dàwěi de biǎo jǐdiǎn le?

5) 莉莉的表 几点了？
Lìli de biǎo jǐdiǎn le?

**4. Practice asking questions and giving answers after the model:**

Model: A: 他几点去 邮局？
Tā jǐdiǎn qù yóujú?

B: 上午 十点。（上午 10:00）
Shàngwǔ shídiǎn. (shàngwǔ 10:00)

1) 起床，6:00
qǐ chuáng, 6:00

2) 吃，早饭，7:15
chī, zǎofàn, 7:15

3) 吃，午饭，12:00
chī, wǔfàn, 12:00

4) 吃，晚饭，5:30
chī, wǎnfàn, 5:30

5) 睡觉，9:55
shuì jiào, 9:55

**5. Practice after the model:**

Model: 现在 我们 去邮局。
Xiànzài wǒmen qù yóujú.

A: 现在 我们 去邮局，好吗？
Xiànzài wǒmen qù yóujú, hǎo ma?

B: 好 吧。
Hǎo ba.

1) 晚上 咱们 去看 电影 。
Wǎnshang zánmen qù kàn diànyǐng.

2) 四点 咱们 去打球。
Sìdiǎn zánmen qù dǎ qiú.

3) 明天 上午 我们 去看 王 先生 。
Míngtiān shàngwǔ wǒmen qù kàn Wáng xiānsheng.

4) 星期天 下午 咱们 去看杂技。
Xīngqītiān xiàwǔ zánmen qù kàn zájì.

5) 现在 去散步。
Xiànzài qù sān bù.

**6. Listen to the dialogue:**

A: 同志，我买 电影票 。
Tóngzhì, wǒ mǎi diànyǐngpiào.

B: 要 哪场 的?
Yào nǎchǎng de?

A: 下午 有 几场 ?
Xiàwǔ yǒu jǐchǎng?

B: 有 四场。一点 的，两 点 五十 的，四点半的，
Yǒu sìchǎng. Yìdiǎn de, liǎngdiǎn wǔshí de, sìdiǎnbàn de,
六点 一刻的。
liùdiǎn yíkè de.

A: 四点半 的 还 有 吗?
Sìdiǎnbàn de hái yǒu ma?

B: 有 。要 几张 ?
Yǒu. Yào jǐzhāng?

A: 两张 。多少 钱 一张 ?
Liǎngzhāng. Duōshao qián yìzhāng?

B: 两毛 。
Liǎngmáo.

A: 给 您 钱 。
Gěi nín qián.

B: 这 是票 和 找 您 的钱，您 看，对吗?
Zhè shì piào hé zhǎo nín de qián, nín kàn, duì ma?

A: 没 错儿。
Méi cuòr.

# 10 Making A Telephone Call
# 打电话 dǎ diànhuà

(Wang Fang telephones Mr. Chen Mingshan.)

| | | |
|---|---|---|
| 王　： | 喂，北京　饭店　吗？① | Hello, is this Beijing Hotel? |
| Wáng: | Wèi, Běijīng Fàndiàn ma? | |
| 话务员： | 对。 | Yes. |
| Huàwùyuán: | Duì. | |
| 王　： | 我　要　五一二四……喂，五一二四　房间　吗？ | I want Room 5124. Hello,is this Room 5124? |
| Wáng: | Wǒ yào wǔyāo'èrsì…… Wèi, wǔyāo'èrsì fángjiān ma? | |
| 艾: | 请　您　说　慢点儿。② | Speak a little slower, please? |
| Ài: | Qǐng nín shuō màn diǎnr. | |

| | | |
|---|---|---|
| 王 :<br>Wáng: | 五一二四 房间 吗?<br>Wǔyāo'èrsì fángjiān ma? | Is this Room 5124? |
| 艾:<br>Ài: | 是。您 找 谁?<br>Shì. Nín zhǎo shuí? | Yes, whom do you want? |
| 王 :<br>Wáng: | 我 找 陈 先 生。<br>Wǒ zhǎo Chén xiānsheng. | I want Mr. Chen. |
| 艾:<br>Ài: | 请 等一下儿。(To Chen) 你 的 电 话。<br>Qǐng děng yíxiàr. Nǐ de diànhuà. | Hold on a minute,please. (To Chen) Your call. |
| 陈 :<br>Chén: | 喂,谁啊?③<br>Wèi, shuí a? | Hello, who's speaking? |
| 王 :<br>Wáng: | 我 是 王 芳。陈 先 生 吗?<br>Wǒ shì Wáng Fāng. Chén xiānsheng ma? | I'm Wang Fang. Is this Mr. Chen? |
| 陈 :<br>Chén: | 哦,王 小姐。我 是 陈 明山。有 什么 事儿 吗?<br>Ò, Wáng xiǎojie. Wǒ shì Chén Míngshān. Yǒu shénme shìr ma? | Oh,Xiao Wang. I'm Chen Mingshan. What can I do for you? |
| 王 :<br>Wáng: | 后天 晚上 有《大闹 天宫》,你们 看 不看?④<br>Hòutiān wǎnshang yǒu《Dà Nào Tiāngōng》, nǐmen kàn bu kàn? | There'll be The Monkey King Creates Havoc in Heaven tomorrow evening.Would you like to go and see it? |
| 陈 :<br>Chén: | 是不是京剧?<br>Shì bu shì jīngjù? | Is it a Beijing opera? |
| 王 :<br>Wáng: | 是。<br>Shì. | Yes. |
| 陈 :<br>Chén: | 在哪儿演?<br>Zài nǎr yǎn? | Where will it be performing? |
| 王 :<br>Wáng: | 人民 剧场。<br>Rénmín Jùchǎng. | At the People's Theater. |
| 陈 :<br>Chén: | 我们 全 家都 去。<br>Wǒmen quán jiā dōu qù. | We would all go. |
| 王 :<br>Wáng: | 明天 晚 上 我 给 你们<br>Míngtiān wǎnshang wǒ gěi nǐmen | I'll give you the tickets tomorrow evening. |

| | | |
|---|---|---|
| | 送 票 去。⑤<br>sòng piào qu. | |
| 陈：<br>Chén: | 好，麻烦你了。⑥<br>Hǎo, máfan nǐ le. | Good. That's very kind of you. |

## • new words • 生词 • shēngcí

| | | | |
|---|---|---|---|
| 1 | 打 | （动）dǎ | to make (a telephone call), to beat, to strike |
| 2 | 电话 | （名）diànhuà | telephone |
| | 打电话 | dǎ diànhuà | to telephone |
| 3 | 喂 | （叹）wèi | hello |
| 4 | 话务员 | （名）huàwùyuán | telephone operator |
| 5 | 说 | （动）shuō | to speak, to talk |
| 6 | 慢 | （形）màn | slow |
| | 说慢点儿 | shuō màn diǎnr | to speak slower |
| 7 | 等 | （动）děng | to wait |
| 8 | 啊 | （助）a | ah, oh |
| 9 | 哦 | （叹）ò | an interjection like "oh" |
| 10 | 后天 | （名）hòutiān | the day after tomorrow |
| 11 | 京剧 | （名）jīngjù | Beijing Opera |
| 12 | 在 | （介）zài | at, in |
| 13 | 演 | （动）yǎn | to perform, to put on a show |
| 14 | 全 | （形）quán | all, whole |
| 15 | 家 | （名）jiā | family, home |
| 16 | 都 | （副）dōu | all, already |
| 17 | 送 | （动）sòng | to send, to take, to present, to see (somebody)……off |

18 麻烦 (动、名、形) máfan to trouble, trouble, troublesome

| 专名 | Zhuānmíng | Proper names |
|---|---|---|
| 北京饭店 | Běijīng Fàndiàn | Beijing Hotel |
| 《大闹天宫》 | "Dà Nào Tiāngōng" | The Monkey King Creates Havoc in Heaven |
| 人民剧场 | Rénmín Jùchǎng | People's Theater |

## study points • 注释 • zhùshì

1 喂，北京饭店吗？ (Wèi, Běijīng Fàndiàn ma? )

This is a common sentence pattern for making a phone call. Here are more examples:

五一二四房间吗？ (Wǔyāo'èrsì fángjiān ma? )

陈先生吗？ (Chén xiānsheng ma? )

In these sentences the subject and the verb 是 (shì) are left out.

2 请您说慢点儿。 (Qǐng nín shuō màn diǎnr. )

Placed after an adjective, "一点儿" (yìdiǎnr) shows a slight change of degree. "一" (yī) can be omitted.

3 喂，谁啊？ (Wèi, shuí a? )

"啊" (a) indicates doubt. When it appears in the middle or at the end of a sentence, its pronunciation often changes with the sound preceding it.

| preceding sound | pronunciation of "啊" |
|---|---|
| a e i o ü | a—— ia |
| u ao ou | a—— ua |
| —n | a—— na |
| —ng | a—— nga |

4 你们看不看？ (Nǐmen kàn bu kàn? )

Putting together the positive and negative forms of a verb is one way of forming questions:

你们去不去？ (Nǐmen qù bu qù? )

Are you going or not?

他是不是你弟弟？ (Tā shì bu shì nǐ dìdi? )

Is he your brother or not?
那个电影好不好？ (Nàge diànyǐng hǎo bu hǎo?)
Is that movie good or not?

5 明天晚上我给你们送票去。(Míngtiān wǎnshang wǒ gěi nǐmen sòng piào qù.)
(See 1 under Study Points of Lesson 22.)

6 麻烦你了。 (Máfan nǐ le.)
This is an idiomatic expression to show appreciation for the help one gets.

## supplementary words • 补充生词 • bǔchōng shēngcí

| | | | | |
|---|---|---|---|---|
| 1 | 位 | （量） | wèi | a measure word for people |
| 2 | 话剧 | （名） | huàjù | play |
| 3 | 歌剧 | （名） | gējù | opera |
| 4 | 占线 | | zhàn xiàn | the line is busy |
| 5 | 电报 | （名） | diànbào | telegram, cable |
| 6 | 电报纸 | （名） | diànbàozhǐ | telegram form |
| 7 | 字 | （名） | zì | character |

| | | |
|---|---|---|
| 华侨大厦 | Huáqiáo Dàshà | Overseas Chinese Hotel |
| 《茶馆》 | 《Cháguǎnr》 | "Tea House", a modern play |
| 首都剧场 | Shǒudū Jùchǎng | Capital Theater |
| 上海 | Shànghǎi | Shanghai |

## exercises • 练习 • liànxí

1 . **Phonetic exercises:**

1) Tones

(1) (3)＋Neutral tone

wǒde
nǐde
Nǐde diànhuà.

Wǎnshang sòng piào.
Wǒmen qù kàn.
Nǎge fàndiàn?

(2) The neutral tone: …不 (bu)…

shì bu shì
kàn bu kàn
qù bu qù
duì bu duì

2) Sound discrimination

| (1) an | ang | (2) ao | ou | (3) s | x |
|---|---|---|---|---|---|
| fàn | fāng | zāo | zǒu | sī | xī |
| shān | shàng | yào | yǒu | sān | xiān |
| bàn | bàng | hào | hòu | sòng | xióng |
| | | chāo | chōu | | |

**2. Practice making telephone calls:**

1) Model:
打电话人：喂，北京饭店吗？
dǎ diànhuà rén: Wèi, Běijīng Fàndiàn ma?
服务员：对，您要哪个房间？
fúwùyuán: Duì, nín yào nǎge fángjiān?
打电话人：我要5013。
dǎ diànhuà rén: Wǒ yào 5013.

(1) 民族饭店，4017
Mínzú Fàndiàn, 4017

(2) 前门饭店，3125
Qiánmén Fàndiàn, 3125

(3) 华侨大厦，1036
Huáqiáo Dàshà, 1036

2) Model:
陈明山：喂，哪位？
Chén Míngshān: Wèi, nǎwèi?
王芳：我是王芳。陈明山先生吗？
Wáng Fāng: Wǒ shì Wáng Fāng. Chén Míngshān xiānsheng ma?
陈明山：哦，王芳同志，您好！我是陈明山，有什么事儿吗？
Chén Míngshān: Ò, Wáng Fāng tóngzhì, nín hǎo! Wǒ shì Chén Míngshān, yǒu shénme shìr ma?

(1) 我 是亨利，赵 先 生 吗？
Wǒ shì Hēnglì, Zhào xiānsheng ma?

(2) 我 是艾琳，李太太 吗？
Wǒ shì Àilín, Lǐ tàitai ma?

(3) 我 是 陈 明 山，张 文汉 同志吗？
Wǒ shì Chén Míngshān, Zhāng Wénhàn tóngzhì ma?

***3. Practice asking questions:**

1) Using "是不是" (shì bu shì)

Model: 《大闹 天 宫》是不是 京剧？
《Dà Nào Tiāngōng》 shì bu shì jīngjù?

(1) 《茶馆》__________？(话剧)
《Cháguǎnr》__________？(huàjù)

(2) 他__________？(张 大中 同志)
Tā__________？(Zhāng Dàzhōng tóngzhì)

(3) 这 位 太太__________？(艾琳)
Zhèwèi tàitai__________？ (Àilín)

2) Using "看不看" (kàn bu kàn)

Model: 今天 晚 上 人民 剧场 演《大闹 天 宫》，
Jīntiān wǎnshang Rénmín Jùchǎng yǎn 《Dà Nào Tiāngōng》,
您 看不看？
nín kàn bu kàn?

(1) 明天 晚上 首都 剧场__________？(《茶馆》)
Míngtiān wǎnshang Shǒudū Jùchǎng__________？(《Cháguǎnr》)

(2) 下午 文化宫__________？(《李 时珍》)
Xiàwǔ Wénhuàgōng__________？(《Lǐ Shízhēn》)

(3) 后天 人民 剧场__________？(歌剧)
Hòutiān Rénmín Jùchǎng__________？(gējù)

3) Using "有没有" (yǒu méi yǒu)

Model: 你 有 没有 八分的 邮票？
Nǐ yǒu méiyǒu bāfēn de yóupiào?

(1) 你__________？(昨天 的报)
Nǐ__________？(zuótiān de bào)

(2) 他__________？(后天的 电影票)
Tā__________？(hòutiān de diànyǐngpiào)

(3) 大伟__________？(《中 国 画报》)
Dàwěi__________？(《Zhōngguó Huàbào》)

4) Using "去不去" (qù bu qù)

Model: 你们 去不去 上海 ?
Nǐmen qù bu qù Shànghǎi?

(1) 他__________?(西安)
Tā__________? (Xī'ān)

(2) 您 下午__________?(故宫)
Nín xiàwǔ__________? (Gùgōng)

(3) 明天 下午 赵 先生 __________?(华侨 大厦)
Míngtiān xiàwǔ Zhào xiānsheng__________? (Huáqiáo Dàshà)

***4. Fill in the blanks using the positive-negative form of the following verbs:**
抽 (chōu), 喝 (hē), 买 (mǎi), 送 (sòng), 演 (yǎn)

(1) 您_____烟?
Nín_____yān?

(2) 他_____茶?
Tā_____chá?

(3) 他们 _____ 电影票 ?
Tāmen_____diànyǐngpiào?

(4) 咱们 _____礼物?
Zánmen_____lǐwù?

(5) 人民 剧场_____《茶馆》?
Rénmín Jùchǎng_____《Cháguǎnr》?

**5. Listen to the dialogues:**

1) 打电话人:喂,北京 饭店吗?
Dǎ diànhuà rén: Wèi, Běijīng Fàndiàn ma?
服务员:是啊,您 要哪儿?
fúwùyuán: Shì a, nín yào nǎr?
打电话人:3064。
Dǎ diànhuà rén: 3064.
服务员:对不起,占 线。
fúwùyuán: Duì bu qǐ, zhàn xiàn.

2) 顾客:同志,我 打 电报。
Gùkè: Tóngzhì, wǒ dǎ diànbào.
营业员:好。这 是 电报纸 。
Yíngyèyuán: Hǎo. Zhè shì diànbàozhǐ.
顾客: 多少 钱 一个字?
Gùkè: Duōshao qián yíge zì?
营业员:三分 钱一个字。您 这 是 十九个字,一共 五
Yíngyèyuán: Sānfēn qián yíge zì. Nín zhè shì shíjiǔge zì, yígòng wǔ-

毛 七。
máo qī.

顾客：给 您 钱 。
Gùkè: Gěi nín qián.

营业员 ：您 给 我 一块，找 您 四毛 三。
Yíngyèyuán: Nín gěi wǒ yíkuài, zhǎo nín sìmáo sān.

# 复习(2) Revision (2) fùxí (2)

1. **Read aloud:**

1) 我爸爸，他妈妈，他弟弟，你姐姐，他朋友，中国人，
wǒ bàba, tā māma, tā dìdi, nǐ jiějie, tā péngyou, Zhōngguórén,
英国电影，美国朋友，加拿大话剧，西德表，
Yīngguó diànyǐng, Měiguó péngyou, Jiā'nádà huàjù, Xīdé biǎo,
我家，我国，他们学校
wǒ jiā, wǒ guó, tāmen xuéxiào

2) 他的表，你的信，他的电报，他们的桌子，弟弟的生日，
tā de biǎo, nǐ de xìn, tā de diànbào, tāmen de zhuōzi, dìdi de shēngrì,
学校的《中国画报》，他姐姐的明信片，
xuéxiào de "Zhōngguó Huàbào", tā jiějie de míngxìnpiàn,
我国的大使馆
wǒ guó de dàshǐguǎn

3) 一(壹)，二(贰)，三(叁)，四(肆)，五(伍)，六(陆)，
yī (yī), èr (èr), sān (sān), sì (sì), wǔ (wǔ), liù (liù),
七(柒)，八(捌)，九(玖)，十(拾)。
qī (qī), bā (bā), jiǔ (jiǔ), shí (shí),

2. **Turn the following statements into questions:**

Model: 他去西安。——他去西安吗？
Tā qù Xī'ān. Tā qù Xī'ān ma?
他去哪儿？
Tā qù nǎr?
他去不去西安？
Tā qù bu qù Xī'ān?

1) 他们看电影。
Tāmen kàn diànyǐng.

2) 她不买杂技票。
Tā bù mǎi zájìpiào.

3) 他们 兑换 美元 。
Tāmen duìhuàn Měiyuán.

4) 我 不 吃 蛋糕。
Wǒ bù chī dàngāo.

5) 他 等 小 王。
Tā děng Xiǎo Wáng.

6) 小 张 填 存款 单子。
Xiǎo Zhāng tián cúnkuǎn dānzi.

7) 大伟 写信。
Dàwěi xiě xìn.

8) 《大闹 天宫》是京剧。
"Dà Nào Tiāngōng" shì jīngjù.

*3. **Fill in the blanks:**

1) 一个 星期 有 七天, 这七天 是 _____, _____,
Yíge xīngqī yǒu qītiān, zhè qītiān shì _____, _____,
_____, _____, _____, _____, _____。
_____, _____, _____, _____, _____.

2) 说说 一个月 有 多少天:
Shuōshuo yíge yuè yǒu duōshaotiān:
_____, _____, _____, _____, _____, _____, _____
_____, _____, _____, _____, _____, _____, _____
有 三十一天。_____, _____, _____, _____有 三十天。
yǒu sānshíyītiān. _____, _____, _____, _____yǒu sānshítiān.
____有 二十八天,或者(or) 二十九天。
____yǒu èrshíbātiān, huòzhě èrshíjiǔtiān.

# 11 Whose Pen Is It?
# 钢笔是谁的 gāngbǐ shì shuí de?

(Xiao Liu, a hotel clerk asks the Chens if any of them has lost a pen. She also tells them that coffee is on sale again at the hotel shop.)

## (一)

| | | |
|---|---|---|
| 小 刘: ① <br> xiǎo Liú: | 早 晨 我 们 在 这 张 <br> Zǎochén wǒmen zài zhèzhāng <br> 桌子上 捡 到 一支 钢 <br> zhuōzishang jiǎn dào yìzhī gāng | We found a pen left on the table this morning. Does it belong to any one of you? |

| | | |
|---|---|---|
| | 笔，②是 你们 哪 一位 的？<br>bǐ, shì nǐmen nǎ yíwèi de? | |
| 伟：<br>Wěi: | 我 看看，③"英 雄"的。④<br>Wǒ kànkan, "Yīngxióng" de.<br>还 是 新的。姐姐，是 你<br>Hái shì xīn de. Jiějie, shì nǐ<br>的吗？<br>de ma? | Let me have a look. It's a "Hero", and a new one, too. Lily, is it yours? |
| 莉：<br>Lì: | 不 是 我 的。我的 在 这儿。<br>Bú shì wǒ de. Wǒ de zài zhèr. | No. I've got mine here. |
| 刘：<br>Liú: | 陈 先生，是 您 太太<br>Chén xiānsheng, shì nín tàitai<br>的 吗？<br>de ma? | Mr. Chen, is it Mrs. Chen's? |
| 陈：<br>Chén: | 不是，她的 是 旧的。<br>Bú shì, tā de shì jiù de. | No. Her's is an old one. |
| 刘：<br>Liú: | 那（么）是 谁 的呢？⑤<br>Nà (me) shì shuí de ne? | I wonder whose is it then? |
| 陈：<br>Chén | 早晨 比利·威 尔 逊 先<br>Zǎochén Bǐlì Wēi'ěrxùn xiān<br>生 也在这儿吃 饭，会 不<br>sheng yě zài zhèr chī fàn, huì bu<br>会 是 他的？⑥<br>huì shì tā de? | Mr. Bailey Wilson also had his breakfast here this morning. Can it be his? |
| 刘：<br>Liú: | 一会儿我问问 他。对了，⑦<br>Yíhuìr wǒ wènwen tā. Duì le,<br>陈 先 生，昨天 您 不<br>Chén xiānsheng, zuótiān nín bú<br>是 要 买 咖啡吗？⑧今天<br>shì yào mǎi kāfēi ma? Jīntiān<br>小卖部 有了。<br>xiǎomàibù yǒu le. | I'll ask him later. Oh, yes, Mr. Chen, you wanted to buy some coffee yesterday, didn't you? They have it at the hotel shop today. |
| 陈：<br>Chén: | 是 吗？⑨ 我 马上 去 买。<br>Shì ma? Wǒ mǎshàng qù mǎi. | Really? I'll go and get some right now. |

## （二） II

| | | |
|---|---|---|
| 陈：<br>Chén: | 同志，我 买 咖啡。<br>Tóngzhì, wǒ mǎi kāfēi. | Comrade, I'd like to buy some coffee. |

| | | |
|---|---|---|
| 售货员：<br>shòuhuòyuán: | 中国的，外国的都有，您要哪一种？<br>Zhōngguó de, wàiguó de dōu yǒu, nín yào nǎ yìzhǒng? | We have both Chinese and foreign coffee. Which kind do you want? |
| 陈：<br>Chén: | 都给我看看，好吗？<br>Dōu gěi wǒ kànkan, hǎo ma? | Will you show me both? |
| 售：<br>shòu: | 好。<br>Hǎo. | Sure. |
| 陈：<br>Chén: | 要两筒中国的。<br>Yào liǎngtǒng Zhōngguó de. | I'll have two cans of Chinese coffee. |
| 售：<br>shòu: | 还要别的吗？<br>Hái yào biéde ma? | Anything else? |
| 陈：<br>Chén: | 再给我一个本子。<br>Zài gěi wǒ yíge běnzi. | Also give me a notebook. |
| 售：<br>shòu: | 这样的行吗？<br>Zhèyàng de xíng ma? | Will this do? |
| 陈：<br>Chén: | 有大的吗？<br>Yǒu dà de ma? | Do you have bigger ones? |
| 售：<br>shòu: | 有。<br>Yǒu. | Yes. We do. |
| 陈：<br>Chén: | 要一个大的。<br>Yào yíge dà de. | I'll have a big one. |

## • new words • 生词 • shēngcí

| | | | |
|---|---|---|---|
| 1 | 钢笔 | （名）gāngbǐ | pen, fountain-pen |
| 2 | 小 | （头、形）xiǎo | little, small, young (used before family names of young people one knows well) |
| 3 | 早晨 | （名）zǎochén | morning |
| 4 | 桌子 | （名）zhuōzi | table |
| 5 | ……上 | （名）…shang | (used after nouns corresponding to "on" or "above") |
| 6 | 捡到 | jiǎn dào | to find, to pick up by chance |

| | | | | |
|---|---|---|---|---|
| 7 | 支 | （量） | zhī | a measure word for cylindrical objects or songs or army units |
| 8 | 位 | （量） | wèi | a measure word used respectfully for people |
| 9 | 新 | （形） | xīn | new, recent |
| 10 | 这儿 | （代） | zhèr | here |
| 11 | 旧 | （形） | jiù | old, out-dated |
| 12 | 那（么） | （连） | nà (me) | then |
| 13 | 吃 | （动） | chī | to eat |
| 14 | 饭 | （名） | fàn | meal |
| 15 | 一会儿 | （名） | yíhuìr | a moment, a little bit later |
| 16 | 问 | （动） | wèn | to ask, to inquire |
| 17 | 对了 | | duì le | by the way |
| 18 | 昨天 | （名） | zuótiān | yesterday |
| 19 | 咖啡 | （名） | kāfēi | coffee |
| 20 | 小卖部 | （名） | xiǎomàibù | small shops at railway stations or hotels, as different from regular shops |
| 21 | 马上 | （副） | mǎshàng | immediately, right away |
| 22 | 售货员 | （名） | shòuhuòyuán | shop assistant |
| 23 | 外国 | （名） | wàiguó | foreign country (ies) |
| 24 | 种 | （量） | zhǒng | kind, sort |
| 25 | 筒 | （量） | tǒng | can, tin |
| 26 | 本子 | （名） | běnzi | notebook |
| 27 | 这样 | （代） | zhèyàng | this, such |
| 28 | 行 | （形） | xíng | all right, O. K., capable |
| 29 | 大 | （形） | dà | big, large, loud, old |

**专名　　Zhuānmíng　　Proper names**

| | | |
|---|---|---|
| 刘 | Liú | a common Chinese family name |

| | | |
|---|---|---|
| 英雄 | Yīngxióng | Hero (here, a brand name of Chinese pens) |
| 比利•威尔逊 | Bǐlì Wēi'ěrxùn | Bailey Wilson-name of Chen Mingshan's American friend |

## study points • 注释 • zhùshì

1 小刘 (Xiǎo Liú)

"小 (xiǎo) + a family name" may be used to address young people whom the speaker knows well and who are younger then the speaker.

2 早晨我们在这张桌子上捡到一支钢笔。(Zǎochén wǒmen zài zhèzhāng zhuōzishang jiǎn dào yìzhī gāngbǐ.)

The phrase "在这张桌子上" (zài zhèzhāng zhuōzishang) is an adverbial phrase of place modifying the verb "捡到 (jiǎn dào). As a rule, the adverbial phrase of place always precedes the verb it modifies.

3 我看看。(Wǒ kànkan.)

Some Chinese verbs can be repeated twice for two reasons:

1) to mean that the duration of the action is short or the action is carried out in a casual manner:

我给你们介绍介绍。(Wǒ gěi nǐmen jièshaojièshao.)
Let me introduce you to each other.
一会儿我问问他。(Yíhuìr wǒ wènwen tā.)
I'll ask him later.

2) "to sample" or "to try something out":

那个电影很好，你去看看。(Nàge diànyǐng hěn hǎo, nǐ qù kànkan. )
That film is good, you can try it out.

With one-syllable verbs, the second character is in the neutral tone; with two-syllable verbs, which is repeated in the form of "ABAB", the second and the fourth syllables are usually in the neutral tone. When one-syllable verbs are repeated, "一" (yī) may be added, for example: "看一看" (kàn yi kàn), "问一问" (wèn yi wèn); however, this is not true of the two-syllable verbs.

4 英雄的 (Yīngxióng de)

The particle "的" (de) is often added to nouns, adjectives, pronouns and measure words to form "qualifiers" which can stand on their own. The nouns they qualify are understood:

这种咖啡是中国的。(Zhèzhǒng kāfēi shì Zhōngguó de.)
This coffee is China's. (noun＋的　中国的＝中国的咖啡)
他的钢笔是新的。(Tā de gāngbǐ shì xīn de.)
His pen is new. (adjective＋的　新的＝新的钢笔)
那封信是你的。(Nàfēng xìn shì nǐ de.)
That letter is yours. (pronoun＋的　你的＝你的信)
这张邮票是八分的。(Zhèzhāng yóupiào shì bāfēn de.)
This stamp is an eight-fen (stamp).
(numeral and measure word＋的　八分的＝八分的邮票)

5 那(么)是谁的呢? (Nà[me] shì shuí de ne?)

The word "那么" (nàme), as a conjunction meaning "then" or "so", serves to introduce a logical deduction:

钢笔不是你的，不是他的，那(么)是谁的呢?
(Gāngbǐ bú shì nǐ de, bú shì tā de, nà(me) shì shuí de ne?)
The pen is not yours, not his, then whose is it?

6 会不会是他的? (Huì bu huì shì tā de?)

The auxiliary verb "会" (huì) indicates possibility in this sentence. Putting together the positive and negative forms of the auxiliary verbs is one way of forming questions:

他会不会去看电影?
(Tā huì bu huì qù kàn diànyǐng?)
Is he going to watch the movie or not?
你要不要买什么东西?
(Nǐ yào bu yào mǎi shénme dōngxi?)
Do you need to buy anything or not?

7 对了 (Duì le)

This phrase is often used in conversation to indicate that the speaker remembers something else and wants to change the subject.

8 昨天您不是要买咖啡吗? (Zuótiān nín bú shì yào mǎi kāfēi ma?)

"不是……吗?" (bú shì…ma?) is a rhetorical question having an affirmative meaning:

他不是要看电影吗?
(Tā bú shì yào kàn diànyǐng ma?)
Doesn't he want to see a movie?

这不是你的信吗？
(Zhè bú shì nǐ de xìn ma?)
Isn't this your letter?

9 是吗？ (Shì ma?)
This expression, which means "Is that so?" or "Really?", is often used as a reply to something unexpected.

## supplementary words • 补充生词 • bǔchōng shēngcí

| | | | | |
|---|---|---|---|---|
| 1 | 块 | （量） | kuài | a measure word (lump, piece, etc.) |
| 2 | 手绢 | （名） | shǒujuànr | handkerchief |
| 3 | 钥匙 | （名） | yàoshi | key |
| 4 | 手套 | （名） | shǒutàor | gloves |
| 5 | 副 | （量） | fù | a measure word (pair) |
| 6 | 只 | （量） | zhī | a measure word |
| 7 | 样 | （名、量） | yàng | appearance, kind; a measure word |
| 8 | 牌儿 | （名） | páir | brand |
| 9 | 红 | （形） | hóng | red |
| 10 | 处理 | （动） | chǔlǐ | to handle, to deal with |
| 11 | 金笔 | （名） | jīnbǐ | gold-tipped pen |
| 12 | 铱金 | （名） | yījīn | iridium |

## • exercises • 练习 • liànxí

1. **Phonetic exercises:**
   1) Tones
      (1) The neutral tone……的 (de):

| (1)＋的 (de) | (2)＋的 (de) | (3)＋的 (de) | (4)＋的 (de) |
|---|---|---|---|
| tā de | shuí de | nǐ de | jiù de |
| xīn de | Yīngxióng de | wǒ de | nǎwèi de |

(2) Neutral tone: The reduplication of verbs

kànkan  wènwen  xièxie  shìshi

2) Sound discrimination

| (1) z | zh | (2) ch | q | (3) ou | uo |
|---|---|---|---|---|---|
| zǎo | zhǎo | chī | qī | dōu | duō |
| zuò | zhuō | chāo | qiáo | zǒu | zuò |
| zì | zhì | chéng | qǐng | shòu | shuō |

***2. Practice asking questions on ownership:**

1) Model: 这支 钢笔是谁 的？（这支钢笔）
Zhèzhī gāngbǐ shì shéi de? (zhèzhī gāngbǐ)

(1) ________是 谁 的？( 这块 手绢 )
________shì shéi de? ( zhèkuài shǒujuànr )

(2) ________是哪位的？(这把 钥匙)
________shì nǎwèi de? ( zhèbǎ yàoshi )

(3) ________是哪个 同志的？(这副手套儿)
________shì nǎge tóngzhì de? ( zhèfù shǒutàor )

2) Model: 莉莉小姐，这支钢笔 是你的 吗？（钢笔）
Lìli xiǎojie, zhèzhī gāngbǐ shì nǐ de ma? (gāngbǐ)

(1) 陈 先生，________？（手套）
Chén xiānsheng, ________? ( shǒutàor )

(2) 史密斯太太，________？（钥匙）
Shǐmìsī tàitai, ________? ( yàoshi )

(3) 大伟，________？( 手绢 )
Dàwěi, ________? ( shǒujuànr )

3) Model: 这支 钢笔是 不 是莉莉的？（莉莉）
Zhèzhī gāngbǐ shì bu shì Lìli de? ( Lìli )

(1) 这块 手绢 ________？( 陈 先生 )
Zhèkuài shǒujuànr ________? ( Chén xiānsheng )

(2) 这只 手套________？（大伟）
Zhèzhī shǒutàor________? ( Dàwěi )

(3) 这把 钥匙________？（史密斯 太太）
Zhèbǎ yàoshi________? ( Shǐmìsī tàitai )

***3. Answer the following questions:**

这支 钢笔 是 你的吗？
Zhèzhī gāngbǐ shì nǐ de ma?

不是我的，是我儿子的。（我儿子）
Bú shì wǒ de, shì wǒ érzi de.（wǒ érzi）

(1) 这块手绢是你的吗？（我弟弟）
Zhèkuài shǒujuànr shì nǐ de ma?（wǒ dìdi）

(2) 这本画报是你姐姐的吗？（她朋友）
Zhèběn huàbào shì nǐ jiějie de ma?（tā péngyou）

(3) 这张桌子是不是你们家的？（我们学校）
Zhèzhāng zhuōzi shì bu shì nǐmen jiā de?（wǒmen xuéxiào）

(4) 这个本子是小刘的吗？（老张）
Zhège běnzi shì Xiǎo Liú de ma?（Lǎo Zhāng）

**4. Listen to the dialogues:**

1) A: 你要给小赵什么礼物？
Nǐ yào gěi Xiǎo Zhào shénme lǐwù?

B: 我要给他一支钢笔。
Wǒ yào gěi tā yìzhī gāngbǐ.

A: 什么样的？
Shénme yàng de?

B: 一定是新的了。
Yídìng shì xīn de le.

A: 是啊，一定不是旧的了。我是问你，
Shì a, yídìng bú shì jiù de le. Wǒ shì wèn nǐ,
什么牌儿的？
shénme páir de?

B: 英雄的，红的。
Yīngxióng de, hóng de.

A: 好。多少钱一支？
Hǎo. Duōshao qián yìzhī?

B: 三块六。
Sānkuài liù.

A: 什么？三块六？不是十几块吗？
Shénme? Sānkuài liù? Bú shì shíjǐkuài ma?
会不会是处理的？
Huì bu huì shì chǔlǐ de?

B: 哪儿啊，十几块的是金笔，这是铱金的。
Nǎr a, shíjǐkuài de shì jīnbǐ, zhè shì yījīn de.

2) 刘：陈太太，你们的信。
Liú: Chén tàitai, nǐmen de xìn.

艾： 谢谢你，小刘。哦，三封呢！
Ài： Xièxie nǐ, Xiǎo Liú. Ó, sānfēng ne!

大伟： 都是谁的？——啊，这封是爸爸的，
Dàwěi: Dōu shì shéi de? —— Ā, zhè fēng shì bàba de,
这封是妈妈的……
zhèfēng shì māma de……

莉莉： 有没有我的？
Lìli : Yǒu méi yǒu wǒ de?

大伟： 没有你的。
Dàwěi: Méi yǒu nǐ de.

莉莉： 那，那一封是谁的？
Lìli : Nà, nà yìfēng shì shéi de?

大伟： 是我……
Dàwěi: Shì wǒ……

莉莉： 是你的？我看看，这不是我的吗！
Lìli : Shì nǐ de? Wǒ kànkan, zhè bú shì wǒ de ma!
怎么是你的？
Zěnme shì nǐ de?

大伟： 我是说，是我姐姐的。
Dàwěi: Wǒ shì shuō, shì wǒ jiějie de.

莉莉： 这个大伟！
Lìli : Zhège Dàwěi!

# 12 Shopping
# 买东西 mǎi dōngxi

(Mr. and Mrs. Chen are in a department store buying an overcoat.)

| | | |
|---|---|---|
| 售货员：<br>shòuhuòyuán: | 您 买 什么？<br>Nín mǎi shénme? | You want to buy something? |
| 陈：<br>Chén: | 我 买 一件大衣。<br>Wǒ mǎi yíjiàn dàyī. | We're looking for an overcoat. |
| 售：<br>shòu: | 您 穿 的 吗？①<br>Nín chuān de ma? | For yourself? |

| | | |
|---|---|---|
| 陈：<br>Chén: | 对。<br>Duì. | Yes. |
| 售：<br>shòu: | 请 这边儿 来。<br>Qǐng zhèbianr lái. | This way, please. |
| 陈：<br>Chén: | 艾琳，你 看， 这件 怎么<br>Àilín, nǐ kàn, zhèjiàn zěnme<br>样 ？②<br>yàng? | What do you think of this one, Irene? |
| 艾：<br>Ài: | 颜色 不 好。<br>Yánsè bù hǎo. | I don't like the color. |
| 陈：<br>Chén: | 那 一件 呢？<br>Nà yíjiàn ne? | How about that one? |
| 艾：<br>Ài: | 那件 颜色 不错，你 试试。<br>Nàjiàn yánsè búcuò, nǐ shìshi. | The color is all right. Try it on. |
| 陈：<br>Chén: | 怎么样 ？③ 合适 吗？<br>Zěnmeyàng? Héshì ma? | How does it look? Does it fit? |
| 艾：<br>Ài: | 太 长。<br>Tài cháng. | A bit too long. |
| 陈：<br>Chén: | 劳 驾，④ 请 换 件 短<br>Láo jià, qǐng huàn jiàn duǎn<br>点儿 的。<br>diǎnr de. | Would you mind getting me a shorter one, please? |
| 艾：<br>Ài: | 嗯， 这件 很 合适，样子<br>Ǹg, zhèjiàn hěn héshì, yàngzi<br>也 比较 好。<br>yě bǐjiào hǎo. | Hm, this fits you and the style's better too. |
| 陈：<br>Chén: | 多少 钱？<br>Duōshao qián? | How much is it? |
| 售：<br>shòu: | 一百八十二块 六（毛）。<br>Yìbǎibāshí'èrkuài liù(máo). | A hundred and eighty-two yuan and sixty fen. |
| 陈：<br>Chén: | 艾琳，你 说 贵 吗？<br>Àilín, nǐ shuō guì ma? | Irene, do you think it's expensive? |
| 艾：<br>Ài: | 不 贵， 要 这件 吧。<br>Bú guì, yào zhèjiàn ba. | No. I think you should take it. |
| 陈：<br>Chén: | 同 志， 给 您 钱。<br>Tóngzhì, gěi nín qián. | Here's the money, Comrade. |
| 售：<br>shòu: | 您 这 是 一百九十块， 找<br>Nín zhè shì yìbǎijiǔshíkuài, zhǎo | A hundred and ninety yuan. Here's your change, |

| | |
|---|---|
| 您 七块 四（毛）。<br>nín qīkuài sì（máo）. | seven yuan forty. |

## • new words • 生词 • shēngcí

| | | | | |
|---|---|---|---|---|
| 1 | 件 | （量）jiàn | | a measure word for overcoats, coats, as well as for things or matters, etc. |
| 2 | 大衣 | （名）dàyī | | overcoat |
| 3 | 穿 | （动）chuān | | to put on, to wear |
| 4 | ……边儿 | （名）…bianr | | (used after words of location to show direction, location, etc.) |
| | 这边儿 | | zhèbianr | here, this way, this side |
| 5 | 怎么样 | （代）zěnmeyàng | | how |
| 6 | 颜色 | （名）yánsè | | color |
| 7 | 不错 | （形）búcuò | | good, fair, not bad |
| 8 | 试 | （动）shì | | to try on, to try |
| 9 | 合适 | （形）héshì | | fit, proper, suitable |
| 10. | 太 | （副）tài | | too, too much |
| 11 | 长 | （形）cháng | | long |
| 12 | 劳驾 | | láo jià | a polite way to ask someone to do something or to make way |
| 13 | 换 | （动）huàn | | to change |
| 14 | 短 | （形）duǎn | | short |
| 15 | 嗯 | （叹）ǹg | | an interjection to express appreciation or consent |
| 16 | 很 | （副）hěn | | very, very much (usually not stressed; stressed only when emphasis is needed) |
| 17 | 样子 | （名）yàngzi | | style, look, model |

18 比较 (副、动) bǐjiào comparatively, relatively, to compare, to contrast

19 贵 (形) guì dear, expensive

## study points • 注释 • zhùshì

1 您穿的吗? (Nín chuān de ma?)
In this case, the verb "穿" (chuān) is used with the particle "的" (de) to mean "for one to wear." The meaning of the whole sentence in the conversation is "an overcoat for yourself to wear?" The "verb+的 (de)" pattern has been explained in Study Point 4 of Lesson 11.

2 这件怎么样? (Zhèjiàn zěnmeyàng?)
The subject in this sentence is the noun phrase "这件" (zhèjiàn) and the predicate is "怎么样" (zěnmeyàng)。Notice the absence of the verb "是" (shì). The following are the common interrogative, negative and affirmative forms:
这件大衣怎么样? (Zhèjiàn dàyī zěnmeyàng?)
How (is) this overcoat?
这件大衣不好。(Zhèjiàn dàyī bù hǎo.)
This overcoat (is) not good.
这件大衣很好。(Zhèjiàn dàyī hěn hǎo.)
This overcoat (is) good.
In the last example, the adverb "很" (hěn) is often used in the affirmative and is often unstressed. In some context, "hěn" may be compared with the English adverb "very", but in this case, it does not indicate degree as "very" does, it helps to indicate the statement in the affirmative.

3 怎么样? (zěnmeyàng?)
This is a colloquial expression often used to ask for somebody's opinion.

4 劳驾 (láo jià)
This is a polite form of asking somebody to do something or to make way for you. People also say "劳你驾" (láo nǐ jià) to mean the same thing.

## supplementary words • 补充生词 • bǔchōng shēngcí

| | | | | |
|---|---|---|---|---|
| 1 | 长短 | （名） | chángduǎnr | Length |
| 2 | 肥瘦儿 | （名） | féishòur | width |
| 3 | 大小 | （名） | dàxiǎor | size |
| 4 | 中式 | （名） | Zhōngshì | Chinese style |
| 5 | 罩衫 | （名） | zhàoshān | a kind of jacket |
| 6 | 条 | （量） | tiáo | a measure word |
| 7 | 裤子 | （名） | kùzi | trousers |
| 8 | 双 | （量） | shuāng | a measure word (pair) |
| 9 | 皮鞋 | （名） | píxié | leather shoes |
| 10 | 瘦 | （形） | shòu | tight, thin |
| 11 | 肥 | （形） | féi | loose |
| 12 | 做 | （动） | zuò | to make |
| 13 | 尺 | （量） | chǐ | a measure word |
| 14 | 布 | （名） | bù | cloth |
| 15 | 够 | （形） | gòu | enough |
| 16 | 得 | （动） | dé | to be ready |
| 17 | 早 | （形） | zǎo | early |

## • exercises • 练习 • liànxí

1. **Phonetic exercises:**

1) Tones

(1) Changes of the tone of "不 (bù)"

| | |
|---|---|
| "不 (bù)" ＋(1) | "不 (bù)" ＋(2) |
| bù xīn | bù cháng |
| bù hē | bù xíng |
| "不 (bù)" ＋(3) | "不 (bù)" ＋(4) |
| bù hǎo | búcuò |
| bù duǎn | bú guì |

(2) The neutral tone……子 (zi):

zhuōzi　　érzi　　běnzi　　yàngzi

(3) Changes of the 3rd tone

hěn xīn　　hěn cháng　　hěn duǎn　　hěn guì

2) Sound discrimination

(1) The retroflex final

| | | |
|---|---|---|
| zhèr | diǎnr | bianr |
| nàr | duǎn diǎnr | zhèbianr |
| shìr | cháng diǎnr | nàbianr |
| yíhuìr | dà diǎnr | shàngbianr |
| | xiǎo diǎnr | xiàbianr |

(2)

| b | p |
|---|---|
| bǎi | pái |
| běn | péng |
| biān | piàn |
| biǎo | piào |

***2. Turn the following into antonyms and negative sentences:**

| | |
|---|---|
| 大 (dà) | |
| 新 (xīn) | |
| 长 (cháng) | |
| 颜色 很 好 (yánsè hěn hǎo) | |
| 样子 很 好 (yàngzi hěn hǎo) | |
| 长短 合适 (chángduǎnr héshì) | |
| 肥瘦儿 合适 (féishòur héshì) | |
| 大小 合适 (dàxiǎor héshì) | |

***3. Make dialogues after the model:**

Model: 顾客：同志，我买大衣。
Gùkè: Tóngzhì, wǒ mǎi dàyī.
售货员：这件 怎么样？
Shòuhuòyuán: Zhèjiàn zěnmeyàng?
顾：太大。有小 点儿的吗？（大，小）
Gù: Tài dà. Yǒu xiǎo diǎnr de ma? (dà, xiǎo)
售：您再试试这件。
Shòu: Nín zài shìshi zhèjiàn.

顾：这件 大小 合适。（大小）
Gù：Zhèjiàn dàxiǎor héshì. （dàxiǎor）

1) 顾：同志，我买件 中式 罩衫。
Gù: Tóngzhì, wǒ mǎi jiàn Zhōngshì zhàoshān.
售 ：这件 行不行？
Shòu: Zhèjiàn xíng bu xíng?
顾：______，______？（大，小）
Gù: ______，______？（dà, xiǎo）
售 ：您再试试这件。
Shòu: Nín zài shìshi zhèjiàn.
顾：________。（大小）
Gù: ________.（dàxiǎor）

2) 顾：同志，我买 条裤子。
Gù: Tóngzhì，wǒ mǎi tiáo kùzi.
售 ：这条 怎么样？
Shòu: Zhètiáo zěnmeyàng?
顾：________？（长，短）
Gù: ________？（cháng, duǎn）
售 ：您再看看 这条。
Shòu: Nín zài kànkan zhètiáo.
顾：________。（长短）
Gù: ________.（chángduǎnr）

3) 顾：同志，我买 双皮鞋。
Gù: Tóngzhì, wǒ mǎi shuāng píxié.
售 ：多少号 的？
Shòu: Duōshaohàor de?
顾：四十号的？
Gù: Sìshíhàor de？
售 ：这双 合适 不合适？
Shòu: Zhèshuāng héshì bu héshì?
顾：________？（瘦，肥）
Gù: ________？（shòu, féi）
售 ：您再试试 这双。
Shòu: Nín zài shìshi zhèshuāng.
顾：________。（肥瘦儿，大小）
Gù: ________.（féishòur, dàxiǎor）

**4. Listen to the dialogue:**

顾客：同志，我要做一件 中式 罩衫，请问，七尺布够不够？
Gùkè: Tóngzhì, wǒ yào zuò yíjiàn Zhōngshì zhàoshān, qǐng wèn, qīchǐ bù gòu bu gòu?

营业员：够。
Yíngyèyuán: Gòu.

顾：我 要肥一点儿的，够 吗？
Gù: Wǒ yào féi yìdiǎnr de, gòu ma?

营：肥一点儿的，七尺也 够。
Yíng: Féi yìdiǎnr de, qīchǐ yě gòu.

顾：那，什么 时候 得呢？
Gù: Nà, shénme shíhour dé ne?

营：一个星期得。
Yíng: Yíge xīngqī dé.

顾：再早一点儿行 不行？
Gù: Zài zǎo yìdiǎnr xíng bu xíng?

营：您 有事儿，要 早 穿？
Yíng: Nín yǒu shìr, yào zǎo chuān?

顾：是啊。
Gù: Shì a.

营：这样 吧，您 下 星期三 来 取。
Yíng: Zhèyàng ba, nín xià xīngqīsān lái qǔ.

顾：好，这样 好。麻烦 您 了。
Gù: Hǎo, zhèyàng hǎo. Máfan nín le.

营：没 什么。喂，同志，您 的 布呢？
Yíng: Méi shénme. Wèi, tóngzhì, nín de bù ne?

顾：啊，我 马上 去 买。一会儿见！
Gù: À, wǒ mǎshàng qù mǎi. Yíhuìr jiàn!

营：一会儿见！
Yíng: Yíhuìr jiàn!

***5. Translate the following into Chinese:**

1) This is a big theater.
2) This fish is not expensive.
3) The coat is well cut.
4) The color is not quite good.
5) This overcoat is a tight sit.

# 13 Going To The Beijing International Airport
# 去国际机场 qù guójì jīchǎng

(Irene asks Xiao Liu to get her a taxi to take her to the Beijing International Airport.)

## (一)

刘：　可以进来吗？①　　May I come in?
Liú:　Kěyǐ jìn lai ma?

艾：　请　进！　　Please do.
Ài:　Qǐng jìn!

| | | |
|---|---|---|
| 刘：<br>Liú: | 陈 太太，陈 先生<br>Chén tàitai, Chén xiānsheng<br>的信。<br>de xìn. | Mrs. Chen, here's a letter for Mr. Chen. |
| 艾：<br>Ài: | 谢谢。小 刘 同志，②<br>Xièxie. Xiǎo Liú tóngzhì,<br>你能 不能 帮 我 叫<br>nǐ néng bu néng bāng wǒ jiào<br>一辆 出租汽车？③<br>yíliàng chūzū qìchē? | Thank you, Comrade Xiao Liu. Can you help me to get a taxi? |
| 刘：<br>Liú: | 什么 时候 要？<br>Shénme shíhour yào? | When do you want it? |
| 艾：<br>Ài: | 半个 小时 以后，我 要<br>Bànge xiǎoshí yǐhòu, wǒ yào<br>去国际 机场。④<br>qù Guójì Jīchǎng. | In half an hour. I want to go to the Beijing International Airport. |
| 刘：<br>Liú: | 好。<br>Hǎo. | O. K. |

## （二） II

| | | |
|---|---|---|
| 艾：<br>Ài: | 同 志，到 国际 机场。<br>Tóngzhì, dào Guójì Jīchǎng. | To Beijing International Airport, Comrade. |
| 司机：<br>sījī : | 好。……您 会 说 中国<br>Hǎo. ……Nín huì shuō Zhōngguó<br>话？⑤<br>huà? | O.K. You speak Chinese? |
| 艾：<br>Ài: | 是啊，还 能 听 懂 吧？⑥<br>Shì a , hái néng tīng dǒng ba? | Yes. Can you understand me? |
| 司：<br>sī : | 能 听 懂。您 的<br>Néng tīng dǒng. Nín de<br>中国话 不错啊！⑦<br>Zhōngguóhuà búcuò a ! | Yes, I can. Your Chinese is not bad! |
| 艾：<br>Ài: | 谢谢。我 先生 是<br>Xièxie. Wǒ xiānsheng shì<br>华侨；⑧我是 美国人。<br>huáqiáo; wǒ shì Měiguórén. | Thank you. My husband is an overseas Chinese. I am an American. Comrade, can we get to |

| | | |
|---|---|---|
| | 同志，一个小时能到 Tóngzhì, yíge xiǎoshí néng dào 机场吗？ jīchǎng ma? | the airport in an hour? |
| 司: sī: | 能，没问题。 Néng, méi wèntí. | No problem at all. |

## • new words • 生词 • shēngcí

| | | | | |
|---|---|---|---|---|
| 1 | 可以 | (助动、形) kěyǐ | | can, may, will do, good enough |
| 2 | 进来 | | jìn lai | to come in |
| 3 | 能 | (助动) néng | | can, to be able to |
| 4 | 帮 | (动) bāng | | to help, to aid |
| 5 | 叫 | (动) jiào | | to call, to order |
| 6 | 辆 | (量) liàng | | a measure word for vehicles |
| 7 | 出租 | (动) chūzū | | to rent out |
| 8 | 汽车 | (名) qìchē | | car, automobile |
| 9 | 小时 | (名) xiǎoshí | | hour |
| 10 | 以后 | (名) yǐhòu | | after |
| 11 | 到 | (动) dào | | to spoken, to reach, to get to |
| 12 | 司机 | (名) sījī | | driver |
| 13 | 中国话 | (名) Zhōngguóhuà | | oral Chinese |
| 14 | 听 | (动) tīng | | to listen, to hear |
| 15 | 懂 | (动) dǒng | | to understand |
| | 听懂 | | tīng dǒng | to understand (by listening) |
| 16 | 机场 | (名) jīchǎng | | airport |
| 17 | 没 | (动、副) méi | | to have not, there is (are) not, no, not |
| 18 | 问题 | (名) wèntí | | problem, question |
| | 没问题 | | méi wèntí | no problem |

## 专名 Zhuānmíng Proper name

国际机场 Guójì Jīchǎng International Airport

## study points • 注释 • zhùshì

1 可以进来吗? (Kěyǐ jìn lai ma?)

The auxiliary verb "可以" (kěyǐ) indicates "request" or "permission":

你可以帮我买点儿东西吗?
(Nǐ kěyǐ bāng wǒ mǎi diǎnr dōngxi ma?) (request)
Can you help me to buy something?

晚上我们可以看电影吗?
(Wǎnshang wǒmen kěyǐ kàn diànyǐng ma?) (permission)
May we go to the cinema in the evening?

2 小刘同志 (Xiǎo Liú tóngzhì)

The pattern "小 (xiǎo) or 老 (lǎo) + the family name + 同志 (tóngzhì)" is a common form of addressing acquaintances in China. In certain context, it implies affection or respect.

3 你能不能帮我叫一辆出租汽车? (Nǐ néng bu néng bāng wǒ jiào yíliàng chūzū qìchē?)

The auxiliary verb "能 (néng) indicates "ability", "request" and "possibility":

他能说中国话。 (Tā néng shuō Zhōngguóhuà.) (ability)
He can speak Chinese.

明天你能给我打个电话吗? (Míngtiān nǐ néng gěi wǒ dǎ ge diànhuà ma?)
Tomorrow, can you give me a telephone call? (request)

汽车一个小时能到机场吗? (Qìchē yíge xiǎoshí néng dào jīchǎng ma?)
Can the car get to the airport in an hour? (possibility)

When used in the sense of "request" or "permission", "能" (néng) and "可以" (kěyǐ) are interchangeable:

你能(可以)等等我吗? (Nǐ néng (kěyǐ) děngdeng wǒ ma?)
明天我们可以(能)去。 (Míngtiān wǒmen kěyǐ (néng) qù.)

4 我要去国际机场。 (Wǒ yào qù Guójì Jīchǎng.)

The auxiliary verb "要" (yào) indicates "will" or "desire":

下午我要给姐姐写信。 (Xiàwǔ wǒ yào gěi jiějie xiě xìn.)

In the afternoon I want to write my sister a letter.

星期六我要去兑换外币。(Xīngqīliù wǒ yào qù duìhuàn wàibì.)

On Saturday, I'll go to get some foreign change.

The negative form of "要" (yào) is "不想" (bùxiǎng):

我不想看杂技。(Wǒ bù xiǎng kàn zájì.)

I don't want to see the acrobatic show.

5 您会说中国话? (Nín huì shuō Zhōngguóhuà?)

The auxiliary verb "会" (huì) has two meanings: 1. "possibility" (See Study Point 6 of Lesson 11), 2. "acquired skill (or habit)":

他会说中国话。(Tā huì shuō Zhōngguóhuà.)

He can speak Chinese.

你会抽烟吗? (Nǐ huì chōu yān mā?)

Do you smoke?

6 还能听懂吧? (Hái néng tīng dǒng ba?)

In this case, the adverb "还" (hái) indicates degree meaning "barely", "by a narrow margin".

7 您的中国话不错啊! (Nín de Zhōngguóhuà búcuò a!)

"啊" (a), serving as an interjection expressing surprise or joy, suggests praise in this sentence.

8 我先生是华侨。(Wǒ xiānsheng shì huáqiáo.)

"我先生" (Wǒ xiānsheng) means "my husband" in this sentence. When used in this sense, the term is often replaced by "爱人" (àirén) literally meaning "beloved person".

## supplementary words • 补充生词 • bǔchōng shēngcí

| | | | | |
|---|---|---|---|---|
| 1 | 当然 | (形、副) | dāngrán | certain, certainly |
| 2 | 这么 | (代) | zhème | so |
| 3 | 跟 | (介) | gēn | with |
| 4 | 酒 | (名) | jiǔ | alcoholic drink |
| 5 | 一起 | (名、副) | yìqǐ | together |

民族饭店 Mínzú Fàndiàn Nationalities Hotel

## • exercises • 练习 • liànxí

**1. Phonetic exercises:**

1) Tones

(1) Changes of the 3rd tone

nǎtiān xiǎoshí kěyǐ yǐhòu

(2) The 4th tone

shēngrì dàngāo tā yào qìchē

xīn jiù dàyī tā qù Gùgōng

2) Sound discrimination

(1)

| g | k |
|---|---|
| gè | kè |
| gàn | kàn |
| gāi | kāi |
| guài | kuài |

(2)

| u | ü |
|---|---|
| chū | qù |
| zhù | jù |
| shù | xù |
| lù | lǚ |
| nǔ | nǚ |

***2. Fill in the blanks with "能" (néng) or "会" (huì) in accordance with the contents of the pictures:**

1) A: 这个小弟弟______走吗?
Zhège xiǎo dìdi______zǒu ma?

B: 不______。
Bú______.

2) A: 这位同志______走吗?
Zhèwèi tóngzhì______zǒu ma?

B: 不______。
Bù______.

3) A: 这位 英国人______说 中国话吗？
Zhèwèi Yīngguórén______shuō Zhōngguó huà ma?

B: 不______。
Bú______.

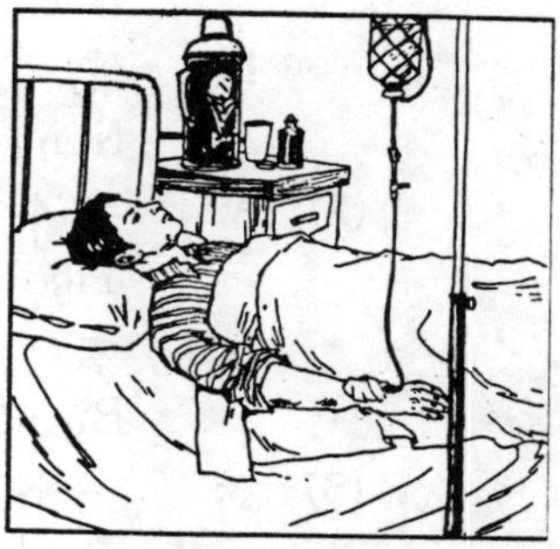

4) A: 他今天______吃点儿东西吗？
Tā jīntiān______chī diǎnr dōngxi ma?

B: 不______。
Bù______.

**3 . Practice asking questions with :**

1) Using "可以……吗？"(kěyǐ……ma?)

Model: A: 可以进来吗？
Kěyǐ jìn lai ma?

B: 请 进。
Qǐng jìn.

(1) A: ______？（走）
______？（zǒu）
B: ______走了。
______Zǒu le .

(2) A: ______？（坐）
______？（zuò）
B: 请 坐吧。
Qǐng zuò ba.

(3) A: ______？（参观）
______？（cānguān）
B: ____参观。
____cānguān.

(4) A: ______？（看看）
______？（kànkan）
B: 当然了。
Dāngrán le.

2) Asking for help

Model: A: 您能帮我叫辆出租汽车吗？
Nín néng bāng wǒ jiào liàng chūzū qìchē ma?

B: 好。
Hǎo.

(1) 寄信
jì xìn

(2) 找一个人
zhǎo yíge rén

(3) 买 电影 票
mǎi diànyǐng piào

(4) 写几个字
xiě jǐge zì

3) Practice after the model:

Model: A: 汽车一个小时能到国际机场吗?
Qìchē yíge xiǎoshí néng dào Guójì Jīchǎng ma?

B: 没问题。
Méi wèntí.

(1) A: 半个小时______?(民族 饭店)
Bànge xiǎoshí______?(Mínzú Fàndiàn)

B: 能。
Néng.

(2) A: 一个小时______?(长城)
Yíge xiǎoshí______?(Chángchéng)

B: 不能。
Bù néng.

(3) A: 一个半小时以后______?(走)
Yígebàn xiǎoshí yǐhòu______?(zǒu)

B: 没问题。
Méi wèntí.

(4) A: 半个小时以后汽车______?(来)
Bànge xiǎoshí yǐhòu qìchē______?(lái)

B: 当然。
Dāngrán.

**4. Listen to the dialogues.**

1) 王 大华:同志,您能帮我找一个人吗?
Wáng Dàhuá: Tóngzhì, nín néng bāng wǒ zhǎo yíge rén ma?

小 刘:您找谁呀,这么晚了?
Xiǎo Liú: Nín zhǎo shéi ya, zhème wǎn le?

王:美国来的陈明山。
Wáng: Měiguó lái de Chén Míngshān.

刘:他住 5128 房间。
Liú: Tā zhù 5128 fángjiān.

王:5128 在哪儿?
Wáng: 5128 zài nǎr?

刘:请跟我来。
Liú: Qǐng gēn wǒ lái.

2) 王 大华:可以进来吗?
Wáng Dàhuá: Kěyǐ jìn lái ma?

陈 明山：哪位呀？
Chén Míngshān: Nǎwèi ya?

王：我是王大华。
Wáng: Wǒ shì Wáng Dàhuá.

陈：哦，大华，是你，你好啊！
Chén: Ò, Dàhuá, shì nǐ, nǐ hǎo a!

王：你好啊！
Wáng: Nǐ hǎo a!

陈：请坐，请坐。我跟艾琳说，这么晚了，
Chén: Qǐng zuò, qǐng zuò. Wǒ gēn Àilín shuō, zhème wǎn le,
你今天大概不会来了。
nǐ jīntiān dàgài bú huì lái le.

王：怎么能不来！
Wáng: Zěnme néng bù lái!

陈：老朋友，会喝酒吗？
Chén: Lǎo péngyou, huì hē jiǔ ma?

王：不会喝呀！
Wáng: Bú huì hē ya!

陈：我也不会喝。今天咱们一定要喝两杯，
Chén: Wǒ yě bú huì hē. Jīntiān zánmen yídìng yào hē liǎngbēi,
是不是？
shì bu shì?

王：对，今天两个老朋友在一起了，
Wáng: Duì, jīntiān liǎngge lǎo péngyou zài yìqǐ le,
不能不喝酒啊！
bù néng bù hē jiǔ a!

陈：是啊，不会喝也要喝。
Chén: Shì a, bú huì hē yě yào hē.

# 14 In A Restaurant
# 在饭馆 zài fànguǎnr

(The Chens are having dinner in a restaurant.)

| | | |
|---|---|---|
| 服务员:<br>fúwùyuán: | 你们 几位 里边儿 请。①<br>Nǐmen jǐwèi lǐbianr qǐng.<br>这 是 菜单, 你们 吃<br>Zhè shì càidān, nǐmen chī<br>什么?<br>shénme? | This way,.please. Here's the menu. What would you have? |

| | | |
|---|---|---|
| 伟 :<br>Wěi: | 爸爸，我 要 吃鱼。<br>Bàba, wǒ yào chī yú . | I want some fish, Dad. |
| 陈 :<br>Chén: | 好 ， 要 个鱼。<br>Hǎo, yào ge yú. | O. K. A fish, please. |
| 服：<br>fú : | 糖醋鱼 还是 红烧鱼？②<br>Tángcùyú háishi hóngshāoyú? | Sweet and sour fish or fish stewed in red sauce? |
| 陈 :<br>Chén: | 听 说 这儿的 糖醋鱼不错，<br>Tīng shuō zhèr de tángcùyú búcuò,<br>来个 糖醋鱼吧。③艾琳，莉莉，<br>lái ge tángcùyú ba. Àilín, Lìli,<br>你们 想 吃 什么？<br>nǐmen xiǎng chī shénme? | I've heard that your sweet and sour fish is very good. Let's have an order of sweet and sour fish. Irene and Lily, what would you like? |
| 艾：<br>Ài: | 要 个 红烧肉 ， 要个<br>Yào ge hóngshāoròu, yào ge<br>炸大虾。<br>zhádàxiā. | Let's have a stewed pork and a fried prawns. |
| 陈 :<br>Chén: | 好。莉莉 呢？<br>Hǎo. Lìli ne? | O. K. What about you, Lily? |
| 莉：<br>Lì : | 要 个 辣子鸡。<br>Yào ge làzijī . | I want chicken cuts fried with hot pepper. |
| 陈 :<br>Chén: | 再 来个豆腐 吧。<br>Zài lái ge dòufu ba. | A bean-curd too. |
| 服：<br>fú : | 要 汤 吗？<br>Yào tāng ma? | How about soup? |
| 陈 :<br>Chén: | 有 鸡蛋汤 没 有？④<br>Yǒu jīdàntāng méi yǒu? | Do you have egg-soup? |
| 服：<br>fú : | 有 。<br>Yǒu. | Yes. |
| 陈 :<br>Chén: | 来一个。<br>Lái yíge. | We'll have an order of that. |
| 服：<br>fú : | 你们 吃 馒头 还是 吃<br>Nǐmen chī mántou háishi chī<br>米饭？<br>mǐfàn? | Would you have steamed bread or rice? |
| 艾：<br>Ài: | 四碗 米饭，两个 馒头。<br>Sìwǎn mǐfàn, liǎngge mántou. | Four bowls of rice and two pieces of steamed bread. |

| | | |
|---|---|---|
| 服： | 要不要酒？ | How about drinks? |
| fú： | Yào bu yào jiǔ? | |
| 莉： | 要 两瓶 啤酒。 | Yes, two bottles of beer. |
| Lì: | Yào liǎngpíng píjiǔ. | |
| 服： | 还 要别的吗？ | Anything else? |
| fú： | Hái yào biéde ma? | |
| 陈： | 就这些 吧。 | I think that'll do. |
| Chén: | Jiù zhèxiē ba. | |
| 服： | 好，你们 等 一 等， | Yes, sir. Your orders will be ready in a minute. |
| fú： | Hǎo, nǐmen děng yi děng, | |
| | 马上 就来。 | |
| | mǎshàng jiù lái. | |

## • new words • 生词 • shēngcí

| | | | | |
|---|---|---|---|---|
| 1 | 饭馆 | （名） | fànguǎnr | restaurant |
| 2 | 里 | （名） | lǐ | a particle used to indicate "within certain time, space or scope" |
| 3 | 里边儿 | （名） | lǐbianr | inside |
| 4 | 菜 | （名） | cài | dish, vegetable |
| | 菜单 | | càidān | menu |
| 5 | 鱼 | （名） | yú | fish |
| 6 | 糖 | （名） | táng | sugar, sweets, candies |
| 7 | 醋 | （名） | cù | vinegar |
| | 糖醋鱼 | | tángcùyú | fish in sweet and sour sauce |
| 8 | 还是 | （连、副） | háishi | or (not used in declarative sentences), still |
| 9 | 红烧 | | hóngshāo | to stew with red sauce (soya bean sauce) |
| | 红烧鱼 | | hóngshāoyú | fish stewed in red sauce |

| | | | | |
|---|---|---|---|---|
| 10 | 听说 | | tīng shuō | to hear, to be told |
| 11 | 想 | （助动、动） | xiǎng | to want, to intend, to think |
| 12 | 肉 | （名） | ròu | meat |
| | 红烧肉 | | hóngshāoròu | meat stewed in red sauce |
| 13 | 炸 | （动） | zhá | to fry |
| 14 | 虾 | （名） | xiā | prawn, shrimp |
| | 炸大虾 | | zhádàxiā | fried prawns |
| 15 | 辣子 | （名） | làzi | hot pepper |
| 16 | 鸡 | （名） | jī | chicken |
| | 辣子鸡 | | làzijī | chicken cuts fried with hot pepper |
| 17 | 豆腐 | （名） | dòufu | bean-curd |
| 18 | 汤 | （名） | tāng | soup |
| 19 | 鸡蛋 | （名） | jīdàn | egg |
| 20 | 馒头 | （名） | mántou | steamed bread in the shape of a half ball |
| 21 | 米饭 | （名） | mǐfàn | cooked rice |
| 22 | 碗 | （名、量） | wǎn | bowl |
| 23 | 酒 | （名） | jiǔ | alcoholic drinks |
| 24 | 瓶 | （量） | píng | bottle |
| 25 | 啤酒 | （名） | píjiǔ | beer |
| 26 | 就 | （副） | jiù | just, only, (as soon as), etc., also used in clauses of result |
| 27 | 些 | （量） | xiē | some, a little (indicating a certain quantity or degree) |
| 28 | 这些 | （代） | zhèxiē | these |

## study points • 注释 • zhùshì

1 你们几位里边请。(Nǐmen jǐwèi lǐbianr qǐng.)

This is a common statement used by waiters in restaurants to greet customers. It corresponds to "This way, please" in English.

2 糖醋鱼还是红烧鱼? (Tángcùyú háishi hóngshāoyú?)

"还是" in this question indicates that there are two alternatives. Study the following examples:

你们吃米饭还是吃馒头? (Nǐmen chī mǐfàn háishi chī mántou?)

Do you want rice or steamed bread?

我们今天去长城还是明天去长城?

(Wǒmen jīntiān qù Chángchéng háishi míngtiān qù Chángchéng?)

Are we going to the Great Wall today or tomorrow?

那支钢笔是新的还是旧的? (Nàzhī gāngbǐ shì xīn de háishi jiù de?)

Is that pen new or is it old?

3 来个糖醋鱼吧。(Lái ge tángcùyú ba.)

"来" here means "要" (yào).

4 有鸡蛋汤没有? (Yǒu jīdàntāng méiyǒu?)

The two forms of asking "有没有" questions are:

1) "有没有……?" (yǒu méi yǒu…?)

2) "有……没有?" (yǒu…méi yǒu?)

## supplementary words • 补充生词 • bǔchōng shēngcí

| | | | | |
|---|---|---|---|---|
| 1 | 饺子 | (名) | jiǎozi | dumplings |
| 2 | 面包 | (名) | miànbāo | bread |
| 3 | 牛奶 | (名) | niúnǎi | milk |
| 4 | 白酒 | (名) | báijiǔ | spirits (alcohol) |
| 5 | 拼盘 | (名) | pīnpánr | mixed cold dish, hors d'oeuvre |
| 6 | 黄瓜 | (名) | huánggua | cucumber |

| | | | | |
|---|---|---|---|---|
| 7 | 面条儿 | （名） | miàntiáor | noodles |
| 8 | 喜欢 | （动） | xǐhuan | to like |
| 9 | 猪肉 | （名） | zhūròu | pork |
| 10 | 牛肉 | （名） | niúròu | beef |
| 11 | 羊肉 | （名） | yángròu | mutton |
| 12 | 盘儿 | （量） | pánr | a measure word (dish, plate) |
| 13 | 花生米 | （名） | huāshēngmǐ | peanuts |
| 14 | 酱肉 | （名） | jiàngròu | cooked meat seasoned in soy sauce. |
| | 青岛 | | Qīngdǎo | a major coastal city, in Shandong Province |

## • exercises • 练习 • liànxí

**1. Phonetic exercises:**

1) Tones

(1) The neutral tone

mántou　　lǐbianr　　làzi　　dòufu

(2) (3)+(1)

Xiǎng chī shénme?　　Mǎi xiē biéde.

Wǒ chī mántou.　　Nǎtiān huí lai?

(3) (3)+(4)

Jǐwèi péngyou?　　mǐfàn liángwǎn

yǒu cài yóu jiǔ　　mǎshàng géi nǐ

2) Sound discrimination

| (1) z | c | (2) c | ch | (3) ian | iang |
|---|---|---|---|---|---|
| zài | cài | céng | chéng | xiān | xiǎng |
| zán | cān | cù | chū | jiǎn | jiǎng |
| zuò | cuò | cì | chī | qián | qiáng |
| zū | cù | | | liǎn | liǎng |

***2. Ask questions using** “有没有”(yǒu méi yǒu):

Model: 同志，有没有饺子?
Tóngzhì, yǒu méi yǒu jiǎozi?

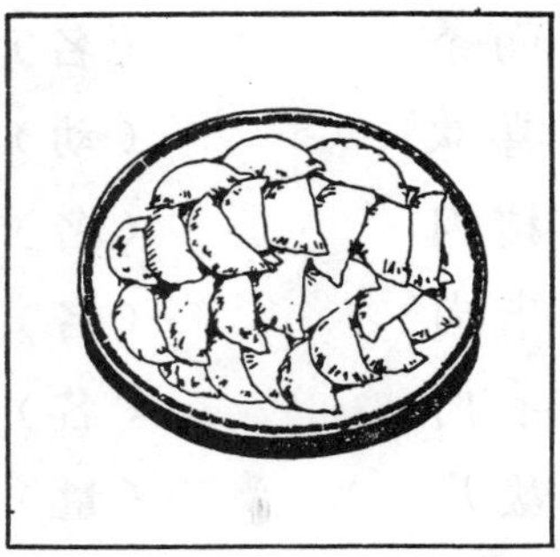

(1) 服务员同志，________?
Fúwùyuán tóngzhì, ________?

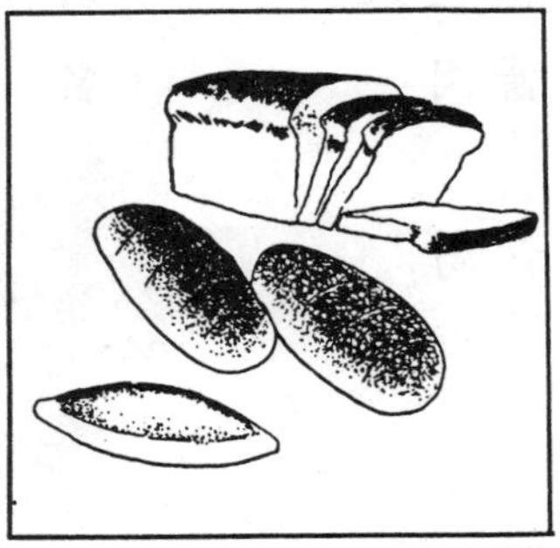

(2) 请问，________?
Qǐng wèn, ________?

(3) 今天晚上________?
Jīntiān wǎnshang________?

2) Ask questions using "……还是……" (…háishi…):

Model: 《大闹天宫》是京剧还是电影?(京剧，电影)
《Dà Nào Tiāngōng》 shì jīngjù háishi diànyǐng? (jīngjù, diànyǐng)

(1) 您要什么酒? ________? (啤酒，白酒)
Nín yào shénme jiǔ? ________? (píjiǔ, báijiǔ)

(2) 您 去_______？（北京 饭店，民族 饭店）
Nín qù_______? ( Běijīng Fàndiàn, Mínzú Fàndiàn )

(3) 你们 _______去 颐和园？（星期六，星期天）
Nǐmen_______qù Yíhéyuán? ( xīngqīliù, xīngqītiān )

(4) _______？（他，你）
_______? ( tā, nǐ )

***3. Complete the following dialogues:**

Model: 服务员：同志，您 吃 什么？
Fúwùyuán: Tóngzhì, nín chī shénme?
顾客：来 个 鱼。
Gùkè: Lái ge yú.
服：糖醋鱼 还是 红烧鱼？
Fú: Tángcùyú háishi hóngshāoyú?
顾：红烧鱼。
Gù: Hóngshāoyú.

1) 服：同志，您 要 什么？
Fú: Tóngzhì, nín yào shénme?
顾：_______。（拼盘）
Gù: _______. ( pīnpánr )
服：您 要 哪种？
Fú: Nín yào nǎzhǒng?
顾：_______。（大拼盘）
Gù: _______. ( dà pīnpánr )

2) 服：您 还 要 什么？
Fú: Nín hái yào shénme?
顾：______。（汤）
Gù: ______. ( tāng )
服：您 要 什么 汤，鸡蛋汤 还是 黄瓜汤？
Fú: Nín yào shénme tāng, jīdàntāng háishi huángguātāng?
顾：_______。（黄瓜汤）
Gù: _______. ( huángguātāng )

3) 服：您 吃 什么？
Fú: Nín chī shénme?
顾：_______。（面条儿，碗）
Gù: _______. ( miàntiáor, wǎn )
服：大碗 的 还是 小碗 的？
Fú: Dàwǎn de háishi xiǎowǎn de?

顾：______。（小碗）
Gù: ______.（xiǎowǎn）

4. **Listen to the dialogues:**

1) A: 咱们 吃 点儿 什么 呢？
Zánmen chī diǎnr shénme ne?
B: 你 喜欢 吃 肉 吧？
Nǐ xǐhuan chī ròu ba?
A: 是 啊，你 呢？
Shì a, nǐ ne?
B: 什么 都 行。
Shénme dōu xíng.
A: 猪肉 你 能 吃，牛 羊 肉 你 也 能 吃？
Zhūròu nǐ néng chī, niú yáng ròu nǐ yě néng chī?
B: 能 吃。
Néng chī.
A: 那，咱们 多 来点儿 肉菜，好 吗？
Nà, zánmen duō lái diǎnr ròucài, hǎo ma?
B: 好 啊。
Hǎo a.

2) 顾客：同志，有 啤酒 没 有？
Gùkè: Tóngzhì, yǒu píjiǔ méi yǒu?
服务员：有，要 青岛 的 还是 北京 的？
Fúwùyuán: Yǒu, yào Qīngdǎo de háishi Běijīng de?
顾：青岛 的。
Gù: Qīngdǎo de.
服：要 几瓶？
Fú: Yào jǐpíng?
顾：两瓶。
Gù: Liǎngpíng.
服：要 什么 菜？
Fú: Yào shénme cài?
顾：来 盘儿 炸花生米，再 来 盘儿 酱肉。
Gù: Lái pánr zháhuāshēngmǐ, zài lái pánr jiàngròu.
服：酱 猪肉 还是 酱 牛肉？
Fú: Jiàngzhūròu háishi jiàngniúròu?
顾：酱牛肉。
Gù: Jiàngniúròu.

# 15 Consulting A Doctor
# 看病 kàn bìng

(David is consulting a doctor in a hospital).

| | | |
|---|---|---|
| 医 生：<br>yīshēng: | 请　坐。你哪儿不舒服？①<br>Qǐng zuò. Nǐ nǎr bù shūfu? | Please sit down. What has gone wrong? |
| 伟：<br>Wěi: | 我 头 疼，发烧，不 想 吃饭。<br>Wǒ tóu téng, fā shāo, bù xiǎng chī fàn. | I've a headache and a fever. I've hardly any appetite. |

| | | |
|---|---|---|
| 医：<br>yī : | 量 一下儿体温吧。<br>Liáng yíxiàr tǐwēn ba. | Let's take your temperature. |
| 伟：<br>Wěi: | 多少度？<br>Duōshaodù? | What is it, doctor? |
| 医：<br>yī : | 三十八度九。② 请 张 开<br>sānshíbādù jiǔ. Qǐng zhāng kāi<br>嘴，我 看看。咳嗽 吗？<br>zuǐ, wǒ kànkan. Késou ma? | Thirty-eight point nine degrees. Please open your mouth. Do you cough? |
| 伟：<br>Wěi: | 有点儿。③<br>Yǒudiǎnr. | A little. |
| 医：<br>yī : | 我 听听。深 呼吸，再 深<br>Wǒ tīngting. Shēn hūxī, zài shēn<br>呼吸，④ 好 了。<br>hūxī, hǎo le. | Take a deep breath in and out. Again in and out. All right. |
| 伟：<br>Wěi: | 大夫，什么 病？<br>Dàifu, shénme bìng? | Doctor, what's wrong? |
| 医：<br>yī : | 感冒。⑤ 打 一针，吃<br>Gǎnmào. Dǎ yìzhēn, chī<br>点儿 药。<br>diǎnr yào. | You get a cold. I'll prescribe an injection and some medicine to take. |
| 伟：<br>Wěi: | 好。<br>Hǎo. | Good. |
| 医：<br>yī : | (Prescribing) 你 叫 什么<br>Nǐ jiào shénme<br>名字？<br>míngzi? | (Prescribing) What's your name? |
| 伟：<br>Wěi: | 陈 大伟。<br>Chén Dàwěi. | David Chen. |
| 医：<br>yī : | 这 是 药方。你 先 到<br>Zhè shì yàofāngr. Nǐ xiān dào<br>药房 取 药，再 到<br>yàofáng qǔ yào, zài dào<br>注射室 打 针。<br>zhùshèshì dǎ zhēn. | Here's the prescription. First of all, go to the dispensary to get your medicine and then get your injection in the Injection Room. |
| 伟：<br>Wěi: | 好。<br>Hǎo. | All right. |
| 医：<br>yī : | 回 去以后，请 按时 吃<br>Huí qu yǐhòu, qǐng ànshí chī | Take the medicine as prescribed. Drink plenty |

| | | |
|---|---|---|
| | 药，多喝开水，⑥ 注意<br>yào, duō hē kāishuǐ, zhùyì<br>休息。<br>xiūxi. | of boiled water and take a good rest. |
| 伟：<br>Wěi: | 谢谢，再见。<br>Xièxie, zàijiàn. | Thank you. Good-bye. |
| 医：<br>yī： | 再见。<br>Zàijiàn. | Good-bye. |

## • new words • 生词 • shēngcí

| | | | | |
|---|---|---|---|---|
| 1 | 看病 | | kàn bìng | to a doctor, doctor examining patient |
| 2 | 医生 | （名） | yīshēng | doctor |
| 3 | 舒服 | （形） | shūfu | well, comfortable |
| | 不舒服 | | bù shūfu | unwell, uncomfortable |
| 4 | 头 | （名） | tóu | head |
| 5 | 疼 | （动） | téng | to ache, to have pain |
| 6 | 发烧 | | fā shāo | to have a fever |
| 7 | 量 | （动） | liáng | to measure, to take measurement |
| 8 | 体温 | （名） | tǐwēn | body temperature |
| 9 | 度 | （量） | dù | degree |
| 10 | 张开 | | zhāng kāi | to open |
| 11 | 嘴 | （名） | zuǐ | mouth |
| 12 | 咳嗽 | （动） | késou | to cough |
| 13 | 有点儿 | | yǒudiǎnr | somewhat, a little bit |
| 14 | 深 | （形） | shēn | deep, profound |
| 15 | 呼吸 | （动） | hūxī | to breathe |
| 16 | 大夫 | （名） | dàifu | doctor |
| 17 | 病 | （动、名） | bìng | to be sick, illness, disease |

| | | | | |
|---|---|---|---|---|
| 18 | 感冒 | (动、名) | gǎnmào | to have a cold, cold, influenza |
| 19 | 打 | (动) | dǎ | to have (injection) |
| 20 | 针 | (名) | zhēn | syringe, needle |
| | 打针 | | dǎ zhēn | to have an injection |
| 21 | 药 | (名) | yào | medicine |
| 22 | 名字 | (名) | míngzi | name |
| 23 | 药方 | (名) | yàofāngr | prescription |
| 24 | 先 | (副) | xiān | firstly, beforehand |
| 25 | 药房 | (名) | yàofáng | dispensary, pharmacy, drug store |
| 26 | 取 | (动) | qǔ | to fetch, to get |
| 27 | 注射 | (动) | zhùshè | to inject |
| 28 | ……室 | (名) | ...shì | room, section |
| | 注射室 | | zhùshèshì | injection room |
| 29 | 回去 | | huí qu | to go back, to return |
| 30 | 按时 | (副) | ànshí | on time |
| 31 | 多 | (副、形) | duō | many, much |
| 32 | 开水 | (名) | kāishuǐ | boiled water |
| 33 | 注意 | (动) | zhùyì | to note, to be sure of, to heed |
| 34 | 休息 | (动) | xiūxi | to rest |

## study points • 注释 • zhùshì

1 你哪儿不舒服？ (Nǐ nǎr bù shūfu?)

The subject of the sentence is "你" and the predicate is "哪儿不舒服"。Within the predicate itself, "哪儿" tends to function as another subject for the rest of the predicate so that the second subject "哪儿" is related to the first subject "你"。 Such a sentence pattern is by no means uncommon in Chinese:

我头疼。(Wǒ tóu téng.)

I have a headache.

他工作很好。(Tā gōngzuò hěn hǎo.)

He works very well.

2 三十八度九 (sānshíbādù jiǔ)

The Centigrade scale is adopted in China for measuring both the air and body temperature.

3 有点儿 (yǒudiǎnr)

When "有点儿" functions as an adverb modifying adjectives or verbs, it means "to a slight degree". In most cases, it tends to suggest dissatisfaction:

这件大衣有点儿短。(Zhè jiàn dàyī yǒudiǎnr duǎn.)

This overcoat is a little bit too short.

他今天有点儿咳嗽。(Tā jīntiān yǒudiǎnr késou.)

Today he has a little cough.

4 深呼吸，再深呼吸。(Shēn hūxī, zài shēn hūxī.)

The main uses of "再" (zài) as an adverb are as follows:

1) to introduce an action which is to be repeated:

深呼吸，再深呼吸。 (Shēn hūxī, zài shēn hūxī.)

今天我给他打电话了，明天我再给他打电话。

(Jīntiān wǒ gěi tā dǎ diànhuà le, míngtiān wǒ zài gěi tā dǎ diànhuà.)

2) to introduce an action which is in addition to another:

要个辣子鸡，再要个豆腐。 (Yào ge làzijī, zài yào ge dòufu.)

3) to indicate that a future action will take place after the one that precedes it. The first action is sometimes introduced by the adverb "先" (xiān):

你先到药房取药，再到注射室打针。

(Nǐ xiān dào yàofáng qǔ yào, zài dào zhùshèshì dǎ zhēn.)

5 感冒 (gǎnmào)

"感冒" (gǎnmào) is a kind of cold with the standard symptoms of coughing, sneezing, headache and high temperature, etc.

6 多喝开水。(Duō hē kāishuǐ.)

Most Chinese are not used to drinking tap water, A Chinese doctor would ask his patient who has a cold to drink a lot of "开水"。

## supplementary words • 补充生词 • bǔchōng shēngcí

1 嗓子 (名) sǎngzi throat

| | | | |
|---|---|---|---|
| 2 | 牙 | （名）yá | tooth |
| 3 | 肚子 | （名）dùzi | stomach |
| 4 | 身体 | （名）shēntǐ | body |
| 5 | 脾气 | （名）píqì | temper |
| 6 | 血压 | （名）xuèyā | blood pressure |
| 7 | 高 | （形）gāo | high |
| 8 | 重 | （形）zhòng | heavy |
| 9 | 白血球 | （名）báixuèqiú | white blood cell |
| 10 | 开始 | （动）kāishǐ | to begin |
| 11 | 医院 | （名）yīyuàn | hospital |
| 12 | 中药 | （名）zhōngyào | Chinese medicine |
| 13 | 西药 | （名）xīyào | Western medicine |

## • exercises • 练习 • liànxí

**1. Phonetic exercises:**

1) Tone

(1) Neutral tone

shūfu　　míngzi　　hǎo le　　dàifu

(2) Four tones

huānyíng qǐng jìn.　　tā méi gǎnmào

sānshíjiǔdù　　xiān lái qǔ yào

2) Sound discrimination

(1)

| s | sh |
|---|---|
| sè | shè |
| sòu | shòu |
| sān | shān |
| sì | shì |

(2)

| i (1) | i (2) | i (3) |
|---|---|---|
| jì | zì | zhì |
| qī | cí | chī |
| xī | sī | shí |
| yì | | rì |

***2. Tell the doctor what is wrong with you:**

Model: 医　生：你哪儿不舒服？
Yīshēng: Nǐ nǎr bù shūfu？

病 人：我 嗓子 疼 。(嗓子)
Bìngrén: Wǒ sǎngzi téng. (sǎngzi)

1) 医 生：您 哪儿不舒服？
Yīshēng: Nín nǎr bù shūfu?
病 人：_______。( 头)
Bìngrén: _______. (tóu)

2) 医 生：您 怎么 不舒服？
Yīshēng: Nín zěnme bù shūfu?
病 人：_______。(牙)
Bìngrén: _______. (yá)

3) 医 生：你 怎么 了？
Yīshēng: Nǐ zěnme le?
病 人：_______。(肚子)
Bìngrén: _______. (dùzi)

***3. Complete the following sentences after the models:**

1) Model: 这个 人 工作 很 好。
Zhège rén gōngzuò hěn hǎo.

(1) _______身体_______。
_______shēntǐ_______.

(2) _______脾气_______。
_______píqì _______.

(3) _______ 中国话 _______。
_______Zhōngguóhuà _______.

2) Model: 你 血压 很 高。
Nǐ xuèyā hěn gāo.

(1) 你_______。(体温，高)
Nǐ _______. (tǐwēn, gāo)

(2) 他 _______。(嗓子，红)
Tā _______. (sǎngzi, hóng)

(3) 我 _______。(头，疼)
Wǒ _______. (tóu, téng)

(4) 他妈妈 _______。(病，重)
Tā māma _______. (bìng, zhòng)

(5) 他弟弟 _______。(白血球，高)
Tā dìdi _______. (báixuèqiú, gāo)

***4. Fill in the blanks with the right phrase or word:**

1) 有点儿，(一)点儿
yǒudiǎnr, (yì) diǎnr

(1) 我 今天 ______不舒服。
Wǒ jīntiān ______bù shūfu .

(2) 大伟，咱们 走 慢______！
Dàwěi, zánmen zǒu màn______!

(3) 他______咳嗽。
Tā______késòu.

(4) 咱们 喝______啤酒吧。
Zánmen hē______píjiǔ ba.

(5) 弟弟的 那件大衣______旧了。买 件 新 的吧。
Dìdi de nàjiàn dàyī ______jiù le, mǎi jiàn xīn de ba.

(6) 他 的 体温______高，休息 两天 吧。
Tā de tǐwēn ______gāo, xiūxi liǎngtiān ba.

2) 还，再
hái, zài

(1) 您 ______要 什 么？
Nín______yào shénme?

(2) 三 个 菜 不 够，______要 一个吧。
Sānge cài bú gòu, ______yào yíge ba.

(3) 我 ______ 想 买几个 信封。
Wǒ______xiǎng mǎi jǐge xìnfēng.

(4) 我 想 ______试试 这双 皮鞋。
Wǒ xiǎng ______shìshi zhèshuāng píxié .

(5) 你______给 我 一本 画报 吧。
Nǐ______gěi wǒ yìběn huàbào ba.

(6) 您 先 吃 点儿菜，______喝酒。
Nín xiān chī diǎnr cài, ______hē jiǔ.

(7) 我 ______有 一个问题。
Wǒ______yǒu yíge wèntí.

5 . **Listen to the dialogues:**

1) 医 生：你 怎么 了？
Yīshēng: Nǐ zěnme le?

病 人：我 头 疼，很 疼。
Bìngrén: Wǒ tóu téng, hěn téng.

医：什么 时候 开始的？
Yī: Shénme shíhour kāishǐ de?

病 ：前天。
Bìng: Qiántiān.

医： 还 有哪儿 不舒服？ 嗓子？
Yī: Hái yǒu nǎr bù shūfu? Sǎngzi?

病 ： 嗓子 不疼。
Bìng: Sǎngzi bù téng.

医： 发 烧 不？
Yī: Fā shāo bù?

病 ： 体温 不高 。
Bìng: Tǐwēn bù gāo.

医： 量量 血压吧。啊，你 血压 高 了。 吃 点儿 药，
Yī: Liángliang xuèyā ba. Ā, nǐ xuèyā gāo le. Chī diǎnr yào,
休息 两天 吧。
xiūxi liǎngtiān ba.

2) A: 你去哪儿了？
Nǐ qù nǎr le?

B: 去 医院 了。
Qù yīyuàn le.

A: 怎么，你 病 了？
Zěnme, nǐ bìng le?

B: 是 啊，感冒 。
Shì a, gǎnmào.

A: 发 烧 吧？
Fā shāo ba?

B: 有点儿发 烧 。
Yǒudiǎnr fā shāo.

A: 多少度 ？
Duōshǎodù?

B: 三十九度四。
Sānshíjiǔdù sì.

A: 啊？ 还 有点儿 发 烧 呢！不 是“有点儿” ，是
Á? Hái yǒudiǎnr fā shāo ne! Bú shì "yǒudiǎnr", shì
比较 高。你要 在 家休息 几天，要 按时吃 药，
bǐjiào gāo. Nǐ yào zài jiā xiūxi jǐtiān, yào ànshí chī yào,
多 喝 开水。
duō hē kāishuǐ.

B: 医生 这么 说，你也 这么 说，都 这么 说。
Yīshēng zhème shuō, nǐ yě zhème shuō, dōu zhème shuō.

A: 不 对 吗？
Bú duì ma?

B: 对，对。
Duì, duì.
A: 医生 给你什么 药？ 中药 还是 西药？
Yīshēng gěi nǐ shénme yào? Zhōngyào háishi Xīyào?
B: 中药 、西药 都 有。
Zhōngyào、Xīyào dōu yǒu.
A: 你 能 吃 中药？
Nǐ néng chī Zhōngyào?
B: 病 了，什么 药 都 能 吃 了。
Bìng le, shénme yào dōu néng chī le.
A: 是 啊，没 有 病，什么 药 也不用 吃。
Shì a, Méi yǒu bìng, shénme yào yě bú yòng chī.

# 复习 (3) Revision (3) fùxí (3)

**1. Turn the following statements into questions:**

Model: 那件 衣服很 新。—— 那件 衣服新吗?
Nàjiàn yīfu hěn xīn. Nàjiàn yīfu xīn ma?
那件 衣服新 不 新?
Nàjiàn yīfu xīn bu xīn?
那件 衣服 怎么样?
Nàjiàn yīfu zěnmeyàng?

1) 这个 本 子 很 好。
Zhège běnzi hěn hǎo.

2) 这种 咖啡 比较 贵。
Zhèzhǒng kāfēi bǐjiào guì.

3) 王 先生 的大衣太 长 。
Wáng xiānsheng de dàyī tài cháng.

4) 他们 的 房间 很大。
Tāmen de fángjiān hěn dà.

5) 她 的 病 不 重 。
Tā de bìng bú zhòng.

***2. Make sentences:**

Model: 这支 钢笔 很 新。
Zhèzhī gāngbǐ hěn xīn.
这支 钢笔 是 新的。( 这, 钢笔, 新)
Zhèzhī gāngbǐ shì xīn de. ( zhè, gāngbǐ, xīn)

1) 那, 面 包, 大
nà, miànbāo, dà

2) 小 王 , 裤子, 长
Xiǎo Wáng, kùzi, cháng

3) 这种 , 蛋 糕, 贵
zhèzhǒng, dàngāo, guì

4) 那，桌子，高
nà, zhuōzi, gāo

5) 她，衣服，红
tā, yīfu, hóng

*3. **Correct the following sentences:**

1) 你 能 给不 给 我 一个 信封？
Nǐ néng gěi bu gěi wǒ yíge xìnfēng?

2) 他 想 吃不 吃 糖醋鱼？
Tā xiǎng chī bu chī tángcùyú?

3) 你 会 抽 不 抽 烟？
Nǐ huì chōu bu chōu yān?

4) 他们 有事儿不可以来了。
Tāmen yǒu shìr bù kěyǐ lái le.

5) 一个 小时 以后，他会 不 会 去 文化宫 吗？
Yíge xiǎoshí yǐhòu, tā huì bu huì qù wénhuàgōng ma?

6) 请 问，半个 小时 能 不 能 到 学校 吗？
Qǐng wèn, bànge xiǎoshí néng bu néng dào xuéxiào ma?

# 16 The Weather In Beijing
# 北京的天气 Běijīng de tiānqì

(The Chens and Ding Shuqin, Li Wenhan's wife, are on their way to the Park of the Fragrant Hills.)

| | | |
|---|---|---|
| 伟：<br>Wěi: | 姐姐，你看，太阳 出来<br>Jiějie, nǐ kàn, tàiyang chū lai<br>了。①<br>le. | Look, Sister, the sun has come out. |
| 莉：<br>Lì: | 昨天 晚上 天气 预报<br>Zuótiān wǎnshang tiānqì yùbào | The weather forecast last night said it would |

| | | |
|---|---|---|
| | 说，阴转　晴 嘛。②<br>shuō, yīn zhuǎn qíng ma. | clear up today. |
| 艾：<br>Ài: | 老 丁，北京 秋天 的<br>Lǎo Dīng, Běijīng qiūtiān de<br>天气真 好，不 冷 也<br>tiānqì zhēn hǎo, bù lěng yě<br>不热。<br>bú rè. | Lao Ding, Beijing's autumn is really nice. It's neither too cold nor too hot. |
| 丁 淑琴：<br>Dīng Shūqín: | 秋天 是 北京 一年里最<br>Qiūtiān shì Běijīng yìniánli zuì<br>好 的季节，你们 秋天 来<br>hǎo de jìjié, nǐmen qiūtiān lái<br>北 京 很合适。<br>Běijīng hěn héshì. | Autumn is the best season of the year. You've chosen the best time to come to Beijing. |
| 莉：<br>Lì: | 听 爸爸 说，③ 北京<br>Tīng bàba shuō, Běijīng<br>夏天 比较热。<br>xiàtiān bǐjiào rè. | Dad said that Beijing's summer is rather hot. |
| 丁：<br>Dīng: | 对。七、八月 还 常常<br>Duì. Qī、bāyuè hái chángchang<br>下雨。<br>xià yǔ. | Yes, and it rains quite often in July and August. |
| 伟：<br>Wěi: | 伯母，听 说 北京 冬天<br>Bómǔ, tīng shuō Běijīng dōngtiān<br>很 冷， 是 吗？④<br>hěn lěng, shì ma? | I've heard that Beijing's winter is very cold. Is that true? |
| 丁：<br>Dīng: | 是，气温 有时候 在 零<br>Shì, qìwēn yǒushíhour zài líng<br>下 十几度。<br>xià shíjǐdù. | Yes, sometimes it's over ten degrees below zero. |
| 莉：<br>Lì: | 北京 冬天 常常 下<br>Běijīng dōngtiān chángcháng xià<br>雪 吗？<br>xuě ma? | Does it often snow in winter in Beijing? |
| 丁：<br>Dīng: | 常常 下，有时候<br>Chángcháng xià, yǒushíhour<br>雪 很 大。<br>xuě hěn dà. | Yes, sometimes it's very heavy too. |

| | | |
|---|---|---|
| 艾：<br>Ai: | 北京 的 春天 怎么样？<br>Běijīng de chūntiān zěnmeyàng? | How's spring in Beijing? |
| 丁：<br>Dīng: | 春天 比较 暖和，但 常常 刮 风。<br>Chūntiān bǐjiào nuǎnhuo, dàn chángcháng guā fēng. | Spring is warmer, but often windy. |
| 莉：<br>Lì: | 现在 秋天 了，香山 一定 很 美。<br>Xiànzài qiūtiān le, Xiāngshān yídìng hěn měi. | Now that it's autumn, the Fragrant Hills must be very beautiful. |
| 丁：<br>Dīng: | 香山 的 树叶儿 都 红 了，⑤ 每天 游览的 人 也 多 了。⑥<br>Xiāngshān de shù yèr dōu hóng le, měitiān yóulǎnde rén yě duō le. | The leaves of the Fragrant Hills have turned red, the number of visitors going there is also getting bigger every day. |

## • new words • 生词 • shēngcí

| | | | | |
|---|---|---|---|---|
| 1 | 天气 | （名） | tiānqì | weather |
| 2 | 太阳 | （名） | tàiyang | sun |
| 3 | 出来 | | chū lai | to come out |
| 4 | 晴 | （形） | qíng | fine (weather) |
| 5 | 预报 | （名、动） | yùbào | forecast |
| 6 | 阴 | （形） | yīn | cloudy, overcast |
| 7 | 转 | （动） | zhuǎn | to turn, to change |
| 8 | 嘛 | （助） | ma | an interjection to give emphasis |
| 9 | 秋天 | （名） | qiūtiān | autumn, fall |
| 10 | 真 | （形） | zhēn | true, real |
| 11 | 冷 | （形） | lěng | cold, chilly |
| 12 | 热 | （形） | rè | hot |

| | | | | |
|---|---|---|---|---|
| 13 | 年 | （名） | nián | year |
| 14 | ……里 | （名） | ...li | (used after nouns meaning "within a certain limit of time or space") |
| 15 | 最 | （副） | zuì | most |
| 16 | 季节 | （名） | jìjié | season |
| 17 | 夏天 | （名） | xiàtiān | summer |
| 18 | 常常 | （副） | chángcháng | often, frequently |
| 19 | 下（雨、雪） | （动） | xià (yǔ、xuě) | to fall (rain, snow) |
| 20 | 雨 | （名） | yǔ | rain |
| 21 | 伯母 | （名） | bómǔ | aunt |
| 22 | 冬天 | （名） | dōngtiān | winter |
| 23 | 气温 | （名） | qìwēn | temperature (weather) |
| 24 | 有时候 | | yǒushíhour | sometimes, occasionally |
| 25 | 零下 | | líng xià | below zero |
| | 零下十几度 | | líng xià shíjǐdù | over ten degrees below zero |
| 26 | 雪 | （名） | xuě | snow |
| 27 | 春天 | （名） | chūntiān | spring |
| 28 | 暖和 | （形） | nuǎnhuo | warm |
| 29 | 但 | （连） | dàn | but, however |
| 30 | 刮（风） | （动） | guā (fēng) | to blow (wind) |
| 31 | 风 | （名） | fēng | wind |
| 32 | 一定 | （副、形） | yídìng | surely, definitely, sure, definite |
| 33 | 美 | （形） | měi | pretty, beautiful |
| 34 | 树 | （名） | shù | tree |
| 35 | 叶儿 | （名） | yèr | leaf |
| | 树叶儿 | | shù yèr | tree leaves |
| 36 | 红 | （形） | hóng | red |
| 37 | 每 | （代） | měi | every, each |
| | 每天 | | měitiān | every day |
| 38 | 游览 | （动） | yóulǎn | to tour, to go sightseeing |

| 专名 | Zhuānmíng | Proper names |
|---|---|---|
| 北京 | Běijīng | Beijing (Peking) |
| 丁淑琴 | Dīng Shūqín | name of Lǐ Wénhàn's wife, a friend of the Chen family |
| 香山 | Xiāngshān | Fragrant Hills (a scenic spot in Beijing, known for its crimson maple leaves in autumn) |

## study points • 注释 • zhùshì

1 太阳出来了。 (Tàiyang chū lai le.)

The particle "了" (le) can be used in many ways. Here it is used to show that a change or a new situation has taken place:

天晴了。 (Tiān qíng le.)

It has cleared up.

现在是秋天了。(Xiànzài shì qiūtiān le.)

Autumn is here now.

我的表停了。 (Wǒ de biǎo tíng le.)

My watch has stopped.

2 阴转晴嘛。 (Yīn zhuǎn qíng ma.)

"嘛" (ma) in this context means that what has been said is evident.

3 听爸爸说 (Tīng bàba shuō.)

The person or persons responsible for giving the information to his or their listeners can be placed in between the two characters of the phrase "听说" (tīng shuō):

听老陈说。(Tīng Lǎo Chén shuō)

Hear Lao Chen say.

听一个同志说。(Tīng yíge tóngzhì shuō)

Hear someone say.

4 北京冬天很冷，是吗？ (Běijīng dōngtiān hěn lěng, shì ma?)

This sentence pattern corresponds to the disjunctive question in English.

5 香山的树叶儿都红了。 (Xiāngshān de shù yèr dōu hóng le.)

"都" (dōu) meaning "already" is unstressed.

6 每天游览的人也多了。 (Měitiān yóulǎn de rén yě duō le.)

1) In Chinese, verbs can be used as attributives, but the particle "的" must be added in between the verb and the noun it modifies:

参观的人 (cānguān de rén)
the people who are visiting
他写的信 (tā xiě de xìn)
the letter he wrote
昨天买的礼物 (zuótiān mǎi de lǐwù)
the gift bought yesterday

2) "也" (yě) may be used in two parallel clauses or only the second clause to show a similarity between the two clauses.

## supplementary words • 补充生词 • bǔchōng shēngcí

| | | | | |
|---|---|---|---|---|
| 1 | 雾 | (名) | wù | fog |
| 2 | 国家 | (名) | guójiā | country, nation |
| 3 | 首都 | (名) | shǒudū | capital |
| 4 | 家乡 | (名) | jiāxiāng | native place |
| 5 | 变 | (动) | biàn | to change |
| 6 | 可不是 | | kěbushì | exactly, indeed |
| 7 | 掉 | (动) | diào | to fall |
| 8 | 气象台 | (名) | qìxiàngtái | weather station |
| 9 | 白天 | (名) | báitiān | day (time) |
| 10 | 云 | (名) | yún | cloud |
| 11 | 阵雨 | (名) | zhènyǔ | shower |
| | 广州 | | Guǎngzhōu | Guangzhou (Canton), capital of Guangdong Province, in south China |

## • exercises • 练习 • liànxí

1. **Ask questions after the model:**

1) Model: 北京秋天的天气怎么样？（北京，秋天）
Běijīng qiūtiān de tiānqì zěnmeyàng? （Běijīng, qiūtiān）

(1) 北京，夏天
Běijīng, xiàtiān

(2) 西安，冬天
Xī'ān, dōngtiān

(3) 广州，春天
Guǎngzhōu, chūntiān

2) Model: 北京冬天常常下雪吗？（冬天，下雪）
Běijīng dōngtiān chángcháng xià xuě ma? （dōngtiān, xià xuě）

(1) 秋天，刮风
qiūtiān, guā fēng

(2) 七、八月，下雨
qī、bāyuè, xià yǔ

(3) 春天，下雾
chūntiān, xià wù

3) Model: 听说，北京冬天很冷，是吗？
Tīng shuō, Běijīng dōngtiān hěn lěng, shì ma?
（冬天，很冷）
（dōngtiān, hěn lěng）

(1) 夏天，比较热
xiàtiān, bǐjiào rè

(2) 秋天，一年里，最好，季节
qiūtiān, yìniánli, zuì hǎo, jìjié

(3) 春天，风，很大
chūntiān, fēng, hěn dà

2. **Answer the following questions in your own words:**

1) 春、夏、秋、冬四个季节的天气怎么样？
Chūn、xià、qiū、dōng sìge jìjié de tiānqì zěnmeyàng?

2) 哪个季节最好？
Nǎge jìjié zuì hǎo?

3) 你 喜欢哪个季节？
Nǐ xǐhuan nǎge jìjié？

3．**Listen to the dialogues:**

弟弟：姐姐，姐姐，不 好 了！
Dìdi：Jiějie，jiějie，bù hǎo le！

姐姐：怎么 了？
Jiějie：Zěnme le？

弟 ： 咱们 不 能 去 颐和园了。
Dì ： Zánmen bù néng qù Yíhéyuán le.

姐： 怎么 不 能 去？
Jiě： Zěnme bù néng qù?

弟： 变 天了。
Dì： Biàn tiān le.

姐： 是吗？ 下雨了吗？
Jiě： Shì ma? Xià yǔ le ma?

弟： 还 没 下。
Dì： Hái méi xià.

姐： 我 看看。可不是 阴天 了。———哎呀！
Jiě： Wǒ kànkan. Kěbushì yīntiān le. ——— Àiya！

开始 掉雨点儿了。
Kāishǐ diào yǔdiǎnr le.

弟： 真 糟糕！ 下大了。
Dì： Zhēn zāogāo! Xià dà le.

姐：大概一会儿 能 停。你 看，那边儿 还 是 晴天 呢。
Jiě： Dàgài yíhuìr néng tíng. Nǐ kàn, nàbianr hái shì qíngtiān ne.

弟： 打 电话 听听 天气 预报 吧。
Dì： Dǎ diànhuà tīngting tiānqì yùbào ba.

姐： 气象台 也不 会 说 咱们 这儿下 不 下 雨。
Jiě： Qìxiàngtái yě bú huì shuō zánmen zhèr xià bu xià yǔ.

听 我 的，一会儿雨 一定 会 停。
Tīng wǒ de, yíhuìr yǔ yídìng huì tíng.

弟： 听 你的？不，我 打 电话 听听 天气 预报。
Dì： Tīng nǐ de? Bù, wǒ dǎ diànhuà tīngting tiānqì yùbào.

天气 预报： 今天 白天，晴 转 多云，有 小 阵雨。
Tiānqì yùbào： Jīntiān báitiān, qíng zhuǎn duō yún, yǒu xiǎo zhènyǔ.

弟：小 阵雨，一会儿雨 能 停。
Dì: Xiǎo zhènyǔ, yíhuìr yǔ néng tíng.

姐：怎么样？我 的 预报 没 错儿。
Jiě: Zěnmeyàng? Wǒ de yùbào méi cuòr.

***4. Translate the following sentences into Chinese using "了":**

1) The sun has come out.
2) Spring's here.
3) Where has he gone?
4) My watch has stopped.
5) I've put on my coat.

# 17 Asking People's Age
## 问年龄 wèn niánlíng

(Mr. Chen Mingshan and his wife are chatting with an elderly man in the Park of the Fragrant Hills.)

| | | |
|---|---|---|
| 陈 ：<br>Chén: | 老 先生，① 您 好啊！<br>Lǎoxiānsheng, nín hǎo a ! | Hello, sir. |
| 老人：<br>lǎorén: | 你们 好！<br>Nǐmen hǎo! | Hello. |
| 艾：<br>Ài: | 老 先生，您 身体<br>Lǎoxiānsheng, nín shēntǐ | Sir, you do look very fit if I may say so. |

| | | |
|---|---|---|
| | 不错 啊！<br>búcuò a！ | |
| 老：<br>lǎo: | 不行 啊，② 老 了。③<br>Bùxíng a， lǎo le. | Not really. I'm old. |
| 陈：<br>Chén: | 您 多大年纪了？④<br>Nín duō dà niánjì le？ | May I ask how old are you? |
| 老：<br>lǎo: | 七十了。<br>Qīshí le. | Seventy. |
| 陈：<br>Chén: | 不 象，象 六十 来 岁的。⑤<br>Bú xiàng, xiàng liùshí lái suì de. | You certainly don't look it. You look a bit over sixty. |
| 老：<br>lǎo: | 哪里。⑥<br>Nǎlǐ. | Not at all. |
| 陈：<br>Chén: | 您 北京人吧？<br>Nín Běijīngrén ba? | You're from Beijing? |
| 老：<br>lǎo: | 是 啊。您 是 华侨 吧？<br>Shì a. Nín shì huáqiáo ba? | Yes. You are an overseas Chinese, aren't you? |
| 陈：<br>Chén: | 对，四一年到 美国 去 的。⑦ 我太太是 美国人。<br>Duì, sìyīnián dào Měiguó qu de. Wǒ tàitai shì Měiguórén. | Yes, I went to the United States in 1941. My wife is an American. |
| 老：<br>lǎo: | 您 的 普通话 很 好。⑧ 老家 在哪儿？<br>Nín de pǔtōnghuà hěn hǎo. Lǎojiā zài nǎr? | You speak very good Putonghua. Where are you from? |
| 陈：<br>Chén: | 也 是 北京。<br>Yě shì Běijīng. | I'm from Beijing too. |
| 老：<br>lǎo: | 怪 不得。<br>Guài bu de. | No wonder! |
| 艾：<br>Ài: | 这 是您 的 小 孙子吧？<br>Zhè shì nín de xiǎo sūnzi ba? | This must be your grandson. |
| 老：<br>lǎo: | 对。小江，叫 爷爷，奶奶。<br>Duì. Xiǎojiāng, jiào yéye, nǎinai. | That's right. Xiaojiang, say hello to grandpa and grandma. |
| 江：<br>Jiāng: | 爷爷，奶奶。<br>Yéye, nǎinai. | Grandpa, Grandma. |

| | | |
|---|---|---|
| 艾: Ài: | 小朋友，你几岁了？ Xiǎopéngyou, nǐ jǐsuì le? | How old are you, little friend? |
| 江： Jiāng: | 九岁了。 Jiǔsuì le. | Nine. |
| 艾: Ài: | 上几年级了？ Shàng jǐ niánjí le? | Which grade are you in? |
| 江： Jiāng: | 小学三年级了。 Xiǎoxué sān niánjí le. | Grade 3 in elementary school. |
| 陈： Chén: | 老先生，常常来公园吧？ Lǎoxiānsheng, chángcháng lái gōngyuánr ba? | Sir, do you come to the park of Fragrant Hills often? |
| 老: lǎo: | 是啊，星期天孩子不上学，带他来玩儿玩儿。 Shì a, Xīngqītiān háizi bú shàng xué, dài tā lai wánrwanr. | Yes, this child does not go to school on Sundays, so I bring him here to play. |

## • new words • 生词 • shēngcí

| | | | | |
|---|---|---|---|---|
| 1 | 年龄 | （名） | niánlíng | age |
| 2 | 老先生 | （名） | lǎoxiānsheng | elderly gentleman |
| 3 | 老人 | （名） | lǎorén | old man (woman), old people |
| 4 | 身体 | （名） | shēntǐ | physical health, body |
| 5 | 不行 | （形） | bùxíng | not so good, not so well |
| 6 | 年纪 | （名） | niánjì | age |
| 7 | 象 | （动） | xiàng | to look like, to resemble |
| 8 | 来 | （助） | lái | approximately |
| 9 | 岁 | （名） | suì | year (of age) |
| 10 | 哪里 | （代） | nǎlǐ | not at all, where |
| 11 | 普通话 | （名） | pǔtōnghuà | common speech (standard modern spoken Chinese) |

| | | | |
|---|---|---|---|
| 12 老家 | （名） | lǎojiā | home town, birthplace |
| 13 怪不得 | | guài bu de | no wonder |
| 14 孙子 | （名） | sūnzi | grandson |
| 15 爷爷 | （名） | yéye | grandpa |
| 16 奶奶 | （名） | nǎinai | grandma |
| 17 小朋友 | （名） | xiǎopéngyou | little friend (children), (a polite way to address a child or children one does not know) |
| 18 上 | （动） | shàng | to be in (with grade or year in school and university) |
| 19 年级 | （名） | niánjí | grade, year |
| 20 小学 | （名） | xiǎoxué | elementary school |
| 21 公园 | （名） | gōngyuán | park |
| 22 孩子 | （名） | háizi | child, children, son (s) and daughter(s) |
| 23 上学 | | shàng xué | to go to school |
| 24 带 | （动） | dài | to take, to bring |
| 25 玩儿 | （动） | wánr | to play, to enjoy oneself |

| 专名 | Zhuānmíng | Proper name |
|---|---|---|
| 小江 | Xiǎojiāng | Xiaojiang, name of the grandson of the old man |

## study points • 注释 • zhùshì

1 老先生（lǎoxiānsheng）
This is a polite form used by urban people to address elderly men on meeting them for the first time.

2 不行啊（bùxíng a）

“不行”is a polite response to a compliment while “啊”gives emphasis to the sentence.

3 老了 (lǎo le)

Another use of “了”(le) is to indicate a certain degree that something or somebody has reached:

七十了。 (Qīshí le.)

Seventy already.

九岁了。 (Jiǔsuì le.)

Nine already.

他上小学三年级了。 (Tā shàng xiǎoxué sān niánjí le.)

He is already in Grade 3.

4 您多大年纪了? (Nín duō dà niánjì le?)

It is very common for the Chinese to ask each other's age in conversation. There are, however, different ways to ask the age of people of different ages:

您多大年纪了? (Nín duō dà niánjì le?)

How old are you?

(used to ask the age of an elderly person)

他多大? (Tā duō dà?)

How old is he?

(used to ask the age of a child or a person about the same age as the speaker)

她几岁了? (Tā jǐsuì le?)

How old is she?

(used to ask a child's age)

In spoken Chinese, the verb “是”(shì) is often omitted in sentences indicating a person's age or birthplace:

陈先生五十八岁。 (Chén xiānsheng wǔshíbāsuì.)

Mr. Chen is 58 years old.

他太太北京人。 (Tā tàitai Běijīngrén.)

His wife is from Beijing.

Questions can be formed by adding “吗”(ma) to these statements:

陈先生五十八岁吗? (Chén xiānsheng wǔshíbāsuì ma?)

Is Mr. Chen 58 years old?

他太太北京人吗? (Tā tàitai Běijīngrén ma?)

Is his wife from Beijing?

5 象六十来岁的。 (Xiàng liùshí lái suì de.)

“来”(lái) is often placed between numerals like “十”(shí), “百”(bǎi),“千”(qiān), etc. and measure words to turn them into approximate numbers.

6 哪里 (nǎli)

Literally meaning "where", this is another polite response to a compliment.

7 四一年到美国去的。 (sìyīnián dào Měiguó qu de.)

1) In spoken Chinese, the first two figures of a certain year are often left out when the year mentioned belongs to the present century. So, "四一年" means 1941.

2) The particle "的" (de) is used here to give emphasis to "四一年".

8 您的普通话很好。 (Nín de pǔtōnghuà hěn hǎo.)

普通话 (pǔtōnghuà) refers to standard modern spoken Chinese.

## supplementary words • 补充生词 • bǔchōng shēngcí

| | | | | |
|---|---|---|---|---|
| 1 | 今年 | (名) | jīnnián | this year |
| 2 | 口音 | (名) | kǒuyīn | accent |
| 3 | 英语 | (名) | Yīngyǔ | English |
| 4 | 句 | (名、量) | jù | sentence, a measure word |
| 5 | 记性 | (名) | jìxing | memory |
| 6 | 阿姨 | (名) | āyí | auntie |
| 7 | 老大爷 | (名) | lǎodàye | grandpa (a polite way to address elderly men) |
| 8 | 空气 | (名) | kōngqì | air |
| 9 | 乖 | (形) | guāi | well-behaved |
| 10 | 孙女 | (名) | sūnnür | grand daughter |
| 11 | 聪明 | (形) | cōngming | intelligent, clever |
| | 李小兰 | | Lǐ Xiǎolán | name of a girl |

## • exercises • 练习 • liànxí

*1. **Fill in the blanks with these phrases:**

多大年纪，多大，几岁
duō dà niánjì, duō dà, jǐsuì

1) 小江 今年______？
Xiǎojiāng jīnnián______？

2) 小江 的爷爷______？
Xiǎojiāng de yéye______？

3) 大伟 今年______？
Dàwěi jīnnián______？

*2. **Ask questions using "几……了" (jǐ…le) and then answer them:**

小王，今天几号了？
Xiǎo Wáng, jīntiān jǐhào le？
三号了。（三号）
Sānhào le. (sānhào)

1) 艾琳，今天______？
Àilín, jīntiān______？
______。（十七号）
______. (shíqīhào)

2) 姐姐，现在______？
Jiějie, xiànzài______？
______。（十一点半）
______. (shíyīdiǎnbàn)

3) 莉莉，你今年______？
Lìli, nǐ jīnnián______？
______。（四年级）
______. (sì niánjí)

*3. **Practice after the model:**

Model: A: 老先生，您的身体真不错啊！（身体）
Lǎoxiānsheng, nín de shēntǐ zhēn búcuò a！(shēntǐ)
B: 不行啊，老了！
Bù xíng a, lǎo le！

1) A: 赵先生，______！（普通话）
Zhào xiānsheng, ______！(pǔtōnghuà)

B: ________, 口音 很 重 啊。
________, kǒuyīn hěn zhòng a.

2) A: 老 王，________！（英语）
Lǎo Wáng, ________！（Yīngyǔ）
B: ________，就会 说 几句。
________, jiù huì shuō jǐjù.

3) A: 刘 太太，________！（记性）
Liú tàitai, ________！（jìxing）
B: ________，年纪 大了。
________, niánjì dà le.

4. **Answer the following questions using the names of the places shown on the map:**

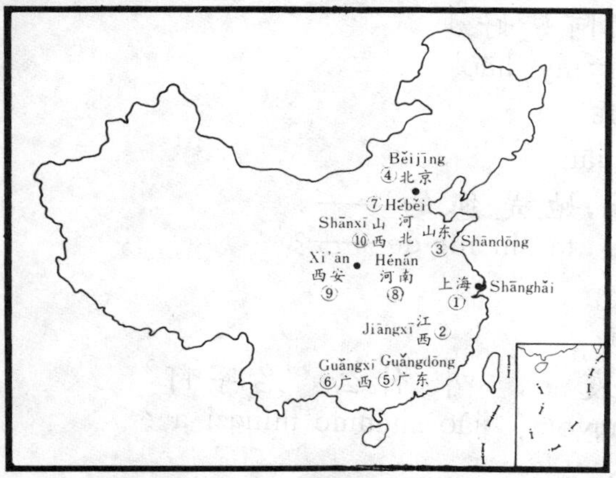


1) 李 先生 哪儿 人？
Lǐ xiānsheng nǎr rén?

2) 张 大中 同志 哪儿人？
Zhāng Dàzhōng tóngzhì nǎr rén?

3) 陈 小姐 哪儿人？
Chén xiǎojie nǎr rén?

4) 那位 太太 哪儿人？
Nàwèi tàitai nǎr rén?

5) 她 先生 哪儿人？
Tā xiānsheng nǎr rén?

6) 赵 阿姨 哪儿人？
Zhào āyí nǎr rén?

7) 老 王 老家 在 哪儿？
Lǎo Wáng lǎojiā zài nǎr?

8) 那位 老 爷爷 老家 在 哪儿？
Nàwèi lǎo yéye lǎojiā zài nǎr?

5. **Listen to the dialogue:**

外国 朋友 男、女：老大爷，早啊！
wàiguó péngyou nán、nǚ: Lǎodàye, zǎo a !

老：你们 早！ 哪国 朋友 啊？
Lǎo: Nǐmen zǎo! Nǎguó péngyou a ?

男、女：英 国。
Nán、nǚ: Yīngguó.

老：欢迎，欢迎！早晨 出来 散散 步啊？
Lǎo: Huānyíng, huānyíng! Zǎochén chūlai sànsan bù a ?

女：是啊，早晨 空气 好。喂，小朋友，来啊！
Nǚ: Shì a , zǎochén kōngqì hǎo. Wèi, xiǎopéngyou , lái a !

小：叔叔、阿姨好！
Xiǎo: Shūshu、āyí hǎo!

男：真 乖。
Nán: Zhēn guāi.

女：老大爷，她 是 您 的——？
Nǚ: Lǎodàye, tā shì nín de——?

老：孙女。
Lǎo: Sūnnǚr.

女：小朋友，叫 什么 名字啊？
Nǚ: Xiǎopéngyou , jiào shénme míngzi a ?

小：李 小兰。
Xiǎo: Lǐ Xiǎolán.

女：多 大 年纪了？
Nǚ: Duō dà niánjì le ?

老：谁？ 问 我吗？
Lǎo: Shéi? Wèn wǒ ma?

女：不，问 小兰。哦，对了，问 小朋友 要 说
Nǚ: Bù, wèn Xiǎolán. Ò , duì le, wèn xiǎopéngyou yào shuō

"几岁"。小 兰，几岁了？
"jǐsuì". Xiǎolán, jǐsuì le ?

小：六岁半。
Xiǎo: Liùsuìbàn.

男：上 学了吗？
Nán: Shàng xué le ma?

小：上 小学 了。
Xiǎo: Shàng xiǎoxué le.

男：会写　多少个　字了？
Nán: Huì xiě duōshaoge zì le?
小：一百　多　了。
Xiǎo: Yìbǎi duō le.
男：真　聪　明。
Nán: Zhēn cōngming.

***6.** **Translate the following questions into Chinese without using "是" (shì):**

1) What's the time now?
2) What's the date today?
3) What day is it?
4) How old is David?
5) Which grade are you in?
6) How old is Xiao Jiang?
7) How old are your grandparents?
8) Where are you from?

# 18 We Visited The Palace Museum Last Week
# 上 星期 我们 参观 故宫了
# shàng xīngqī wǒmen cānguān Gùgōng le

(The Chens and Ding Shuqin are on their way back after a trip to the Fragrant Hills.)

| | | |
|---|---|---|
| 艾:<br>Ài: | 香山 的 风景 太 美 了!<br>Xiāngshān de fēngjǐng tài měi le! | The scenery of the Fragrant Hills is so beautiful. |
| 丁 :<br>Dīng: | 你们 来得 正 是 时<br>Nǐmen lái de zhèng shì shí | You came at the right time. Mrs. Chen, are you |

| | | |
|---|---|---|
| | 候 。① 陈 太太，累了吧？<br>hour. Chén tàitai, lèi le ba? | tired? |
| 艾：<br>Ài: | 还 好。②<br>Hái hǎo. | I'm all right. |
| 丁 ：<br>Dīng: | 你们 参观 故宫 了吗？③<br>Nǐmen cānguān Gùgōng le ma? | Have you visited the Forbidden City yet? |
| 艾：<br>Ài: | 上 星期 参观 了。<br>Shàng xīngqī cānguān le. | Yes, we went there last week. |
| 丁 ：<br>Dīng: | 几个大 公园 都 去了吗？<br>Jǐge dà gōngyuánr dōu qù le ma? | Have you been to all the major parks in Beijing? |
| 陈 ：<br>Chén: | 北 海，天坛，颐和园 都 去了。<br>Běihǎi, Tiāntán, Yíhéyuán dōu qù le. | We've been to the Beihai Park, the Temple of Heaven and the Summer Palace. |
| 丁 ：<br>Dīng: | 中山 公园 呢？<br>Zhōngshān Gōngyuán ne? | And the Zhongshan Park? |
| 陈 ：<br>Chén: | 没 去，这次时间 不够，不 去了。<br>Méi qù, zhècì shíjiān bú gòu, bú qù le. | No, there wouldn't be time for it this time. |
| 丁 ：<br>Dīng: | 长城 去了没有？<br>Chángchéng qù le méiyǒu? | Have you been to the Great Wall? |
| 陈 ：<br>Chén: | 还 没有呢。<br>Hái méiyǒu ne. | Not yet. |
| 丁 ：<br>Dīng: | 什么 时候 去？<br>Shénme shíhour qù? | When are you going? |
| 陈 ：<br>Chén: | 后天 或者 大后天吧。<br>Hòutiān huòzhě dàhòutiān ba.<br>明天 想 带他们 到<br>Míngtiān xiǎng dài tāmen dào<br>燕山 中学 看看。<br>Yānshān Zhōngxué kànkan.<br>从 三二年 到 三八年<br>Cóng sān'èrnián dào sānbānián<br>我 一直在那儿念 书。不<br>wǒ yìzhí zài nàr niàn shū. Bú<br>过，那时不叫 燕山<br>guò, nà shí bú jiào Yānshān | Probably the day after tomorrow or the day after. I want to take Lily and David to Yanshan High School for a visit tomorrow. I was there from thirty-six to thirty-eight, though it wasn't called Yanshan High School at the time. |

| | | |
|---|---|---|
| | 中学。<br>Zhōngxué. | |
| 丁：<br>Dīng: | 几十年了，旧地重游，<br>Jǐshínián le, jiù dì chóng yóu,<br>一定会很有意思。好<br>yídìng huì hěn yǒu yìsi. Hǎo<br>了，④ 我在这儿下车了。<br>le, wǒ zài zhèr xià chē le.<br>你们可能累了，回去<br>Nǐmen kěnéng lèi le, huí qu<br>好好儿休息休息。明天<br>hǎohāor xiūxixiūxi. Míngtiān<br>见。⑤<br>jiàn. | It should be very meaningful to revisit a place one used to know well after so many years. I'll get off here. You must all be tired. Take a good rest after getting home. See you tomorrow. |
| 陈：<br>Chén:<br>艾：<br>Ài: | 明天见。<br>Míngtiān jiàn. | See you tomorrow. |

## new words • 生词 • shēngcí

| | | | | |
|---|---|---|---|---|
| 1 | 风景 | （名） | fēngjǐng | scenery |
| 2 | 得 | （助） | de | (used before compliment to indicate degree or possibility) |
| 3 | 正 | （副） | zhèng | just, exactly, (indicating an action in progress) |
| 4 | 累 | （形） | lèi | tired, weary |
| 5 | 上 | （名） | shàng | last, previous, above, on top of, on the surface of |
| 6 | 次 | （量） | cì | time, (a measure word) |
| 7 | 时间 | （名） | shíjiān | time |

| | | | | |
|---|---|---|---|---|
| 8 | 够 | （形） | gòu | enough, adequate |
| 9 | 或者 | （连） | huòzhě | or |
| 10 | 大后天 | （名） | dàhòutiān | two days from today |
| 11 | 他们 | （代） | tāmen | they, them |
| 12 | 从 | （介） | cóng | since, from |
| 13 | 从……到…… | | cóng…dào… | from…to… |
| 14 | 一直 | （副） | yìzhí | ever, all along |
| 15 | 念书 | | niàn shū | to study, to read a book, to go to school |
| 16 | 不过 | （连） | búguò | yet, however |
| 17 | ……时 | （名） | …shí | time |
| 18 | 旧地重游 | | jiù dì chóng yóu | to revisit a place that one used to know well |
| 19 | 有意思 | | yǒu yìsi | interesting, meaningful |
| 20 | 好了 | | hǎo le | enough (used to wind up a remark and introduce the next one) |
| 21 | 下 | （动） | xià | to get off, to disembark |
| 22 | 车 | （名） | chē | vehicle |
| 23 | 可能 | （助动、形） | kěnéng | possible, may |
| 24 | 好好儿 | （副） | hǎohāor | well, sufficiently |
| 25 | 见 | （动） | jiàn | to see, to meet |
| | 明天见 | | míngtiān jiàn | See you tomorrow |

## 专名 Zhuānmíng Proper names

| | | |
|---|---|---|
| 北海 | Běihǎi | Beihai Park, an imperial garden built and expanded during the Liao, Jin, Yuan, Ming and Qing dynasties, is one of the best-known parks in Beijing. Its White Pagoda has drawn |

| | | |
|---|---|---|
| | | worldwide acclaim. |
| 天坛 | Tiāntán | Temple of Heaven, used to be the place where the Ming and Qing emperors worshipped gods and prayed for good harvests, is now known for its architectual beauty. |
| 颐和园 | Yíhéyuán | Summer Palace, an imperial garden during the Jin, Yuan, Ming and Qing dynasties, is the biggest and perhaps the most beautiful park in Beijing. |
| 中山公园 | Zhōngshān Gōngyuán | Zhongshan Park, to the west of the Palace Museum, is named after Dr. Sun Yet-sam, a great revolutionary in the Chinese democratic revolution. |
| 燕山中学 | Yānshān Zhōngxué | name of the middle school where Mr. Chen studied |

## study points • 注释 • zhùshì

1 你们来得正是时候。(Nǐmen lái de zhèng shì shíhour.)
"正是时候" (zhèng shì shíhour) means "just in time" and it tends to function as an adverbial phrase modifying the action "来" (lái), "come". This kind of adverbial phrase will be further explained in Study Point 1 of Lesson 28.

2 还好 (hái hǎo)
The literal meaning of this expression is "still well". In this context, it means "I am tired, but not too tired."

3 你们参观故宫了吗? (Nǐmen cānguān Gùgōng le ma?)
One of the uses of the particle "了" (le), as in this case, is to indicate that something has already taken place:

上星期我们去香山公园了。(Shàng xīngqī wǒmen qù Xiāngshān Gōngyuán le.)

Last week we [already] went to Fragrant Hills Park.

昨天他病了。(Zuótiān tā bìng le.)

Yesterday, he felt ill.

To form the negative of this kind of "le" sentences, we can replace "了" (le) with either "没有" (méiyǒu) or simply "没" (méi), e.g.

昨天我们没(有)去颐和园。(Zuótiān wǒmen méi(yǒu) qù Yíhéyuán).

Yesterday, we did not go to the Summer Palace.

We can form a question with this kind of sentence in two ways:

昨天晚上你吃没(有)吃药? (Zuótiān wǎnshang nǐ chī méi(yǒu) chī yào?)

Did you or did you not take the medicine last night?

昨天晚上你吃药了没有? (Zuótiān wǎnshang nǐ chī yào le méiyǒu?)

Did you take the medicine last night or not?

4 好了 (hǎo le)

In the context, this expression shows that the speaker is winding up a topic and is starting a new one.

5 明天见 (míngtiān jiàn)

"再见" (zàijiàn), "good-bye", is the general expression we use when we are taking leave. But if the time of our next meeting is definite, we may use this pattern: "time of the next meeting + 见 (jiàn), 'see'":

明天见。(Míngtiān jiàn) See you tomorrow.

晚上见。(Wǎnshang jiàn) See you to-night.

下星期见。(xià xīngqī jiàn) See you next week.

## supplementary words • 补充生词 • bǔchōng shēngcí

| | | | | |
|---|---|---|---|---|
| 1 | 马戏 | (名) | mǎxì | circus |
| 2 | 节目 | (名) | jiémù | program |
| 3 | 好玩儿 | (形) | hǎowánr | enjoyable |
| 4 | 狗 | (名) | gǒu | dog |
| 5 | 作 | (动) | zuò | to do |
| 6 | 算术 | (名) | suànshù | arithmetic |
| 7 | 看够 | | kàn gòu | to see enough of |

## • exercises • 练习 • liànxí

1. **Questions and answers:**

1) Model: A: 星期天 你们去哪儿了？
Xīngqītiān nǐmen qù nǎr le?
B: 我们 去 香山 了。（香山）
Wǒmen qù Xiāngshān le. （Xiāngshān）

(1) 昨天 ＿＿＿＿？（天坛 公园）
Zuótiān＿＿＿＿? （Tiāntán Gōngyuán）

(2) 上午 ＿＿＿＿？（前门 饭店）
Shàngwǔ＿＿＿＿? （Qiánmén Fàndiàn）

(3) 前天 晚上 ＿＿＿＿？（人民 剧场，看 京剧）
Qiántiān wǎnshang＿＿＿＿? （Rénmín Jùchǎng, kàn jīngjù）

2) Model: A: 星期天 你们 去 香山 了没有？
Xīngqītiān nǐmen qù Xiāngshān le méiyǒu?
B: 没有，我们 去 北海了。（香山，北海）
Méiyǒu, wǒmen qù Běihǎi le. （Xiāngshān, Běihǎi）

(1) 上 星期三＿＿＿＿？（中山 公园，天坛）
Shàng xīngqīsān＿＿＿＿? （Zhōngshān Gōngyuán, Tiāntán）

(2) 昨天 晚上 ＿＿＿＿？（民族 饭店，国际 机场）
Zuótiān wǎnshang＿＿＿＿? （Mínzú Fàndiàn, Guójì Jīchǎng）

(3) 前天＿＿＿＿？（故宫，长城）
Qiántiān＿＿＿＿? （Gùgōng, Chángchéng）

*2. **Practice making sentences with "都" "dōu" and "没都" "méi dōu":**

Model: A: 几个 大 公园 都 去 了 吗？（公园）
Jǐge dà gōngyuánr dōu qù le ma? （gōngyuánr）
B: 时间 不够，没 都 去。
Shíjiān bú gòu, méi dōu qù.

1) A: 几个 ＿＿＿＿去 了吗？（学校）
Jǐge ＿＿＿＿ qù le ma? （xuéxiào）
B: 太 累 了，＿＿＿＿。
Tài lèi le, ＿＿＿＿.

2) A: 几个 ＿＿＿＿去 了吗？（老 朋友 家）
Jǐge ＿＿＿＿ qù le ma? （lǎo péngyou jiā）

B: 时间不够，________。
Shíjiān bú gòu, ________.

3) A: 几个________看了？（电影）
Jǐge ________ kàn le?（diànyǐng）

B: 有点儿别的事儿，________。
Yǒu diǎnr biéde shìr, ________.

3. **Listen to the dialogue:**

A: 昨天你们没去天坛公园吧？
Zuótiān nǐmen méi qù Tiāntán Gōngyuán ba?

B: 没去。我们去看马戏了。
Méi qù. Wǒmen qù kàn mǎxì le.

A: 马戏？那一定很有意思。都演什么节目了？
Mǎxì? Nà yídìng hěn yǒu yìsi. Dōu yǎn shénme jiémù le?

B: 节目真多，有十七、八个。最好玩儿的是小狗作算术，孩子们没看够。
Jiémù zhēn duō, yǒu shíqī、bā ge. Zuì hǎowánr de shì xiǎogǒur zuò suànshù, háizimen méi kàn gòu.

A: 是吗？下星期我也带孩子去看看。
Shì ma? Xià xīngqī wǒ yě dài háizi qu kànkan.

B: 天坛怎么样？
Tiāntán zěnmeyàng?

A: 啊，很好。那儿还有一个画展，孩子们很喜欢。我和老赵都累了，没好好儿看。
À, hěn hǎo. Nàr hái yǒu yíge huàzhǎn, háizimen hěn xǐhuan. Wǒ hé Lǎo Zhào dōu lèi le, méi hǎohāor kàn.

*4. **Translate the following sentences into Chinese:**

1) Where did you go tonight?
2) They went to the Summer Palace yesterday.
3) What did you do the night before last?
4) Did you go to the Palace Museum last Tuesday?
5) He didn't come the day before yesterday.

# 19 We Were Just Talking About You
# 我们正在说你呢
# wǒmen zhèngzài shuō nǐ ne

(The Chens are getting ready to go to the Friendship Store.)

## (一)

| | | |
|---|---|---|
| 艾: | 王　小姐一会儿来吗? | Is Miss Wang coming in a while? |
| Ài: | Wáng xiǎojie yíhuìr lái ma? | |
| 陈: | 来，这不，① 我 正 等 | Yes, I'm waiting for her now. |
| Chén: | Lái, zhè bù, wǒ zhèng děng | |

| | | |
|---|---|---|
| | 她 呢。②<br>tā ne. | |
| 艾：<br>Ài: | 那 今天 我们 还 去 不 去 友谊 商店？<br>Nà jīntiān wǒmen hái qù bu qù Yǒuyì Shāngdiàn? | Are we still going to the Friendship Store? |
| 陈：<br>Chén: | 去 吧。过 几天 我们 就 要 离开 北京 了。③ 今天 不 去，以后 没 时间 了。<br>Qù ba. Guò jǐtiān wǒmen jiù yào líkāi Běijīng le. Jīntiān bú qù, yǐhòu méi shíjiān le. | I think so. We're leaving Beijing in just a few days and if we don't go today, we won't have time later. |
| 艾：<br>Ài: | 几点 去？<br>Jǐdiǎn qù? | When are we going then? |
| 陈：<br>Chén: | 跟 王 小姐 谈 完 就 去。她 说 八点半 到。<br>Gēn Wáng xiǎojie tán wán jiù qù. Tā shuō bādiǎnbàn dào. | As soon as I've had a talk with Miss Wang. She said she'd be here at eight-thirty. |
| 艾：<br>Ài: | 现在 已经 八点半 了。<br>Xiànzài yǐjīng bādiǎnbàn le.<br>(Wang Fang arrives.) | It's eight-thirty now. |
| 王：<br>Wáng: | 你们 好！<br>Nǐmen hǎo! | Hello! |
| 陈：<br>Chén: | 你 好！<br>Nǐ hǎo! | Hello! |
| 艾：<br>Ài: | 王 小姐，我们 正 说 你 呢。<br>Wáng xiǎojie, wǒmen zhèng shuō nǐ ne. | We were just talking about you, Miss Wang. |
| 王：<br>Wáng: | 是 吗？说 曹 操，曹 操 就 到。<br>Shì ma? Shuō Cáo Cāo, Cáo Cāo jiù dào. | Were you? Talk of the devil, huh? |
| 艾：<br>Ài: | 哈 哈……<br>Hā hā…… | Ha, ha··· |
| 王：<br>Wáng: | | Ha, ha··· |

## （二）　　　　II

| | | |
|---|---|---|
| 艾：<br>Ài: | 大伟，你在干　什么？<br>Dàwěi, nǐ zài gàn shénme? | David, what are you doing? |
| 伟：<br>Wěi: | 我　在　听　收音机　呢。爸爸<br>Wǒ zài tīng shōuyīnjī ne. Bàba<br>还　在　跟　王　小姐　谈　话<br>hái zài gēn Wáng xiǎojie tán huà<br>呢　吗？④<br>ne ma? | Listening to the radio. Is Dad still talking with Miss Wang? |
| 艾：<br>Ài: | 没有，王　小姐　已经<br>Méiyǒu, Wáng xiǎojie yǐjīng<br>走　了。<br>zǒu le. | No, she has left. |
| 伟：<br>Wěi: | 咱们　走吧，快　十点　了。<br>Zánmen zǒu ba, kuài shídiǎn le. | Let's go then. It's almost ten. |
| 艾：<br>Ài: | 你　姐姐呢？<br>Nǐ jiějie ne? | Where's your sister? |
| 伟：<br>Wěi: | 她　没　在　看　书　吗？<br>Tā méi zài kàn shū ma? | Isn't she reading? |
| 艾：<br>Ài: | 没有　。<br>Méiyǒu. | No. |
| 伟：<br>Wěi: | 刚才　我　找　她的　时候，<br>Gāngcái wǒ zhǎo tā de shíhour,<br>她　正在　看　医学　杂志呢。<br>tā zhèngzài kàn yīxué zázhì ne. | When I saw her just now, she was reading a medical journal. |
| 艾：<br>Ài: | 那　上　哪儿　了呢？⑤<br>Nà shàng nǎr le ne? | I wonder where she has gone. |
| 伟：<br>Wěi: | 等　她一会儿吧。<br>Děng tā yíhuìr ba. | Let's wait for her for a while. |
| 艾：<br>Ài: | 大伟，今天　外边儿　有<br>Dàwěi, jīntiān wàibianr yǒu<br>一点儿风，你去　多　穿<br>yìdiǎnr fēng, nǐ qù duō chuān<br>一件衣服。<br>yíjiàn yīfu. | It's a bit windy today, David. Go and put on something more. |

## • new words • 生词 • shēngcí

| | | | | |
|---|---|---|---|---|
| 1 | 正在 | （副） | zhèngzài | in the process of, in the middle of |
| | 正在……呢 | | zhèngzài…ne | (an emphatic way of saying that an action is in progress) |
| 2 | 这不 | | zhè bù | (used to call attention to something that is obvious) |
| 3 | 过 | （动） | guò | to pass, to spend |
| 4 | 要……了 | | yào…le | to be going to (an adverb used to indicate something about to happen) |
| 5 | 离开 | （动） | líkāi | to leave |
| 6 | 谈 | （动） | tán | to talk |
| 7 | 完 | （动） | wán | to finish, to end |
| | 谈完 | | tán wán | to finish talking |
| 8 | 说曹操，曹操就到 | | shuō Cáo Cāo, Cáo Cāo jiù dào | Talking of the devil and the devil comes. |
| 9 | 哈 | （象声） | hā | ha |
| 10 | 在 | （副） | zài | an adverb to indicate something is in progress |
| | 在……呢 | | zài…ne | (See Study Points.) |
| 11 | 收音机 | （名） | shōuyīnjī | radio |
| 12 | 跟 | （介、连） | gēn | with, and |
| 13 | 谈话 | | tán huà | to talk, to speak |
| | 跟……谈话 | | gēn…tán huà | to talk with (to), to speak with (to) |
| 14 | 已经 | （副） | yǐjīng | already |
| 15 | 快 | （副、形） | kuài | soon, quick, fast |
| 16 | 书 | （名） | shū | book |
| | 看书 | | kàn shū | to read a book |

| | | | | |
|---|---|---|---|---|
| 17 | 刚才 | (名) | gāngcái | just now, a moment ago |
| 18 | 医学 | (名) | yīxué | medical science |
| 19 | 杂志 | (名) | zázhì | magazine, journal |
| 20 | 上 | (动) | shàng | to go, to get on, to board |
| | 上哪儿 | | shàng nǎr | where to go |
| 21 | 外 | (名) | wài | outside |
| 22 | 外边儿 | | wàibianr | open air, outside, outdoors |
| 23 | 衣服 | (名) | yīfu | clothes, clothing |

| 专名 | Zhuānmíng | Proper name |
|---|---|---|
| 友谊商店 | Yǒuyì Shāngdiàn | Friendship Store, a store for foreigners and overseas Chinese |

## study points • 注释 • zhùshì

1 这不 (zhè bù)

This is a phrase used in conversation to show that what is going to be said is evident.

2 我正等她呢。 (Wǒ zhèng děng tā ne.)

To indicate that an action is in progress, we can add "正在" (zhèngzài) or "正" (zhèng) or "在" (zài) before the verb or add "呢" (ne) at the end of the sentence. "正在" or "正" or "在" can be used with "呢" at the same time:

他正在写信。 (Tā zhèngzài xiě xìn.)
他正写信。 (Tā zhèng xiě xìn.)
他在写信。 (Tā zài xiě xìn.)
他写信呢。 (Tā xiě xìn ne.)
他正在写信呢。 (Tā zhèngzài xiě xìn ne.)
他正写信呢。 (Tā zhèng xiě xìn ne.)
他在写信呢。 (Tā zài xiě xìn ne.)

The negative form is:

他没(有)在写信。 (Tā méi(yǒu) zài xiě xìn.)

The action in progress can be either in the present or in the past:

刚才我去找他的时候，他正在看杂志呢。

(Gāngcái wǒ qù zhǎo tā de shíhour, tā zhèng zài kàn zázhì ne.)

3 过几天我们就要离开北京了。 (Guò jǐtiān wǒmen jiù yào líkāi Běijīng le.)

1) “要……了”(yào…le) or “快……了” (kuài…le) can be used to indicate that something is going to happen soon:

他们要去西安了。 (Tāmen yào qù Xī'ān le.)

They will be going to Xian.

老李快来了。(Lǎo Lǐ kuài lái le.)

Lao Li is going to come soon.

2) The adverb “就” (jiù) means “in a short while”:

你等一会儿，我就来。 (Nǐ děng yíhuìr, wǒ jiù lái.)

Wait a moment. I'll come soon.

3) The pattern “就要……了” (jiù yào…le) means that there is little time left before something is going to happen:

冬天就要到了。 (Dōngtiān jiù yào dào le.)

Winter is going to come soon.

4 爸爸还在跟王小姐谈话呢吗? (Bàba hái zài gēn Wáng xiǎojie tán huà ne ma?)

“还” (hái) here indicates that the action is still in progress.

5 那上哪儿了呢? (Nà shàng nǎr le ne?)

那 (nà) here is a simplified form of the conjunction “那么” (nàme). (See Study Point 5 of Lesson 11.)

## supplementary words • 补充生词 • bǔchōng shēngcí

| | | | | |
|---|---|---|---|---|
| 1 | 报告 | (动、名) | bàogào | to report, report |
| 2 | 比赛 | (动、名) | bǐsài | to compete, match |
| 3 | 刚 | (副) | gāng | just |
| 4 | 开球 | | kāi qiú | to serve the ball |
| 5 | 客人 | (名) | kèrén | guest |
| 6 | 告别 | (动) | gàobié | to say good-bye |
| 7 | 上楼 | | shàng lóu | to go upstairs |

| | | | |
|---|---|---|---|
| 8 | 开（车） | （动）kāi (chē) | (a vehicle) to start |
| 9 | 水果 | （名）shuǐguǒ | fruit |
| 10 | 广播 | （动、名）guǎngbō | to broadcast, broadcast |
| 11 | 旅客 | （名）lǚkè | passenger |
| 12 | 列车 | （名）lièchē | train |
| 13 | 分钟 | （名）fēnzhōng | minute |
| | 小同 | Xiǎotóng | name of a boy |

## • exercises • 练习 • liànxí

*1. **Fill in the blanks using:** 就要 (jiù yào) or 正（在）(zhèng (zài)):

1) A: 他们 谈 完 了吗?
Tāmen tán wán le ma?
B: 没有，________谈呢。
Méiyǒu, ________tán ne.

2) A: 报告 开始 了吗？
Bàogào kāishǐ le ma?
B: 没有，________开始了。
Méiyǒu, ________kāishǐ le.

3) A: 比赛开始 了吗？
Bǐsài kāishǐ le ma?
B: 刚 开始，你 看，________开 球 呢。
Gāng kāishǐ, nǐ kàn, ________kāi qiú ne.

4) A: 客人 走 了吗?
Kèrén zǒu le ma?
B: ________走 了，________告别 呢。
________zǒu le, ________gàobié ne.

5) A: 你 爸爸回 来 了吗？
Nǐ bàba huí lai le ma?
B: 回 来 了，那不，________上 楼呢。
Huí lai le, nà bù, ________shàng lóu ne.

**＊2. Answer the questions in accordance with the contents of the pictures:**

Model: A: 他 干 什么 呢？
Tā gàn shénme ne?
B: 听 收音机 呢。
Tīng shōuyīnjī ne.

1) A: 他 干 什么 呢？
Tā gàn shénme ne?
B: ＿＿＿＿＿＿。
＿＿＿＿＿＿.

2) A: 她 在 干 什么？
Tā zài gàn shénme?
B: ＿＿＿＿＿＿。
＿＿＿＿＿＿.

3) A: 她 在 干 什么 呢？
Tā zài gàn shénme ne?
B: ＿＿＿＿＿＿。
＿＿＿＿＿＿.

**3. Listen to the dialogue:**

A: 怎么 弟弟 还不 回来 呀！
Zěnme dìdi hái bù huí lai ya!

B: 早不买，晚不买，车快开了，还去买什么
Zǎo bù mǎi, wǎn bù mǎi, chē kuài kāi le, hái qù mǎi shénme
水果。
shuǐguǒ.

A: 还有多少时间？
Hái yǒu duōshao shíjiān?

B: 时间就要到了。这不，正在广播呢。
Shíjiān jiù yào dào le. Zhè bù, zhèngzài guǎngbō ne.

(Voice from the loudspeaker) "旅客同志们请注意，九次
"Lǚkè tóngzhìmen qǐng zhùyì, jiǔcì
列车还有十分钟就要开车了，去广州的
lièchē hái yǒu shífēnzhōng jiù yào kāi chē le, qù Guǎngzhōu de
旅客，请快上车。"
lǚkè, qǐng kuài shàng chē."

A: 这个小同啊，就他事儿多。
Zhège Xiǎotóng a, jiù tā shìr duō.

B: 他干什么都这么慢。姐姐，小同回来了。
Tā gàn shénme dōu zhème màn. Jiějie, Xiǎotóng huí lai le.

A: 哪儿呢？
Nǎr ne?

B: 那不，正上楼呢。小同！小同！快点儿吧！要
Nà bù, zhèng shàng lóu ne. Xiǎotóng! Xiǎotóng! Kuài diǎnr ba! Yào
开车了！
kāi chē le!

C: 哪儿啊！还有七分钟呢！
Nǎr a! Hái yǒu qīfēnzhōng ne!

***4. Translate the following sentences into Chinese:**

1) I'm nearly fifty.
2) They're leaving Beijing soon.
3) Mr. Wang arrived as we were talking about him.
4) What are you doing?
5) They are not talking.
6) He was writing a letter when I came in.

# 20 Saying Good-Bye
## 辞行 cí xíng

(Mr. Smith, interpreter for a U.S. trade delegation, comes to Mr. Chen's room to say good-bye and they talk about what they see in Beijing.)

| | | |
|---|---|---|
| 史：<br>Shǐ: | 陈 先生，我 向 你辞 行 来了。<br>Chén xiānsheng, wǒ xiàng nǐ cí xíng lái le. | Mr. Chen, I'm here to say good-bye. |
| 陈：<br>Chén: | 怎么，你要 回 国了？<br>Zěnme, nǐ yào huí guó le? | Why, you're going home? |

| | | |
|---|---|---|
| 史：<br>Shǐ: | 是的，① 国内 来 电报，<br>Shì de, guó nèi lái diànbào,<br>有 重要 事情，要 我们<br>yǒu zhòngyào shìqing, yào wǒmen<br>赶快 回去。<br>gǎnkuài huí qu. | Yes. We got a cable from home telling us to get back quickly because of some urgent matters. |
| 陈：<br>Chén: | 你们 的 贸易 谈判 结束了？<br>Nǐmen de màoyì tánpàn jiéshù le? | Have you finished your business talks? |
| 史：<br>Shǐ: | 结束 了。昨天 下午 签<br>Jiéshù le. Zuótiān xiàwǔ qiān<br>订了 一个 合同，② 双<br>dìngle yíge hétóng, shuāng<br>方 都 比较 满意。<br>fāng dōu bǐjiào mǎnyì. | Yes, we have. We signed a contract yesterday afternoon to the satisfaction of both sides. |
| 陈：<br>Chén: | 什么 时候 走？<br>Shénme shíhour zǒu? | When will you be leaving? |
| 史：<br>Shǐ: | 今天 下午 准备准备，<br>Jīntiān xiàwǔ zhǔnbeizhǔnbei,<br>晚上 就 上 飞机了。<br>wǎnshang jiù shàng fēijī le. | We'll be getting everything ready this afternoon and will be boarding the plane in the evening. |
| 陈：<br>Chén: | 这么 急？哎哟，今天 晚<br>Zhème jí? Āiyō, jīntiān wǎn<br>上 有一个 朋友 请<br>shang yǒu yíge péngyou qǐng<br>吃 饭，没有 时间去 送<br>chī fàn, méi yǒu shíjiān qù sòng<br>你 了，实在对 不起。<br>nǐ le, shízài duì bu qǐ. | So soon? I've been asked to dinner tonight by a friend of mine. I'm really sorry I won't be able to see you off. |
| 史：<br>Shǐ: | 没 关系，不 用 送 了。<br>Méi guānxi, bú yòng sòng le.<br>昨天 给 你们打了几次<br>Zuótiān gěi nǐmen dǎle jǐcì<br>电话，你们 都 不在，<br>diànhuà, nǐmen dōu bú zài,<br>上 哪儿 去了？<br>shàng nǎr qù le? | Forget it. There's really no need. I tried to phone you several times yesterday. None of you was in. Where were you? |
| 陈：<br>Chén: | 昨天 我们 吃了 早饭 就<br>Zuótiān wǒmen chīle zǎofàn jiù | We went out right after breakfast yesterday. We |

| | | |
|---|---|---|
| | 出 去 了。 上午 看了<br>chū qu le . Shàngwǔ kànle<br>《唐代 绘画 展览》，<br>“Tángdài Huìhuà Zhǎnlǎn ”,<br>下午到 琉璃厂 买了点儿<br>xiàwǔ dào Liúlíchǎng mǎile diǎnr<br>古玩 。<br>gǔwán . | visited an exhibition of Tang paintings in the morning and in the afternoon we went to Liulichang where we bought a few pieces of antiques. |
| 史：<br>Shǐ: | 你这次来北京， 收获 不<br>Nǐ zhècì lái Běijīng, shōuhuò bù<br>少 吧？<br>shǎo ba? | You must have gained quite a bit from your present visit to Beijing. |
| 陈 ：<br>Chén: | 是 啊， 看望了 老 朋友，<br>Shì a , kànwàngle lǎo péngyou,<br>买了 不 少 书，也 游览了<br>mǎile bù shǎo shū, yě yóulǎnle<br>许多 地方。北京 的 变化<br>xǔduō dìfang. Běijīng de biànhuà<br>真 不 小 啊！<br>zhēn bù xiǎo a ! | Yes. I've seen my old friends, bought a few books and toured many places. Beijing has changed a lot. |
| 史：<br>Shǐ: | 北京 没有 亲戚了？<br>Běijīng méi yǒu qīnqi le ? | Don't you have any relatives in Beijing now? |
| 陈 ：<br>Chén: | 没有 了。<br>Méi yǒu le . | No. |
| 史：<br>Shǐ: | 你们 什么 时候 去西安？<br>Nǐmen shénme shíhour qù Xī'ān? | When will you be leaving for Xian? |
| 陈 ：<br>Chén: | 星期五。<br>Xīngqīwǔ. | This Friday. |
| 史：<br>Shǐ: | 票 买了 没有？③<br>Piào mǎile méiyǒu? | Have you got the tickets yet? |
| 陈 ：<br>Chén: | 还 没有 呢。 王 小姐<br>Hái méiyǒu ne. Wáng xiǎojie<br>说 她 给 买。④<br>shuō tā gěi mǎi. | Not yet. Miss Wang said she'd take care of that. |
| 史：<br>Shǐ: | 时间 不早了， 我 该<br>Shíjiān bù zǎo le , wǒ gāi<br>走 了。一个 月 以后<br>zǒu le . Yíge yuè yǐhòu | Well, it's getting late and I should be going. See you in the U. S. a month later. |

| | | |
|---|---|---|
| | 美国 见！<br>Měiguó jiàn! | |
| 陈：<br>Chén: | 回 美国 以后，一定 去<br>Huí Měiguó yǐhòu, yídìng qù<br>看 你。 祝 你们 一路<br>kàn nǐ. Zhù nǐmen yílù<br>平安！⑤<br>píng'ān! | I'll go and see you when we get back.Bon voyage. |

## • new words • 生词 • shēngcí

| | | | | |
|---|---|---|---|---|
| 1 | 辞行 | | cí xíng | to say good-bye, to take leave |
| 2 | 向 | （介） | xiàng | to, towards |
| 3 | 回 | （动） | huí | to come back, to return |
| 4 | 的 | （助） | de | a particle indicating affirmation |
| 5 | 内 | （名） | nèi | inside, (usually used in written language) |
| | 国内 | | guó nèi | inside the country |
| 6 | 电报 | （名） | diànbào | telegram, cable |
| | 来电报 | | lái diànbào | telegram sent by (from) |
| 7 | 重要 | （形） | zhòngyào | important |
| 8 | 事情 | （名） | shìqing | matter, business |
| 9 | 要 | （动） | yào | to ask somebody to do something |
| 10 | 赶快 | （副） | gǎnkuài | as quickly as possible, quickly |
| 11 | 贸易 | （动、名） | màoyì | to trade, trade |
| 12 | 谈判 | （动） | tánpàn | to negotiate |
| 13 | 结束 | （动） | jiéshù | to finish, to be over |
| 14 | 签订 | （动） | qiāndìng | to sign |
| 15 | 合同 | （名） | hétóng | contract |

| | | | |
|---|---|---|---|
| 16 双方 | （名） | shuāngfāng | both sides |
| 17 满意 | （动、形） | mǎnyì | to be satisfied, satisfactory |
| 18 准备 | （动、名） | zhǔnbèi | to prepare, to get ready, preparation |
| 19 飞机 | （名） | fēijī | airplane, aircraft |
| 上飞机 | | shàng fēijī | to board a plane |
| 20 这么 | （代） | zhème | so, such |
| 21 急 | （形） | jí | urgent, hurried, impatient |
| 22 哎哟 | （叹） | āiyō | an interjection expressing surprise, pain, etc. |
| 23 实在 | （副、形） | shízài | really, so real, honest, substantial |
| 24 早饭 | （名） | zǎofàn | breakfast |
| 25 出去 | | chū qu | to go out |
| 26 古玩 | （名） | gǔwán | antique |
| 27 收获 | （名、动） | shōuhuò | results, yield, to harvest |
| 28 看望 | （动） | kànwàng | to visit, to see |
| 29 许多 | （形） | xǔduō | many, a lot of |
| 30 地方 | （名） | dìfang | place |
| 31 变化 | （名） | biànhuà | change |
| 32 亲戚 | （名） | qīnqi | relative, kin |
| 33 祝 | （动） | zhù | to wish, to congratulate |
| 34 一路 | （名） | yílù | the whole journey, all the way |
| 35 平安 | （形） | píng'ān | safe, free from dangers |
| 一路平安 | | yílù píng'ān | bon voyage, a pleasant trip |

## 专名 Zhuānmíng Proper names

| | | |
|---|---|---|
| 唐代绘画展览 | Tángdài Huìhuà Zhǎnlǎn | Exhibition of the Paintings of the Tang Dynasty |
| 琉璃厂 | Liúlíchǎng | a famous street in Beijing for selling Chinese paintings, calligraphy, stationaries and antiques |

## study points • 注释 • zhùshì

1 是的 (shì de)
The particle "的" (de) is for emphasis here.

2 昨天下午签订了一个合同。(Zuótiān xiàwǔ qiāndìngle yíge hétóng.)
"了" (le) can serve as an aspect particle or as a modal particle. When functioned as an aspect particle, "了" (le) is placed after the verb to indicate the completion of an action:

昨天我们看了一个展览。(Zuótiān wǒmen kànle yíge zhǎnlǎn.)
Yesterday we saw (visited) an exhibition.
昨天他们签订了一个合同。(Zuótiān tāmen qiāndìngle yíge hétóng.)
Yesterday they signed a contract.

When a past action is a habitual one or there is no need to emphasize its completion, "了" (le) is not used.

去年她常常来。(Qùnián tā chángcháng lái.)
Last year, she came frequently.

When functioned as a modal particle, "了" is used to assert that something has already taken place. Compare the following two sentences:

1) 我买水果。 (Wǒ mǎi shuǐ guǒ.)
2) 我买水果了。 (Wǒ mǎi shuǐ guǒ le.)

In sentence 1) "了" shows that the action "买水果" has not yet been completed. In sentence 2) "了" is used to show that the action has already taken place. Study the following sentence and notice the difference in function between the first and second "了".

昨天他看了展览了。 (Zuótiān tā kànle zhǎnlǎn le.)
Yesterday he saw the exhibition.

The first "了" is an aspect particle which is placed after the verb "看" (kàn) to indicate the completion of the action. Placed at the end of the sentence the second "了" is a modal particle used to show the state of affairs.
The negative is formed by adding "没(有)" (méi (yǒu)) before the verb and leaving out "了":
(Positive) 昨天他去看了一个朋友。(Zuótiān tā qù kànle yíge péngyou.)
(Negative) 昨天他没(有)去看朋友。(Zuótiān tā méi(yǒu) qù kàn péngyou.)

3 票买了没有? (Piào mǎile méiyǒu?)

Here, “了”functions as an aspect particle to show the perfect aspect of the action “买”.

4 她给买。(Tā gěi mǎi.)
In this sentence, the object “我们” has been left out because it is understood. The whole sentence should be“她给我们买”。(Tā gěi wǒmen mǎi) “She buys for us”.

5 祝你们一路平安! (Zhù nǐmen yílù píng'ān!)
This is a common Chinese expression people use when seeing their friends or relatives off for a long trip.

## supplementary words • 补充生词 • bǔchōng shēngcí

| | | | |
|---|---|---|---|
| 1 | 借 | (动) jiè | to borrow, to lend |
| 2 | 点(菜) | (动) diǎn (cài) | order (dishes) |
| 3 | 胶卷 | (名) jiāojuǎnr | film |
| 4 | 忙 | (形) máng | busy |
| 5 | 外地 | (名) wàidì | other places |
| 6 | 陪 | (动) péi | to accompany |
| 7 | 火车 | (名) huǒchē | train |

地下宫殿 Dìxià Gōngdiàn Underground Palace

## • exercises • 练习 • liànxí

*1. **Fill in the blanks using the following verbs:**

说, 吃, 买, 看, 喝, 写, 叫, 寄, 借, 参观, 看望
shuō, chī, mǎi, kàn, hē, xiě, jiào, jì, , jiè, cānguān, kànwàng

1) 她 Tā ______ ______ ______ ______ ______ ______ ______ ______ ______ 了一本书。 le yìběn shū.

2) 他 Tā
______ 了一个学校。 le yíge xuéxiào.
______ 了一场新电影。 le yìchǎng xīn diànyǐng.
______ 了两句中国话。 le liǎngjù Zhōngguóhuà.
______ 了几位朋友。 le jǐwèi péngyou.
______ 了几件衣服。 le jǐjiàn yīfu.
______ 了一杯茶。 le yìbēi chá.
______ 了半个馒头。 le bànge mántou.
______ 了一辆出租汽车。 le yíliàng chūzū qìchē.

**∗2. Fill in the blanks with relevant phrases:**

1) 他 Tā
买了一筒 ________。 mǎile yìtǒng ________.
点了四个 ________。 diǎnle sìge ________.
试了两件 ________。 shìle liǎngjiàn ________.
喝了一瓶 ________。 hēle yìpíng ________.
吃了一碗 ________。 chīle yìwǎn ________.

要了　一杯________。
yàole　yìbēi________.
寄了　两封________。
jìle　liǎngfēng________.
借了　三本________。
jièle　sānběn________.
填了　一张________。
tiánle　yìzhāng________.
兑换了　一些________。
duìhuànle　yìxiē________.

2) 她　看了 / Tā kànle
________。
________.
________。
________.
________。
________.
________。
________.

**＊3. Rearrange the following words and phrases into proper sentences:**

1) 我，出去，了，看，一个，亲戚，昨天
wǒ, chū qu, le, kàn, yíge, qīnqi, zuótiān

2) 他，去，了，机场，下午
tā, qù, le, jīchǎng, xiàwǔ

3) 她，晚饭，吃，没，睡，了，就
tā, wǎnfàn, chī, méi, shuì, le, jiù

4) 他们，吃，了，饭
tāmen, chī, le, fàn

**＊4) Answer the questions using "了" (le):**

1) A: 你　买　什么　了？
Nǐ mǎi shénme le?
B: ________。（一个　胶卷）
________.（yíge jiāojuǎnr）

2) A: 你　买的　什么？
Nǐ mǎi de shénme?
B: ________。（两斤　大　虾）
________.（liǎngjīn dà xiā）

3) A: 你　买了　什么　了？
Nǐ mǎile shénme le?

B: __________。（两本 杂志）
__________. (liǎngběn zázhì)

*5. **Fill in the blanks using "了" and also in accordance with the contents of the pictures:**

1) 她________就出去了。
Tā________ jiù chū qu le.

2) 我们________就回家。
Wǒmen________ jiù huí jiā.

3) 他们一家________就去地下宫殿。
Tāmen yìjiā________ jiù qù Dìxià Gōngdiàn.

4) 小王________就去友谊商店。
Xiǎo Wáng________ jiù qù Yǒuyì Shāngdiàn.

6 . **Listen to the dialogue:**

A: 前天，昨天，我 找了 你几次，你 都 不 在。
Qiántiān, zuótiān, wǒ zhǎole nǐ jǐcì, nǐ dōu bú zài.

B: 真 对不起，前天 早晨，我吃了饭 就 出去了，这 两 天一直 在 外边儿 忙 。昨天 晚上 回 到家，都 快 十一点 了，你 哪 能 找 到 我。
Zhēn duì bu qǐ, qiántiān zǎochén, wǒ chīle fàn jiù chū qu le, zhè liǎngtiān yìzhí zài wàibianr máng. Zuótiān wǎnshang huí dào jiā, dōu kuài shíyīdiǎn le, nǐ nǎ néng zhǎo dào wǒ.

A: 有 什么 事儿，这么 忙？
Yǒu shénme shìr, zhème máng?

B: 我们 家亲戚 多，事儿就 多。这 几天，有 两个 外地 亲戚 来这儿，我 陪 他们 游览，看 画展，买 东西，给 他们 买 车票，送 他们 上 火车。实在 是 忙 。
Wǒmen jiā qīnqi duō, shìr jiù duō. Zhè jǐtiān, yǒu liǎngge wàidì qīnqi lái zhèr, wǒ péi tāmen yóulǎn, kàn huàzhǎn, mǎi dōngxi, gěi tāmen mǎi chēpiào, sòng tāmen shàng huǒchē. Shízài shì máng.

A: 怪 不得 见 不 到 你。
Guài bu de jiàn bu dào nǐ.

B: 他们 走了，我 可以好好儿休息休息了。啊，你 找 我，一定 有 重要 事儿。
Tāmen zǒu le, wǒ kěyǐ hǎohāor xiūxixiūxi le. À, nǐ zhǎo wǒ, yídìng yǒu zhòngyào shìr.

A: 也 不是 什么 重要 事儿。后 天，我 要 去 上海，你 那儿也有 不 少 亲戚，是不是？
Yě bú shì shénme zhòngyào shìr. Hòutiān, wǒ yào qù Shànghǎi, nǐ nàr yě yǒu bù shǎo qīnqi, shì bu shì?

B: 是 啊。
Shì a.

A: 你 有 什么 事儿没 有？带 不 带 东西 给 他们？
Nǐ yǒu shénme shìr méi yǒu? Dài bu dài dōngxi gěi tāmen?

B: 当然 要 带 了。你 看，今天 和 明天 我 还 要 忙 啊。
Dāngrán yào dài le. Nǐ kàn, jīntiān hé míngtiān wǒ hái yào máng a.

*7. **Translate the following sentences into Chinese:**

1) Lily bought a magazine.
2) We visited a school yesterday.
3) He went out after supper.
4) We'll go to the Summer Palace after he's come.
5) He went to see films every day last week.

# 复习 (4) fùxí (4) Revision (4)

***1. Turn the following statements into five forms of questions:**

Model: 他们 的 贸易 谈判 明天 结束。
Tāmen de màoyì tánpàn míngtiān jiéshù.
他们 的 贸易 谈判 明天 结束?
Tāmen de màoyì tánpàn míngtiān jiéshù?
他们 的 贸易 谈判 明天 结束吗?
Tāmen de màoyì tánpàn míngtiān jiéshù ma?
他们 的 贸易 谈判 什么 时候 结束?
Tāmen de màoyì tánpàn shénme shíhour jiéshù?
他们 的 贸易 谈判 明天 结束 不结束?
Tāmen de màoyì tánpàn míngtiān jiéshù bu jiéshù?
他们 的 贸易 谈判 明天 结束 还是 后天 结束?
Tāmen de màoyì tánpàn míngtiān jiéshù háishi hòutiān jiéshù?

1) 这些 古玩是 赵 先生 的。
Zhèxiē gǔwán shì Zhào xiānsheng de.

2) 他们 有 一辆 新汽车。
Tāmen yǒu yíliàng xīn qìchē.

3) 她 的 休息 时间 很 多。
Tā de xiūxi shíjiān hěn duō.

4) 他 买 两 瓶 啤酒。
Tā mǎi liǎngpíng píjiǔ.

5) 他们 昨天 去 看 画展 了。
Tāmen zuótiān qù kàn huàzhǎn le .

***2. Fill in the blanks with "不" (bù) or "没(有)" (méi (yǒu)):**

1) 昨天 他去 长城 了, _____ 去 故宫。
Zuótiān tā qù Chángchéng le , _____ qù Gùgōng.

2) 到 现在 他还_____来, 我_____ 等 他 了。
Dào xiànzài tā hái_____lái, wǒ_____ děng tā le .

3) 今天 她 病 了，______能 去 学校 了。
Jīntiān tā bìng le, ______néng qù xuéxiào le.

4) 听 说 那个 电影 不 怎么样，我______想 看 了。
Tīng shuō nàge diànyǐng bù zěnmeyàng, wǒ______xiǎng kàn le.

5) 上午 有 点儿 别的 事儿，我______去 看 病。
Shàngwǔ yǒu diǎnr biéde shìr, wǒ______qù kàn bìng.

6) 他 的 记性 不 太 好，票______带 来。
Tā de jìxing bú tài hǎo, piào______dài lai.

7) 我 的 亲戚 昨天 还______走，今天 我 还 得 陪 他，______去 看 杂技 了。
Wǒ de qīnqi zuótiān hái______zǒu, jīntiān wǒ hái děi péi tā, ______qù kàn zájì le.

8) 那位 售货员 同志 很 忙，昨天 是 星期天，他 也______休息。
Nàwèi shòuhuòyuán tóngzhì hěn máng, zuótiān shì xīngqītiān, tā yě______xiūxi.

***3. Correct the mistakes in the following sentences:**

1) 昨天 下午 没 签订 合同 了。
Zuótiān xiàwǔ méi qiāndìng hétóng le.

2) 他 上午 写 信 了 就 出去 了。
Tā shàngwǔ xiě xìn le jiù chū qu le.

3) 明天 我 看望 老 朋友 了，就 去 了 琉璃厂。
Míngtiān wǒ kànwàng lǎo péngyou le, jiù qùle Liúlíchǎng.

4) 昨天 的 电视 我 看，真 好！
Zuótiān de diànshì wǒ kàn, zhēn hǎo!

5) 上星期 你们 参观了 没有 故宫？
Shàngxīngqī nǐmen cānguānle méiyǒu Gùgōng?

6) 王 先生 说 明天 他 给 买了 飞机票。
Wáng xiānsheng shuō míngtiān tā gěi mǎile fēijīpiào.

# 21 A Chance Meeting
## 相遇 xiāngyù

(Mr. Chen runs into Wang Fang in a book store.)

| | | |
|---|---|---|
| 陈 :<br>Chén: | 小　王，小　王！①<br>Xiǎo Wáng, Xiǎo Wáng! | Xiao Wang, Xiao Wang! |
| 王 :<br>Wáng: | 哦，　是 你 啊。②　陈　太太<br>Ò，　shì nǐ　a .　Chén tàitai<br>他 们 呢？ ③<br>tāmen　ne? | Oh, it's you, Mr. Chen. Where are Mrs. Chen and the children? |

| | | |
|---|---|---|
| 陈：<br>Chén: | 他们 没来。艾琳 在家给<br>Tāmen méi lái. Àilín zài jiā gěi<br>她 妹妹 写 信；④ 莉莉、<br>tā mèimei xiě xìn; Lìli、<br>大伟 跟 朋友 一起看 电<br>Dàwěi gēn péngyou yìqǐ kàn diàn<br>影 去了。你今天 怎么 有<br>yǐng qu le . Nǐ jīntiān zěnme yǒu<br>空儿来 逛 书店？<br>kòngr lái guàng shūdiàn? | They have not come. Irene's at the hotel writing to her sister. Lily and David went to the cinema with some friends. Well, how come you've time today to browse in a book store? |
| 王：<br>Wáng: | 我 去 看 我 哥哥，他 病 了。<br>Wǒ qù kàn wǒ gēge, tā bìng le.<br>我 刚 从 他那儿来，路过<br>Wǒ gāng cóng tā nàr lái, lùguò<br>这儿，给侄子 买 几本书。⑤<br>zhèr, gěi zhízi mǎi jǐběn shū.<br>我 正 打算 晚上 到<br>Wǒ zhèng dǎsuàn wǎnshang dào<br>你那儿去，跟你 说 一下儿<br>nǐ nàr qu, gēn nǐ shuō yíxiàr<br>买 火车票 的事儿。⑥ 没<br>mǎi huǒchēpiào de shìr. Méi<br>想 到在这儿遇见 你。<br>xiǎng dào zài zhèr yù jiàn nǐ.<br>现在 跟 你 说一下儿吧。<br>Xiànzài gēn nǐ shuō yíxiàr ba. | I went to see my brother, he's ill. I just left his place and dropped by here to pick up a few books for my nephew. I was thinking of going to your hotel and talking to you about the train tickets tonight. Now that you're here, I might as well talk to you now. |
| 陈：<br>Chén: | 好。<br>Hǎo. | Sure. |
| 王：<br>Wáng: | 七号 的 快车票 没有了，<br>Qīhào de kuàichēpiào méi yǒu le,<br>六号的、八号 的还 有。<br>liùhào de、bāhào de hái yǒu.<br>你 看 怎么 办？<br>Nǐ kàn zěnme bàn? | The express train tickets for the seventh are all sold out. There are tickets for the sixth and the eighth though. What do you think we should do? |
| 陈：<br>Chén: | 七号 有 特快的 吗？<br>Qīhào yǒu tèkuài de ma? | Any special express tickets for the seventh? |

王：也 没有了。⑦
Wáng: Yě méi yǒu le.
They are sold out too.

陈：那 就买八号的吧。⑧
Chén: Nà jiù mǎi bāhào de ba.
In that case we'll get the tickets for the eighth.

王：明天 买了票，我给你打 电话。
Wáng: Míngtiān mǎile piào, wǒ gěi nǐ dǎ diànhuà.
I'll give you a call tomorrow after i get the tickets.

陈：我 明天 上午 不在家，你下午 给 我打吧。
Chén: Wǒ míngtiān shàngwǔ bú zài jiā, nǐ xiàwǔ gěi wǒ dǎ ba.
I won't be home tomorrow morning. Will you give me a call in the afternoon?

王：好。你买 什么 书 了？
Wáng: Hǎo. Nǐ mǎi shénme shū le?
Sure. What books have you got?

陈：我 刚 到，还 没 买呢。⑨ 莉莉 想 买一本《汉 英 词典》，我 想 买一些 古代 历史 方面 的书，为 今后 的 研究 工作 作 点儿 准备。
Chén: Wǒ gāng dào, hái méi mǎi ne. Lìli xiǎng mǎi yìběn "Hàn Yīng Cídiǎn", wǒ xiǎng mǎi yìxiē gǔdài lìshǐ fāngmiàn de shū, wèi jīnhòu de yánjiū gōngzuò zuò diǎnr zhǔnbèi.
Nothing yet. I just got here. Lily wants a copy of *The Chinese-English Dictionary* and I am looking for books on ancient history that would help me to prepare well for my future research work.

王：词典 和历史书 都 在 那 边儿。你 到 那边儿去 看 看。我 先 走 了。
Wáng: Cídiǎn hé lìshǐ shū dōu zài nà biānr. Nǐ dào nàbianr qù kàn kan. Wǒ xiān zǒu le.
Dictionaries and history books are over there. Why don't you walk over and have a look. I have to go now.

陈：明天 下午 我 等 你的 电话。
Chén: Míngtiān xiàwǔ wǒ děng nǐ de diànhuà.
I'll be waiting for your call tomorrow afternoon.

## • new words • 生词 • shēngcí

| | | | | |
|---|---|---|---|---|
| 1 | 相遇 | (动) | xiāngyù | to meet |
| 2 | 他们 | (代) | tāmen | they, them |
| 3 | 妹妹 | (名) | mèimei | younger sister |
| 4 | 一起 | (副、名) | yìqǐ | together, being together |
| | 跟……一起 | | gēn…yìqǐ | together with |
| 5 | 怎么 | (代) | zěnme | why, how, what |
| 6 | 空儿 | (名) | kòngr | free time, spare time |
| | 有空儿 | | yǒu kòngr | to be free, to have spare time |
| 7 | 逛 | (动) | guàng | to saunter, to go (shopping) |
| 8 | 书店 | (名) | shūdiàn | book store |
| 9 | 哥哥 | (名) | gēge | elder brother |
| 10 | 刚 | (副) | gāng | just, barely |
| 11 | 那儿 | (代) | nàr | there |
| 12 | 路过 | (动) | lùguò | to pass |
| 13 | 侄子 | (名) | zhízi | nephew |
| 14 | 打算 | (动) | dǎsuàn | to intend, to plan |
| 15 | 火车 | (名) | huǒchē | train |
| 16 | 没想到 | | méi xiǎng dào | unexpected, out of expectation |
| 17 | 遇见 | | yù jiàn | to meet, to come upon |
| 18 | 快车 | (名) | kuàichē | express train |
| 19 | 办 | (动) | bàn | to do, to handle, to carry out |
| 20 | 怎么办 | | zěnme bàn | how to do, what to do |
| 21 | 特快 | (名) | tèkuài | special express train |
| 22 | 一些 | (量) | yìxiē | some, several |
| 23 | 古代 | (名) | gǔdài | ancient times |
| 24 | 历史 | (名) | lìshǐ | history |

| | | | |
|---|---|---|---|
| 25 | 方面 | （名）fāngmiàn | aspect, side |
| 26 | 为 | （介）wèi | for |
| 27 | 今后 | （名）jīnhòu | future |
| 28 | 研究 | （动、名）yánjiū | to study, research |
| 29 | 作 | （动）zuò | to do, to work |
| 30 | 词典 | （名）cídiǎn | dictionary |

**专名　Zhuānmíng　Proper name**

| | | |
|---|---|---|
| 《汉英词典》 | Hàn Yīng Cídiǎn | *The Chinese-English Dictionary* |

## study points • 注释 • zhùshì

1　小王，小王！ (Xiǎo Wáng, Xiǎo Wáng!)

The name is often repeated in public places (to make sure it is heard)

2　是你啊。(Shì nǐ a.)

1) "是" (shí) here emphasizes a sudden realization. "你" (nǐ) must be stressed.

2) "啊" (a) indicates affirmation.

3　陈太太她们呢？ (Chén tàitai tāmen ne?)

"她们" (tāmen), when placed after a name, or a title indicates the person or persons associated with that name or title. Here it refers to Mrs. Chen and her son and daughter.

4　艾琳在家给她妹妹写信。(Àilín zài jiā gěi tā mèimei xiě xìn.)

When followed by their objects prepositions like "从" (cóng), "跟" (gēn), "在" (zài), "给" (gěi), "为" (wèi), etc., form prepositional structures. They must precede the verbs they modify when used as adverbials:

他们从美国来。(Tāmen cóng Měiguó lái.)

They came from the U.S.A.

老王跟他朋友一起去看杂技了。

(Lǎo Wáng gēn tā péngyou yìqǐ qù kàn zájì le.)

Lao Wang has gone to see the acrobatics with his friends.

他在邮局寄信。(Tā zài yóujú jì xìn.)

He is in the post-office mailing a letter.

我给我侄子买书。(Wǒ gěi wǒ zhízi mǎi shū.)

I am buying books for my nephew.

他要为今后的研究工作作点儿准备。

(Tā yào wèi jīnhòu de yánjiū gōngzuò zuò diǎnr zhǔnbèi.)

He has to make preparations for his future research.

The objects of the prepositions "在" and "从" must be nouns or phrases of place or nominals like 这儿 (zhèr) or 那儿 (nàr):

他刚从我这儿去。(Tā gāng cóng wǒ zhèr qù.)

He left my place a moment ago.

昨天晚上老李在他哥哥那儿看电影了。

(Zuótiān wǎnshang Lǎo Lǐ zài tā gēge nàr kàn diànyǐng le.)

Lao Li was at his brother's place last night watching a movie.

5 给侄子买几本书。(Gěi zhízi mǎi jǐběn shū.)

In Chinese sons and daughters of your brother are your 侄子 (zhízi) and 侄女 (zhínǚ) respectively, while sons and daughters of your sister are your 外甥 (wàisheng) and 外甥女 (wàishengnǚ).

6 跟你说一下儿买火车票的事儿。(Gēn nǐ shuō yíxiàr mǎi huǒchēpiào de shìr.)

In Chinese, the structure "verb+object" can be used attributively and the word it modifies is a noun of procedure. Here "买火车票" is attributive to "事儿". The structural particle "的" has to be placed between the structure and the noun. (See Study Point 6 of Lesson 16 and 4 of Lesson 23 )

7 也没有了。(Yě méi yǒu le.)

The Chinese adverb "也" (yě) can be used together with the negative adverb "没" (méi), "不" (bù).

8 那就买八号的吧。(Nà jiù mǎi bāhào de ba.)

"就" (jiù) here indicates that "under the circumstances or in that case, we have no other choice". In this sentence it is used to express the idea that since there are no tickets for the 6th or the 7th, then we must get tickets for the 8th.

9 还没(有)……呢。(Hái méi(yǒu)…ne.)

"还没(有)……呢" (hái méi(yǒu) …ne) indicates something that has not happened yet.

## supplementary words • 补充生词 • bǔchōng shēngcí

| | | | | |
|---|---|---|---|---|
| 1 | 同学 | （名） | tóngxué | school-mate |
| 2 | 翻译 | （动、名） | fānyì | to translate; translation |
| 3 | 洋娃娃 | （名） | yángwáwa | doll |
| 4 | 开玩笑 | | kāi wánxiào | to make jokes |
| 5 | 接 | （动） | jiē | to take, to receive |
| 6 | 出发 | （动） | chūfā | to start off |
| 7 | 照 | （动） | zhào | to take (photos) |
| 8 | 照片 | （名） | zhàopiàn | photo |
| 9 | 照相馆 | （名） | zhàoxiàngguǎn | photo studio |
| 10 | 洗（照片） | （动） | xǐ (zhàopiàn) | to develop (photos) |

## • exercises • 练习 • liànxí

*1. **Answer the following questions:**

1) Model: 你 从 哪儿来？
Nǐ cóng nǎr lái?
我 从 我 哥哥 那儿来。（我哥哥）
Wǒ cóng wǒ gēge nàr lái. （wǒ gēge）

(1) 李 先生 从 哪儿来？
Lǐ xiānsheng cóng nǎr lái?
______________。（他妹妹）
______________. （tā mèimei）

(2) 你们 两位 从 哪儿来？（张 大中 同志）
Nǐmen liǎngwèi cóng nǎr lái? （Zhāng Dàzhōng tóngzhì）
______________。
______________.

2) Model: 你 到哪儿去？
Nǐ dào nǎr qù?
我 到我弟弟那儿去。（我 弟弟）
Wǒ dào wǒ dìdi nàr qu. （wǒ dìdi）

(1) 你们 到哪儿去？
Nǐmen dào nǎr qù?

______________。（陈　伯伯）
______________.（Chén bóbo）

(2) 陈　小姐 到哪儿去了？
Chén xiǎojie dào nǎr qu le?

______________。（她　朋友）
______________.（tā péngyou）

***2. Complete the dialogues between A and B by using the prepositions:**
在 (zài), 给 (gěi), 跟 (gēn) and their objects:

1) A: 你弟弟呢？
Nǐ dìdi ne?

B: ____________。
____________.

A: 在家作什么呢？
Zài jiā zuò shénme ne?

B: ________ 写信呢。
________ xiě xìn ne.

A: ________ 写信呢？
________ xiě xìn ne?

B: 给一个同学。
Gěi yíge tóngxué.

2) 妹妹：姐姐，________ 去看话剧《茶馆》吧。
mèimei: Jiějie, ________ qù kàn huàjù "Cháguǎnr" ba.

姐姐：我不________去，我还有事儿呢。
jiějie: Wǒ bù ________ qù, wǒ hái yǒu shìr ne.

妹妹：好姐姐，去吧，我不懂的地方，你________翻译一下儿。
mèimei: Hǎo jiějie, qù ba, wǒ bù dǒng de dìfang, nǐ ________ fānyì yíxiàr.

姐姐：那你怎么谢我呢？
jiějie: Nà nǐ zěnme xiè wǒ ne?

妹妹：我________买个大洋娃娃。
mèimei: Wǒ ________ mǎi ge dà yángwáwa.

姐姐：谁________开玩笑。
jiějie: Shuí ________ kāi wánxiào.

妹妹：好，好，我请两块好糖。
mèimei: Hǎo, hǎo, wǒ qǐng liǎngkuài hǎo táng.

***3. Rearrange the following words and phrases into proper sentences:**

Model: 张 先生，来，从，英国
Zhāng xiānsheng, lái, cóng, Yīngguó
张 先生 从 英国 来。
Zhāng xiānsheng cóng Yīngguó lái.

1) 他们，来，从，日本
tāmen, lái, cóng, Rìběn

2) 哪儿，你，到，去
nǎr, nǐ, dào, qu

3) 他，打球，去，一起，跟，同学
tā, dǎ qiú, qu, yìqǐ, gēn, tóngxué

4) 老刘，要，说，一件，事儿，跟，小陈
Lǎo Liú, yào, shuō, yíjiàn, shìr, gēn, Xiǎo Chén

5) 我，介绍，一下儿，你们，给
wǒ, jièshào, yíxiàr, nǐmen, gěi

***4. Complete the following sentences:**

1) Model: 我正打算去找你，没想到在这儿遇见了你。（遇见）
Wǒ zhèng dǎsuàn qù zhǎo nǐ, méi xiǎng dào zài zhèr yù jiànle nǐ.（yù jiàn）

(1) 我正打算下午去看你，__________。（看我）
Wǒ zhèng dǎsuàn xiàwǔ qù kàn nǐ, __________. (kàn wǒ)

(2) __________，没想到你给我送来了。（取票）
__________, méi xiǎng dào nǐ gěi wǒ sòng lai le. (qǔ piào)

(3) 我正打算给你借那本杂志看看，__________
Wǒ zhèng dǎsuàn gěi nǐ jiè nàběn zázhì kànkan, __________
__________。（买来）
__________.（mǎi lai）

2) Model: A: 七号、八号的飞机票都没有了，你看怎么办？
Qīhào、bāhào de fēijīpiào dōu méiyǒu le, nǐ kàn zěnme bàn?
B: 那就买九号的吧。（九号）
Nà jiù mǎi jiǔhào de ba.（jiǔhào）

(1) A: 两点半、四点一刻的电影票都没有了，你看怎么办？
Liǎngdiǎnbàn、sìdiǎn yíkè de diànyǐngpiào dōu méiyǒu le, nǐ kàn zěnme bàn?

B: 那 就_______________。（六点 五十）
Nà jiù_______________.（liùdiǎn wǔshí）

(2) A: 旅游局的 电话 占线，没 人接，
Lǚyóujú de diànhuà zhànxiàn, méi rén jiē,
你说 怎么办？
nǐ shuō zěnme bàn?

B: 那 就_______________。（ 等 ）
Nà jiù_______________.（děng）

(3) A: 天气 预报 说 有雨，明天 不能 去 长城 了，
Tiānqi yùbào shuō yǒu yǔ, míngtiān bù néng qù Chángchéng le,
你看 怎么办？
nǐ kàn zěnme bàn?

B: 那 就_______________。（以后）
Nà jiù_______________.（yǐhòu）

5. **Listen to the dialogue:**

王 芳：喂，陈 先生 吗？我是王芳。火车票 我给您 买了，八号的 快车，302次。到 西安 去的 快车 每天 有 三次，这 一次 时间 最好，早晨 九点 从 北京 出发，第二天 五点 多 到 西安。您 看 怎么样？
Wáng Fāng: Wèi, Chén xiānsheng ma? Wǒ shì Wáng Fāng. Huǒchē piào wǒ gěi nín mǎi le, bāhào de kuàichē, sānlíng'èrcì. Dào Xī'ān qù de kuàichē měitiān yǒu sāncì, zhè yícì shíjiān zuì hǎo, zǎochén jiǔdiǎn cóng Běijīng chūfā, dì'èr tiān wǔdiǎn duō dào Xī'ān. Nín kàn zěnmeyàng?

陈：很 好啊，就 这样 吧。
Chén: Hěn hǎo a, jiù zhèyàng ba.

王：那我 晚上 就给您 送 去。
Wáng: Nà wǒ wǎnshang jiù gěi nín sòng qu.

陈：太 麻烦 你了。
Chén: Tài máfan nǐ le.

王：您 不要 跟我这么 客气。还有别的事儿吗？
Wáng: Nín bú yào gēn wǒ zhème kèqi. Hái yǒu biéde shìr ma?

陈：还 有点儿 小事儿。
Chén: Hái yǒu diǎnr xiǎo shìr.

王：您 说 吧，什么事儿？
Wáng: Nín shuō ba, shénme shìr?

陈：你跟我们一起在长城照的照片不是送照相馆去洗了吗？等照片得了，麻烦你给我寄去。到西安以后，我马上就给你写信。
Chén: Nǐ gēn wǒmen yìqǐ zài Chángchéng zhào de zhàopiàn bú shì sòng zhàoxiàngguǎn qù xǐ le ma? Děng zhàopiàn dé le, máfan nǐ gěi wǒ jì qu. Dào Xī'ān yǐhòu, wǒ mǎshàng jiù gěi nǐ xiě xìn.

王：好，您的信到了，我就给您寄去。
Wáng: Hǎo, nín de xìn dàole, wǒ jiù gěi nín jì qu.

***6. Translate the following sentences into Chinese:**

1) Where are you from?
2) I am going to Britain.
3) Mr. Wang has bought some books for the children.
4) Will you give me a ring this afternoon?
5) What did he tell you about?
6) Mr. Zhao asked Lao Liu to go to the Fragrant Hills with them.

# 22 We Went To The Great Wall
# 我们游览长城去了
# wǒmen yóulǎn Chángchéng qu le

(Lily has a conversation with Liu, an attendant at the hotel while waiting for the elevator.)

| | | |
|---|---|---|
| 莉: | 下 去吗？① | Going down? |
| Lì: | Xià qu ma? | |
| 服: | 对 不起，现 在 电梯 往 | Sorry, it's going up. |
| fú: | Duì bu qǐ, xiànzài diàntī wǎng | Please wait a moment. |
| | 上 ，请 等 一会儿， | It'll be down in a mi- |
| | shàng, qǐng děng yíhuìr , | nute. |

| | | |
|---|---|---|
| | 马上 就 下 来。<br>mǎshàng jiù xià lai. | |
| 刘：<br>Liú： | 莉莉 小姐，我 正 要 找<br>Lìli xiǎojie, wǒ zhèng yào zhǎo<br>你去，你 上 哪儿？<br>nǐ qu, nǐ shàng nǎr ? | Miss Chen, I was looking for you. Are you going somewhere? |
| 莉：<br>Lì: | 我 上 邮局 寄 包裹 去。<br>Wǒ shàng yóujú jì bāoguǒ qu.<br>有 什么 事儿？<br>Yǒu shénme shìr ? | I'm going to the post office to send this parcel. What is it? |
| 刘：<br>Liú: | 上午 十点半，有 一个<br>Shàngwǔ shídiǎnbàn, yǒu yíge<br>人 来 找 你。她 给 你<br>rén lái zhǎo nǐ. Tā gěi nǐ<br>送 来了 这 两本 杂志，<br>sòng lai le zhè liǎngběn zázhì,<br>你 不在。<br>nǐ bú zài. | A lady came and asked for you at 10:30 this morning. You were out. She left these two magazines for you. |
| 莉：<br>Lì: | 谢谢 你，小 刘。她 说<br>Xièxie nǐ, Xiǎo Liú. Tā shuō<br>什么 了 没有？<br>shénme le méiyǒu? | Thank you, Xiao Liu. Did she say anything? |
| 刘：<br>Liú: | 没有。她 给 你 留了 个<br>Méiyǒu. Tā gěi nǐ liúle ge<br>电话 号码儿。<br>diànhuà hàomǎr. | No, but she left you her phone number. |
| 莉：<br>Lì: | 好，一会儿 我 给 她 打 个<br>Hǎo, yíhuìr wǒ gěi tā dǎ ge<br>电话。上午 我们 游览<br>diànhuà. Shàngwǔ wǒmen yóulǎn<br>长城 去 了。<br>Chángchéng qu le. | All right. I'll give her a call later. We went to the Great Wall this morning. |
| 刘：<br>Liú: | 怎么样？<br>Zěnmeyàng? | How did you find it? |
| 莉：<br>Lì: | 好 极 了！② 太 雄伟 了！<br>Hǎo jí le! Tài xióngwěi le!<br>真 是 百闻 不如 一见<br>Zhēn shì bǎi wén bùrú yí jiàn | Simply wonderful! Just magnificent. Seeing is believing. Imagine it was built by the Chinese |

| | | |
|---|---|---|
| | 啊！③ 两千 多 年 以<br>a ! Liǎngqiān duō nián yǐ<br>前， 中国 人民 就有<br>qián, Zhōngguó rénmín jiù yǒu<br>这样 伟大的 创造，④<br>zhèyàng wěidà de chuàngzào,<br>实在 了不起！<br>shízài liǎobuqǐ ! | people more than two thousand years ago Amazing! |
| 刘：<br>Liú: | 你们 都 爬 上 去 了吗？⑤<br>Nǐmen dōu pá shang qu le ma? | Did you all make it to the top? |
| 莉：<br>Lì: | 都 爬 上 去 了。爸爸 说<br>Dōu pá shang qu le . Bàba shuō<br>不 到 长城 非 好汉。⑥<br>bú dào Chángchéng fēi hǎohàn.<br>刘 小姐，明天 下午<br>Liú xiǎojie, míngtiān xiàwǔ<br>我们 就要 走 了。感谢<br>wǒmen jiù yào zǒu le . Gǎnxiè<br>你 半个 月 来 对 我们<br>nǐ bànge yuè lái duì wǒmen<br>的 帮助。⑦<br>de bāngzhù. | Yes, we did. Dad said you could not call yourself a true man if you had not visited the Great Wall. Miss Liu, we are leaving tomorrow afternoon. Thank you for all your help during the past two weeks. |
| 刘：<br>Liú: | 别 客气。⑧ 这 是 我 应<br>Bié kèqi . Zhè shì wǒ yīng<br>该 做的。 欢迎 你们 以<br>gāi zuò de. Huānyíng nǐmen yǐ<br>后 再来。<br>hòu zài lái. | Don't mention it. I only did my job. Hope you'll come back again sometime. |
| 莉：<br>Lì: | 十天 以后 我们 还 回 这儿<br>Shítiān yǐhòu wǒmen hái huí zhèr<br>来。<br>lai . | We'll be back in ten days. |
| 刘：<br>Liú: | 你们 不是 回 美国 去吗？<br>Nǐmen bú shì huí Měiguó qu ma? | Aren't you going back to the States? |
| 莉：<br>Lì: | 不，我们 到 西安 去，还<br>Bù, wǒmen dào Xī'ān qu, hái<br>要 回 来的。<br>yào huí lai de. | Not yet. We'll come back after visiting Xian. |

| | | | |
|---|---|---|---|
| 刘： | 欢迎 你们，祝 你们旅途 愉快！⑨ | | You're always welcome here. Wish you a pleasant trip. |
| Liú: | Huānyíng nǐmen, zhù nǐmen lǚtú yúkuài! | | |
| 莉： | 谢谢。 | | Thank you. |
| Lì: | Xièxie. | | |
| 刘： | 电梯 下 来 了。 | | The elevator's here. |
| Liú: | Diàntī xià lai le. | | |
| 服： | 下 去 吗？ 请 进 来。 | | Going down? Please come in. |
| fú: | Xià qu ma? Qǐng jìn lai. | | |
| 刘： | 进 去吧。 | | Please. |
| Liú: | Jìn qu ba. | | |
| 莉： | 再 见！ | | Good-bye. |
| Lì: | Zàijiàn! | | |

## • new words • 生词 • shēngcí

| | | | | |
|---|---|---|---|---|
| 1 | 下去 | | xià qu | to go down |
| 2 | 电梯 | （名） | diàntī | lift, elevator |
| 3 | 往 | （动） | wǎng | to go |
| 4 | 下来 | | xià lai | to come down |
| 5 | 包裹 | （名） | bāoguǒ | parcel |
| 6 | 留 | （动） | liú | to leave behind |
| 7 | 号码儿 | （名） | hàomǎr | number |
| 8 | 极 | （形、副、名） | jí | utmost, extremely, pole |
| | 好极了 | | hǎo jí le | extremely good, wonderful |
| 9 | 雄伟 | （形） | xióngwěi | magnificent |
| 10 | 百闻不如一见 | | bǎi wén bùrú yí jiàn | Seeing is believing. (Hearing a hundred times is not as good as seeing once.) |

| | | | | |
|---|---|---|---|---|
| 11 | 人民 | （名） | rénmín | people |
| 12 | 伟大 | （形） | wěidà | great |
| 13 | 创造 | （名、动） | chuàngzào | creation, to create |
| 14 | 上去 | | shàng qu | to go up |
| 15 | 了不起 | （形） | liǎobuqǐ | great (in praise of...) |
| 16 | 爬 | （动） | pá | to climb, to crawl |
| 17 | 不到长城非好汉 | | bú dào Cháng chéng fēi hǎohàn | We are no true heroes if we do not reach the Great Wall. |
| 18 | 感谢 | （动） | gǎnxiè | to thank |
| 19 | ……来 | （名） | ...lái | since |
| 20 | 对 | （介） | duì | for |
| 21 | 帮助 | （动、名） | bāngzhù | to help, help |
| 22 | 别 | （副） | bié | do not |
| 23 | 客气 | （形） | kèqi | polite, courteous |
| | 别客气 | | bié kèqi | Please feel at home. Do not stand on ceremony. |
| 24 | 应该 | （助动） | yīnggāi | should, ought to |
| 25 | 做 | （动） | zuò | to do, to make |
| 26 | 旅途 | （名） | lǚtú | journey, trip |
| 27 | 愉快 | （形） | yúkuài | happy, enjoyable |
| 28 | 进去 | | jìn qu | to go in, to enter |

## study points • 注释 • zhùshì

1 下去吗？(Xià qu ma?)

"来"(lái) and "去"(qù), besides being full verbs, also function as direction indicators in which case they are placed after the verb. The general pattern is:

For intransitive verbs:

他们上来了。(Tāmen shàng lai le.)

They have come up.

你下去吗?(Nǐ xià qu ma?)

Are you going down?

For transitive verbs:

十天以后我们还回这儿来。(Shítiān yǐhòu wǒmen hái huí zhèr lai.)

We will be back in ten days.

他带了一本词典去。(Tā dàile yìběn cídiǎn qu.)

He took one dictionary with him.

A variation of the general pattern is also possible by placing the object at the end of the sentence. It is, therefore, common to use the following pattern to express past time: Subject＋verb＋来 (or 去)＋了＋object.

你朋友给你送来了两本杂志。(Nǐ péngyou gěi nǐ sòng lai le liǎngběn zázhì.)

Your friend left two magazines for you.

我已经寄去了三封信。(Wǒ yǐjīng jì qu le sānfēng xìn.)

I have sent three letters.

他们已送来了你的行李。(Tāmen yǐ sòng lai le nǐ de xíngli.)

They have sent your luggage here.

2 好极了。(Hǎo jí le.)

An adjective＋极了(jí le) indicates a very high degree, such as "冷极了" (lěng jí le), "累极了" (lèi jí le).

3 真是百闻不如一见。(Zhēn shì bǎi wén bùrú yí jiàn.)

This is a Chinese idiom equivalent to "Seeing is believing".

4 两千多年以前，中国人民就有这样伟大的创造。

(Liǎngqiān duō nián yǐqián, Zhōngguó rénmín jiù yǒu zhèyàng wěidà de chuàngzào.)

"就" here emphasizes that something happened such a long time ago.

5 你们都爬上去了吗? (Nǐmen dōu pá shang qu le ma?)

"上来" (shàng lai), "上去" (shàng qu), "下来" (xià lai), "下去" (xià qu), "进来" (jìn lai), "进去" (jìn qu), "出来" (chū lai), "出去" (chū qu), "回来" (huí lai), "回去" (huí qu), "过来" (guò lai), "过去" (guò qu), "起来" (qǐ lai) —— all these 13 expressions can be placed after other verbs to show the direction of an action:

他们都爬上来了。(Tāmen dōu pá shang lai le.)

They have all climbed up.

我们走回去吧。(Wǒmen zǒu hui qu ba.)

Let us go back on foot.

Here the function of "来" and "去" is the same as Study Point 1 of this lesson.

6 不到长城非好汉。(Bú dào Chángchéng fēi hǎohàn.)
See Mao Zedong's (毛泽东) poem *Mount Liupan.*

7 感谢你半个月来对我们的帮助。
(Gǎnxiè nǐ bànge yuè lái duì wǒmen de bāngzhù.)
"来" (lái) or "以来" (yǐlái) indicates a period of time from the past till the present.

一个星期来 (yíge xīngqī lái)
for the last week
四十年来 (sìshí nián lái)
for the last forty years

8 别客气 (bié kèqi)
You can either say "别客气" (bié kèqi) or "不客气" (bú kèqi) in response to the gratitude expressed by somebody.

9 祝你们旅途愉快。(Zhù nǐmen lǚtú yúkuài.)
This expression is equivalent to "Wish you a pleasant journey" in English.

## supplementary words • 补充生词 • bǔchōng shēngcí

| | | | | |
|---|---|---|---|---|
| 1 | 长途 | (名) | chángtú | long distance |
| 2 | 拿 | (动) | ná | to bring |
| 3 | 台 | (名) | tái | station |
| 4 | 口 | (量) | kǒu | a measure word |
| 5 | 儿媳妇 | (名) | érxífu | daughter-in-Law (son's wife) |
| 6 | 托儿所 | (名) | tuō'érsuǒ | nursery |
| 7 | 工资 | (名) | gōngzī | wage, pay |
| 8 | 退休金 | (名) | tuìxiūjīn | retire pension |
| 9 | 够用 | | gòu yòng | enough (for a purpose) |
| 10 | 房租 | (名) | fángzū | rent |
| 11 | 水电费 | (名) | shuǐdiànfèi | payment for water and electricity |
| 12 | 托儿费 | (名) | tuō'érfèi | payment for child care |

13 统筹医疗费 tǒngchóu yīliáofèi payment for co-operative medical care

14 大人 （名）dàren grown-up

15 公费医疗 gōngfèi yīliáo free medical care

王大娘 Wáng dàniáng Auntie Wang

## • exercises • 练习 • liànxí

*1. **Practise the following questions after the model:**

Model: 你 上 哪儿？
Nǐ shàng nǎr？
我 上 邮局 取 包裹 去。（取 包裹）
Wǒ shàng yóujú qǔ bāoguǒ qu.（qǔ bāoguǒ）

1) 你 上 哪儿？
Nǐ shàng nǎr？
____________。（打 长途 电话）
____________.（dǎ chángtú diànhuà）

2) 你 上 哪儿 去？
Nǐ shàng nǎr qu？
____________。（兑换 外币）
____________.（duìhuàn wàibì）

3) 你 干 什么 去？
Nǐ gàn shénme qu？
____________。（找 小 陈）
____________.（zhǎo Xiǎo Chén）

4) 你们 干 什么 去 了？
Nǐmen gàn shénme qu le？
____________。（到 故宫）
____________.（dào Gùgōng）

5) 他 到 这儿 干 什么 来 了？
Tā dào zhèr gàn shénme lai le？
____________。（给 赵 先生 送 书）
____________.（gěi Zhào xiānsheng sòng shū）

6) 小 王 打算 晚上 到老刘那儿干什么去?
Xiǎo Wáng dǎsuàn wǎnshang dào Lǎo Liú nàr gàn shénme qu?
__________________。(送 火车票)
__________________. (sòng huǒchēpiào)

**∗2. Complete the sentences in accordance with the contents of the pictures**

1) 她__________了。
Tā__________le.

2) 他们 爬__________了。
Tāmen pá__________le.

3) 大伟__________了。
Dàwěi__________le.

4) 请__________吧。
Qǐng__________ba.

***3. Rearrange the following words and phrases into proper sentences:**

1) 他们，回，去，不，英国，现在
tāmen, huí, qù, bù, Yīngguó, xiànzài

2) 老刘，要，上，去，楼
Lǎo Liú, yào, shàng, qù, lóu

3) 请，进，来，屋，吧
qǐng, jìn, lái, wū, ba

4) 莉莉，拿，来，茶，呀
Lìli, ná, lái, chá, ya

5) 张 先生，送，一本，《汉 英 词 典》，
Zhāng xiānsheng, sòng, yìběn, "Hàn Yīng Cídiǎn",
来，了，上午
lái, le, shàngwǔ

***4. Complete the dialogues:**

1) Model: A: 电梯下去吗？
Diàntī xià qu ma?
B: 对不起，请等一会儿。
Duì bu qǐ, qǐng děng yíhuìr.

(1) A: 可以进来吗？
Kěyǐ jìn lai ma?
B: ______，请等一会儿。
______, qǐng děng yíhuìr.

(2) A: 喂，长途台吗？我要美国。
Wèi, chángtútái ma? Wǒ yào Měiguó.
B: 对不起，__________。
Duì bu qǐ, __________.

(3) A: 现在能给我看病吗？
Xiànzài néng gěi wǒ kàn bìng ma?
B: 人多，__________，__________。
Rén duō, __________, __________.

2) Model: A: 怎么样？ 长城 好玩儿吗？
Zěnmeyàng? Chángchéng hǎowánr ma?
B: 好玩儿极了。
Hǎowánr jí le.

(1) A: ______？那儿的风景美吗？
______? Nàr de fēngjǐng měi ma?

B: ________ 极 了。
________ jí le .

(2) A: ________? 那 地方 的 天气 热 吗?
________? Nà dìfang de tiānqì rè ma?

B: ________ 极 了。
________ jí le .

(3) A: ________? 颐和园 人 多吗?
________? Yíhéyuán rén duō ma?

B: ________ 极 了。
________ jí le .

***5. Practice the following sentences after the model:**

Model: A: 感 谢 你 对 我们 的 帮 助。
Gǎnxiè nǐ duì wǒmen de bāngzhù.

B: 别 客气。这 是 我 应 该 做 的。
Bié kèqi . Zhè shì wǒ yīnggāi zuò de.

1) A: 太 感谢 你们 了。
Tài gǎnxiè nǐmen le .

B: ________。这 是 我 应 该 做 的。
________. Zhè shì wǒ yīnggāi zuò de.

2) A: 您 对 我们 太 好 了。
Nín duì wǒmen tài hǎo le .

B: 客气 什么。________。
Kèqi shénme. ________.

3) A: 您 对 我 的 帮 助 这么 大, 怎么 感谢 您 好 呢?
Nín duì wǒ de bāngzhù zhème dà, zěnme gǎnxiè nín hǎo ne?

B: 说 这个 干 什么。________。
Shuō zhège gàn shénme. ________.

**6 . Listen to the dialogue:**

王 大娘: 请 进 来 吧。
Wáng dàniáng: Qǐng jìn lai ba.

艾琳: 谢 谢 您。您 家 几 口 人?
Àilín : Xièxie nín. Nín jiā jǐkǒu rén ?

王 : 五 口 。这 不, 都 在 这 上边 呢!
Wáng: Wǔkǒu. Zhè bù, dōu zài zhè shàngbianr ne!

艾: 啊 , 这 是 您 全 家 的 照 片 , 我 看 看。
Ài: À , zhè shì nín quán jiā de zhàopiàn, wǒ kànkan.

王 : 这 是 儿子、儿 媳 妇 , 这 是 我 女 儿 。
Wáng: Zhè shì érzi 、érxífu , zhè shì wǒ nǚ'ér .

艾：女儿 也 跟 你们 一起住？
Ài: Nǚ'ér yě gēn nǐmen yìqǐ zhù?
王：是 啊。
Wáng: Shì a.
艾：您 这 小 孙子 哪儿去 了？
Ài: Nín zhè xiǎo sūnzi nǎr qù le?
王：送 托儿所 了。早晨 送 去，晚上 接 回 来。
Wáng: Sòng tuō'érsuǒ le. Zǎochén sòng qu, wǎnshàng jiē hui lai.
艾：您 一家 每个 月 收入 多 少？有 二百 多吧？
Ài: Nín yìjiā měige yuè shōurù duōshao? Yǒu èrbǎi duō ba?
王：是 啊，他们 三个 人 的 工资 和 我 的 退休金 一共 二百 三十块。
Wáng: Shì a, tāmen sānge rén de gōngzī hé wǒ de tuì xiūjīn yígòng èrbǎi sānshíkuài.
艾：五口 人，二百 多 块 够 用 吗？
Ài: Wǔkǒu rén, èrbǎi duō kuài gòu yòng ma?
王：够 啊。你 看，房租、水电费 八块，吃 饭 每 人 二十块，托儿费 三块 五，小 孙子 统筹 医疗费 六毛，四个 大人 看 病 有 公费 医疗。
Wáng: Gòu a. Nǐ kàn, fángzū、shuǐdiànfèi bākuài, chī fàn měi rén èrshíkuài, tuō'érfèi sānkuài wǔ, xiǎo sūnzi tǒng chóu yīliáofèi liùmáo, sìge dàrén kàn bìng yǒu gōngfèi yīliáo.
艾：是 啊，够 用 啊。
Ài: Shì a, gòu yòng a.

*7. **Translate the following phrases into English:**

1) 上 来 shàng lai
2) 上 去 shàng qu
3) 下 来 xià lai
4) 下 去 xià qu
5) 进 来 jìn lai
6) 进 去 jìn qu
7) 出 来 chū lai
8) 出 去 chū qu
9) 回 来 huí lai
10) 回 去 huí qu

# 23 Invitation To A Dinner
## 宴请 yànqǐng

(Mr. and Mrs. Li Wenhan invite the Chens to a Beijing Duck dinner at Quan Ju De.)

| | | |
|---|---|---|
| 李：<br>Lǐ: | 来，① 大家都 请吧，别<br>Lái, dàjiā dōu qǐng ba, bié<br>客气。<br>kèqi . | Come, help yourselves and don't stand on ceremony. |
| 丁：<br>Dīng: | 陈 先生 ，在 美国<br>Chén xiānsheng, zài Měiguó | Mr. Chen, do you use chopsticks in the United |

| | | |
|---|---|---|
| | 用　筷子吃饭吗？② <br> yòng kuàizi chī fàn ma? | States? |
| 陈　： <br> Chén: | 不　经常　用，不太熟练　了。 <br> Bù jīngcháng yòng, bú tài shú liàn le. | Not very often, so I'm out of practice. |
| 丁　： <br> Dīng: | 陈　太太，怎么样？你能　用　筷子吃饭吗？ <br> Chén tàitai, zěnmeyàng? Nǐ néng yòng kuàizi chī fàn ma? | How about you, Mrs. Chen? Can you use chopsticks? |
| 艾： <br> Ài: | 不行，我还得用　刀子、叉子　吃。 <br> Bù xíng, wǒ hái děi yòng dāo zi、chāzi chī. | No, I can't. I'll have to use knife and fork. |
| 李： <br> Lǐ: | 用　西方　的刀子、叉子吃　中国　饭，这也可以　说　是　一种　中　西结合吧。 <br> Yòng Xīfāng de dāozi、chāzi chī Zhōngguó fàn, zhè yě kěyǐ shuō shì yìzhǒng Zhōng Xī jiéhé ba. | To use knife and fork for a Chinese meal can be considered as a happy combination of the East and West, right? |
| 莉： <br> Lì: | 这儿的烤鸭　味道　确实好，真　是　名　不虚传　。③ <br> Zhèr de kǎoyā wèidao quèshí hǎo, zhēn shì míng bù xū chuán. | The duck here is really delicious. It deserves the reputation it enjoys. |
| 艾： <br> Ài: | 听　说　全聚德　烤鸭店已经　有一百　多　年　的历史了，不　知道　确实不　确实。 <br> Tīng shuō Quánjùdé Kǎoyādiàn yǐjīng yǒu yìbǎi duō nián de lìshǐ le, bù zhīdao quèshí bu quèshí. | I've been told Quan Ju De has a history of over a hundred years, is that true? |
| 李： <br> Lǐ: | 是，有一百　多　年　了。来北京　游览的外国　朋友 <br> Shì, yǒu yìbǎi duō nián le. Lái Běijīng yóulǎn de wàiguō péngyou | Yes, its' over a hundred years old now. Foreign friends visiting Beijing invariably come here to |

| | | |
|---|---|---|
| | 都 喜欢 到这儿来 尝<br>dōu xǐhuan dào zhèr lai cháng<br>尝 北京 烤鸭。④<br>chang Běijīng kǎoyā. | taste the Beijing duck. |
| 伟：<br>Wěi: | 爸爸，为什么 叫 全<br>Bàba, wèi shénme jiào Quán-<br>聚德？<br>jùdé? | Dad, why is the restaurant called Quan Ju De? |
| 莉：<br>Lì: | 是 啊，全聚德 是 什么<br>Shì a, Quánjùdé shì shénme<br>意思？<br>yìsi? | Yes, what does the name mean? |
| 陈 ：<br>Chén: | 意思 是 美德之家。<br>Yìsi shì měidé zhī jiā. | Well, it means the home of the virtuous. |
| 丁 ：<br>Dīng: | 来，来，来，别 净 说<br>Lái, lái, lái, bié jìng shuō<br>话，大家 一边 吃 一边 说。<br>huà, dàjiā yìbiān chī yìbiān shuō. | Come, don't just talk, we'll chat over the food. |
| 李：<br>Lǐ: | 今天 老 朋友 相会，是<br>Jīntiān lǎo péngyou xiānghuì, shì<br>很 值得 高兴 的事儿。来，<br>hěn zhíde gāoxìng de shìr. Lái,<br>为 陈 先生 一家的<br>wèi Chén xiānsheng yìjiā de<br>健康 干杯！⑤<br>jiànkāng gān bēi! | Reunion of old friends is something to be celebrated. Come, let's drink to the health of the Chens! |
| 陈 ：<br>Chén: | 酒 逢知己 千杯 少。⑥<br>Jiǔ féng zhījǐ qiānbēi shǎo.<br>今天 能 有机会 回 来<br>Jīntiān néng yǒu jīhui huí lai<br>参观 访问，确实 是<br>cānguān fǎngwèn, quèshí shì<br>一件 值得 高兴 的 事儿。<br>yíjiàn zhíde gāoxìng de shìr.<br>来，我敬 老 李，老 丁<br>Lái, wǒ jìng Lǎo Lǐ, Lǎo Dīng<br>一杯！<br>yìbēi! | Even a thousand cups aren't enough when good friends meet. To be able to come back for a visit after so many years is really something to be happy about. Come, Lao Li and Lao Ding, drink a toast. |

| | | |
|---|---|---|
| 丁：<br>Dīng: | 为 陈 先生 一家 旅游<br>Wèi Chén xiānsheng yìjiā lǚyóu<br>愉快 干一杯！<br>yúkuài gān yìbēi! | Let's drink to the pleasant trip of the Chen family! |
| 艾：<br>Ài: | 为 我们 两家 的 友谊<br>Wèi wǒmen liǎngjiā de yǒuyì<br>干 杯！<br>gān bēi! | Drink to the friendship of our two families. |

## • new words • 生词 • shēngcí

| | | | |
|---|---|---|---|
| 1 | 宴请 | （动）yànqǐng | to host a dinner party, to give a banquet |
| 2 | 用 | （动）yòng | to use |
| 3 | 筷子 | （名）kuàizi | chopsticks |
| 4 | 经常 | （形）jīngcháng | often |
| 5 | 熟练 | （形）shúliàn | skilled, skillful |
| 6 | 得 | （助动、动）děi | must, should, to have to, to need |
| 7 | 刀子 | （名）dāozi | knife |
| 8 | 叉子 | （名）chāzi | fork |
| 9 | 结合 | （动、名）jiéhé | to combine, combination |
| | 中西结合 | Zhōng Xī jiéhé | combination of things Chinese and Western |
| 10 | 烤 | （动）kǎo | to roast |
| 11 | 鸭（子） | （名）yā(zi) | duck |
| | 烤鸭 | （名）kǎoyā | roast duck |
| 12 | 味道 | （名）wèidào | taste, flavor |
| 13 | 确实 | （形）quèshí | really, truly |
| 14 | 名不虚传 | míng bù xū chuán | to live up to its name |

| | | | | |
|---|---|---|---|---|
| 15 | 知道 | （动） | zhīdao | to know |
| 16 | 喜欢 | （动） | xǐhuan | to like |
| 17 | 尝 | （动） | cháng | to taste, to sample |
| 18 | 意思 | （名） | yìsi | meaning |
| | ……是什么意思 | | ···shì shénme yìsi | what is the meaning |
| 19 | 美德之家 | | měidé zhī jiā | home of the virtuous |
| 20 | 净 | （副） | jìng | only |
| 21 | 说话 | | shuō huà | to talk |
| 22 | 大家 | （代） | dàjiā | everybody, all |
| 23 | 一边……一边…… | | yìbiān···yìbiān··· | at the same time, ···while··· |
| 24 | 相会 | （动） | xiānghuì | to meet, to come together |
| 25 | 值得 | （动） | zhíde | to be worth |
| 26 | 高兴 | （形） | gāoxìng | happy |
| 27 | 一家 | （名） | yìjiā | family |
| | 陈明山一家 | | Chén Míngshān yìjiā | the Chens |
| 28 | 健康 | （名、形） | jiànkāng | health, healthy |
| 29 | 干杯 | | gān bēi | bottoms up, cheers |
| | 为……干杯 | | wèi···gān bēi | to drink to |
| 30 | 酒逢知己千杯少 | | jiǔ féng zhījǐ qiānbēi shǎo | Even a thousand cups are not enough when good friends meet |
| 31 | 机会 | （名） | jīhuì | opportunity |
| 32 | 访问 | （动、名） | fǎngwèn | to visit, visit |
| 33 | 敬 | （动） | jìng | to toast; to respect |
| 34 | 杯 | （量） | bēi | cup, glass |
| | 敬……一杯 | | jìng···yìbēi | to propose a toast to, to drink to |
| 35 | 旅游 | （动） | lǚyóu | to visit as a tourist |
| 36 | 友谊 | （名） | yǒuyì | friendship |

| 专名 | Zhuānmíng | Proper names |
|---|---|---|
| 全聚德烤鸭店 | Quánjùdé Kǎoyā Diàn | Quan Ju De Roast Duck Restaurant (the best-known Beijing Duck restaurant in Beijing) |
| 西方 | Xīfāng | the West |

## study points • 注释 • zhùshì

1 来，大家都请吧。(Lái, dàjiā dōu qǐng ba.)
"来" (lái) here introduces a suggestion to do something.

2 陈先生，在美国用筷子吃饭吗？(Chén xiānsheng, zài Měiguó yòng kuàizi chī fàn ma?)
The Chinese structure "verb+object" can be used as an adverb to describe how the action is carried out:

他用刀子、叉子吃饭。(Tā yòng dāozi、chāzi chī fàn.)
He eats with knife and fork.
我用钢笔写信。(Wǒ yòng gāngbǐ xiě xìn.)
I write my letters with a pen.
他们坐汽车去故宫参观。(Tāmen zuò qìchē qù Gùgōng cānguān.)
They are going to the Palace Museum by bus.

3 真是名不虚传。(Zhēn shì míng bù xū chuán.)
This is a Chinese idiom to describe a very famous person or thing that has lived up to his or its fame.

4 来北京游览的外国朋友都喜欢到这儿来尝尝北京烤鸭。(Lái Běijīng yóulǎn de wài guó péngyou dōu xǐhuan dào zhèr lai chángchang Běijīng kǎoyā.)
This is another example of using the verbal structure attributively. "的" which is placed between the attributive and the noun it modifies shows the function of the structure as an attributive.

每天去长城游览的人很多。(Měi tiān qù Chángchéng yóulǎn de rén hěn duō.)
Each day, lots of people go and tour the Great Wall.

5 为陈先生一家的健康干杯。(Wèi Chén xiānsheng yìjiā de jiànkāng gān bēi.)
It is the Chinese custom to give toasts throughout a feast.

6 酒逢知己千杯少。(Jiǔ féng zhījǐ qiānbēi shǎo.)

This is a Chinese idiom, meaning that when good friends meet, no amount of wine is enough for the happy occasion.

## supplementary words • 补充生词 • bǔchōng shēngcí

| | | | | |
|---|---|---|---|---|
| 1 | 汉语 | (名) | Hànyǔ | Chinese |
| 2 | 地铁 | (名) | dìtiě | underground railway, subway |
| 3 | 女士 | (名) | nǚshì | lady |
| 4 | 自己 | (代) | zìjǐ | self |
| 5 | 生活 | (动、名) | shēnghuó | to live, life |
| 6 | 幸福 | (形、名) | xìngfú | happy |
| 7 | 夹 | (动) | jiā | to pick up |
| 8 | 不如 | (动) | bùrú | not as good as, not as well as |
| 9 | 方便 | (形) | fāngbiàn | convenient |
| 10 | 容易 | (形) | róngyì | easy |
| 11 | 西餐 | (名) | xīcān | western food |
| 12 | 端 | (动) | duān | to take, to hold |
| 13 | 刬 | (动) | chǎn | to lift |
| 14 | 扒 | (动) | pá | to gather up, to rake up |
| | 唐人街 | | Tángrénjiē | China town |

## • exercises • 练习 • liànxí

*1. **Questions and answers:**

1) Model: A: 中国人　用　什么　吃饭？

Zhōngguórén yòng shénme chī fàn?

B: 中国人　用　筷子吃饭。（筷子）

Zhōngguórén yòng kuàizi chī fàn. (kuàizi)

(1) A: 西方人　用　什么　吃饭？

Xīfāngrén yòng shénme chī fàn?

B: ________________。（刀子，叉子）
________________.（dāozi，chāzi）

(2) A: 电报纸 用 什么 笔 写？
Diànbàozhǐ yòng shénme bǐ xiě？
B: ________________。（钢笔）
________________.（gāngbǐ）

(3) A: 你们 两个 用 英语谈话 还是 用 汉语 谈话？
Nǐmen liǎngge yòng Yīngyǔ tán huà háiski yòng Hànyǔ tàn huà？
B: ________________________。（汉语）
________________________.（Hànyǔ）

2) Questions and answers on different means of transportation:

Model: A: 他 每天 怎么去学校？
Tā měitiān zěnme qù xuéxiào?
B: 他 每天 坐 地铁去 学校。
Tā měitiān zuò dìtiě qù xuéxiào.

(1) A: 他 坐 什么 车去国际 机场？
Tā zuò shénme chē qù Guójì Jīchǎng?
B: ________________。
________________.

(2) A: 约翰 先生 坐飞机去 上海 还是坐 火车 去？
Yuēhàn xiānsheng zuò fēijī qù Shànghǎi háishi zuò huǒchē qù?
B: ________________________。
________________________.

(3) A: 他们 一家 怎么 回 英国？
Tāmen yìjiā zěnme huí Yīngguó?
B: ______________。
______________.

**2. Complete the following sentences, using either "来" (lái) or "得" (děi):**

1) Model: A: 来，大家 都 请 吧。
Lái, dàjiā dōu qǐng ba.
B: 请 。
Qǐng.

(1) A: ______，女士们， 先生们 ，请 吧。
______, nǚshìmen, xiānshengmen, qǐng ba.
B: 请 。
Qǐng.

(2) A: 这位 是______？
Zhèwèi shì______?
B: ______，我 给 你们 介绍 一下儿。
______, wǒ gěi nǐmen jièshao yíxiàr.

(3) A: ______， 尝尝 这个。
______, chángchang zhège.
B: 好，我 自己 来。
Hǎo, wǒ zìjǐ lái.

2) Model: 我 不会 用 筷子，我 得 用 刀子、叉子。
Wǒ bú huì yòng kuàizi, wǒ děi yòng dāozi、chāzi.

(1) 要 晚 了，我______ 走 了。
Yào wǎn le, wǒ______ zǒu le.

(2) 别 感冒 了，您 ______再 穿 件 衣服。
Bié gǎnmào le, nín ______ zài chuān jiàn yīfu.

(3) 太 高兴 了，我们 ______ 多 喝 几杯。
Tài gāoxìng le, wǒmen______ duō hē jǐbēi.

***3. Make sentences with "一边……一边……" (yìbiān··· yìbiān···):**

Model: 大家 一边 吃 一边 说。
Dàjiā yìbiān chī yìbiān shuō.

(1) 她，走，看。
tā, zǒu, kàn.

(2) 他们，参观，谈话。
tāmen, cānguān, tán huà.

(3) 很多人，工作，上学。
hěn duō rén, gōngzuò, shàngxué.

4. **Practice proposing a toast:**

Model: 为陈先生一家旅游愉快干杯！
Wèi Chén xiānsheng yìjiā lǚyóu yúkuài gān bēi!

(1) 您的健康
nín de jiànkāng

(2) 我们两家的友谊
wǒmen liǎngjiā de yǒuyì

(3) 我们两国人民的友谊
wǒmen liǎng guó rénmín de yǒuyì

(4) 你们生活幸福
nǐmen shēnghuó xìngfú

5. **Listen to the dialogue:**

中国人：你会用筷子吗？
Zhōngguórén: Nǐ huì yòng kuàizi ma?

外国人：不会。我去唐人街中国饭馆儿学了两次，也没学会。
wàiguórén: Bú huì. Wǒ qù Tángrénjiē Zhōngguó fànguǎnr xuéle liǎngcì, yě méi xué huì.

中：你看，这样拿，就能夹住东西。来，试试。
Zhōng: Nǐ kàn, zhèyàng ná, jiù néng jiā zhù dōngxi. Lái, shìshi.

外：好，我试试。
wài: Hǎo, wǒ shìshi.

中：对，就这样，夹菜。
Zhōng: Duì, jiù zhèyàng, jiā cài.

外：还不行。我看用筷子吃饭没有用刀叉方便。
wài: Hái bùxíng. Wǒ kàn yòng kuàizi chī fàn méiyǒu yòng dāo chā fāngbiàn.

中：那要看吃什么。吃面条儿，用筷子夹，很容易就夹起来，用刀叉就不行。吃
Zhōng: Nà yào kàn chī shénme. Chī miàntiáor, yòng kuàizi jiā, hěn róngyì jiù jiā qi lai, yòng dāo chā jiù bùxíng. Chī

| | |
|---|---|
| | 西餐 一定 要 用 刀叉；吃 中国 饭 一定<br>xīcān yídìng yào yòng dāo chā; chī Zhōngguó fàn yídìng<br>要 用 筷子。<br>yào yòng kuàizi. |
| 外：<br>wài: | 也不一定。吃 花生米 用 筷子 一次 夹<br>Yě bù yídìng. Chī huāshēngmǐ yòng kuàizi yícì jiā<br>一个，太 慢 了。<br>yíge, tài màn le. |
| 中：<br>Zhōng: | 那 还是 你 不会 用。你看，得 这样 拿，用<br>Nà háishì nǐ bú huì yòng. Nǐ kàn, děi zhèyàng ná, yòng<br>筷子 向 上 刬。<br>kuàizi xiàng shàng chǎn. |
| 外：<br>wài: | 那，我也可以用 刀叉吃 面条。<br>Nà, wǒ yě kěyǐ yòng dāo chā chī miàntiáor. |
| 中：<br>Zhōng: | 怎么 吃？<br>Zěnme chī? |
| 外：<br>wài: | 端 起 碗 来，往 嘴里 扒。<br>Duān qi wǎn lai, wàng zuǐli pá. |
| 中：<br>Zhōng: | 啊？当然，这也行。<br>Á? Dāngrán, zhè yě xíng. |

***6. Translate the sentences into Chinese:**

1) The Chinese eat their meals with chopsticks.
2) Nearly all foreign visitors touring Beijing wish to go to see the Great Wall.
3) Come on, everybody! Let's drink to our friendship.
4) We've got to go back now.

# 24 Seeing People Off At The Railway Station
## 车站送行 chēzhàn sòng xíng

(The Chens are leaving Beijing for Xian. Mr. and Mrs. Li Wenhan have come to the station to see them off.)

| | | |
|---|---|---|
| 陈 :<br>Chén: | 这次 在 北京 给 你们 添<br>Zhècì zài Běijīng gěi nǐmen tiān<br>了 不 少 麻烦。①<br>le bù shǎo máfan. | We've given you much trouble while in Beijing. |
| 李:<br>Lǐ: | 别 这样 说，有 什么<br>Bié zhèyàng shuō, yǒu shénme | Don't say that, no trouble at all. |

麻烦 啊。
máfan a .

| | | |
|---|---|---|
| 艾：<br>Ài: | 对 你们的 热情 帮助 和<br>Duì nǐmen de rèqíng bāngzhù hé<br>款待，我们 全 家 都<br>kuǎndài, wǒmen quán jiā dōu<br>表示 感谢。<br>biǎoshì gǎnxiè. | My family and I must thank you for your fervent help and warm reception. |
| 丁：<br>Dīng: | 您 太客气了。<br>Nín tài kèqi le . | You are too kind. |
| 陈：<br>Chén: | 相见 时 难别 亦 难。②<br>Xiāngjiàn shí nán bié yì nán.<br>几十年 没见 面 了，真<br>Jǐshínián méi jiàn miàn le , zhēn<br>想 多 呆 几天。<br>xiǎng duō dāi jǐtiān . | It is just as difficult to say goodbye as it is to get together. We haven't seen each other for decades. How I wish to stay longer. |
| 李：<br>Lǐ: | 是 啊，你们这次来，时间<br>Shì a , nǐmen zhècì lái, shíjiān<br>太 短 了。<br>tài duǎn le. | Ah, yes. Your stay here has been far too short. |
| 陈：<br>Chén: | 从 西安 回 来 以后，在<br>Cóng Xī'ān huí lai yǐhòu, zài<br>北京 只 能 呆 两 天。<br>Běijīng zhǐ néng dāi liǎngtiān.<br>今后 只要 有 可能，争<br>Jīnhòu zhǐyào yǒu kěnéng, zhēng<br>取 每年 回 来一次。<br>qǔ měinián huí lai yícì. | And we have only two days in Beijing after our return from Xian. If at all possible,I'll try to come back once every year. |
| 李：<br>Lǐ: | 希望 每 年 都 能 在<br>Xīwàng měinián dōu néng zài<br>北京 欢迎 你们。<br>Běijīng huānyíng nǐmen. | Hope I'll be able to welcome you here each year. |
| 艾：<br>Ài: | 我们 也 希望 能 在 美<br>Wǒmen yě xīwàng néng zài Měi<br>国 欢迎 你们。<br>guó huānyíng nǐmen. | We hope to be able to welcome you in America too. |
| 丁：<br>Dīng: | 谢谢。我 想 会 有 机会<br>Xièxie. Wǒ xiǎng huì yǒu jīhui | Thank you. I think the day will come. |

| | | |
|---|---|---|
| | 的。<br>de. | |
| 李：<br>Lǐ: | 你们 还 有 什么 事儿<br>Nǐmen hái yǒu shénme shìr<br>需要 帮 忙 的吗？<br>xūyào bāng máng de ma? | Is there anything else I can do for you? |
| 陈：<br>Chén: | 那几本 书 买 到以后，③<br>Nà jǐběn shū mǎi dào yǐhòu,<br>麻烦 你直接给我寄 到<br>máfan nǐ zhíjiē gěi wǒ jì dào<br>美国 。<br>Měiguó. | I'll trouble you to send those books to the United States after you get them. |
| 李：<br>Lǐ: | 前天 我打电话 问了，<br>Qiántiān wǒ dǎ diànhuà wèn le,<br>今天 上午 我 又打电<br>jīntiān shàngwǔ wǒ yòu dǎ diàn<br>话 问了，④ 都 说 还<br>huà wèn le, dōu shuō hái<br>没 到。你 放心 吧，买<br>méi dào. Nǐ fàngxīn ba, mǎi<br>到 了 马上 就 给 你 寄<br>dào le mǎshàng jiù gěi nǐ jì<br>去。到 西安 一定 找 老<br>qu. Dào Xī'ān yídìng zhǎo Lǎo<br>张 去。老 张 就 住<br>Zhāng qu. Lǎo Zhāng jiù zhù<br>在 钟楼 附近，⑤离 你们<br>zài Zhōnglóu fùjìn, lí nǐmen<br>住 的 地方 不 远。<br>zhù de dìfang bù yuǎn. | I called the book store the day before yesterday and again this morning. They said the books had not arrived yet. Don't worry, I'll have them sent to you as soon as I get them. Be sure to call Lao Zhang when you arrive at Xian. He lives near the Bell Tower which isn't far from where you'll be staying. |
| 丁：<br>Dīng: | 老 张 的地址，你们 知<br>Lǎo Zhāng de dìzhǐ, nǐmen zhī<br>道 吧？<br>dao ba? | You've his address, right? |
| 陈：<br>Chén: | 知道 。<br>Zhīdao. | Yes. |
| 丁：<br>Dīng: | 还 有 五分钟 火车<br>Hái yǒu wǔfēnzhōng huǒchē | The train will start in five minutes. You'd better |

| | | |
|---|---|---|
| | 就开了，你们上车吧。<br>jiù kāi le，nǐmen shàng chē ba. | get on. |
| 艾：<br>Ài: | 莉莉，行李放好了吗？⑥<br>Lìli，xíngli fàng hǎo le ma? | Lily, have you had our luggage put on a rack? |
| 莉：<br>Lì: | 放好了。<br>Fàng hǎo le. | Yes. |
| 艾：<br>Ài: | 票呢？<br>Piào ne? | Where are the tickets? |
| 莉：<br>Lì: | 票和护照一起放在手提包里了。<br>Piào hé hùzhào yìqǐ fàng zài shǒutíbāoli le. | They are in the handbag with the passports. |
| 陈：<br>Chén: | 你们请回吧，谢谢你们！<br>Nǐmen qǐng huí ba，xièxie nǐmen! | You'd better go now. Thanks for coming. |
| 李：<br>Lǐ: | 见到老张，请代我问好。<br>Jiàn dào Lǎo Zhāng，qǐng dài wǒ wèn hǎo. | Give Lao Zhang our regards when you see him. |
| 陈：<br>Chén: | 好，一定。时间不早了，请回吧！<br>Hǎo，yídìng. Shíjiān bù zǎo le，qǐng huí ba! | Sure. It's getting late, you better go. |
| 李：<br>Lǐ:<br>丁：<br>Dīng: | 祝你们一路顺风！<br>Zhù nǐmen yílù shùn fēng! | Have a pleasant journey! |
| 陈：<br>Chén:<br>艾：<br>Ài: | 谢谢你们。再见！<br>Xièxie nǐmen. Zàijiàn! | Thank you. Good-bye. |

## • new words • 生词 • shēngcí

1 车站 （名）chēzhàn station

| | | | | |
|---|---|---|---|---|
| 2 | 送行 | | sòng xíng | to see somebody off |
| 3 | 添 | （动） | tiān | to add |
| 4 | 少 | （形） | shǎo | less, little, few |
| 5 | 热情 | （形、名） | rèqíng | warm, warm-heartedness |
| 6 | 款待 | （动、名） | kuǎndài | to entertain, hospitality |
| 7 | 表示 | （动） | biǎoshì | to show, to express |
| 8 | 相见时难别亦难 | | xiāngjiàn shí nán bié yì nán | difficult to meet, difficult to part. |
| 9 | 见面 | | jiàn miàn | to meet |
| 10 | 只 | （副） | zhǐ | only |
| 11 | 呆 | （动） | dāi | to stay |
| 12 | 只要 | （连） | zhǐyào | if only, so long as |
| 13 | 争取 | （动） | zhēngqǔ | to try; to manage |
| 14 | 希望 | （动） | xīwàng | to wish, to hope |
| 15 | 需要 | （动、名） | xūyào | to need, need |
| 16 | 帮忙 | | bāng máng | to help, help |
| 17 | 直接 | （形） | zhíjiē | direct, straight |
| 18 | 前天 | （名） | qiántiān | day before yesterday |
| 19 | 放心 | （动） | fàngxīn | to rest assured, to be at ease |
| 20 | 又 | （副） | yòu | again |
| 21 | 附近 | （名） | fùjìn | vicinity |
| 22 | 离 | （介、动） | lí | from, to leave |
| 23 | 远 | （形） | yuǎn | far, distant |
| | 离……不远 | | lí…bù yuǎn | not far from |
| 24 | 地址 | （名） | dìzhǐ | address |
| 25 | 分钟 | （量） | fēnzhōng | minute |
| 26 | 开 | （动） | kāi | to start, to drive |
| 27 | 行李 | （名） | xíngli | luggage, baggage |
| 28 | 放 | （动） | fàng | to put |
| 29 | 护照 | （名） | hùzhào | passport |

| | | | | |
|---|---|---|---|---|
| 30 | 手提包 | （名） | shǒutíbāo | handbag |
| 31 | 代 | （动） | dài | to do something on someone's behalf |
| 32 | 问好 | | wèn hǎo | to send regards, to ask after |
| 33 | 早 | （形） | zǎo | early |
| 34 | 一路顺风 | | yīlù shùn fēng | bon voyage, a pleasant trip |

| 专名 | Zhuānmíng | Proper name |
|---|---|---|
| 钟楼 | Zhōnglóu | Bell Tower, here it refers to the bell tower in Xian. |

## study points • 注释 • zhùshì

1 给你们添了不少麻烦。(Géi nǐmen tiānle bù shǎo máfan.)
This is to show your gratitude to people who have done something for you. You can also say "给你们添麻烦了" (géi nǐmen tiān máfan le). The usual response is "不麻烦" (Bù máfan), To be more emphatic, you can say "有什么麻烦呢？" (yǒu shénme máfan ne?) or "有什么麻烦啊。" (yǒu shénme máfan a.)

2 相见时难别亦难。(Xiāngjiàn shí nán bié yì nán.)
See the poem "Without a Title" by the Tang poet Li Shangyin. (李商隐)

3 那几本书买到以后。(Nà jǐběn shū mǎi dào yǐhòu.)
In compound verbs like "买到" (mǎi dào), "放好" (fàng hǎo) and "住在" (zhù zài) the second constituents (到，好，在，etc.) are used to show the completion of an action:

你们见到老张，请代我问好。
(Nǐmen jiàn dào Lǎo Zhāng, qǐng dài wǒ wèn hǎo.)
昨天晚上他们谈到九点半。
(Zuótiān wǎnshang tāmen tán dào jiǔdiǎnbàn.)
下星期我们还要回到北京来。
(Xià xīngqī wǒmen hái yào huí dào Běijīng lai.)
他们已经把菜弄好了。
(Tāmen yǐjing bǎ cài nòng hǎo le.)

When followed by the aspect particle "了" (le) these verbs indicate completed action:

昨天我看到王先生了。(Zuótiān wǒ kàn dào Wáng xiāngsheng le.)

他写好了信了。(Tā xiě hǎo le xìn le.)

The negative is formed by adding "没(有)" (méi(yǒu)):

上午他没(有)买到书。(Shàngwǔ tā méi(yǒu) mǎi dào shū.)

4 今天上午我又打电话问了。(Jīntiān shàngwǔ wǒ yòu dǎ diànhuà wèn le.)

Both the adverbs "又" (yòu) and "再" (zài) can be used to show repetition of an action; but "又" is used for an already completed action, while "再" is for action yet to take place, for example:

昨天他来了，今天上午他又来了。

(Zuótiān tā lái le, jīntian shàngwǔ tā yòu lái le.)

我昨天问他了，明天再问问他。

(Wǒ zuótiān wèn tā le, míngtiān zài wènwen tā.)

5 老张就住在钟楼附近。(Lǎo Zhāng jiù zhù zài Zhōnglóu fùjìn.)

1) "就" (jiù) is for emphasis here.

2) The verb "在" (zài) indicate the result of the action. It is often used to show that action has reached a certain place, therefore it must be followed by a word of place, for example:

他家住在西安。(Tā jiā zhù zài Xī'ān)

火车票放在手提包里了。(Huǒchēpiào fàng zài shǒutíbāolǐ le.)

6 行李放好了吗? (Xíngli fàng hǎo le ma?)

"好" here is an adjective to indicate the result as well as the completion of an action:

我写好信了。(Wǒ xiě hǎo xìn le.)

他们谈好了没有? (Tāmen tán hǎo le méiyǒu?)

## supplementary words • 补充生词 • bǔchōng shēngcí

| | | | | |
|---|---|---|---|---|
| 1 | 行李架 | (名) | xínglijià | luggage rack |
| 2 | 收 | (动) | shōu | to receive, to keep |
| 3 | 手续 | (名) | shǒuxù | procedure |

| | | | |
|---|---|---|---|
| 4 | 办 | （动）bàn | to go through |
| 5 | 讨论 | （动）tǎolùn | to discuss |
| 6 | 旅行 | （动、名）lǚxíng | to travel, travel |
| 7 | 口袋 | （名）kǒudài | pocket |
| 8 | 衣帽钩 | （名）yīmàogōur | pegs for coats and hats |
| 9 | 忘 | （动）wàng | to forget |
| 10 | 西服 | （名）xīfú | suit |
| 11 | 眼镜盒儿 | （名）yǎnjìnghér | case for keeping glasses |
| 12 | 丢 | （动）diū | to lose |
| 13 | 保险 | （形、名）bǎoxiǎn | safe, security |

## • exercises • 练习 • liànxí

*1. **Answer the following questions:**

1) Model: A: 张 先生 住在 什么 地方？
Zhāng xiānsheng zhù zài shénme dìfang?
B: 他 住在 钟楼 附近。（钟楼）
Tā zhù zài Zhōnglóu fùjìn .（Zhōnglóu）

(1) A: 李文汉 同志 住在 什么 地方？
Lǐ Wénhàn tóngzhì zhù zài shénme dìfang？
B: ________________。（人民 剧场）
________________.（Rénmín Jùchǎng）

(2) A: 小 陈 住在 几层？
Xiǎo Chén zhù zài jǐcéng？
B: ________________。（四层）
________________.（sìcéng）

(3) A: 票 放在哪儿了？
Piào fàng zài nǎr le ？
B: ________________。（手提包）
________________.（shǒutíbāo）

(4) A: 手提包 放 在哪儿了？
Shǒutíbāo fàng zài nǎr le ?

B: ____________。(行李架)
____________. (xínglijià)

2) Model: A: 行李 放 好 了吗？
Xíngli fàng hǎo le ma?

B: 放 好 了。
Fàng hǎo le .

(1) A: 准备 好 了吗？
Zhǔnbèi hǎo le ma?

B: ____________。
____________.

(2) A: 票 收 好 了 吗？
Piào shōu hǎo le ma?

B: ____________。
____________.

(3) A: 手续 办 好 了吗？
Shǒuxù bàn hǎo le ma?

B: ____________。
____________.

3) Model: A: 明天 的 特快 买 到 了吗？
Míngtiān de tèkuài mǎi dào le ma?

B: 没 买 到。
Méi mǎi dào.

(1) A: 《汉 英 词典》借 到 了吗？
"Hàn Yīng Cídiǎn" jiè dào le ma?

B: ____________。
____________.

(2) A: 你见 到老 李 了 吗？
Nǐ jiàn dào Lǎo Lǐ le ma?

B: ____________。
____________.

(3) A: 他 寄给 你的包裹 收 到 了吗？
Tā jì gěi nǐ de bāoguǒ shōu dào le ma?

B: ____________。
____________.

***2. Practice the following questions after the model:**

Model: 还 有 什么 事儿需要 帮 忙 的吗?
Hái yǒu shénme shìr xūyào bāng máng de ma?
（事儿，帮 忙 ）
( shìr , bāng máng )

(1) 问题，讨论
wèntí , tǎolùn

(2) 手续 ，办
shǒuxù, bàn

(3) 工作 ，研究
gōngzuò, yánjiū

**3. Fill in the blanks:**

Model: 见 到老 张 ，请 代 我 问 好 。
Jiàn dào Lǎo Zhāng, qǐng dài wǒ wèn hǎo.

(1) 见 到老 刘，__________。（我们）
Jiàn dào Lǎo Liú, __________. ( wǒmen )

(2) __________，请 代 我 向 他 问 好 。（老 李）
__________, qǐng dài wǒ xiàng tā wèn hǎo. ( Lǎo Lǐ )

(3) __________，你 给 我 带 个 好儿 吧。（ 小 陈 ）
__________, nǐ gěi wǒ dài ge hǎor ba. ( Xiǎo Chén )

**4. Fill in the blanks:**

Model: 祝 你们 一路 平安！
Zhù nǐmen yílù píng'ān!

(1) ______一路 顺 风！（你）
______ yílù shùn fēng! ( nǐ )

(2) ______ 旅行 愉快！（你们 一家）
______ lǚxíng yúkuài! ( nǐmen yìjiā )

**5. Listen to the dialogues:**

1) 陈 明 山： 票 收 好 了 吗？
Chén Míngshān: Piào shōu hǎo le ma?
莉莉： 收 好 了。
Lìli : Shōu hǎo le .
陈 ： 放 在哪儿了？
Chén: Fàng zài nǎr le ?
莉： 放 在我的大衣 口袋里了。
Lì: Fàng zài wǒ de dàyī kǒudàili le .
陈 ： 你的 大衣 呢？
Chén: Nǐ de dàyī ne?

| | | |
|---|---|---|
| | 莉： | 挂 在 衣帽钩上 了。 |
| | Lì: | Guà zài yīmàogōushang le. |
| | 陈 ： | 快 拿来，还是 放 在 我 这儿吧。 |
| | Chén: | Kuài ná lai, háishi fàng zài wǒ zhèr ba. |
| 2) | 王 太太： | 刘 先生 他们 家 住哪儿？你 知道 吗？ |
| | Wáng tàitai: | Liú xiānsheng tāmen jiā zhù nǎr ? Nǐ zhīdao ma? |
| | 王 先 生： | 老 李 不是 给 咱们 写了个 地址 吗？ |
| | Wáng xiānsheng: | Lǎo Lǐ bú shì gěi zánmen xiěle ge dìzhǐ ma? |
| | 太太： | 拿 来，我 看看 。 |
| | tàitai: | Ná lai, wǒ kànkan. |
| | 先 生 ： | 哎呀，我 忘了 放 在哪儿了。你没 看到？ |
| | xiānsheng: | Āiyā, wǒ wàngle fàng zài nǎr le. Nǐ méi kàn dào? |
| | 太太： | 没 看 到。会 不会 放 在西服口袋里了？ |
| | tàitai: | Méi kàn dào. Huì bu huì fàng zài xīfú kǒudàili le? |
| | 先 生 ： | 没 放 在 口袋里。 |
| | xiānsheng: | Méi fàng zài kǒudàili. |
| | 太太： | 看看 眼镜盒儿里 有 没有 ？ |
| | tàitai: | Kànkan yǎnjìnghérli yǒu méiyǒu? |
| | 先 生 ： | 也 没有 。 |
| | xiānsheng: | Yě méiyǒu. |
| | 太太： | 再 找 找 别的 地方。 |
| | tàitai: | Zài zhǎozhao biéde dìfang. |
| | 先 生 ： | 还 能 在哪儿？ 能 找 的 地方 我 都 找 了。没有 地址，怎么 办呢？ |
| | xiānsheng: | Hái néng zài nǎr ? Néng zhǎo de dìfang wǒ dōu zhǎo le. Méiyǒu dìzhǐ, zěnme bàn ne? |
| | 太太： | 你 怎么不 放 好呢！ |
| | tàitai: | Nǐ zěnme bú fàng hǎo ne! |
| | 先 生 ： | 我 放 好 了。 |
| | xiānsheng: | Wǒ fàng hǎo le. |
| | 太太： | 什么 放 好 了！ 一定 是 丢 了。 |
| | tàitai: | Shénme fàng hǎo le! Yídìng shì diū le. |
| | 先 生 ： | 不会，不会 丢。 |
| | xiānsheng: | Bú huì, bú huì diū. |
| | 太太： | 那，你再 好好儿 想想 。 |
| | tàitai: | Nà, nǐ zài hǎohāor xiǎngxiang. |
| | 先 生 ： | 啊，对 了 对 了。 |
| | xiānsheng: | À, duì le duì le. |

太太： 放 在哪儿了？
tàitai : Fàng zài nǎr le ?

先生 ： 这 不，夹在 这本 书里了。我 说 放 好 了嘛。
xiānsheng: Zhè bù, jiā zài zhèběn shūli le . Wǒ shuō fàng hǎo le ma.

太太： 我 说 你 放 的这个地方也太“保险”了。
tàitai : Wǒ shuō nǐ fàng de zhège dìfang yě tài “bǎoxiǎn” le .

# 25 Chinese Forms Of Address
# 中国人的称呼 zhōngguórén de chēnghu

(The Chens talk about Chinese ways of addressing people before they go to see Zhang Xin.)

| | | |
|---|---|---|
| 陈：<br>Chén: | 刚才 我给老 张 打<br>Gāngcái wǒ gěi Lǎo Zhāng dǎ<br>电 话 了。<br>diànhuà le . | I just called Lao Zhang. |
| 艾：<br>Ài: | 打 通 了 吗？<br>Dǎ tōng le ma? | Did you get through? |

| | | |
|---|---|---|
| 陈：<br>Chén: | 打通了。他让我们明天上午去。① 他和他太太在家等我们。<br>Dǎ tōng le. Tā ràng wǒmen míngtiān shàngwǔ qù. Tā hé tā tàitai zài jiā děng wǒmen. | Yes. He wants us over tomorrow morning. He and his wife will be waiting for us. |
| 伟：<br>Wěi: | 爸爸，明天见面时怎么叫他们呢？<br>Bàba, míngtiān jiàn miàn shí zěnme jiào tāmen ne? | Oh Dad, what shall I call them when we meet tomorrow? |
| 陈：<br>Chén: | 叫"伯伯"、"伯母"。<br>Jiào "bóbo"、"bómǔ". | You call them "Bo Bo" and "Bo Mu". |
| 伟：<br>Wěi: | 为什么叫"伯伯"、"伯母"，不叫"叔叔"、"阿姨"呢？<br>Wèi shénme jiào "bóbo"、"bómǔ", bú jiào "shūshu"、"āyí" ne? | Why "Bo Bo" and "Bo Mu" and not "Shu Shu" and "Ah Yi"? |
| 陈：<br>Chén: | 因为老张比我大好几岁。②<br>Yīnwei Lǎo Zhāng bǐ wǒ dà hǎo jǐsuì. | Because Lao Zhang is a few years older than me. |
| 伟：<br>Wěi: | 在北京常常听见孩子们叫"叔叔"、"阿姨"，③ 这是怎么回事儿呢？<br>Zài Běijīng chángcháng tīng jiàn háizimen jiào "shūshu"、"āyí", zhè shì zěnme huí shìr ne? | In Beijing I often hear children addressing grown-ups as "Shu Shu" and "Ah Yi". Why do they do that? |
| 陈：<br>Chén: | 孩子们管那些跟自己父亲、母亲年龄差不多的叫"叔叔"、"阿姨"。<br>Háizimen guǎn nàxiē gēn zìjǐ fùqin、mǔqin niánlíng chà bu duō de jiào "shūshu"、"āyí". | Children usually call people about the age of their parents "Shu Shu" and "Ah Yi". |
| 莉：<br>Lì: | 爸爸，中国人的称<br>Bàba, Zhōngguórén de chēng | Oh Dad, the Chinese way of addressing |

| | | |
|---|---|---|
| | 呼太复杂了，什么“老<br>hu tài fùzá le, shénme “Lǎo<br>张　”、“小刘”、“同志”、<br>Zhāng”、“Xiǎo Liú”、“tóngzhì”、<br>“　先生　”。④我　都糊涂<br>“xiānsheng”.　Wǒ dōu hútu<br>了。到底该怎么用，您<br>le. Dàodǐ gāi zěnme yòng, nín<br>给我　讲讲　吧。<br>gěi wǒ jiǎngjiang ba. | people is too complicated. "Lao Zhang", "Xiao Liu","Comrade", "Mr.". I get them all mixed up. You'd better give me some ideas as to how they're used. |
| 陈：<br>Chén: | 你叫我讲，我也只<br>Nǐ jiào wǒ jiǎng, wǒ yě zhǐ<br>能　简单地讲一下儿。⑤<br>néng jiǎndān de jiǎng yíxiàr.<br>现在　有的　情况　我也<br>Xiànzài yǒude qíngkuàng wǒ yě<br>不　清楚。<br>bù qīngchu. | I can only give you a rough idea. I'm not familiar with some of the present conditions myself. |
| 莉：<br>Lì: | 您　先　讲　一　讲　“同志”。<br>Nín xiān jiǎng yi jiǎng “tóngzhì”. | First of all, tell us about "Comrade". |
| 陈：<br>Chén: | “同志”是中国人　现<br>“Tóngzhì” shì Zhōngguórén xiàn<br>在常　用　的一个普通<br>zài cháng yòng de yíge pǔtōng<br>称呼　。不认识的人见<br>chēnghu. Bú rènshi de rén jiàn<br>面　时，可以　互相　称<br>miàn shí, kěyǐ hùxiāng chēng<br>呼“同志”。知道　对方<br>hu “tóngzhì”. Zhīdao duìfāng<br>姓名　的，可以称呼<br>xìngmíng de, kěyǐ chēnghu<br>“某　同志”，或者“某<br>“mǒu tóngzhì”, huòzhě “mǒu<br>某　某　同志”。<br>mǒu mǒu tóngzhì”. | "Comrade" is the most common term Chinese use to address people nowadays. When strangers meet, they can call each other "comrade". If you know his name you can call him "Comrade so-and-so", using either surname or full name. |
| 莉：<br>Lì: | 什么　时候　叫“老　什<br>Shénme shíhour jiào “lǎo shén | And when do you use "Lao" and "Xiao"? |

| | | |
|---|---|---|
| | 么"、"小 什么"呢?<br>me"、"xiǎo shénme"ne? | |
| 陈:<br>Chén: | 比较 熟悉的人，年龄 大的对 年龄 小 的可以称呼 "小 什么"；年龄 小 的对 年龄 大的，或者 年龄 差 不 多的，可以 称呼 "老 什么"。这样 听 起来 亲切 一些。<br>Bǐjiào shúxi de rén, niánlíng dà de duì niánlíng xiǎo de kěyǐ chēnghu "xiǎo shénme"; niánlíng xiǎo de duì niánlíng dà de, huòzhě niánlíng chà bu duō de, kěyǐ chēnghu "lǎo shénme". Zhèyàng tīng qilai qīnqiè yìxiē. | That's for people you're familiar with. Older ones can call those younger than they are "Xiao something" while younger ones can call those older or about the same age as they are "Lao something". It sounds more intimate that way. |
| 伟:<br>Wěi: | 在 美国，"先生"不 离 口，可是在 这儿，我 只 听 见 有 人 这样 称 呼您，这 是 为 什么?<br>Zài Měiguó, "xiānsheng" bù lí kǒu, kěshì zài zhèr, wǒ zhǐ tīng jiàn yǒu rén zhèyàng chēnghu nín, zhè shì wèi shénme? | In the United States, we call everybody Mr. so-and-so. But here I hear people addressing nobody but you as Mr. Chen. Why's that? |
| 陈:<br>Chén: | 现 在 中国 国 内 很 少 称呼 "先 生"了。<br>Xiànzài Zhōngguó guó nèi hěn shǎo chēnghu "xiānsheng" le. | At present you seldom use Mr. to address people in China. |
| 伟:<br>Wěi: | "太太"、"小 姐"呢?<br>"Tàitai"、"xiǎojie" ne? | What about Mrs. and Miss? |
| 陈:<br>Chén: | "太太"、"小姐"都 不 用 了。"先 生"、"太 太"、"小 姐"现在 主要 是 用来 称 呼 外国 人<br>"Tàitai"、"xiǎojie" dōu bú yòng le. "Xiānsheng"、"tàitai"、"xiǎojie" xiànzài zhǔyào shì yònglái chēnghu wàiguó rén | Neither are used now. Mr., Mrs., Miss are used mostly to address foreigners and overseas Chinese visiting here. |

和回国参观探亲的
hé huí guó cānguān tànqīn de
华侨。
huáqiáo.

| | | |
|---|---|---|
| 艾: Ài: | 我们走吧，八点半了。 Wǒmen zǒu ba, bādiǎnbàn le. | Let's go. It's eight-thirty. |
| 陈: Chén: | 没关系，老张让我们十点半到他家。 Méi guānxi, Lǎo Zhāng ràng wǒmen shídiǎnbàn dào tā jiā. | No hurry. Lao Zhang expects us at half past ten. |

## • new words • 生词 • shēngcí

| | | | | |
|---|---|---|---|---|
| 1 | 称呼 | (名、动) | chēnghu | a form of address, to address, to call |
| 2 | 通 | (动) | tōng | to be through, to lead to |
| | 电话打通了 | | diànhuà dǎ tōng le | The phone call has been put through. |
| 3 | 让 | (动) | ràng | to ask, to let, to give up |
| 4 | 为什么 | | wèi shénme | why |
| 5 | 叔叔 | (名) | shūshu | uncle |
| 6 | 阿姨 | (名) | āyí | aunt (what children call young women) |
| 7 | 因为 | (连) | yīnwei | because |
| 8 | 比 | (介、动、名) | bǐ | than, to compare, comparison |
| 9 | 好 | (副) | hǎo | well, quite |
| | 好几岁 | | hǎo jǐsuì | quite a few years (of age) |
| 10 | 听见 | | tīng jiàn | to hear |
| 11 | 回 | (量) | huí | a measure word for time or round |
| | 这是怎么回事儿? | | Zhè shì zěnme huí shìr? | What is the matter? What is the meaning of this? |
| 12 | 管 | (介、动) | guǎn | as, (to call)…as |

| | | | | |
|---|---|---|---|---|
| | 管……叫…… | | guǎn···jiào··· | to call···as |
| 13 | 那些 | (代) | nàxiē | those |
| 14 | 父亲 | (名) | fùqin | father |
| 15 | 母亲 | (名) | mǔqin | mother |
| 16 | 差不多 | | chà bu duō | nearly, more or less |
| | 跟……差不多 | | gēn··· chà bu duō | more or less the same as··· |
| 17 | 复杂 | (形) | fùzá | complicated |
| 18 | 糊涂 | (形) | hútu | confused |
| 19 | 到底 | (副) | dàodǐ | after all, in the final analysis, how on earth |
| 20 | 讲 | (动) | jiǎng | to explain, to say, to talk |
| 21 | 叫 | (动) | jiào | to call, to address |
| 22 | 简单 | (形) | jiǎndān | simple |
| 23 | 地 | (助) | de | a particle added to adjectives as adverbial |
| 24 | 有的 | (代) | yǒude | some |
| 25 | 情况 | (名) | qíngkuàng | situation |
| 26 | 清楚 | (形) | qīngchu | clear |
| 27 | 常 | (形、副) | cháng | regular, frequent, often |
| 28 | 普通 | (形) | pǔtōng | ordinary, common |
| 29 | 认识 | (动、名) | rènshi | to know, understanding |
| 30 | 互相 | (副) | hùxiāng | each other |
| 31 | 对方 | (名) | duìfāng | the other party (side) |
| 32 | 姓名 | (名) | xìngmíng | full name |
| 33 | 某 | (代) | mǒu | certain |
| 34 | 熟悉 | (形) | shúxi | familiar |
| 35 | ……之间 | | ···zhījiān | between, among |
| 36 | ……起来 | | ···qilai | an expression indicating that an action is in progress |
| 37 | 亲切 | (形) | qīnqiè | friendly, warm |

| | | | | |
|---|---|---|---|---|
| 38 | 口 | （名） | kǒu | mouth |
| | “先生”不离口 | | “xiānsheng” bù lí kǒu | saying “Mr.” all the time |
| 39 | 可是 | （连） | kěshì | but, however |
| 40 | 主要 | （形） | zhǔyào | main |
| 41 | 用来 | | yòng lái | to be used purposely |
| 42 | 探亲 | | tàn qīn | to visit relatives |

## study points • 注释 • zhùshì

1 他让我们明天上午去。(Tā ràng wǒmen míngtiān shàngwǔ qù.)

In Chinese, there is a kind of sentence in which the object of its first verb is at the same time the subject of the second "subject-predicate" structure. Verbs like “请”(qǐng), “叫” (jiào), “让” (ràng), etc. often serve as the first verb in such sentences:

李先生请他吃饭。(Lǐ xiānsheng qǐng tā chī fàn.)

你叫我讲，我也只能简单地讲一下儿。

(Nǐ jiào wǒ jiǎng, wǒ yě zhǐ néng jiǎndān de jiǎng yíxiàr.)

老张让我们十点半到他家。

(Lǎo Zhāng ràng wǒmen shídiǎnbàn dào tā jiā.)

2 老张比我大好几岁。(Lǎo Zhāng bǐ wǒ dà hǎo jǐsuì.)

1) “比” (bǐ) is the most common comparison indicator. The general pattern is: A＋比＋B＋the result or the difference of the comparison:

今天比昨天冷。(Jīntiān bǐ zuótiān lěng.)

你的书比他的书多吗? (Nǐ de shū bǐ tā de shū duō ma?)

老李比我大三岁。(Lǎo Lǐ bǐ wǒ dà sānsuì.)

The negative form is:

他不比我大。(Tā bù bǐ wǒ dà.)

2) “好” (hǎo) is an adverb here, meaning "quite", "a good many", etc.

3 在北京常常听见孩子们叫“叔叔”，“阿姨”。

(Zài Běijīng chángcháng tīng jiàn háizǐmen jiào “shūshu”, “āyí”.)

The verb “见” (jiàn) is often placed after the verbs “听” (tīng) and “看”

(kàn) to mean "to have heard" and "to have seen".

4 什么"老张"，"小刘"，"同志"，"先生"。
(Shénme "Lǎo Zhāng", "Xiǎo Liú", "tóngzhì", "xiānsheng".)
"什么" (Shénme) when placed before a series of parallel elements shows that there are too many to be listed.

5 我也只能简单地讲一下儿。(Wǒ yě zhǐ néng jiǎndān de jiǎng yīxiàr.)
When a two-syllable adjective is used as an adverbial, the structural particle "地" is usually placed between it and the verb:

他高兴地说："我已经买了汽车了。"
(Tā gāoxìng de shuō: "Wǒ yǐjīng mǎile qìchē le.")
他热情地介绍了很多情况。
(Tā rèqíng de jièshàole hěn duō qíngkuàng.)

## supplementary words • 补充生词 • bǔchōng shēngcí

| | | | | |
|---|---|---|---|---|
| 1 | 主持人 | (名) | zhǔchírén | chairperson |
| 2 | 历史学家 | (名) | lìshǐxuéjiā | historian |
| 3 | 不敢当 | | bù gǎndāng | not at all (literally, I don't deserve it.) |
| 4 | 进行 | (动) | jìnxíng | to proceed |
| 5 | 学术 | (名) | xuéshù | scholarship, academic subject |
| 6 | 交流 | (动) | jiāoliú | to exchange |
| 7 | 面前 | (名) | miànqián | before, in front of |
| 8 | 班门弄斧 | | Bān mén nòng fǔ | to display one's slight skill before an expert |
| 9 | 指正 | (动) | zhǐzhèng | to criticize |
| 10 | 耽误 | (动) | dānwu | to take up (one's time) |
| 11 | 衷心 | (形) | zhōngxīn | heartfelt |
| 12 | 座谈 | (动) | zuòtán | to discuss (informally) |
| 13 | 解答 | (动) | jiědá | to answer |

## • exercises • 练习 • liànxí

*1. **Fill in the blanks with the right words:**

几点，哪天，谁，哪儿，什么
jǐdiǎn, nǎtiān, shuí, nǎr, shénme

1) A: 老张要请______吃饭？
Lǎo Zhāng yào qǐng______ chī fàn?

B: 请陈先生全家。
Qǐng Chén xiānsheng quán jiā.

2) A: 老张请他们______去？
Lǎo Zhāng qǐng tāmen______ qù?

B: 明天。
Míngtiān.

3) A: 老张请他们去______？
Lǎo Zhāng qǐng tāmen qù______?

B: 去他家。
Qù tā jiā.

4) A: 老张让他们______到他家？
Lǎo Zhāng ràng tāmen______ dào tā jiā?

B: 十点半。
Shídiǎnbàn.

5) A: 莉莉叫陈先生讲______？
Lìli jiào Chén xiānsheng jiǎng______?

B: 讲中国人的称呼。
Jiǎng Zhōngguórén de chēnghu.

*2. **Rearrange the following words and phrases into proper sentences:**

1) 北京饭店，高，比，民族饭店
Běijīng Fàndiàn, gāo, bǐ, Mínzú Fàndiàn

2) 莉莉，三岁，大，比，大伟
Lìli, sānsuì, dà, bǐ, Dàwěi

3) 老丁，一点儿，瘦，比，陈太太
Lǎo Dīng, yìdiǎnr, shòu, bǐ, Chén tàitai

4) 这件，上衣，样子，好，比，那件
zhèjiàn, shàngyī, yàngzi, hǎo, bǐ, nàjiàn

5) 这个 国家， 差 不 多，跟，那个国家 ，大
zhège guójiā， chà bu duō， gēn， nàge guójiā，dà

6) 他，年纪，大，差不多，跟，他
tā，niánji，dà，chà bu duō，gēn，tā

**3. Answer the following questions:**

1) 莉莉叫 老 张 什么？
Lìli jiào Lǎo Zhāng shénme?

2) 孩子们 管 谁 叫“叔叔”、“阿姨”?
Háizimen guǎn shuí jiào “shūshu”、“āyí”?

3) 什么 人 见面 时 互相 称呼 “同志”?
Shénme rén jiànmiàn shí hùxiāng chēnghu “tóngzhì”?

4) “太太”、“小姐”主要 用 来 称 呼 哪些 人？
“Tàitai”、“xiǎojie” zhǔyào yòng lái chēnghu nǎxiē rén？

**4. Listen to the dialogue:**

(Mr. Smith, a historian, gives a talk at a symposium at a university.)

主持人： 今天， 我们 请 到了美国 历史学家史密斯 先生 来 作报告。史密斯 先生 对 中国 历史 很 有研究。
zhǔchírén: Jīntiān, wǒmen qǐng dào le Měiguó lìshǐxuéjiā Shǐmìsī xiānsheng lái zuò bàogào. Shǐmìsī xiānsheng duì Zhōngguó lìshǐ hěn yǒu yánjiū.

史密斯： 不 敢当，不 敢当 。
Shǐmìsī: Bù gǎndāng, bù gǎndāng.

主： 现在，让 我们 欢迎 史密斯 先生 作 报告。
zhǔ: Xiànzài, ràng wǒmen huānyíng Shǐmìsī xiānsheng zuò bàogào.

史： 今天 有 机会 和 中国 朋友 进行 学术 交流，我 很 高兴 。不过，在 中国 朋友 面前 谈 中国 历史 方面 的问题，实在 是 班 门 弄 斧。请 朋友们 多多 指正 。
Shǐ: Jīntiān yǒu jīhui hé Zhōngguó péngyou jìnxíng xuéshù jiāoliú, wǒ hěn gāoxìng. Búguò, zài Zhōngguó péngyou miànqián tán Zhōngguó lìshǐ fāngmiàn de wèntí, shízài shì Bān mén nòng fǔ. Qǐng péngyoumen duōduō zhǐzhèng.

* * *

史： 今天 我 要 讲 的就 是 这些， 耽误 大家 不 少
Shǐ: Jīntiān wǒ yào jiǎng de jiù shì zhèxiē, Dānwu dàjiā bù shǎo

时间，谢谢。
shíjiān, xièxie.

主：史密斯 先生 给 我们 作了 一个 很 好 的 学术 报告，让 我们 向 史密斯 先生 表示衷心 的 感谢。下边儿 史密斯 先生 还 想 跟 我们 座谈座谈。大家 有 问题 可以 请 史密斯 先生 解答。
zhǔ: Shǐmìsī xiānsheng gěi wǒmen zuòle yíge hěn hǎo de xuéshù bàogào, ràng wǒmen xiàng Shǐmìsī xiānsheng biǎoshì zhōngxīn de gǎnxiè. Xiàbianr Shǐmìsī xiānsheng hái xiǎng gēn wǒmen zuòtanzuòtan. Dàjiā yǒu wèntí kěyǐ qǐng Shǐmìsī xiānsheng jiědá.

史：不是 我 解答 问题，我 是 跟 你们 一起 谈谈，交流交流 情况。座谈 嘛，在这儿的 先生、女士 都 要 谈，好不好？
Shǐ: Bú shì wǒ jiědá wèntí, wǒ shì gēn nǐmen yìqǐ tántan, jiāoliujiāoliu qíngkuàng. Zuòtán ma, zài zhèr de xiānsheng、nǚshì dōu yào tán, hǎo bu hǎo?

主：啊，都不要客气了。开始吧。
zhǔ: À, dōu bú yào kèqi le. Kāishǐ ba.

**＊5. Translate the following sentences into Chinese:**

1) What's your name, please?
2) David calls Wang Dazhong uncle.
3) She asked Mr. Chen to tell her how to address the Chinese people.
4) Come in, please!
5) Could you please tell me where comrade Xiao Zhang lives?
6) Lao Chen invited Xiao Li and his family to his place.

# 复习 (5) Revision (5) fùxí (5)

***1. Give their antonyms:**

| | | | |
|---|---|---|---|
| 长 ______ cháng ______ | 大 ______ dà ______ | 冷 ______ lěng ______ | 对 ______ duì ______ |
| 多 ______ duō ______ | 快 ______ kuài ______ | 早 ______ zǎo ______ | 新 ______ xīn ______ |
| 肥 ______ féi ______ | 复杂 ______ fùzá ______ | 上 ______ shàng ______ | 里 ______ lǐ ______ |
| 这 ______ zhè ______ | 以前 ______ yǐqián ______ | 买 ______ mǎi ______ | 来 ______ lái ______ |
| 进 ______ jìn ______ | 开始 ______ kāishǐ ______ | 出国 ______ chū guó ______ | 国内 ______ guó nèi ______ |

***2. Fill in the blanks with the right words:**

给，管，往，在，从，跟，对，让，为
gěi, guǎn, wàng, zài, cóng, gēn, duì, ràng, wèi

1) 我 刚 ______ 张 先生 那儿来。
Wǒ gāng ______ Zhāng xiānsheng nàr lái.

2) 他 要 ______ 今后的 研究 工作 作些 准备 了。
Tā yào ______ jīnhòu de yánjiū gōngzuò zuò xiē zhǔnbèi le.

3) ______ 这儿 遇见 你，我 真 高兴。
______ zhèr yùjiàn nǐ, wǒ zhēn gāoxìng.

4) 你 ______ 他 帮 你 一下儿，他 还 能 不 帮？
Nǐ ______ tā bāng nǐ yíxiàr, tā hái néng bù bāng?

5) 我 怎么 能 ______ 他 比 呢，他 多 会 办 事儿 啊。
Wǒ zěnme néng ______ tā bǐ ne, tā duō huì bàn shìr a.

6) 他 ______ 我的 帮助 太 大 了，我 得 好好儿 谢谢 他。
Tā ______ wǒ de bāngzhù tài dà le, wǒ děi hǎohāor xièxie tā.

7) ______ 你 这儿 吃 饭，我 还 客气？ 咱们 是 谁 ______ 谁 呀!
______ nǐ zhèr chī fàn, wǒ hái kèqi? Zánmen shì shuí ______ shuí ya!

8) 小王______你早点儿去，他说他______汽车站等你。
Xiǎo Wáng______nǐ zǎo diǎnr qù, tā shuō tā ______ qìchēzhàn děng nǐ .

9) 快______他们送票去吧，他们就别______咱们这儿跑了。
Kuài______tāmen sòng piào qu ba, tāmen jiù bié______zánmen zhèr pǎo le .

10) 你们______张明叫“老张”，可我们都______他叫“小张”，他比我们小啊。
Nǐmen______Zhāng Míng jiào “Lǎo Zhāng”, kě wǒmen dōu______tā jiào “Xiǎo Zhāng”, tā bǐ wǒmen xiǎo a .

***3. Correct the mistakes in the sentences:**

1) 他来刚从小赵家。
Tā lái gāng cóng Xiǎo Zhào jiā.

2) 我们去看小刘明天下午。
Wǒmen qù kàn Xiǎo Liú míngtiān xiàwǔ.

3) 晚上他们回英国从中国。
Wǎnshang tāmen huí Yīngguó cóng Zhōngguó.

4) 陈先生买了一些历史方面的书在那个书店。
Chén xiānsheng mǎile yìxiē lìshǐ fāngmiàn de shū zài nàge shūdiàn.

5) 后天晚上演杂技，王小姐给一张票她朋友。
Hòutiān wǎnshang yǎn zájì, Wáng xiǎojie gěi yìzhāng piào tā péngyou.

6) 小张游览长城跟大伟他们一起。
Xiǎo Zhāng yóulǎn Chángchéng gēn Dàwěi tāmen yìqǐ .

7) 他回学校从他哥哥那儿。
Tā huí xuéxiào cóng tā gēge nàr .

8) 前天我问了，又今天上午我问了。
Qiántiān wǒ wèn le, yòu jīntiān shàngwǔ wǒ wèn le .

9) 你们去广州什么时候？
Nǐmen qù Guǎngzhōu shénme shíhour?

10) 时间这么晚了，他们不会来一定了。
Shíjiān zhème wǎn le, tāmen bú huì lái yídìng le .

# 26 Asking The Way
## 问路 wèn lù

(The Chens are on their way to Zhang Xin's home.)

(一) I

| | | |
|---|---|---|
| 陈：<br>Chén: | 艾琳，今天咱们上老<br>Àilín, jīntiān zánmen shàng Lǎo<br>张家，走路去，好不<br>Zhāng jiā, zǒu lù qù, hǎo bu | Irene, let's walk to Lao Zhang's place, shall we? |

| | | |
|---|---|---|
| | 好？①<br>hǎo? | |
| 艾：<br>Ài: | 咱们 不认识路啊！<br>Zánmen bú rènshi lù a! | But we don't know the way. |
| 陈：<br>Chén: | 鼻子下边儿有嘴呢，②不<br>Bízi xiàbianr yǒu zuǐ ne, bú<br>认识就问嘛。<br>rènshi jiù wèn ma. | We've got mouths. We can ask. |
| 艾：<br>Ài: | 好，听你的。<br>Hǎo, tīng nǐ de. | All right, as you say. |
| 陈：<br>Chén: | 老张就住在钟楼<br>Lǎo Zhāng jiù zhù zài Zhōnglóu<br>附近，我们先到钟楼。<br>fùjìn, wǒmen xiān dào Zhōnglóu. | He lives close to Bell Tower, so let's go to Bell Tower first. |

## （二） II

| | | |
|---|---|---|
| 陈：<br>Chén: | 请问，前边儿是钟<br>Qǐng wèn, qiánbianr shì Zhōng<br>楼吗？<br>lóu ma? | Excuse me, is that Bell Tower over there? |
| 路人甲：<br>lùrén jiǎ: | 对。<br>Duì. | That's right. |
| 陈：<br>Chén: | 和平新村在哪儿？<br>Hépíng Xīn Cūn zài nǎr? | Where's New Peace Village then? |
| 路人甲：<br>lùrén jiǎ: | 钟楼的东边儿是剧<br>Zhōnglóu de dōngbianr shì jù<br>院，和平新村就在<br>yuàn, Hépíng Xīn Cūn jiù zài<br>剧院的北边儿。您到<br>jùyuàn de běibianr. Nín dào<br>那儿再问问。<br>nàr zài wènwen. | There's a theater to the east of Bell Tower, and New Peace Village is to the north of it. Ask again when you get there. |
| 陈：<br>Chén: | 谢谢。<br>Xièxie. | Thank you. |

## （三） III

| | | |
|---|---|---|
| 莉：<br>Lì: | 请问，这是和平新村吗？<br>Qǐng wèn, zhè shì Hépíng Xīn Cūn ma? | Excuse me, is this New Peace Village? |
| 路人乙：<br>lùrén yǐ: | 这不是和平新村，和平新村在南边儿。<br>Zhè bú shì Hépíng Xīn Cūn, Hépíng Xīn Cūn zài nánbianr. | No, New Peace Village is in the south. |
| 伟：<br>Wěi: | 请问怎么走呢？③<br>Qǐng wèn zěnme zǒu ne? | Could you tell me how to get there? |
| 路人乙：<br>lùrén yǐ: | 顺这条路一直往前走，到路口向右拐。<br>Shùn zhètiáo lù yìzhí wàng qián zǒu, dào lùkǒu xiàng yòu guǎi. | You go straight along this road, then turn right when you come to the end of it. |
| 莉：<br>Lì:<br>伟：<br>Wěi: | 谢谢，麻烦您啦。④<br>Xièxie, máfan nín la. | Thank you. |

## （四） IV

| | | |
|---|---|---|
| 陈：<br>Chén: | 劳驾，我问一下儿，这儿是和平新村吗？<br>Láojià, wǒ wèn yíxiàr, zhèr shì Hépíng Xīn Cūn ma? | Excuse me, is this New Peace Village? |
| 路人丙：<br>lùrén bǐng: | 对。<br>Duì. | Yes. |
| 陈：<br>Chén: | 哪儿是三号楼？<br>Nǎr shì sānhào lóu? | Could you tell me which is No 3 Building? |
| 路人丙：<br>lùrén bǐng: | 您看，那是二号楼，二号楼后边儿是三号楼。<br>Nín kàn, nà shì èrhào lóu, èrhào lóu hòubianr shì sānhào lóu. | Look, that's No 2 Building. No 3 is behind it. |
| 陈：<br>Chén: | 谢谢。<br>Xièxie. | Thank you. |

## • new words • 生词 • shēngcí

| | | | | |
|---|---|---|---|---|
| 1 | 路 | （名） | lù | road, street, way |
| 2 | 走路 | | zǒu lù | to walk |
| 3 | 鼻子 | （名） | bízi | nose |
| 4 | 下边儿 | （名） | xiàbianr | underneath, below |
| 5 | 前 | （名） | qián | front |
| 6 | 前边儿 | （名） | qiánbianr | in front, ahead |
| 7 | 路人 | （名） | lùrén | passerby |
| 8 | 甲 | （名） | jiǎ | A |
| 9 | 东 | （名） | dōng | east |
| 10 | 东边儿 | （名） | dōngbianr | to the east, in the east |
| 11 | 剧院 | （名） | jùyuàn | theater |
| 12 | 北 | （名） | běi | north |
| 13 | 北边儿 | （名） | běibianr | to the north, in the north |
| 14 | 乙 | （名） | yǐ | B |
| 15 | 南 | （名） | nán | south |
| 16 | 南边儿 | （名） | nánbianr | to the south, in the south |
| 17 | 顺 | （介） | shùn | along |
| 18 | 条 | （量） | tiáo | a measure word for something elongated in shape |
| 19 | 往 | （介） | wàng | toward |
| 20 | 路口 | （名） | lùkǒu | end of a road (street) |
| 21 | 右 | （名） | yòu | right |
| 22 | 拐 | （动） | guǎi | to turn |
| 23 | 啦 | （助） | la | a modal particle |
| 24 | 丙 | （名） | bǐng | C |

25 号 （名）hào number
26 楼 （名）lóu building
27 后 （名）hòu back
28 后边儿 （名）hòubianr behind, back

**专名 Zhuānmíng Proper name**

和平新村 Hépíng Xīn Cūn New Peace Village (a residential area in Xian)

## study points • 注释 • zhùshì

1 走路去，好不好？(Zǒu lù qù, hǎo bu hǎo?)
"好不好？" (hǎo bu hǎo?) is a form of asking for an opinion. (See Study Point 3 of Lesson 9).

2 鼻子下边儿有嘴呢。(Bízi xiàbianr yǒu zuǐ ne.)
In Chinese, "上边儿" (shàngbianr), "下边儿" (xiàbianr), "里边儿" (lǐbianr), "外边儿" (wàibianr), "旁边儿" (pángbiānr), "东边儿" (dōngbianr), "西边儿" (xībianr), "南边儿" (nánbianr), "北边儿" (běibianr), etc. are expressions of location. They can be used independently as nominal structures or they can follow nouns that modify them:

里边儿有小卖部。(Lǐbianr yǒu xiǎomàibù.)
二号楼后边儿是三号楼。(Èrhào lóu hòubianr shì sānhào lóu.)
和平新村在剧院的北边儿。(Hépíng Xīn Cūn zài jùyuàn de běibianr.)

3 怎么走呢？(Zěnme zǒu ne?)
The particle "呢" (ne) at the end of the question takes out its bluntness.

4 麻烦您啦。(Máfan nín la.)
This is a common expression to show your thanks for somebody who has helped you.

## supplementary words • 补充生词 • bǔchōng shēngcí

| | | | |
|---|---|---|---|
| 1 | 打听 | （动）dǎting | to ask, to find out |
| 2 | 路 | （量）lù | a measure word |
| 3 | 售票员 | （名）shòupiàoyuán | conductor |
| 4 | 方向 | （名）fāngxiàng | direction |
| 5 | 左边儿 | （名）zuǒbianr | left side |
| 6 | 跑 | （动）pǎo | to run |
| 7 | 错 | （形）cuò | wrong |
| 8 | 反 | （形）fǎn | the other way round |
| 9 | 马路 | （名）mǎlù | street, road |
| 10 | 对面 | （名）duìmiàn | opposite side |
| | 中国书店 | Zhōngguó Shūdiàn | China Book Store |

## • exercises • 练习 • liànxí

*1. **Fill in the blanks in accordance with the contents of the pictures:**

北边儿，东边儿，前边儿，后边儿，
běibianr, dōngbianr, qiánbianr, hòubianr,

三号楼前边儿那个楼就是二号楼。
Sānhào lóu qiánbianr nàge lóu jiù shì èrhào lóu.

1) 钟楼 ________ 是剧院。
Zhōnglóu ________ shì jùyuàn.

2) 和平新村在剧院 ________。
Hépíng XīnCūn zài jùyuàn ________.

3) 一号楼 ______ 有一家饭馆儿。
Yīhào lóu ______ yǒu yìjiā fànguǎnr.

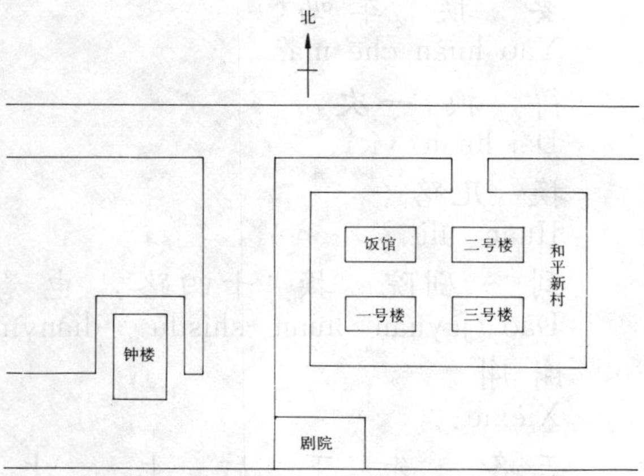


4) 二号 楼 ________ 那个 楼 就是 三号 楼。
Èrhào lóu ________ nàge lóu jiù shì sānhào lóu.

***2. Complete the questions with your own words:**

1) A: 今天 咱们 上 老 李家，________？
Jīntiān zánmen shàng Lǎo Lǐ jiā, ________？

B: 走 路去吧。
Zǒu lù qù ba.

2) A: 劳 驾，我想 跟您 打听打听，去友谊 医院 ________？
Láo jià, wǒ xiǎng gēn nín dǎtingdǎting, qù Yǒuyì Yīyuàn ________？

B: 顺 这条路一直向 前 走。
Shùn zhètiáo lù yìzhí xiàng qián zǒu.

3) A: 劳 您 驾，我 打听一下儿，人民 剧场 ________？
Láo nín jià, wǒ dǎting yíxiàr, Rénmín Jùchǎng________？

B: 在 饭馆儿 南边儿。
Zài fànguǎnr nánbianr.

4) A: 同志，请 问 ________ 三号 楼？
Tóngzhì, qǐng wèn ________ sānhào lóu？

B: 最 后边儿 那个楼 就是。
Zuì hòubianr nàge lóu jiù shì.

**3. Listen to the dialogues:**

1) 陈 明 山：劳 驾，我 打听一下儿，去 中国 书店 怎么 坐 车？
Chén Míngshān: Láo jià, wǒ dǎting yíxiàr, qù Zhōngguó Shūdiàn zěnme zuò chē?

路人：坐 一路、十路汽车 都 可以。
lùrén: Zuò yílù、shílù qìchē dōu kěyǐ.

陈　：　要　换　车吗？
Chén:　Yào huàn chē ma?

路人：　得　换　一次。
lùrén：　Děi huàn yícì.

陈　：　换　几路？
Chén:　Huàn jǐlù？

路人：　到　剧院　换　十四路，电影院　下。
lùrén：　Dào jùyuàn huàn shísìlù, diànyǐngyuàn xià.

陈　：　谢谢。
Chén:　Xièxie.

2) 售　票　员：　三路，先　下　后　上，上了　车　请　往　里　走。
shòupiàoyuán:　Sānlù, xiān xià hòu shàng, shàngle chē qǐng wàng lǐ zǒu.

大伟：　同志，是　三路　汽车　吗？
Dàwěi:　Tóngzhì, shì sānlù qìchē ma?

售　票　员：　对。
shòupiàoyuán:　Duì.

大伟：　快　上！
Dàwěi:　Kuài shàng!

莉莉：　大伟，来的　时候　怎么　没　看　见　右　边儿　这个　大楼？
Lìli：　Dàwěi, lái de shíhour zěnme méi kàn jiàn yòu bianr zhège dàlóu？

大伟：　是　啊。
Dàwěi:　Shì a.

莉莉：　妈，您　说　咱们　这　车　在　往　哪个　方　向　走？
Lìli：　Mā, nín shuō zánmen zhè chē zài wàng nǎge fāng xiàng zǒu？

艾琳：　往　南　啊。
Àilín:　Wàng nán a.

陈　明山：　是　吗？你　看，太阳　在　哪儿？
Chén Míngshān:　Shì ma? Nǐ kàn, tàiyang zài nǎr？

艾琳：　太阳　在　车的　左边儿。
Àilín：　Tàiyang zài chē de zuǒbianr.

陈　：　前边儿　是　南，左边儿就　是……
Chén:　Qiánbianr shì nán, zuǒbianr jiù shì…

大伟： 东。
Dàwěi: Dōng.

陈 ： 你 看看，下午 五点钟 的 太阳 怎么 跑 到 东边儿 去了？
Chén: Nǐ kànkan, xiàwǔ wǔdiǎnzhōng de tàiyang zěnme pǎo dào dōngbianr qù le ?

艾琳： 那么 说，车 坐 错 了！
Àilín : Nàme shuō, chē zuò cuò le !

莉莉： 车 没 坐 错，是 三路。大概 方向 不 对。
Lìli : Chē méi zuò cuò, shì sānlù. Dàgài fāngxiàng bú duì.

大伟： 姐姐，你 快 去 问问 售票员 同志 吧。
Dàwěi: Jiějie, nǐ kuài qù wènwen shòupiàoyuán tóngzhì ba.

莉莉： 同志，这 车 是 开 往 钟楼 的吗？
Lìli : Tóngzhì, zhè chē shì kāi wǎng Zhōnglóu de ma?

售票员： 不 对，你们 坐 反 了。快 下 车，到 马路 对面 去 上。
shòupiàoyuán: Bú duì, nǐmen zuò fǎn le. Kuài xià chē, dào mǎlù duìmiàn qù shàng.

***4. Translate the following sentences into Chinese:**

1) What can you see from the bell tower?
2) On the east side of the theater is the Roast Duck Restaurant.
3) Lili was sitting on the right side of Aunt Ding.
4) Is the Peace Housing Estate somewhere ahead?
5) Excuse me, could you show me the way to China Bookstore?
6) Go straight ahead, take the first turning on the right and you can't miss it.

# 27 When Old Friends Meet
# 老友重逢 lǎoyǒu chóngféng

(Mr. Chen Mingshan and Zhang Xin talk about what has become of them since they last met.)

| | | |
|---|---|---|
| 陈 ： <br> Chén: | 老 张 ，分别 四十年 了， <br> Lǎo Zhāng, fēnbié sìshínián le , <br> 今天 我们 能 在这儿见 <br> jīntiān wǒmen néng zài zhèr jiàn <br> 面 ，实在 太 高兴 了。 <br> miàn, shízài tài gāoxìng le . | Lao Zhang, it's really nice to see you again after a period of forty years. |

| | | |
|---|---|---|
| 张：<br>Zhāng: | 可不是吗？① 国庆前接到你的信，② 知道你要到西安来，全家人都高兴极了。昨天上午接到你的电话后，我就告诉了玉珍。下午她就买好了菜，还特意买了黄油、面包，准备今天好好儿招待你们。<br>Kě bu shì ma? Gúoqìng qián jiē dào nǐ de xìn, zhīdao nǐ yào dào Xī'ān lai, quán jiā rén dōu gāoxìng jí le. Zuótiān shàngwǔ jiē dào nǐ de diànhuà hòu, wǒ jiù gàosule Yùzhēn. Xiàwǔ tā jiù mǎi hǎo le cài, hái tèyì mǎile huángyóu、miànbāo, zhǔn bèi jīntiān hǎohāor zhāodài nǐ men. | Yes, isn't it? We were all overjoyed when we got your letter before the National Day saying that you were coming to Xian. I told Yuzhen about your coming right after. I got your call yesterday morning. She went grocery shopping in the afternoon and had everything ready for today's dinner. The bread and butter are specially prepared for you. |
| 陈：<br>Chén: | 太感谢了。老张，你这儿离我们住的地方很近啊。<br>Tài gǎnxiè le. Lǎo Zhāng, nǐ zhèr lí wǒmen zhù de dìfang hěn jìn a. | You are all too kind. Lao Zhang, your residence is very close to the place where we are staying. |
| 张：<br>Zhāng: | 刚才你们是怎么来的？③ 是坐公共汽车来的吗？<br>Gāngcái nǐmen shì zěnme lái de? Shì zuò gōnggòng qìchē lái de ma? | How did you get here? By bus? |
| 陈：<br>Chén: | 不，我们是走来的。路上问了几个人。<br>Bù, wǒmen shì zǒu lái de. Lùshang wènle jǐge rén. | No, we walked. We asked several people on our way. |
| 张：<br>Zhāng: | 你们这次在北京呆了<br>Nǐmen zhècì zài Běijīng dāile | How long did you stay in Beijing? |

| | | |
|---|---|---|
| | 多长时间？<br>duō cháng shíjiān? | |
| 陈：<br>Chén: | 我们是上个月二十三号到北京的。在北京呆了两个星期。<br>Wǒmen shi shàngge yuè èrshí sānhào dào Běijing de. Zài Běijing dāile liǎngge xīngqī. | We arrived in Beijing on the 23rd of last month, and stayed there for two weeks. |
| 张：<br>Zhāng: | 你还记得四十年前，我们分别的情景吗？<br>Nǐ hái jìde sìshínián qián, wǒmen fēnbié de qíngjǐng ma? | Do you still remember how we parted forty years ago? |
| 陈：<br>Chén: | 忘不了。我们是在昆明的一个汽车站分别的。那是一九四〇年十一月八号。④<br>Wàng bu liǎo. Wǒmen shì zài Kūnmíng de yíge qìchēzhàn fēnbié de. Nà shi yījiǔsìlíngnián shíyīyuè bāhào. | I'll never forget it. We bid each other farewell at a bus station in Kunming. It was on the 8th of November, 1940. |
| 张：<br>Zhāng: | 我是四二年大学毕业后来西安的，快四十年了，一直就在西安。<br>Wǒ shì sì'èrnián dàxué bì yè hòu lái Xī'ān de, kuài sìshínián le, yìzhí jiù zài Xī'ān. | I came to Xian after I graduated from the university in 1942 nearly forty years ago, and I've been here ever since. |
| 陈：<br>Chén: | 分别时，我们都是二十来岁的人，现在见面时都成老头儿了。<br>Fēnbié shí, wǒmen dōu shì èrshí lái suì de rén, xiànzài jiàn miàn shí dōu chéng lǎo tóur le. | We were in our early twenties then, but we are old men now. |
| 张：<br>Zhāng: | 自然规律嘛！孩子们大了，我们也老了。<br>Zìrán guīlǜ ma! Háizimen dà le, wǒmen yě lǎo le. | Ah, it's the law of nature! Our children have grown up, and we have grown old. |

| | | |
|---|---|---|
| 陈：<br>Chén: | 你几个孩子都在身边吗？⑤<br>Nǐ jǐge háizi dōu zài shēnbiān ma? | Are your children still with you? |
| 张：<br>Zhāng: | 三个孩子都在西安。老大跟老二都是医院的医生，⑥ 老三上中学呢。<br>Sānge háizi dōu zài Xī'ān. Lǎodà gēn lǎo'èr dōu shì yīyuàn de yīshēng, lǎosān shàng zhōngxué ne. | All three of them are in Xian. The elder two are doctors. The youngest is still in high school. |
| 陈：<br>Chén: | 老大、老二结婚了吗？<br>Lǎodà、lǎo'èr jié hūn le ma? | Are the elder ones married? |
| 张：<br>Zhāng: | 老大去年结的婚。⑦ 他爱人在工厂工作，⑧ 是个工程师。老二还没结婚，有对象了。<br>Lǎodà qùnián jié de hūn. Tā àiren zài gōngchǎng gōngzuò, shì ge gōngchéngshī. Lǎo'ér hái méi jié hūn, yǒu duìxiàng le. | The eldest was marriec last year. His wife is an engineer in a factory. The second isn't married yet but he's got a fiancée. |
| 陈：<br>Chén: | 什么时候结婚啊？<br>Shénme shíhour jié hūn a? | When are they going to get married? |
| 张：<br>Zhāng: | 元旦。现在正在准备。前几天刚买了床、桌子、椅子、沙发、衣柜。<br>Yuándàn. Xiànzài zhèng zài zhǔnbèi. Qián jǐtiān gāng mǎile chuáng、zhuōzi、yǐzi、shāfā、yīguì. | On the New Year's Day. They are getting everything ready. They've bought a bed, a table, a few chairs, two sofas and a wardrobe just a few days ago. |
| 陈：<br>Chén: | 老二的对象也是医生吗？<br>Lǎo'èr de duìxiàng yě shì yīshēng ma? | Is his fiancée also a doctor? |
| 张：<br>Zhāng: | 不，是个舞蹈演员。我<br>Bù, shì ge wǔdǎo yǎnyuán. Wǒ | No, she is a dancer. I've asked them to come |

| | | |
|---|---|---|
| | 让 他们 中午 下 班 都<br>ràng tāmen zhōngwǔ xià bān dōu<br>回 来 跟 你们 见见 面。<br>huí lai gēn nǐmen jiànjian miàn. | after work to meet you all this noon. |
| 陈：<br>Chén: | 太 好 了。老 张，你<br>Tài hǎo le. Lǎo Zhāng, nǐ<br>这个 家庭 真 是 个 幸福<br>zhège jiātíng zhēn shì ge xìngfú<br>的 家庭啊！<br>de jiātíng a! | Excellent! Lao Zhang, your family is indeed a happy one. |
| 张：<br>Zhāng: | 是 啊。十二点 了，他们<br>Shì a. Shí'èrdiǎn le, tāmen<br>也 快 回 来了。咱们 准<br>yě kuài huí lai le. Zánmen zhǔn<br>备 吃 饭 吧，一边 吃 一边<br>bèi chī fàn ba, yìbiān chī yìbiān<br>聊。今天 请 你 尝尝<br>liáo. Jīntiān qǐng nǐ chángchang<br>玉 珍 的 手艺。<br>Yùzhēn de shǒuyì. | Yes, indeed. Well, it's twelve o'clock now. They will be home soon. Let's eat first. We can chat while we eat. You can try Yuzhen's cooking. |

## • new words • 生词 • shēngcí

| | | | | |
|---|---|---|---|---|
| 1 | 老友重逢 | | lǎoyǒu chóngféng | reunion of old friends |
| 2 | 分别 | (动) | fēnbié | to part, to separate |
| 3 | 可不是 | | kě bu shì | isn't it |
| 4 | 国庆 | (名) | guóqìng | National Day |
| 5 | 接 | (动) | jiē | to receive, to take, to connect |
| | 接到 | | jiē dào | to receive |
| 6 | 告诉 | (动) | gàosu | to tell |
| 7 | 特意 | (副) | tèyì | specially |
| 8 | 黄油 | (名) | huángyóu | butter |

| | | | | |
|---|---|---|---|---|
| 9 | 面包 | （名） | miànbāo | bread |
| 10 | 招待 | （动） | zhāodài | to entertain |
| 11 | 近 | （形） | jìn | near, close |
| 12 | 公共 | （形） | gōnggòng | public |
| | 公共汽车 | | gōnggòng qìchē | public bus (service) |
| 13 | 路上 | （名） | lùshang | (on the) road, (on the) way |
| 14 | 记得 | （动） | jìde | to remember |
| 15 | 情景 | （名） | qíngjǐng | situation, scene |
| 16 | 忘 | （动） | wàng | to forget |
| | 忘不了 | | wàng bu liǎo | unforgettable, not to forget |
| 17 | 站 | （名） | zhàn | station, stop |
| 18 | 0 | （数） | líng | zero, nil |
| 19 | 大学 | （名） | dàxué | university |
| 20 | 毕业 | | bì yè | to graduate |
| 21 | 成 | （动） | chéng | to become |
| 22 | 老头儿 | （名） | lǎotóur | old man |
| 23 | 自然 | （形、名、副） | zìrán | natural, nature, naturally |
| 24 | 规律 | （名） | guīlǜ | law |
| 25 | 身边 | （名） | shēnbiān | one's side |
| 26 | 老大 | （名） | lǎodà | the eldest (son, daughter) |
| | 老二 | | lǎo'èr | the second (eldest) |
| | 老三 | | lǎosān | the third (eldest) |
| 27 | 医院 | （名） | yīyuàn | hospital |
| 28 | 中学 | （名） | zhōngxué | high school |
| 29 | 结婚 | | jié hūn | to marry |
| 30 | 爱人 | （名） | àiren | wife, husband, fiancée, fiancé |
| 31 | 工厂 | （名） | gōngchǎng | factory |
| 32 | 工程师 | （名） | gōngchéngshī | engineer |
| 33 | 对象 | （名） | duìxiàng | fiancée, fiance, object |
| 34 | 元旦 | （名） | yuándàn | New Year's Day |

| | | | |
|---|---|---|---|
| 35 | 床 | （名）chuáng | bed |
| 36 | 椅子 | （名）yǐzi | chair |
| 37 | 沙发 | （名）shāfā | sofa |
| 38 | 衣柜 | （名）yīguì | wardrobe |
| 39 | 舞蹈 | （名）wǔdǎo | dance |
| 40 | 演员 | （名）yǎnyuán | actor, actress |
| 41 | 中午 | （名）zhōngwǔ | noon |
| 42 | 下班 | xià bān | to come or go off work |
| 43 | 家庭 | （名）jiātíng | family |
| 44 | 幸福 | （形）xìngfú | happy |
| 45 | 聊 | （动）liáo | to chat |
| 46 | 手艺 | （名）shǒuyì | skill |

| 专名 | Zhuānmíng | Proper names |
|---|---|---|
| 张新 | Zhāng Xīn | name of a friend of Mr. Chen Mingshan |
| 张 | Zhāng | a common Chinese family name |
| 玉珍 | Yùzhēn | name of Lao Zhang's wife |
| 昆明 | Kūnmíng | Kunming, capital of Yunan Province in the southwest of China |

## study points • 注释 • zhùshì

1 可不是吗？(Kě bu shì ma?)

This is a common expression to show your agreement.

2 国庆前接到你的信。(Guóqìng qián jiē dào nǐ de xìn.)

“国庆” (guóqìng) here refers to the National Day of the People's Republic of China. The PRC was founded on October 1st, 1949.

3 刚才你们是怎么来的？(Gāngcái nǐmen shì zěnme lái de?)

The "是…的" (shì…de) structure is often used to emphasize the time, place and manner of an action which has already taken place:

他们是上个月二十三号到北京的。
(Tāmen shì shàngge yuè èrshísānhào dào Běijīng de.) (time)

我们是在昆明的一个火车站分别的。
(Wǒmen shì zài Kūnmíng de yíge huǒchēzhàn fēnbié de.) (place)

你们是坐公共汽车来的吗？
(Nǐmen shì zuò gōnggòng qìchē lái de ma?) (manner)

"是" (shì) is sometimes omitted in the structure. The object, if there is one, can be placed between the verb and "的" (de), or after "的":

他（是）昨天到中国的。(Tā (shì) zuótiān dào Zhōngguó de.) or
他（是）昨天到的中国。(Tā (shì) zuótiān dào de Zhōngguó.)

The negative form of this structure is "不是…的" (bú shì…de). In the negative, "是" cannot be omitted:

他们不是坐公共汽车来的。
(Tāmen bú shì zuò gōnggòng qìchē lái de.)
张先生不是从美国来的。
(Zhāng xiānsheng bú shì cóng Měiguó lái de.)

4 那是一九四〇年十一月八号。(Nà shì yījiǔsìlíngnián shíyīyuè bāhào.)

In Chinese, the order of date is: _年 (nián) _月 (yuè) _日 (rì) or (号) (hào), the opposite of that in English.

5 你几个孩子都在身边吗? (Nǐ jǐge háizi dōu zài shēnbiān ma?)

"在身边" (zài shēnbiān) here means to live together with.

6 老大跟老二都是医院的医生。(Lǎodà gēn lǎo'èr dōu shì yīyuàn de yīshēng.)

"老大" (lǎodà) is a colloquial expression meaning the first son or daughter of the family. "老二" (lǎo'èr) is the second, "老三" (lǎosān) the third, so on and forth up to "十" (shí).

7 老大去年结的婚。(Lǎodà qùnián jié de hūn.)

"结" (jié) is a verb while "婚" (hūn) is the object of it. The normal way of using this expression is A 跟 (gēn) B 结婚。

8 他爱人在工厂工作。(Tā àiren zài gōngchǎng gōngzuò.)

The Chinese nowadays call their spouses "爱人" (àiren) instead of "丈夫" (zhàngfu, husband) or 妻子 (qīzi, wife). "先生" (xiānsheng) and "太太" (tàitai) are no longer used either.

## supplementary words • 补充生词 • bǔchōng shēngcí

| | | | | |
|---|---|---|---|---|
| 1 | 失散 | （动） | shīsàn | to lose |
| 2 | 羊肉泡馍 | | yángròu pào mó | a popular dish in the northwest of China |
| 3 | 特产 | （名） | tèchǎn | special produce |
| 4 | 各 | （代） | gè | every |
| 5 | 满 | （形） | mǎn | full |
| 6 | 鱼翅 | （名） | yúchì | shark's fin |
| 7 | 难得 | （形） | nándé | rare |
| 8 | 席 | （名） | xí | banquet, table |
| 9 | 名贵 | （形） | míngguì | valuable |
| 10 | 练 | （动） | liàn | to practice |
| 11 | 洗尘 | （动） | xǐchén | to celebrate someone's homecoming |
| 12 | 恭敬不如从命 | | gōngjìng bùrú cóngmìng | The best way to show respect is to obey. |

## • exercises • 练习 • liànxí

*1. **Answer the following questions:**

Model: A: 你是怎么来的？
Nǐ shì zěnme lái de?

B: 我是走来的。（走）
Wǒ shì zǒu lái de. （zǒu）

1) A: 他们 一家是 怎么去 上海 的?
Tāmen yìjiā shì zěnme qù Shànghǎi de?
B: ________________。( 火车 )
________________. ( huǒchē )

2) A: 他们 是 什么 时候儿 到 北京 的?
Tāmen shì shénme shíhòur dào Běijīng de?
B: ________________。( 九月 五日下午 )
________________. ( jiǔyuè wǔrì xiàwǔ )

3) A: 你 家老大 是 哪年 结的婚?
Nǐ jiā lǎodà shì nǎnián jié de hūn?
B: ________________。( 去年 )
________________. ( qùnián )

4) A: 他们 是 在哪儿分别 的?
Tāmen shì zài nǎr fēnbié de?
B: ________________。( 汽车站 )
________________. ( qìchēzhàn )

5) A: 你是 在哪儿 学 的 汉语?
Nǐ shì zài nǎr xué de Hànyǔ?
B: ________________。( 中国 )
________________. ( Zhōngguó )

***2. Complete the sentences after the model:**

Model: 见 到你，我很 高兴。( 很 )
Jiàn dào nǐ, wǒ hěn gāoxing. ( hěn )

1) 今天 有 机会来 你们 国家 参观、访问，________
Jīntiān yǒu jīhui lái nǐmen guójiā cānguān、fǎngwèn, ________
________。( 很 )
________. ( hěn )

2) 接 到你的 来信，________。(……极 了)
Jiē dào nǐ de lái xìn, ________. (…… jí le)

3) 这次回 国探亲，找 到了 失散 多年 的 孩子，________
Zhècì huí guó tànqīn, zhǎo dàole shīsàn duōnián de háizi, ________
________。(太 …… 了)
________。( tài …… le )

**3. Fill in the blanks after the model:**

Model: 今天 请 你 尝尝 她的 手艺。( 你 )
Jīntiān qǐng nǐ chángchang tā de shǒuyì. ( nǐ )

1) ____________ 西安的 羊肉 泡 馍。
____________ Xī'ān de yángròu pào mó.

2) ＿＿＿＿＿＿ 我 家乡 的 特产。
＿＿＿＿＿＿ wǒ jiāxiāng de tèchǎn.

3) ＿＿＿＿＿＿ 北京 烤鸭 。
＿＿＿＿＿＿ Běijīng kǎoyā.

**4. Listen to the dialogue:**

赵 太太： 哎呀，你们 太 客气 了。看，这 满满 的 一 桌子。
Zhào tàitai: Āiyā, nǐmen tài kèqi le. Kàn, zhè mǎnmǎn de yì zhuōzi.

刘 太太： 也 没 什么 东西。坐，坐。
Liú tàitai: Yě méi shénme dōngxi. Zuò, zuò.

赵 先生： 不 要 这么 麻烦 嘛。老 刘，今天 咱们 主要 是 好好儿 聊聊。
Zhào xiānsheng: Bú yào zhème máfan ma. Lǎo Liú, jīntiān zánmen zhǔyào shì hǎohāor liáoliao.

刘 先生： 要 好好儿 聊聊，也 要 好好儿 喝喝。来，先 为 咱们 两家 的 重逢 干 一杯！
Liú xiānsheng: Yào hǎohāor liáoliao, yě yào hǎohāor hēhe. Lái, xiān wèi zánmen liǎngjiā de chóngféng gān yìbēi!

赵 先生： 干！
Zhào xiānsheng: Gān!

刘 太太： 你们 尝尝 这个。
Liú tàitai: Nǐmen chángchang zhège.

赵 先生： 这 是 鱼翅 吧？很 难得 呀！
Zhào xiānsheng: Zhè shì yúchì ba? Hěn nándé ya!

刘 先生： 是 我 哥哥 寄 来 的。
Liú xiānsheng: Shì wǒ gēge jì lai de.

赵 太太： 鱼翅 是 中国 席上 最 名贵 的 菜 呀！
Zhào tàitai: Yúchì shì Zhōngguó xíshang zuì míngguì de cài ya!

刘 太太： 都 这么 说。大概 就 名贵 在 难得 上 了。夹 菜 呀！
Liú tàitai: Dōu zhème shuō. Dàgài jiù míngguì zài nándé shang le. Jiā cài ya!

赵 太太： 好，我 自己 来。
Zhào tàitai: Hǎo, wǒ zìjǐ lái.

赵 先生： 味道 真 好！没 想 到 刘 太太 你 还
Zhào xiānsheng: Wèidao zhēn hǎo! Méi xiǎng dào Liú tàitai nǐ hái

有 这么高的手艺，跟谁 学的？
yǒu zhème gāo de shǒuyì, gēn shuí xué de?

| | |
|---|---|
| 刘太太： | 自己慢慢儿练的，做得不好。 |
| Liú tàitai : | Zìjǐ mànmānr liàn de, zuò de bù hǎo. |
| 刘先生： | 今天为老赵全家洗尘，应该干三杯。请，请。 |
| Liú xiānsheng: | Jīntiān wèi Lǎo Zhào quán jiā xǐchén, yīnggāi gān sānbēi. Qǐng, qǐng. |
| 赵先生： | 请。 |
| Zhào xiānsheng: | Qǐng. |
| 刘太太： | 赵太太，来呀。 |
| Liú tàitai : | Zhào tàitai, lái ya. |
| 赵太太： | 哎呀，我就能喝一杯。 |
| Zhào tàitai : | Āiyā, wǒ jiù néng hē yìbēi. |
| 赵先生： | 恭敬不如从命，你喝啤酒吧。 |
| Zhào xiānsheng: | Gōngjìng bùrú cóngmìng, nǐ hē píjiǔ ba. |
| 刘先生： | 好，添上，添上。 |
| Liú xiānsheng: | Hǎo, tiān shang, tiān shang. |

*5. **Translate the sentences into Chinese. Note the difference in meaning between the two sentences in each group.**

1) It was in April, 1952 that I returned from abroad.
   I returned from abroad on April, 1952.
2) It was in the Uuited States that Lao Zhang got to know Lao Liu.
   Lao Zhang got to know Lao Liu in the United States.
3) It was with his father that he went to Britain.
   He went to Britain with his father.

# 28 Talking About Learning Chinese
# 谈汉语学习 tán hànyǔ xuéxí

(After dinner Guo Yuzhen, Lao Zhang's wife, talks to Lily about learning Chinese.)

| | | |
|---|---|---|
| 郭玉珍：<br>Guō Yùzhēn: | 莉莉，你汉语 说 得 真<br>Lìli, nǐ Hànyǔ shuō de zhēn<br>好，① 又流利又清楚。②<br>hǎo, yòu liúlì yòu qīngchu. | Lily, you speak excellent Chinese, fluent and clear. |
| 莉：<br>Lì: | 伯母，您 过奖 了。③ 我<br>Bómǔ, nín guòjiǎng le. Wǒ | Oh Auntie, you're flattering me. I don't |

| | | |
|---|---|---|
| | 说 得不好。<br>shuō de bù hǎo. | speak well at all. |
| 郭：<br>Guō: | 不，你的 声调 、语调 都<br>Bù, nǐ de shēngdiào、yǔdiào dōu<br>很 自然，跟 从 小 生<br>hěn zìrán, gēn cóng xiǎo shēng<br>活 在 北京 的 人 差 不<br>huó zài Běijīng de rén chà bu<br>多 。<br>duō. | No, you have such natural tone and intonation, just like people raised in Beijing. |
| 张 ：<br>Zhāng: | 莉莉，你 听听，④ 你 伯母 是<br>Lìli, nǐ tīngting, nǐ bómǔ shì<br>教 外国 留学生 汉语<br>jiāo wàiguó liúxuéshēng Hànyǔ<br>的，⑤ 三句 话 不离 本行。⑥<br>de, sānjù huà bù lí běnháng. | Listen to her, Lily. Your Aunt teaches foreign students Chinese. She always talks shop. |
| 莉：<br>Lì: | 我 正 想 请 伯母 帮<br>Wǒ zhèng xiǎng qǐng bómǔ bāng<br>助 我 学 汉语 呢。不 知<br>zhù wǒ xué Hànyǔ ne. Bù zhī<br>道 伯母 愿意 不 愿意 收<br>dao bómǔ yuànyì bu yuànyì shōu<br>我 这个 学 生 。<br>wǒ zhège xuésheng. | And I was thinking of asking Auntie to help me with my Chinese. Would you take me as your student, Auntie? |
| 郭 ：<br>Guō: | 你 从 小 就 开始 学 的 吧？<br>Nǐ cóng xiǎo jiù kāishǐ xué de ba? | You must have started learning Chinese when you were very young? |
| 莉：<br>Lì: | 从 十一岁 起，爸爸 就 教<br>Cóng shíyīsuì qǐ, bàba jiù jiāo<br>我。我 每天 都 起 得<br>wǒ. Wǒ měitiān dōu qǐ de<br>很 早，睡 得 很 晚。早<br>hěn zǎo, shuì de hěn wǎn. Zǎo<br>上 起 床 以后，我 就<br>shang qǐ chuáng yǐhòu, wǒ jiù<br>自己 念 啊，背 啊， 说 啊。⑦<br>zìjǐ niàn a, bèi a, shuō a.<br>下午 听 录音 ，写 汉字。<br>Xiàwǔ tīng lùyīn, xiě Hànzì. | Dad started teaching me Chinese when I was eleven. I get up very early every morning and go to bed late. I read, recite and speak on my own in the morning. In the afternoon I practice writing Chinese characters and listen to tapes; at night I practice spoken |

| | | |
|---|---|---|
| | 晚上 跟爸爸练习说<br>Wǎnshang gēn bàba liànxí shuō<br>汉语。<br>Hànyǔ. | Chinese with Dad. |
| 郭：<br>Guō: | 怪不得你学得这样<br>Guài bu de nǐ xué de zhèyàng<br>好。莉莉，你觉得汉语难<br>hǎo. Lìli, nǐ juéde Hànyǔ nán<br>吗？<br>ma? | No wonder your Chinese is so good. Do you find Chinese difficult, Lily? |
| 莉：<br>Lì: | 我觉得语音、语法不太难，<br>Wǒ juéde yǔyīn、yǔfǎ bú tài nán,<br>汉字比较难。<br>Hànzì bǐjiào nán. | Pronunciation and grammar aren't too difficult, but Chinese characters are. |
| 郭：<br>Guō: | 你汉字写得怎么样？<br>Nǐ Hànzì xiě de zěnmeyàng? | How's your Chinese handwriting? |
| 莉：<br>Lì: | 不好。伯母，您看看，这<br>Bù hǎo. Bómǔ, nín kànkan, zhè<br>就是我写的汉字。<br>jiù shì wǒ xiě de Hànzì. | Bad. Auntie, look, I wrote these. |
| 郭：<br>Guō: | 很好，很好。莉莉，听<br>Hén hǎo, hén hǎo. Lìli, tīng<br>说你会好几种语言，<br>shuō nǐ huì hǎo jǐzhǒng yǔyán,<br>是吗？<br>shì ma? | Good, very good! Lily, I was told you speak many languages. Is that right? |
| 莉：<br>Lì: | 除了英语、汉语以外，<br>Chúle Yīngyǔ、Hànyǔ yǐwài,<br>法语、日语也能说一<br>Fǎyǔ、Rìyǔ yě néng shuō yì<br>点儿。⑧<br>diǎnr. | Besides English and Chinese, I also speak a little French and Japanese. |
| 陈：<br>Chén: | 莉莉，时间不早了，我们<br>Lìli, shíjiān bù zǎo le, wǒmen<br>该走了吧？<br>gāi zǒu le ba? | It's getting late, Lily. Shouldn't we be leaving? |
| 莉：<br>Lì: | 伯母，耽误了您不少时<br>Bómǔ, dānwule nín bù shǎo shí | Auntie, I've taken up much of your time. |

| | | |
|---|---|---|
| | 间，谢谢您。<br>jiān, xièxie nín. | Thank you. |
| 郭：<br>Guō: | 没什么。⑨陈先生，<br>Méi shénme. Chén xiānsheng,<br>你女儿可真招人喜<br>nǐ nǚ'ér kě zhēn zhāo rén xǐ<br>欢啊！⑩<br>huan a ! | Oh, it's nothing. Mr. Chen, you've such a lovely daughter. |

## • new words • 生词 • shēngcí

| | | | | |
|---|---|---|---|---|
| 1 | 汉语 | （名） | Hànyǔ | the Chinese language |
| 2 | 学习 | （动、名） | xuéxí | to learn, study |
| 3 | 流利 | （形） | liúlì | fluent |
| 4 | 过奖 | （动） | guòjiǎng | overpraise, flatter |
| 5 | 声调 | （名） | shēngdiào | tone |
| 6 | 语调 | （名） | yǔdiào | intonation |
| 7 | 生活 | （动、名） | shēnghuó | to live, life |
| 8 | 教 | （动） | jiāo | to teach |
| 9 | 留学生 | （名） | liúxuéshēng | foreign students, students studying abroad |
| 10 | 三句话不离本行 | | sānjù huà bù lí běnháng | talking shop |
| 11 | 愿意 | （助动） | yuànyì | to be willing |
| 12 | 收 | （动） | shōu | to accept, to keep |
| 13 | 学生 | （名） | xuésheng | student, pupil |
| 14 | 开始 | （动） | kāishǐ | to begin, to start |
| 15 | 学 | （动） | xué | to learn |
| 16 | 从……起 | | cóng…qǐ | from, starting from |

| | | | | |
|---|---|---|---|---|
| 17 | 起 | (动) | qǐ | to rise |
| 18 | 睡 | (动) | shuì | to go to bed, to sleep |
| 19 | 早上 | (名) | zǎoshang | morning |
| 20 | 起床 | | qǐ chuáng | to get out of bed, to get up |
| 21 | 自己 | (代) | zìjǐ | self |
| 22 | 念 | (动) | niàn | to read |
| 23 | 背 | (动) | bèi | to recite, to learn by heart |
| 24 | 录音 | (名) | lùyīn | recording |
| 25 | 汉字 | (名) | Hànzì | Chinese character |
| 26 | 练习 | (动、名) | liànxí | to practice, practice |
| 27 | 觉得 | (动) | juéde | to feel, to think |
| 28 | 难 | (形) | nán | difficult |
| 29 | 语音 | (名) | yǔyīn | pronunciation, phonetics |
| 30 | 语法 | (名) | yǔfǎ | grammar |
| 31 | 语言 | (名) | yǔyán | language |
| 32 | 除了 | (介) | chúle | besides, except |
| 33 | 以外 | (名) | yǐwài | apart from |
| | 除了……以外 | | chúle…yǐwài | besides, except |
| 34 | 英语 | (名) | Yīngyǔ | the English language |
| 35 | 法语 | (名) | Fǎyǔ | the French language |
| 36 | 日语 | (名) | Rìyǔ | the Japanese language |
| 37 | 耽误 | (动) | dānwu | to hold up, to delay |
| 38 | 可 | (副) | kě | (for emphasis) |
| 39 | 招 | (动) | zhāo | to attract |

## 专名　Zhuānmíng　Proper Name

| | | |
|---|---|---|
| 郭玉珍 | Guō Yùzhēn | the name of the wife of Zhang Xin, a friend of Chen Mingshan's |
| 郭 | Guō | a Chinese common family name |

## study points • 注释 • zhùshì

1 你汉语说得真好。(Nǐ Hànyǔ shuō de zhēn hǎo.)

To show the extent of an action, the following pattern is used:

subject+verb+"得" (de) + adjective:

每天我起得很早。(Měitiān wǒ qǐ de hěn zǎo.)

他学得很好。(Tā xué de hěn hǎo.)

If there is an object, the pattern is as follows:

subject + verb + object + verb repeated+"得" +adjective:

他写汉字写得很快。(Tā xiě Hànzì xiě de hěn kuài.)

我做饭做得很好。(Wǒ zuò fàn zuò de hěn hǎo.)

If the object is to be emphasized, the following two patterns are used:

a. subject+object+verb+"得"+ adjective:

他汉字写得很快。(Tā Hànzì xiě de hěn kuài.)

他饭做得很好。(Tā fàn zuò de hěn hǎo.)

b. object + subject + verb +"得"+adjective:

汉字他写得很快。(Hànzì tā xiě de hěn kuài.)

饭他做得很好。(Fàn tā zuò de hěn hǎo.)

The negative is formed by putting the adverb"不"(bù) before the adjective:

昨天晚上他睡得不晚。(Zuótiān wǎnshang tā shuì de bù wǎn.)

我英语说得不好。(Wǒ Yīngyǔ shuō de bù hǎo.)

The alternative question is:

你休息得好不好? (Nǐ xiūxi de hǎo bu hǎo?)

他法语说得流利不流利? (Tā Fǎyǔ shuō de liúlì bu liúlì?)

2 又流利又清楚(yòu liúlì yòu qīngchu)

"又 (yòu) …… 又 ……" shows two conditions or situations complementary to each other.

3 您过奖了。(Nín guòjiǎng le.)

"过奖" (guòjiǎng) is an expression to show modesty. It means the praise for one is too much.

4 你听听。(Nǐ tīngting.)

This is an parenthesis used to draw the attention of the listener.

5 你伯母是教外国留学生汉语的。(Nǐ bómǔ shì jiāo wàiguó liúxuéshēng Hànyǔ de.)

"subject +"是" (shì) + verb + object + "的" (de) "can be used to show one's profession:

他是开车的。(Tā shì kāi chē de.)

我是教历史的。(Wǒ shì jiāo lìshǐ de.)

6 三句话不离本行。(Sānjù huà bù lí běnháng.)

This is an idiom.

7 念啊，背啊，说啊。(Niàn a , bèi a, shuō a.)

The modal particle "啊" can be used in the following ways:

1) To be placed after each verb of a series:

我每天念啊，背啊，说啊。(Wǒ měitiān niàn a, bèi a, shuō a.)

2) To be placed at the end of a sentence to show a praise in surprise:

您的中国话不错啊！(Nín de Zhōngguóhuà búcuò a!) (Lesson 13)

北京的变化真不小啊！(Běijīng de biànhuà zhēn bù xiǎo a!) (Lesson 20)

真是百闻不如一见啊！(Zhēn shì bǎi wén bùrú yí jiàn a!) (Lesson 22)

3) To be placed at the end of a sentence to show affirmation:

是你啊。(Shì nǐ a.) (Lesson 21)

你这儿离我们住的地方很近啊。(Nǐ zhèr lí wǒmen zhù de dìfang hěn jìn a.) (Lesson 27)

4) To be placed at the end of a sentence to form questions:

谁啊？(Shuí a?) (Lesson 10)

什么时候结婚啊？(Shénme shíhòur jié hūn a?) (Lesson 27)

8 除了英语、汉语以外，法语、日语也能说一点儿。

(Chúle Yīngyǔ、Hànyǔ yǐwài，Fǎyǔ、Rìyǔ yě néng shuō yìdiǎnr.)

"除了 (chúle) …… 以外 (yǐwài), …… 也 (yě) " means that there are other things besides something.

9 没什么 (méi shénme)

The praise here means "It does not matter."

10 你女儿可真招人喜欢啊！(Nǐ nǚ'ér kě zhēn zhāo rén xǐhuan a!)

"可" (kě) here is for emphasis.

## supplementary words • 补充生词 • bǔchōng shēngcí

| | | | | |
|---|---|---|---|---|
| 1 | 出差 | | chū chāi | to be sent out on business |
| 2 | 空儿 | （名） | kòngr | spare time |

| | | | |
|---|---|---|---|
| 3 | 圈 | （名、量）quān | circle, round |
| 4 | 呀 | （助）ya | a modal particle |
| 5 | 运动 | （动、名）yùndòng | to do exercises, sports |
| 6 | 球迷 | （名）qiúmí | fan (ball games) |
| 7 | 网球 | （名）wǎngqiú | tennis |
| 8 | 台球 | （名）táiqiú | billiards |
| 9 | 高尔夫球 | （名）gāo'ěrfūqiú | golf |
| 10 | 跳高 | （名）tiàogāo | high jump |
| 11 | 个子 | （名）gèzi | height |
| 12 | 篮球 | （名）lánqiú | basket-ball |
| 13 | 中锋 | （名）zhōngfēng | cente (a position in ball games) |
| 14 | 米 | （量）mǐ | mete |
| | 王力 | Wáng Lì | a well-known professor of Chinese linguistics |

## • exercises • 练习 • liànxí

***1. Answer the questions:**

1) Model: A: 这个司机开 车开得 怎么样？
Zhège sījī kāi chē kāi de zěnmeyàng?

B: 他开 车开得很好。
Tā kāi chē kāi de hěn hǎo.

(1) A: 郭 伯母 做菜 做得 怎么样？
Guō bómǔ zuò cài zuò de zěnmeyàng?

B: ____________________。
____________________.

(2) A: 这个大夫看 病 看得 怎么样？
Zhège dàifu kàn bìng kàn de zěnmeyàng?

B: ____________________。
____________________.

(3) A: 他 念 书 念 得 怎么样？
Tā niàn shū niàn de zěnmeyàng?

B: ________________。
________________.

2) Model: A: 她 起 得 早 不 早？
Tā qǐ de zǎo bu zǎo?

B: 她 起 得 很 早。
Tā qǐ de hěn zǎo.

(1) A: 雨 下 得 大 不 大？
Yǔ xià de dà bu dà?

B: ________________。
________________.

(2) A: 车 开 得 快 不 快？
Chē kāi de kuài bu kuài?

B: ________________。
________________.

(3) A: 她 回答 得 对 不 对？
Tā huídá de duì bu duì?

B: ________________。
________________.

***2. Fill in the blanks:**

Model: A: 您 汉语 说得真 好!
Nín Hànyǔ shuō de zhēn hǎo!
B: 您 过奖了。我说 得不好。
Nín guòjiǎng le . Wǒ shuō de bù hǎo.

(1) A: 您 字__________!
Nín zì__________!
B: 您 过奖了。我写得不好。
Nín guòjiǎng le . Wǒ xiě de bù hǎo.

(2) A: 你球 __________!
Nǐ qiú __________!
B: 您 过 奖了。我打得不好。
Nín guòjiǎng le . Wǒ dǎ de bù hǎo.

(3) A: 您 京剧__________!
Nín jīngjù__________!
B: 您 过奖了。我 演得不好。
Nín guòjiǎng le . Wǒ yǎn de bù hǎo.

***3. Practice"怪不得"** (guài bu de):

Model: A: 他是在英国 上 的 小学 和 中 学。
Tā shì zài Yīngguó shàng de xiǎoxué hé zhōngxué.
B: 怪 不得他 英语这么 好。
Guài bu de tā Yīngyǔ zhème hǎo.

(1) A: 他是 语言学家 王 力的 学生 。
Tā shì yǔyánxuéjiā Wáng Lì de xuésheng.
B: ____________。(汉语)
____________. (Hànyǔ)

(2) A: 你 体温 三十八度九。
Nǐ tǐwēn sānshíbādù jiǔ.
B: __________。(不舒服)
__________. (bù shūfu)

(3) A: 他 出 差 了,你 不 知道?
Tā chū chāi le , nǐ bù zhīdao?
B: __________。(见)
__________. (jiàn)

***4. Complete the sentences:**

1) Model: 我 想 请 叔叔 帮 我 学 算术,不 知道
Wǒ xiǎng qǐng shūshu bāng wǒ xué suànshù, bù zhīdao

叔叔有空儿没有。(空儿)
shūshu yǒu kòngr méiyǒu. (kòngr)

(1) 我想请您帮我买飞机票,不知道您______
Wǒ xiǎng qǐng nín bāng wǒ mǎi fēijīpiào, bù zhīdao nín______
______。(时间)
______. (shíjiān)

(2) 我想请您和您太太明天带孩子来玩儿
Wǒ xiǎng qǐng nín hé nín tàitai míngtiān dài háizi lai wánr
一天,不知道你们______。(别的活动)
yìtiān, bù zhīdao nǐmen______. (biéde huódòng)

(3) 我想请他下午来一下儿,不知道他______
Wǒ xiǎng qǐng tā xiàwǔ lái yíxiàr, bù zhīdao tā ______
______。(事儿)
______. ( shìr )

2) Model: 除了英语、汉语以外,法语、日语他也会一点儿。(会)
Chúle Yīngyǔ、Hànyǔ yǐwài, Fǎyǔ、Rìyǔ tā yě huì yì diǎnr. (huì)

(1) 除了美元以外,英镑我______。(兑换)
Chúle Měiyuán yǐwài, Yīngbàng wǒ______. (duìhuàn)

(2) ______,别的地方他们都没去。(北京,上海)
______, biéde dìfang tāmen dōu méi qù. (Běijīng. Shànghǎi)

(3) 这次回来______,我还想看看老朋友。(参观,游览)
Zhècì huí lai ______, wǒ hái xiǎng kànkan lǎo péngyou. (cānguān, yóulǎn)

3) Model: 从十二岁起,我就跟妈妈学汉语。
Cóng shí'èrsuì qǐ, wǒ jiù gēn māma xué Hànyǔ.

(1) ______,我就在这儿等你了。(九点)
______, wǒ jiù zài zhèr děng nǐ le. (jiǔdiǎn)

(2) ______,他就开始了新的生活。(这一天)
______, tā jiù kāishǐle xīn de shēnghuó. (zhè yìtiān)

(3) ______,我就不抽烟了。(明天)
______, wǒ jiù bù chōu yān le. (míngtiān)

5 . **Listen to the dialogue:**

A: 哦，你 都 跑 回 来 了，起 得 真 早 啊。
Ó，nǐ dōu pǎo hui lai le，qǐ de zhēn zǎo a.

B: 五 点 半 从 家里 出 去，跑 一 大 圈 回 来，不 到 六 点。早饭 前，还 有 不 少 时间 念念 日语。
Wǔdiǎnbàn cóng jiāli chū qu，pǎo yí dà quān huí lai，bú dào liù diǎn. Zǎofàn qián，hái yǒu bù shǎo shíjiān niànnian Rìyǔ.

A: 你 天天 跑 吗？
Nǐ tiāntiān pǎo ma?

B: 除了 大 风 大 雨 天，都 跑。
Chúle dà fēng dà yǔ tiān，dōu pǎo.

A: 怪 不得 你 身体 这么 好。
Guài bu de nǐ shēntǐ zhème hǎo.

B: 你 身体 也 不错 呀，一定 也 很 喜欢 运动 吧？
Nǐ shēntǐ yě búcuò ya，yídìng yě hěn xǐhuan yùndòng ba？

A: 大家 都 管 我 叫 球迷，网 球、台球、高尔夫球 都 喜欢。
Dàjiā dōu guǎn wǒ jiào qiúmí，wǎngqiú、táiqiú、gāo'ěrfūqiú dōu xǐhuan.

B: 那 一定 打得 很 好。
Nà yídìng dǎ de hěn hǎo.

A: 不 好。打 一会儿 就 累得 不 行。你 喜欢 什么 运动？
Bù hǎo. Dǎ yíhuìr jiù lèi de bù xíng. Nǐ xǐhuan shénme yùndòng?

B: 跳高。
Tiàogāo.

A: 啊，个子 高。那 你 篮球 大概 也 打 得 不错！ 高大 的 中锋 啊！
Ā，gèzi gāo. Nà nǐ lánqiú dàgài yě dǎ de búcuò！ Gāodà de zhōngfēng a！

B: 不，打 中 锋，我 的 个子 还 不 够 高。你 知道 咱们 国 家 最 高 的 中锋 多 高？ 两米 二 还 多 呢！
Bù，dǎ zhōngfēng，wǒ de gèzi hái bú gòu gāo. Nǐ zhīdao zánmen guójiā zuì gāo de zhōngfēng duō gāo? Liǎngmǐ èr hái duō ne!

A: 谁 能 跟 他 比 呀！ 全 国 不 就 一个 吗？
Shuí néng gēn tā bǐ ya! Quán guó bú jiù yíge ma?

# 29 The "Man" In The Shop Window
# 橱窗里的"人"chúchuāngli de "rén"

(A dialogue between Lily and David in front of a shop window)

| | | |
|---|---|---|
| 伟：<br>Wěi: | 姐姐，你 说 现在 冷 不 冷？<br>Jiějie, nǐ shuō xiànzài lěng bu lěng? | Would you say it's cold now, Lily? |
| 莉：<br>Lì: | 一点儿 也 不 冷。① 我们 不<br>Yìdiǎnr yě bù lěng. Wǒmen bù | Not at all. We are only wearing sweaters, aren't |

都 是 穿 一件 毛衣 吗？ we?
dōu shì chuān yíjiàn máoyī ma?

伟：对 啊，可是 我 看见 有 个 人 身上 穿着 皮 大衣，② 脚上 穿着 皮 靴子，头上 戴着 皮 帽子，脖子上 围着 毛 围巾，手上 戴着 皮 手套。
Wěi: Duì a, kěshì wǒ kàn jiàn yǒu ge rén shēnshang chuānzhe pí dàyī, jiǎoshang chuānzhe pí xuēzi, tóushang dàizhe pí màozi, bózishang wéizhe máo wéijīn, shǒushang dàizhe pí shǒutàor.
That's right, but I just saw someone wearing fur coat, high boots, fur hat, scarf and gloves.

莉：哦，我 不 相信。
Lì: Ó, wǒ bù xiāngxìn.
Oh no, I don't believe it.

伟：不 相信？他 还 笑着 向 我 招 手 呢。③
Wěi: Bù xiāngxìn? Tā hái xiàozhe xiàng wǒ zhāo shǒu ne.
You don't? That person even smiled and waved at me.

莉：那 说 不 定 是 个 疯子。
Lì: Nà shuō bu dìng shì ge fēngzi.
It might be someone crazy.

伟：他 一点儿 也 不 疯。
Wěi: Tā yìdiǎnr yě bù fēng.
No, not at all.

莉：那 准 是 个 傻子。
Lì: Nà zhǔn shì ge shǎzi.
Then he must be an idiot.

伟：他 长着 一对 聪明 的 大 眼睛。
Wěi: Tā zhǎngzhe yíduì cōngming de dà yǎnjing.
No, that person has a pair of big, intelligent eyes.

莉：男 的 还是 女 的？
Lì: Nán de háishi nǚ de?
A man or a woman?

伟：男 的。
Wěi: Nán de.
A man.

莉：你 认识 他 吗？
Lì: Nǐ rènshi tā ma?
Do you know him?

伟：不 认 识。
Wěi: Bú rènshi.
I don't.

| | | |
|---|---|---|
| 莉：<br>Lì: | 你不认识他，他怎么会笑着向你招手呢？<br>Nǐ bú rènshi tā, tā zěnme huì xiàozhe xiàng nǐ zhāo shǒu ne? | If you don't know him, why did he smile and wave at you? |
| 伟：<br>Wěi: | 他向谁都笑着招手。④<br>Tā xiàng shuí dōu xiàozhe zhāo shǒu. | He smiles and waves at everybody. |
| 莉：<br>Lì: | 你跟他说话了吗？<br>Nǐ gēn tā shuō huà le ma? | Did you speak to him? |
| 伟：<br>Wěi: | 没有，他不说话。<br>Méiyǒu, tā bù shuō huà. | No, he doesn't speak. |
| 莉：<br>Lì: | 大伟，你怎么了？⑤你说得我都糊涂了。⑥你在哪儿看见的？<br>Dàwěi, nǐ zěnme le? Nǐ shuō de wǒ dōu hútu le. Nǐ zài nǎr kàn jiàn de? | What's wrong with you, David? You've got me all confused. Where did you see this person? |
| 伟：<br>Wěi: | 远在天边，近在眼前。⑦那不，他在橱窗里站着呢。<br>Yuǎn zài tiānbiān, jìn zài yǎn qián. Nà bù, tā zài chúchuāng li zhànzhe ne. | If you look far, he is ten thousand miles away, but if you look close, he is right in front of you. He is standing in the show window. |
| 莉：<br>Lì: | 你这个调皮鬼！<br>Nǐ zhège tiáopíguǐ! | You naughty boy! |

## • new words • 生词 • shēngcí

| | | | | |
|---|---|---|---|---|
| 1 | 橱窗 | （名） | chúchuāng | show window |
| 2 | 毛衣 | （名） | máoyī | sweater, jumper, pull-over |
| 3 | 看见 | | kàn jiàn | to see |
| 4 | 身上 | （名） | shēnshang | on the body |

| | | | | |
|---|---|---|---|---|
| 5 | 着 | （助） | zhe | a particle placed after verbs to show continuation of an action or state. |
| 6 | 皮 | （名） | pí | fur, hide, skin |
| 7 | 脚 | （名） | jiǎo | foot |
| 8 | 靴子 | （名） | xuēzi | boots |
| 9 | 戴 | （动） | dài | to wear (hats, gloves and glasses, etc.) |
| 10 | 帽子 | （名） | màozi | hat, cap, head-gear |
| 11 | 脖子 | （名） | bózi | neck |
| 12 | 围 | （动） | wéi | to wrap, to surround |
| 13 | 毛 | （名） | máo | wool |
| 14 | 围巾 | （名） | wéijīn | scarf, muffler |
| 15 | 手 | （名） | shǒu | hand |
| 16 | 手套 | （名） | shǒutàor | gloves, mittens |
| 17 | 相信 | （动） | xiāngxìn | to believe |
| 18 | 笑 | （动） | xiào | to laugh, to smile |
| 19 | 招手 | | zhāo shǒu | to wave |
| 20 | 说不定 | | shuō bu dìng | perhaps, probably |
| 21 | 疯子 | （名） | fēngzi | madman |
| 22 | 疯 | （形） | fēng | mad, crazy |
| 23 | 准 | （形） | zhǔn | sure, certain |
| 24 | 傻子 | （名） | shǎzi | fool, idiot |
| 25 | 长 | （动） | zhǎng | to grow |
| 26 | 对 | （量） | duì | pair |
| 27 | 聪明 | （形） | cōngming | intelligent, bright, clever |
| 28 | 眼睛 | （名） | yǎnjing | eyes |
| 29 | 男 | （名） | nán | man, male |
| 30 | 女 | （名） | nǚ | woman, female |
| 31 | 怎么了 | | zěnme le | What is wrong? What is the matter? |

| | | | |
|---|---|---|---|
| 32 | 远在天边，近在眼前 | yuǎn zài tiānbiān, jìn zài yǎnqián | If you look far, it is ten thousand miles away, and if you look near, it is right in front of you. |
| 33 | 那不 | nà bù | an expression to direct people's attention to something obvious |
| 34 | 站 | (动) zhàn | to stand |
| 35 | 调皮鬼 | (名) tiáopíguǐ | naughty or mischievous person |

## study points • 注释 • zhùshì

1 一点儿也不冷。(Yīdiǎnr yě bù lěng.)

"一点儿也不"＋ adjective has an exact paralell in English which is "not a bit" ＋ adjective.

2 我看见有个人身上穿着皮大衣。

(Wǒ kàn jiàn yǒu ge rén shēnshang chuānzhe pí dàyī.)

"着" (zhe) here functions as a continuation indicator:

他的脚上穿着皮靴子。( Tā de jiǎoshang chuānzhe pí xuēzi.)

他在橱窗里站着。(Tā zài chúchuāngli zhànzhe.)

桌子上放着手提包。(Zhuōzishang fàngzhe shǒutíbāo.)

The negative is formed by putting "没有" (méiyǒu) before the verb:

他的头上没有戴着皮帽子。(Tā de tóushang méiyǒu dàizhe pí màozi.)

"verb ＋ 着" can sometimes be used adverbially to modify the verb that follows:

他笑着向我招手。(Tā xiàozhe xiàng wǒ zhāo shǒu.)

他们坐着谈话。(Tāmen zuòzhe tán huà.)

3 他还笑着向我招手呢。(Tā hái xiàozhe xiàng wǒ zhāo shǒu ne.)

The main uses of the adverb "还" (hái) are:

1) to show something you have not expected to happen or to be so but has actually happened or is so:

他还笑着向我招手呢。(Tā hái xiàozhe xiàng wǒ zhāo shǒu ne.)

2) to show an increase or an addition:

我还要五张八分邮票。(Wǒ hái yào wǔzhāng bāfēn yóupiào.)(Lesson 6)

还要别的吗？(Hái yào biéde ma?) (Lesson 11)

七、八月还常常下雨。(Qī、bāyuè hái chángcháng xià yǔ.) (Lesson 16)

3) to show a moderate extent:

还能听懂吧? (Hái néng tīng dǒng ba?) (Lesson 13)

陈太太，累了吧? (Chén tàitai, lèi le ba?)

还好。(Hái hǎo.) (Lesson 18)

4) to show a state or an action still in progress:

爸爸还在跟王小姐谈话吗?

(Bàba hái zài gēn Wáng xiǎojie tán huà ma?) (Lesson 19)

我还得用刀子、叉子吃饭。

(Wǒ hái děi yòng dāozi、chāzi chī fàn.) (Lesson 23)

4 他向谁都招手。(Tā xiàng shuí dōu zhāo shǒu.)

谁 (shuí) here means anybody or everybody is general.

5 你怎么了? (Nǐ zěnme le?)

“怎么”(zěnme) here is used to inquire about what has happened.

6 你说得我都糊涂了。(Nǐ shuō de wǒ dōu hútu le.)

“我都糊涂了”。 (Wǒ dōu hútu le) indicates the result of the action “说” (shuō).

7 远在天边，近在眼前。(Yuǎn zài tiānbiān, jìn zài yǎnqián.)

This is an idiom.

## supplementary words • 补充生词 • bǔchōng shēngcí

| | | | | |
|---|---|---|---|---|
| 1 | 白 | (形) | bái | white |
| 2 | 俩 | (数量) | liǎ | two |
| 3 | 门口儿 | (名) | ménkǒur | door-way |
| 4 | 盯 | (动) | dīng | to stare |
| 5 | 打伞 | | dǎ sǎn | to hold an umbrella |
| 6 | 雨衣 | (名) | yǔyī | raincoat |
| 7 | 喊 | (动) | hǎn | to shout |
| 8 | 跳 | (动) | tiào | to jump |
| 9 | 抬 | (动) | tái | to carry (on shoulder) |
| 10 | 箱子 | (名) | xiāngzi | suitcase, trunk |

11 拉 (动) lā to pull
12 指 (动) zhǐ to point

## • exercises • 练习 • liànxí

*1. **Fill in the blanks using the structure "verb+着"(zhe):**

1) 这个女服务员，身上____白衣服，头上____白帽子，一只手____五碗米饭，一只手____一大把筷子。
Zhège nǚ fúwùyuán, shēnshang____ bái yīfu, tóushang____ bái màozi, yìzhī shǒu____ wǔwǎn mǐfàn, yìzhī shǒu____ yí dà bǎ kuàizi.

2) 一个男顾客____烟，眼睛____菜单，嘴里____菜名，一个服务员在他的左边儿____，手里____笔在纸上____。
Yíge nán gùkè ____ yān, yǎnjing____ càidān, zuǐli ____ càimíng, yíge fúwùyuán zài tā de zuǒbianr____, shǒuli____ bǐ zài zhǐ shang____.

3) 椅子上____一个小男孩儿，小脸上____一对聪明的大眼睛，脖子上____一块大手绢儿，身上____小红毛衣，脚上____小皮鞋，____向人招手。
Yǐzishang____ yíge xiǎo nánháir, xiǎo liǎnshang____ yíduì cōngming de dà yǎnjing, bózishang____ yíkuài dà shǒujuànr, shēnshang____ xiǎo hóng máoyī, jiǎoshang____ xiǎo píxié, ____ xiàng rén zhāo shǒu.

*2. **Complete the dialogues in accordance with the contents of the pictures:**

Model: A: 我的毛衣哪儿去了？
Wǒ de máoyī nǎr qù le?
B: 在你身上穿着呢。
Zài nǐ shēnshang chuānzhe ne.

1) A: 你 哥哥呢？
Nǐ gēge ne?
B: 在 那边儿__________呢。
Zài nàbianr __________ ne.

2) A: 信 写了吗？
Xìn xiěle ma?
B: 这 不 正 __________？
Zhè bù zhèng __________？

3) A: 我 要 写 字 了，你注意 看啊！
Wǒ yào xiě zì le, nǐ zhùyì kàn a!
B: 我 不是__________？
Wǒ bú shì__________？

4) A: 邮局 什么 时候 休息？
Yóujú shénme shíhour xiūxi?
B: 上 边 儿________呢。
Shàngbianr ________ ne.

3. **Rephrase the sentences using "说不定" (shuō bu dìng) and "准" (zhǔn):**
Model: 他是个 演员。——说 不 定 他是 个 演员。
Tā shì ge yǎnyuán. ——Shuō bú dìng tā shì ge yǎnyuán.
他 准 是 个 演员。
Tā zhǔn shì ge yǎnyuán.

1) 他 病 了。
Tā bìng le .

2) 他们 不 来 了。
Tāmen bù lái le .

3) 车 开 走 了。
Chē kāi zǒu le .

4) 他 是 个 外国人。
Tā shì ge wàiguórén.

5) 他们 去 长城 了。
Tāmen qù Chángchéng le .

6) 那 地方 冷 啊。
Nà dìfang lěng a .

7) 那儿 是 个 学校。
Nàr shì ge xuéxiào.

8) 他们 俩 喜欢 吃 中国菜 。
Tāmen liǎ xǐhuan chī Zhōngguócài.

**4 . Listen to the dialogue.**

A: 听 说，你 认识 我们 书店 的 小 赵 ？
Tīng shuō, nǐ rènshi wǒmen shūdiàn de Xiǎo Zhào?

B: 认识 啊。
Rènshi a .

A: 你们 怎么 认识的？ 说 说 好 吗？
Nǐmen zěnme rènshi de? Shuōshuo hǎo ma?

B: 那 是 夏天 的事儿 了。我 妹妹 回 家 探 亲，我 去 汽
Nà shì xiàtiān de shìr le . Wǒ mèimei huí jiā tàn qīn , wǒ qù qì
车站 接 她。天 下着 雨，雨 大 了，我 就 在 书店
chēzhàn jiē tā . Tiān xiàzhe yǔ , yǔ dà le , wǒ jiù zài shūdiàn
门口儿 等着。
ménkǒur děngzhe.

A: 啊，这样 认识的？
Á , zhèyàng rènshi de?

B: 你 听 啊 。 公共 汽车 来 了，我 跑 到 车站，眼睛
Nǐ tīng a . Gōnggòng qìchē lái le, wǒ pǎo dào chēzhàn, yǎnjing
盯 着 一个一个 下 车 的 人。先 下 来 几个 大人，有 的
dīngzhe yíge yíge xià chē de rén. Xiān xià lái jǐge dàren, yǒude
打着 伞，有的 穿着 雨衣。我 看了 看，都 不 是。
dǎzhe sǎn, yǒude chuānzhe yǔyī . Wǒ kànle kàn, dōu bú shì.

"下雨了！好玩儿啊！"一个小男孩儿喊着，跳着下了车，他妈妈跟着也下了车。
"Xià yǔ le! Hǎo wánr a!" Yíge xiǎo nánháir hǎnzhe, tiàozhe xiàle chē, tā māma gēnzhe yě xiàle chē.

A: 你妹妹还没来？
Nǐ mèimei hái méi lái?

B: 没有啊，等下一辆吧。我正想着，车上下来了两个女的。她俩抬着一个箱子。啊，来了！
Méiyǒu a, děng xià yíliàng ba. Wǒ zhèng xiǎngzhe, chēshang xià lai le liǎngge nǚ de. Tā liǎ táizhe yíge xiāngzi. À, lái le!

A: 你俩妹妹？
Nǐ liǎ mèimei?

B: 不是。我妹妹说："哥，这是我在汽车上认识的，她帮了我不少忙。"她拉着那女同志的手说："走，到我家去坐一会儿。"那女同志用手指着书店说："不，工作时间到了。"
Bú shì. Wǒ mèimei shuō: "Gē, zhè shì wǒ zài qìchēshang rènshi de, tā bāngle wǒ bù shǎo máng." Tā lāzhe nà nǚ tóngzhì de shǒu shuō: "Zǒu, dào wǒ jiā qu zuò yíhuìr." Nà nǚ tóngzhì yòng shǒu zhǐzhe shūdiàn shuō: "Bù, gōngzuò shíjiān dào le."

A: 这准是小赵！她真热情，是不是？
Zhè zhǔn shì Xiǎo Zhào! Tā zhēn rèqíng, shì bu shì?

*5. **Translate the following into Chinese:**

1) The child is in a red wollen jacket.
2) It was raining heavily outside.
3) Today's newspaper is on my table.
4) He waved at me with a smile.

# 30 How To Write Chinese Letters
# 怎 样 写 中 文 信
# zěnyàng xiě zhōngwén xìn

(After receiving a letter from Li Wenhan, Mr. Chen teaches David how to write Chinese letters.)

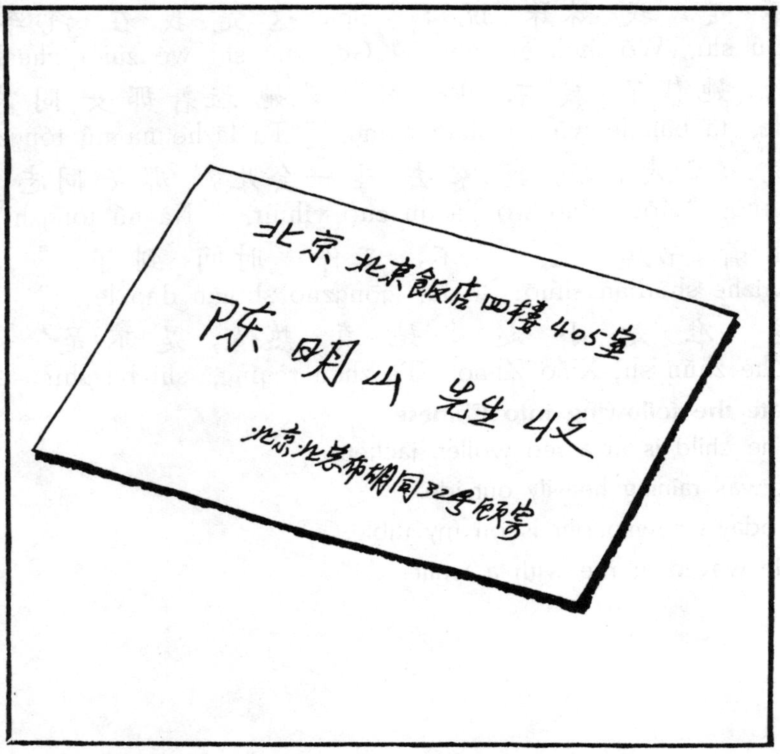


| | | |
|---|---|---|
| 伟 ：<br>Wěi: | 爸爸，信！ 服务员 送 来 的。<br>Bàba, xìn! Fúwùyuán sòng lai de. | Dad, it's a letter. The attendant delivered it. |
| 陈 ：<br>Chén: | 给 我。<br>Gěi wǒ. | Give it to me. |

| | | |
|---|---|---|
| 伟：<br>Wěi: | 是谁寄来的？<br>Shì shuí jì lai de? | Who is it from? |
| 陈：<br>Chén: | 李伯伯。<br>Lǐ bóbo. | Uncle Li. |
| 伟：<br>Wěi: | 爸爸，中文信跟英文信的写法一样吗？①<br>Bàba, Zhōngwén xìn gēn Yīngwén xìn de xiěfǎ yíyàng ma? | Dad, is the way of writing Chinese letters the same as English ones? |
| 陈：<br>Chén: | 你看看，信封是怎么写的？<br>Nǐ kànkan, xìnfēng shì zěnme xiě de? | See how the envelope is written. |
| 伟：<br>Wěi: | 收信人的地址写在信封上边儿，②信封中间儿写收信人姓名，下边儿写寄信人地址。<br>Shōuxìnrén de dìzhǐ xiě zài xìnfēng shàngbianr, xìnfēng zhōngjiànr xiě shōuxìnrén xìngmíng, xiàbianr xiě jìxìnrén dìzhǐ. | The address's at the top, the name in the middle, and the address of the sender at the bottom. |
| 陈：<br>Chén: | 这跟英文信的写法一样吗？<br>Zhè gēn Yīngwén xìn de xiěfǎ yíyàng ma? | Is that the same as English letters? |
| 伟：<br>Wěi: | 不一样。英文信是在信封的正面写收信人的姓名和地址，③在左上角或背面写寄信人的地址。<br>Bù yíyàng. Yīngwén xìn shì zài xìnfēng de zhèngmiàn xiě shōuxìnrén de xìngmíng hé dìzhǐ, zài zuǒ shàng jiǎo huò bèimiàn xiě jìxìnrén de dìzhǐ. | No, it isn't. The English way is to write the name and then the address in the center of the envelope. The address of the sender is written in the upper left-hand corner or on the back of the envelope. |
| 陈：<br>Chén: | 对了。写中文信，信封上的地址要先写<br>Duì le. Xiě Zhōngwén xìn, xìnfēngshang de dìzhǐ yào xiān xiě | That's right. For Chinese letters, you put down the province or city first, then the county or di- |

大 地名，后 写 小 地名，
dà dìmíng, hòu xiě xiǎo dìmíng,
也 就 是 说，④ 先 写 省
yě jiù shì shuō, xiān xiě shěng
（市）、再 写 县（区）、村（街），
（shì）、zài xiě xiàn（qū）、cūn（jiē），
最 后 写 门牌 号码儿。⑤
zuìhòu xiě ménpái hàomǎr.
如 果 是 从 外国 寄 来的，
Rúguǒ shì cóng wàiguó jì lai de,
首先 要 写 中华 人
shǒuxiān yào xiě Zhōnghuá Rén
民 共和国。
mín Gònghéguó.

strict, then the village or street, the number always comes last. If it is an overseas letter, People's Republic of China should be written first.

伟：
Wěi:
爸爸，这 封 信 怎么 不 写
Bàba, zhèfēng xìn zěnme bù xiě
日期和 写信人 的 地点呢？
rìqī hé xiěxìnrén de dìdiǎn ne?

Dad, why is there no date or the sender's address on the letter?

陈：
Chén:
你 先 看，看 完 再 说。
Nǐ xiān kàn, kàn wán zài shuō.

Read it first, then you'll see.

伟：
Wěi:
哦，中文 信 是 先 写
Ò, Zhōngwén xìn shì xiān xiě
完 内容，最后 才 写日期
wán nèiróng, zuìhòu cái xiě rìqī
的。怎么 没有 写 信 的
de. Zěnme méiyǒu xiě xìn de
地点 呢？
dìdiǎn ne?

Ah, the body of the letter comes first, the date is written at the end. But why is there no sender's address?

陈：
Chén:
写 信 的 地点 可以 不 写，
Xiě xìn de dìdiǎn kěyi bù xiě,
这 一点 也 跟 英文 信
zhè yìdiǎn yě gēn Yīngwén xìn
不 一样。大伟，你去 问 问
bù yíyàng. Dàwěi, nǐ qù wènwen
你 姐姐，给 你 老爷 的 信
nǐ jiějie, gěi nǐ lǎoye de xìn
写 完 了 没有。现在 有
xiě wán le méiyou. Xiànzài yǒu

It can be omitted and this is one of the differences between Chinese and English letters. David, go and ask your sister if she has finished her letter to Grandpa. In the meantime I'll write a reply to Lao Li, and we can mail the two

| | | |
|---|---|---|
| | 空儿，我给老李回封<br>kòngr, wǒ gěi Lǎo Lǐ huí fēng<br>信，一会儿一起寄。<br>xìn, yíhuìr yìqǐ jì. | letters together. |
| 伟：<br>Wěi: | 给我老爷的信，姐姐昨<br>Gěi wǒ lǎoye de xìn, jiějie zuó<br>天 晚上 就写 完了。<br>tiān wǎnshang jiù xiě wán le. | Lily finished her letter to Grandpa last night. |
| 陈：<br>Chén: | 那你来，我一边写一边<br>Nà nǐ lái, wǒ yìbiān xiě yìbiān<br>再给你说一说。⑥<br>zài gěi nǐ shuō yi shuō. | Then come. I'll explain to you the way of writing a Chinese letter as I write. |

## • new words • 生词 • shēngcí

| | | | | |
|---|---|---|---|---|
| 1 | 怎样 | （代）zěnyàng | how |
| 2 | 中文 | （名）Zhōngwén | Chinese |
| 3 | 英文 | （名）Yīngwén | English |
| 4 | 写法 | （名）xiěfǎ | the way to write |
| 5 | 一样 | （形）yíyàng | same |
| | 跟……一样 | gēn…yíyàng | same as |
| 6 | 上边儿 | （名）shàngbianr | upper part |
| 7 | 中间儿 | （名）zhōngjiànr | middle |
| 8 | 正面 | （名）zhèngmiàn | front |
| 9 | 左 | （名）zuǒ | left |
| 10 | 角 | （名）jiǎo | corner |
| 11 | 或 | （连）huò | or |
| 12 | 背面 | （名）bèimiàn | back |
| 13 | 后 | （副）hòu | then, later |
| | 先……后…… | xiān…hòu… | first…then |

| | | | | |
|---|---|---|---|---|
| 14 | 地名 | （名） | dìmíng | name of a place |
| 15 | 也就是说 | | yě jiù shì shuō | that is to say |
| 16 | 省 | （名） | shěng | province |
| 17 | 市 | （名） | shì | city, municipality |
| 18 | 县 | （名） | xiàn | county |
| 19 | 区 | （名） | qū | district |
| 20 | 村 | （名） | cūn | village |
| 21 | 街 | （名） | jiē | street |
| 22 | 最后 | （名） | zuìhòu | last |
| 23 | 门牌 | （名） | ménpái | number (of a house) |
| 24 | 如果 | （连） | rúguǒ | if |
| 25 | 首先 | （副、名） | shǒuxiān | first, beginning |
| 26 | 日期 | （名） | rìqī | date |
| 27 | 内容 | （名） | nèiróng | content, body |
| 28 | 才 | （副） | cái | only then |
| 29 | 地点 | （名） | dìdiǎn | place, locality, address |
| 30 | 点 | （量） | diǎn | point |
| 31 | 回信 | | huí xìn | reply |
| 32 | 老爷 | （名） | lǎoye | maternal grandfather |

**专名　　Zhuānmíng　　Proper name**

| | | |
|---|---|---|
| 中华人民共和国 | Zhōnghuá Rénmín Gònghéguó | The People's Republic of China |

## study points • 注释 • zhùshì

1　中文信跟英文信的写法一样吗？
(Zhōngwén xìn gēn Yīngwén xìn de xiěfǎ yíyàng ma?)

"……跟……一样" is a way of equating two items:

他的毛衣跟我的毛衣一样。(Tā de máoyī gēn wǒ de máoyī yíyàng.)

这张桌子跟那张桌子一样。(Zhèzhāng zhuōzi gēn nàzhāng zhuōzi yíyàng.)

The negative is formed by putting "不" (bù) before "一样" (yíyàng); the question form has a "吗" (ma) at the end.

2 收信人的地址写在信封上边儿。
(Shōuxìnrén de dìzhǐ xiě zài xìnfēng shàngbianr.)
This sentence is passive in meaning. (See Study Point 1 of Lesson 34.)

3 英文信是在信封的正面写收信人的姓名和地址。
(Yīngwén xìn shì zài xìnfēng de zhèngmiàn xiě shōuxìnrén de xìngmíng hé dìzhǐ.)
"是" (shì) is for emphasis here.

4 也就是说 (yě jiù shì shuō)
The expression means "that is to say".

5 先写省(市),再写县(区)、村(街),最后写门牌号码儿。
(Xiān xiě shěng(shì), zài xiě xiàn(qū)、cūn(jiē), zuìhòu xiě ménpái hàomǎr.)
There are thirty provinces, cities and autonomous regions (including Taiwan) in China. See appendix for their names and names of their capitals.

6 我一边写一边再给你说一说。(Wǒ yìbiān xiě yìbiān zài gěi nǐ shuō yi shuō.)
"说一说" here means "to explain briefly".
Similar expressions like "等一等" (děng yi děng), "看一看" (kàn yi kàn), etc. all carry the connotation of doing something briefly.

## supplementary words • 补充生词 • bǔchōng shēngcí

| | | | | |
|---|---|---|---|---|
| 1 | 文章 | (名) | wénzhāng | article, composition |
| 2 | 声 | (名) | shēng | voice, sound |
| 3 | 打开 | | dǎkāi | to open |
| 4 | 人数 | | rén shù | number of people |
| 5 | 扇子 | (名) | shànzi | fan |
| 6 | 画 | (动) | huà | to draw, to paint |
| 7 | 幅 | (量) | fú | a measure word for pictures and |

| | | | | |
|---|---|---|---|---|
| | | | | paintings |
| 8 | 画儿 | (名) | huàr | drawing, painting |
| 9 | 改 | (动) | gǎi | to make changes |
| 10 | 石头 | (名) | shítou | stone |
| 11 | 黑 | (形) | hēi | black |
| 12 | 金 | (名) | jīn | gold |
| 13 | 难看 | (形) | nánkàn | ugly |

## • exercises • 练习 • liànxí

***1. Fill in the blanks with the right words:**

见，到，完，在，好
jiàn, dào, wán, zài, hǎo

1) 这本书他看_____了。
Zhèběn shū tā kàn_____ le.

2) 爸爸寄来的包裹他收_____了。
Bàba jì lai de bāoguǒ tā shōu_____ le.

3) 给哥哥的信他写_____了。
Gěi gēge de xìn tā xiě _____ le.

4) 帽子、手套儿全都戴_____了。
Màozi、shǒutàor quán dōu dài_____ le.

5) 他们坐_____前边儿。
Tāmen zuò_____ qiánbianr.

6) 他的表找_____了。
Tā de biǎo zhǎo_____ le.

7) 对，四十分钟就能走_____。
Duì, sìshífēnzhōng jiù néng zǒu_____.

8) 文章不长，二十分钟就看_____了。
Wénzhāng bù cháng, èrshífēnzhōng jiù kàn_____ le.

9) 飞机声他们早就听_____了。
Fēijī shēng tāmen zǎo jiù tīng_____ le.

***2. Make short dialogues using** “……跟……一样” (…gēn…yíyàng):

Model: A: 中文　信 跟 英文 信 的写法 一样吗？
Zhōngwén xìn gēn Yīngwén xìn de xiěfǎ yíyàng ma?

B: 写法 不一样。
Xiěfǎ bù yíyàng.

1) 这种，那种，字，写法
zhèzhǒng, nàzhǒng, zì, xiěfǎ

2) 这个，那个，字，声调
zhège, nàge, zì, shēngdiào

3) 这件，那件，衣服，颜色
zhèjiàn, nàjiàn, yīfu, yánsè

4) 这个，那个，孩子，年龄
zhège, nàge, háizi, niánlíng

5) 你们，他们，学校，人数
nǐmen, tāmen, xuéxiào, rén shù

6) 你，他，工作，时间
nǐ, tā, gōngzuò, shíjiān

**3. Listen to the dialogue:**

老王：老丁，你看，这是我新买的扇子。
Lǎo Wáng: Lǎo Dīng, nǐ kàn, zhè shì wǒ xīn mǎi de shànzi.

老丁：真好。如果这上边儿再画上一幅好画儿，那才好呢！
Lǎo Dīng: Zhēn hǎo. Rúguǒ zhè shàngbianr zài huà shang yìfú hǎo huàr, nà cái hǎo ne!

老王：我买了扇子一直在想，请谁给画一幅画儿呢。听说，你会画……
Lǎo Wáng: Wǒ mǎile shànzi yìzhí zài xiǎng, qǐng shuí gěi huà yìfú huàr ne. Tīng shuō, nǐ huì huà……

老丁：啊，会一点儿。那，我试试。画什么呢？
Lǎo Dīng: Á, huì yìdiǎnr. Nà, wǒ shìshi. Huà shénme ne?

老王：你想画什么就画什么吧。
Lǎo Wáng: Nǐ xiǎng huà shénme jiù huà shénme ba.

老丁：那好。一个星期就能画好。
Lǎo Dīng: Nàhǎo. Yíge xīngqī jiù néng huà hǎo.

老王：我先谢谢了。
Lǎo Wáng: Wǒ xiān xièxie le.

（一个星期以后）
( Yíge xīngqī yǐhòu )

老　王：老　丁，我那扇子？
Lǎo Wáng: Lǎo Dīng, wǒ nà shànzi?

老　丁：啊，我给你画上了大树。
Lǎo Dīng: À, wǒ gěi nǐ huà shang le dà shù.

老　王：行　啊。
Lǎo Wáng: Xíng a.

老　丁：可是，那大树画得太大了，只画了几个树叶儿，不好，不好。我看，再改改，画块大石头吧。
Lǎo Dīng: Kěshì, nà dà shù huà de tài dà le, zhǐ huàle jǐge shùyèr, bù hǎo, bù hǎo. Wǒ kàn, zài gǎigai, huà kuài dà shítou ba.

老　王：也行。
Lǎo Wáng: Yě xíng.

老　丁：老　王，你再给我三天时间，三天准能画好。
Lǎo Dīng: Lǎo Wáng, nǐ zài gěi wǒ sāntiān shíjiān, sāntiān zhǔn néng huà hǎo.

（三天以后）
(Sāntiān yǐhòu)

老　丁：老　王啊，那大石头我画完了，可是太黑了。我再改改。改什么呢？对，这样，扇子全都画黑了，再写上几个大金字，你看怎么样？
Lǎo Dīng: Lǎo Wáng a, nà dà shítou wǒ huà wán le, kěshì tài hēi le. Wǒ zài gǎigai. Gǎi shénme ne? Duì, zhèyàng, shànzi quán dōu huà hēi le, zài xiě shang jǐge dà jīn zì, nǐ kàn zěnmeyàng?

老　王：那跟买的黑扇子一样了。
Lǎo Wáng: Nà gēn mǎi de hēi shànzi yíyàng le.

老　丁：不一样。这是我画的呀。
Lǎo Dīng: Bù yíyàng. Zhè shì wǒ huà de ya.

老　王：太感谢了。画完了，你自己用吧。
Lǎo Wáng: Tài gǎnxiè le. Huà wán le, nǐ zìjǐ yòng ba.

老　丁：那合适吗？
Lǎo Dīng: Nà héshì ma?

老　王：还说什么呢？你用跟我用都一样难看啊！
Lǎo Wáng: Hái shuō shénme ne? Nǐ yòng gēn wǒ yòng dōu yíyàng nán kàn a!

Appendix: A sketch of the provinces (with their capitals), cities and autonomous reaions(with their capitals).

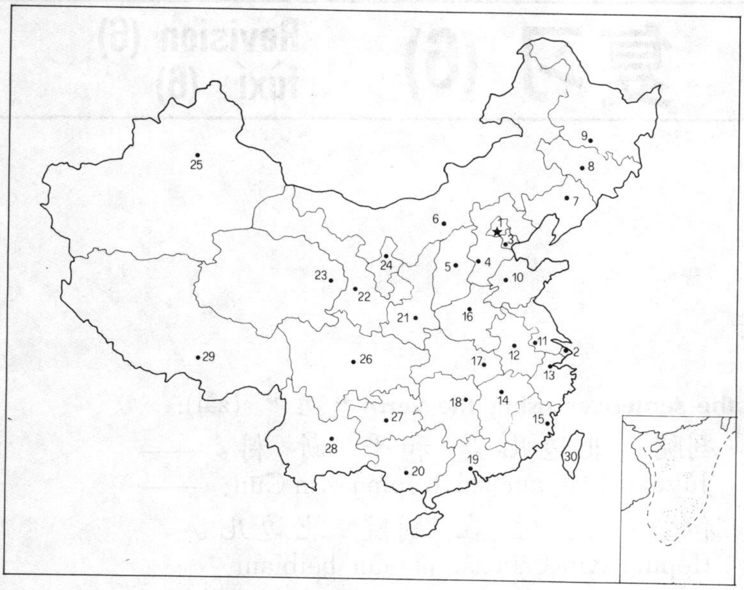


| | Names of cities, provinces and autonomous regions | Capitals of provinces and autonomous regions |
|---|---|---|
| 1 | 北京市<br>Běijīng shì | |
| 2 | 上海 市<br>Shànghǎi shì | |
| 3 | 天津 市<br>Tiānjīn shì | |
| 4 | 河北 省<br>Héběi shěng | 石家庄<br>Shíjiāzhuāng |
| 5 | 山西省<br>Shānxī shěng | 太原<br>Tàiyuán |
| 6 | 内蒙古自治区<br>Nèi Měnggǔ zìzhìqū | 呼和浩特<br>Hūhéhàotè |
| 7 | 辽 宁 省<br>Liáoníng shěng | 沈 阳<br>Shěnyáng |
| 8 | 吉林 省<br>Jílín shěng | 长 春<br>Chángchūn |
| 9 | 黑龙 江 省<br>Hēilóngjiāng shěng | 哈尔滨<br>Hā'ěrbīn |
| 10 | 山 东 省<br>Shāndōng shěng | 济南<br>Jǐnián |
| 11 | 江 苏 省<br>Jiāngsū shěng | 南京<br>Nánjīng |
| 12 | 安徽 省<br>Ānhuī shěng | 合肥<br>Héféi |
| 13 | 浙 江 省<br>Zhèjiāng shěng | 杭 州<br>Hángzhōu |
| 14 | 江 西 省<br>Jiāngxī shěng | 南 昌<br>Nánchāng |
| 15 | 福建 省<br>Fújiàn shěng | 福 州<br>Fúzhōu |

| | Names of cities, provinces and autonomous regions | Capitals of provinces and autonomous regions |
|---|---|---|
| 16 | 河南 省<br>Hénán shěng | 郑 州<br>Zhèngzhōu |
| 17 | 湖北 省<br>Húběi shěng | 武汉<br>Wǔhàn |
| 18 | 湖南 省<br>Húnán shěng | 长 沙<br>Chángshā |
| 19 | 广东 省<br>Guǎngdōng shěng | 广 州<br>Guǎngzhōu |
| 20 | 广西壮族自治区<br>Guǎngxī zhuàngzú zìzhìqū | 南 宁<br>Nánníng |
| 21 | 陕 西 省<br>Shǎnxī shěng | 西安<br>Xī'ān |
| 22 | 甘肃 省<br>Gānsù shěng | 兰 州<br>Lánzhōu |
| 23 | 青 海 省<br>Qīnghǎi shěng | 西 宁<br>Xīníng |
| 24 | 宁 夏 回族自治区<br>Níngxià Huízú zìzhìqū | 银 川<br>Yínchuān |
| 25 | 新 疆 维吾尔自治区<br>Xīnjiāng Wéiwúěr zìzhìqū | 乌鲁木齐<br>Wūlǔmùqí |
| 26 | 四 川 省<br>Sìchuān shěng | 成 都<br>Chéngdū |
| 27 | 贵 州 省<br>Guìzhōu shěng | 贵 阳<br>Guìyáng |
| 28 | 云 南 省<br>Yúnnán shěng | 昆 明<br>Kūnmíng |
| 29 | 西藏自治 区<br>Xīzàng zìzhìqū | 拉萨<br>Lāsà |
| 30 | 台 湾 省<br>Táiwān shěng | 台北<br>Táiběi |

# 复习 (6) Revision (6) fùxí (6)

*1. **Rewrite the sentences using the verb "在" (zài):**

Model: 剧院 北边儿 是 和平 新 村。——
Jùyuàn běibianr shì Hépíng Xīn Cūn. ——
和平 新村 在 剧院 北边儿。
Hépíng Xīn Cūn zài jùyuàn běibianr.

1) 三号 楼 后边儿是 四号 楼。
Sānhào lóu hòubianr shì sìhào lóu.

2) 剧院 南边儿 有 个 汽车站。
Jùyuàn nánbianr yǒu ge qìchēzhàn.

3) 他 房间 的 左边儿 是 我 的 房间。
Tā fángjiān de zuǒbianr shì wǒ de fángjiān.

4) 张 先生 右边儿 坐的是 陈 先生。
Zhāng xiānsheng yòubianr zuò de shì Chén xiānsheng.

5) 她们 三个人 这样 站着: 中间儿 是 刘 小姐, 左边儿是 王 小姐, 右边儿是 赵 小姐。
Tāmen sānge rén zhèyàng zhànzhe: zhōngjiànr shì Liú xiǎojie, zuǒbianr shì Wáng xiǎojie, yòubianr shì Zhào xiǎojie.

6) 前边儿 是 小 汽车, 后边儿是 大 汽车。
Qiánbianr shì xiǎo qìchē, hòubianr shì dà qìchē.

*2. **Rewrite the following sentences using "是……的" (shì…de):**

Model: 他 坐飞机去 上海 了。——
Tā zuò fēijī qù Shànghǎi le. ——
他 是 坐飞机去 上海 的。
Tā shì zuò fēijī qù Shànghǎi de.

1) 他俩 走着 去 友谊 商店 了。
Tā liǎ zǒuzhe qù Yǒuyì Shāngdiàn le.

2) 上 星期 他 跟 王 伯伯 一起 参观 画展 了。
Shàng xīngqī tā gēn Wáng bóbo yìqǐ cānguān huàzhǎn le.

3) 中午　十二点他回　到了家里。
Zhōngwǔ shí'èrdiǎn tā huí dào le jiāli.

4) 去年　国庆节，他结了　婚。
Qùnián Guóqìngjié, tā jiéle hūn.

5) 你　跟他在哪儿见了　面　？
Nǐ gēn tā zài nǎr jiànle miàn?

6) 十　年　前　的　秋天，　我们　分别　了。
Shínián qián de qiūtiān, wǒmen fēnbié le.

7) 那些　书　九月　六号借来了。
Nàxiē shū jiǔyuè liùhào jiè lai le.

8) 他　在那个大　商店　买了　电视机。
Tā zài nàge dà shāngdiàn mǎile diànshìjī.

***3. Fill in the blanks with "得" (de) or "的" (de):**

1) 他 ______ 普通话　真　好。
Tā ______ pǔtōnghuà zhēn hǎo.

2) 他　俩　汉语　都　说 ______ 不错。
Tā liǎ Hànyǔ dōu shuō ______ búcuò.

3) 这　地方 ______ 东西　真　贵　呀，比　你们那儿贵　多　了！
Zhè dìfang ______ dōngxi zhēn guì ya, bǐ nǐmen nàr guì duō le!

4) 你们　家 ______ 那张　画儿画 ______ 多　好啊！
Nǐmen jiā ______ nàzhāng huàr huà ______ duō hǎo a!

5) 赵　先生　每天　都来 ______ 很早，走 ______ 很　晚。
Zhào xiānsheng měitiān dōu lái ______ hěn zǎo, zǒu ______ hén wǎn.

6) 他 ______ 话不大好懂，说 ______ 也太快，很　多人
Tā ______ huà bú dà hǎo dǒng, shuō ______ yě tài kuài, hěn duō rén
没　听懂。
méi tīng dǒng.

7) 他 ______ 车你可别坐，开 ______ 太快了！
Tā ______ chē nǐ kě bié zuò, kāi ______ tài kuài le!

8) 昨天　是　小　刘 ______ 生日，他请　我们　在他家吃
Zuótiān shì Xiǎo Liú ______ shēngrì, tā qǐng wǒmen zài tā jiā chī
______ 饭，菜　做 ______ 不错。
______ fàn, cài zuò ______ búcuò.

# 31 We Are In The Same Profession
## 我们是同行 wǒmen shì tóngháng

(Mr. Chen Mingshan chats with a young teacher at the entrance of Qian Ling Museum before it opens.)

| | | |
|---|---|---|
| 陈 :<br>Chén: | 请 问，博物馆 几点 开 门？<br>Qǐng wèn, Bówùguǎn jǐdiǎn kāi mén? | Could you tell me when the museum opens, please? |
| 青 年 :<br>qīngnián: | 八点。您 也 是 来 参观<br>Bādiǎn. Nín yě shì lái cānguān | Eight o'clock. You've come to visit the mu- |

| | | |
|---|---|---|
| | 的？<br>de? | seum too? |
| 陈：<br>Chén: | 是 啊。我 是 华 侨，在<br>Shì a . Wǒ shì huáqiáo, zài<br>美国 一个 大学 教 中<br>Měiguó yíge dàxué jiāo Zhōng<br>国 历史。<br>guó lìshǐ . | Yes. I'm an overseas Chinese. I teach Chinese history at an American university. |
| 青：<br>qīng: | 您 是 搞 古代史 的？<br>Nín shì gǎo gǔdài shǐ de? | Ancient history? |
| 陈：<br>Chén: | 我 主要 是 研究 唐 史。<br>Wǒ zhǔyào shì yánjiū Táng shǐ.<br>唐 代 三百年，西安 是<br>Táng dài sānbǎinián, Xī'ān shì<br>当时 全 国 政治、经济、<br>dāngshí quán guó zhèngzhì、jīngjì、<br>文化 的中心。西安是很<br>wénhuà de zhōngxīn. Xī'ān shì hěn<br>值得 参观 的。① 你对历史<br>zhíde cānguān de. Nǐ duì lìshǐ<br>也 有 兴趣？<br>yě yǒu xìngqù? | I study the history of Tang dynasty. Throughout the three hundred years of Tang dynasty, Xian was the political, economic and cultural center of the country; it is indeed the place to visit. You are also interested in history? |
| 青：<br>qīng: | 我 也是 搞 历史的。我 在<br>Wǒ yě shì gǎo lìshǐ de. Wǒ zài<br>西安 大学 历史系 工作。<br>Xī'ān Dàxué lìshǐ xì gōngzuò. | History is also my specialty. I work in the History Department of Xian University. |
| 陈：<br>Chén: | 我们 是 同行 啊！太 好<br>Wǒmen shì tóngháng a ! Tài hǎo<br>了！请 问，您 贵 姓？②<br>le ! Qǐng wèn, nín guì xìng? | Then we are in the same profession. How wonderful! May I ask your name? |
| 青：<br>qīng: | 我 姓 林，叫 林 小东。<br>Wǒ xìng Lín, jiào Lín Xiǎodōng. | My name is Lin, Lin Xiaotung. |
| 陈：<br>Chén: | 我 叫 陈 明 山。你 在<br>Wǒ jiào Chén Míngshān. Nǐ zài<br>西安大学 工作 几年了？③<br>Xī'ān Dàxué gōngzuò jǐnián le? | And my name is Chen Mingshan. How long have you been teaching at Xian University? |
| 青：<br>qīng: | 我 是 前年 毕业的，刚<br>Wǒ shì qiánnián bì yè de, gāng | I graduated the year before last, so I've been |

| | | |
|---|---|---|
| | 工作了 两年 多，是个<br>gōngzuòle liǎngnián duō, shì ge<br>助教。您 教 中国 历史<br>zhùjiào. Nín jiāo Zhōngguó lìshǐ<br>教了 多 长 时间 了？<br>jiāole duō cháng shíjiān le ? | working for only two years. I'm a teaching assistant. How long have you been teaching Chinese history? |
| 陈：<br>Chén: | 三十年 了。<br>Sānshínián le . | Thirty years. |
| 青：<br>qīng: | 您 对 中国 历史一定<br>Nín duì Zhōngguó lìshǐ yídìng<br>很 有 研究 喽。<br>hěn yǒu yánjiū lou . | Then you must be an expert on Chinese history. |
| 陈：<br>Chén: | 哪里！在 国外 研究 中<br>Nǎlǐ ! Zài guówài yánjiū Zhōng<br>国 历史，怎么也不如你们<br>guó lìshǐ , zěnme yě bùrú nǐmen<br>在 国内。④<br>zài guónèi . | Oh come. To study Chinese history outside China is not quite as good as within the country. |
| 青：<br>qīng: | 也不一定。有的人在国<br>Yě bù yídìng . Yǒude rén zài guó<br>外 研究也很有 成<br>wài yánjiū yě hěn yǒu chéng<br>就。今天 参观 这个 乾<br>jiù . Jīntiān cānguān zhège Qián<br>陵 博物馆 对 您 研究<br>Líng Bówùguǎn duì nín yánjiū<br>唐 代历史一定会有很<br>Táng dài lìshǐ yídìng huì yǒu hěn<br>大帮助。<br>dà bāngzhù . | Not necessarily. Some people are also doing very well (in their study of Chinese history) outside China. You'll find this Qian Ling Museum a great help to your study of Tang history. |
| 陈：<br>Chén: | 是 啊。西安 简直 是 个 大<br>Shì a . Xī'ān jiǎnzhí shì ge dà<br>博物 馆，可惜 时间 太 短<br>bówùguǎn, kěxī shíjiān tài duǎn<br>了，不 能 都 去 参观 。<br>le , bù néng dōu qù cānguān. | Yes. Xian is a big museum. It's a pity that my stay here is too short and I can't visit all the places. |
| 青：<br>qīng: | 来 西安几天了？<br>Lái Xī'ān jǐtiān le ? | How long have you been in Xian? |

| | | |
|---|---|---|
| 陈 ： Chén: | 六天 了。过 两天 就 得 走了。⑤ Liùtiān le . Guò liǎntiān jiù děi zǒu le . | Six days. I'll have to leave in a few days. |
| 青 ： qīng: | 以后 有 机会再来。 Yǐhòu yǒu jīhui zài lái . | Come again when you have the chance. |
| 陈 ： Chén: | 那 一定。 Nà yídìng . | Of course. |
| 青 ： qīng: | 开 门 了，我们 进 去 吧。 Kāi mén le, wǒmen jìn qu ba. | The museum has opened. Let's go inside. |

## • new words • 生词 • shēngcí

| | | | | |
|---|---|---|---|---|
| 1 | 同行 | （名）tóngháng | | someone of the same trade or profession |
| 2 | 博物馆 | （名）bówùguǎn | | museum |
| 3 | 青年 | （名）qīngnián | | youth, young man (men) |
| 4 | 开 | （动）kāi | | to open |
| 5 | 门 | （名）mén | | door, gate |
| 6 | 开门 | | kāimén | to open the door, open to the public |
| 7 | 搞 | （动）gǎo | | to do, to carry on, to be engaged in |
| 8 | ……史 | （名）… shǐ | | history |
| 9 | 代 | （名）dài | | dynasty, generation |
| 10 | 当时 | （名）dāngshí | | at the time |
| 11 | 政治 | （名）zhèngzhì | | politics |
| 12 | 经济 | （名）jīngjì | | economy, economics |
| 13 | 文化 | （名）wénhuà | | culture |
| 14 | 中心 | （名）zhōngxīn | | center |
| 15 | 兴趣 | （名）xìngqù | | interest |

| | | | | |
|---|---|---|---|---|
| | 对……有兴趣 | | duì…yǒu xìngqù | to be interested in |
| 16 | 系 | （名） | xì | department |
| 17 | 贵姓 | | guì xìng | a polite way of asking someone's family name |
| | 你（您）贵姓？ | | Nǐ (nín) guì xìng? | May I ask your name? |
| 18 | 姓 | （动、名） | xìng | one's family name is…, family name |
| 19 | 前年 | （名） | qiánnián | the year before last |
| 20 | 助教 | （名） | zhùjiào | teaching assistant |
| 21 | 喽 | （助） | lou | a particle meaning "naturally" |
| 22 | 不如 | （动） | bùrú | not as good as, not as well as |
| 23 | 成就 | （名） | chéngjiù | achievements |
| | 有成就 | | yǒu chéngjiù | to enjoy success or to win recognition |
| 24 | 简直 | （副） | jiǎnzhí | simply (for emphasis) |
| 25 | 可惜 | （形） | kěxī | unfortunate, the pity is |

## 专名 Zhuānmíng Proper names

| | | |
|---|---|---|
| 唐 | Táng | Tang, an early dynasty in the history of China, between 618 and 907 A. D. |
| 林 | Lín | a common Chinese family name |
| 林小东 | Lín Xiǎodōng | name of a staff member of Xian University |
| 西安大学 | Xī'ān Dàxué | Xian University |
| 乾陵博物馆 | Qián Líng Bówùguǎn | Qian Ling Museum, the museum for the unearthed artifacts from the Qian Tomb which is the tomb of the well-known Tang emperor, Tang Gao Zong. |

## study points • 注释 • zhùshì

1 西安是很值得参观的。(Xī'ān shì hěn zhíde cānguān de.)
"是……的" (shì···de) is for emphasis here.

2 您贵姓? (Nín guì xìng?)
"贵" (guì) is a word of respect. "贵姓" (guì xìng) is a polite way to ask someone's family name. A less cordial way is "你姓什么?" (Nǐ xìng shénme?)

3 你在西安大学工作几年了? (Nǐ zài Xī'ān Dàxué gōngzuò jǐnián le?)
In Chinese, the way to express the duration of an action or a situation is to put the time element at the end: Subject + action word + time element.
For monosyllabic action words, the pattern is as follows:

他工作六年多了。(Tā gōngzuò liùnián duō le.)

他们谈了半个小时了。(Tāmen tánle bànge xiǎoshí le.)

If there is an object, the verb has to be repeated and the time element placed after the repeated verb, for example:

他教中国历史教了三十年了。(Tā jiāo Zhōngguó lìshǐ jiāole sānshínián le.)

我找你找了一个小时了。(Wǒ zhǎo nǐ zhǎole yíge xiǎoshí le.)

If the object is not a pronoun or a name of a place, the time element can be placed between the verb and the object, for example:

他教了三十年中国历史了。(Tā jiāole sānshínián Zhōngguó lìshǐ le.)

This saves the trouble of repeating the first syllable.

4 怎么也不如你们在国内。(Zěnme yě bùrú nǐmen zài guónèi.)
"怎么也" (zěnme yě) means "no matter how".

5 过两天就得走了。(Guò liǎngtiān jiù děi zǒu le.)
"两天" (liǎngtiān) does not literally mean "two days" here. It shows an approximation and is unstressed.

## supplementary words • 补充生词 • bǔchōng shēngcí

| | | | | |
|---|---|---|---|---|
| 1 | 钟头 | (名) | zhōngtóu | hour |
| 2 | 划(船) | (动) | huá (chuán) | to row |
| 3 | 船 | (名) | chuán | boat |

| | | | |
|---|---|---|---|
| 4 | 真是的 | zhēn shi de | a mild disapproval |
| 5 | 岸 | （名）àn | shore |
| 6 | 小说 | （名）xiǎoshuōr | novel |
| 7 | 能力 | （名）nénglì | ability |
| 8 | 眼 | （名、量）yǎn | eye, look |
| 9 | 教育 | （名、动）jiàoyù | education, to educate |
| 10 | 教书 | jiāo shū | to teach |

## • exercises • 练习 • liànxí

*1. **Practice the following expressions of time:**

Ask questions in two different forms as shown in the models.

A. 几（小时，天，星期，月，年）
jǐ（xiǎoshí，tiān，xīngqī，yuè，nián）

B. 多 长 时间
duō cháng shíjiān

Model: 你 工作 —— 你 工作 几年了？
nǐ gōngzuò —— Nǐ gōngzuò jǐnián le？
你 工作 多 长 时间了？
Nǐ gōngzuò duō cháng shíjiān le？

1) 他 大学 毕业
tā dàxué bì yè

2) 他 俩 认识
tā liǎ rènshi

3) 他们 聊
tāmen liáo

4) 他 出去
tā chū qu

5) 你们 分别
nǐmen fēnbié

6) 你们 等 他
nǐmen děng tā

2 . **Practice** "搞什么（工作）的" (gǎo shénme (gōngzuò) de)

Model: 经济——A: 他是 搞 什么 （ 工 作 ）的？
jīngjì—— Tā shì gǎo shénme ( gōngzuò ) de?
B: 他是 搞 经济的。
Tā shì gǎo jīngjì de.

1) 贸易
màoyì
2) 旅游
lǚyóu
3) 话剧
huàjù
4) 语言
yǔyán
5) 历史
lìshǐ
6) 舞蹈
wǔdǎo

*3. **Make short dialogues after the model:**

Model: A: 你 打了 多 长 时间 电话 ？
Nǐ dǎle duō cháng shíjiān diànhuà?
B: 打了 一分钟 的 电话 。（电 话， 一分钟）
Dǎle yì fēnzhōng de diànhuà. (diànhuà, yìfēnzhōng)

1) 听 广播， 半个 钟头
tīng guǎngbō, bànge zhōngtóu
2) 学 历史， 三年半
xué lìshǐ, sānniánbàn
3) 研究 中文 ， 二十 多 年
yánjiū Zhōngwén, èrshí duō nián
4) 坐 飞机， 三个 小时
zuò fēijī, sānge xiǎoshí
5) 画 画儿， 半天
huà huàr, bàntiān

4 . **Listen to the dialogues:**

1) 小 赵 ：划 船 真 好玩儿。
Xiǎo Zhào: Huá chuán zhēn hǎowánr .
小 刘： 咱们 划了 多 长 时间 了？
Xiǎo Liú: Zánmen huále duō cháng shíjiān le ?

小　赵：大概 划了 两个　钟头　了。
Xiǎo Zhào: Dàgài huále liǎngge zhōngtóu le.
小　刘：累 了 吧？ 让 我 划 一会儿。
Xiǎo Liú: Lèi le ba? Ràng wǒ huá yíhuìr.
小　赵：你 这个 人 可 真 是 的。我 才 划了 十几分钟，累 什么？
Xiǎo Zhào: Nǐ zhège rén kě zhēn shi de. Wǒ cái huále shíjǐfēn zhōng, lèi shénme?
小　刘：那，咱们 再 划 半个 钟头 就 上 岸 吧。
Xiǎo Liú: Nà, zánmen zài huá bànge zhōngtóu jiù shàng àn ba.
小　赵：好，听 你 的。
Xiǎo Zhào: Hǎo, tīng nǐ de.

2) 老　王：老 李，听说，你们 写 小说 的 人 有 一种 能力，就是 你 看 一眼，就 知道 这个 人 是 干 什么 工作 的。
Lǎo Wáng: Lǎo Lǐ, tīng shuō, nǐmen xiě xiǎoshuōr de rén yǒu yì zhǒng nénglì, jiù shì nǐ kàn yìyǎn, jiù zhīdao zhège rén shì gàn shénme gōngzuò de.
老　李：我 们 是 写 人 的，就是 要 研究 人。在 这 方面 我 还 可以 说 有 一定 的 能力。
Lǎo Lǐ: Wǒmen shì xiě rén de, jiù shì yào yánjiū rén. Zài zhè fāngmiàn wǒ hái kěyǐ shuō yǒu yídìng de nénglì.
老　王：真 的？那，你 说说，那边儿 那个 男 的，他 是 搞 什么 的？
Lǎo Wáng: Zhēn de? Nà, nǐ shuōshuo, nàbianr nàge nán de, tā shì gǎo shénme de?
老　李：他 呀，他 是 搞 教育 的，他 已经 教了 十几年 书 了。他 不是 北京人，可是 他 在 北京 学习、工作、生活了 十五年 了。他 大学 还 是 在 北京 上 的 呢。
Lǎo Lǐ: Tā ya, tā shì gǎo jiàoyù de, tā yǐjīng jiāole shíjǐnián shū le. Tā bú shì Běijīngrén, kěshì tā zài Běijīng xuéxí、gōngzuò、shēnghuóle shíwǔnián le. Tā dàxué hái shì zài Běijīng shàng de ne.
老　王：你 说 完 了 吧？ 我 去 问问 他。
Lǎo Wáng: Nǐ shuō wán le ba? Wǒ qù wènwen tā.
老　李：你 问 去，准 没 错儿。
Lǎo Lǐ: Nǐ wèn qu, zhǔn méi cuòr.

老　王：　对 不起，想 麻烦 您 一下儿。啊！是 你 呀，
Lǎo Wáng: Duì bu qǐ，xiǎng máfan nín yíxiàr．Ā！Shì nǐ ya，
老 李 的 弟弟。哈哈，老 李，你 对 你弟弟
Lǎo Lǐ de dìdi． Hāhā，Lǎo Lǐ，nǐ duì nǐ dìdi
研究 得 真 好，你 说 的 确实 一点儿 也 没
yánjiū de zhēn hǎo，nǐ shuō de quèshí yìdiǎnr yě méi
错 ！
cuòr！

# 32 What's On The Radio And Television
# 现在什么节目 xiànzài shénme jiémù

(Lily and David listen to the radio and watch the TV. )

| | | |
|---|---|---|
| 伟： | 姐姐，现在 什么 节目? | Lily, what's on the radio |
| Wěi: | Jiějie, xiànzài shénme jiémù? | now? |
| 莉： | 国际 新闻。有 好 几条 | International news. A few |
| Lì: | Guójì xīnwén. Yǒu hǎo jǐtiáo | items are about the Unit- |
| | 关于 美国 的 消息。现 | ed States. They are read- |
| | guānyú Měiguó de xiāoxi. Xiàn | ing the headlines now, |

| | | |
|---|---|---|
| | 在正播送标题呢。一会儿有详细内容，你来听听。<br>zài zhèng bōsòng biāotí ne. Yí huìr yǒu xiángxì nèiróng, nǐ lái tīngting. | the details will follow in a minute. Come and listen. |
| 伟：<br>Wěi: | 好，等一会儿我就来。新闻节目完了是什么？<br>Hǎo, děng yíhuìr wǒ jiù lái. Xīnwén jiémù wánle shì shénme? | All right. I'll be with you in a minute. What's on after the news. |
| 莉：<br>Lì: | 音乐。<br>Yīnyuè. | Music. |
| 伟：<br>Wěi: | 姐姐，声音太小，听不清楚。① 你开大一点儿。<br>Jiějie, shēngyīn tài xiǎo, tīng bu qīngchu. Nǐ kāi dà yìdiǎnr. | The volume is too low, Lily. I can't hear it clearly. Make it a bit louder. |
| 莉：<br>Lì: | 行了吗？听得清楚吗？<br>Xíng le ma? Tīng de qīngchu ma? | Is that O. K.? Clear now? |
| 伟：<br>Wěi: | 行了。<br>Xíng le. | O. K. |
| | (They listen together.) | |
| 莉：<br>Lì: | 音乐节目完了。<br>Yīnyuè jiémù wán le. | That's the end of the music program. |
| 伟：<br>Wěi: | 关了吧，别听了。七点了，咱们看电视吧。<br>Guān le ba, bié tīng le. Qīdiǎn le, zánmen kàn diànshì ba. | Turn it off. No more of this. It's seven now, let's watch TV. |
| 莉：<br>Lì: | 今天晚上电视有什么节目？<br>Jīntiān wǎnshang diànshì yǒu shénme jiémù? | What's on TV this evening? |
| 伟：<br>Wěi: | 刚才我看《广播电视节目报》，中央台第一套节目是话剧《茶<br>Gāngcái wǒ kàn "Guǎngbō Diànshì Jiémù Bào", Zhōngyāngtái dìyītào jiémù shì huàjù "Chá | I just looked on the TV Guide. The first program of the Central Station is "Tea House", which is a play and the second program is Beijing opera. |

| | | |
|---|---|---|
| | 馆 》,② 第二套 节目 是<br>guǎnr”, dì'èrtào jiémù shì<br>京剧。<br>jīngjù. | |
| 莉:<br>Lì: | 我们 看 话剧《茶 馆》吧。京剧 看 不 懂。<br>Wǒmen kàn huàjù“Cháguǎnr”ba. Jīngjù kàn bu dǒng. | Let's watch the play "Tea House". We can't understand Beijing Opera anyway. |
| 伟:<br>Wěi: | 好,就 看 话剧吧。<br>Hǎo, jiù kàn huàjù ba. | All right. Let's watch the play then. |
| 莉:<br>Lì: | 第一套节目 几 频道,你 知 道 吗?<br>Dìyītào jiémù jǐ píndào, nǐ zhīdao ma? | Which channel is program one, do you know? |
| 伟:<br>Wěi: | 知 道。第一套节目 是二 频 道。<br>Zhīdao. Dìyītào jiémù shì èr píndào. | Yes, it's on channel 2. |
| 莉:<br>Lì: | 图象 不 太 清 楚,你 调 一下儿。<br>Túxiàng bú tai qīngchu, nǐ tiáo yíxiàr. | The picture is not clear. Will you adjust it? |
| 伟:<br>Wěi: | 我 调 不 好,你 来 吧。<br>Wǒ tiáo bu hǎo, nǐ lái ba. | No, I can't make it clear. You try it, Lily. |
| 莉:<br>Lì: | 你 调 一 调 天线。好 了,图象 清 楚 了。声 音 太 大 了,你 调 小 一点儿。<br>Nǐ tiáo yi tiáo tiānxiàn. Hǎo le, túxiàng qīngchu le. Shēngyīn tài dà le, nǐ tiáo xiǎo yìdiǎnr. | Adjust the (direction of the) aerial. O.K. The picture is clear now, but the volume is too high. Turn it down a bit. |
| 伟:<br>Wěi: | 这样 行 了吗?<br>Zhèyàng xíng le ma? | Is that O.K.? |
| 莉:<br>Lì: | 再 小 一点儿,③ 好了。<br>Zài xiǎo yìdiǎnr, hǎo le. | No, turn it down a bit more. O.K. |

## • new words • 生词 • shēngcí

| | | | | |
|---|---|---|---|---|
| 1 | 节目 | （名） | jiémù | program |
| 2 | 国际 | （名） | guójì | international (community) |
| 3 | 新闻 | （名） | xīnwén | news |
| 4 | 关于 | （介） | guānyú | about, on |
| 5 | 消息 | （名） | xiāoxi | news |
| 6 | 播送 | （动） | bōsòng | to broadcast |
| 7 | 标题 | （名） | biāotí | title, headline |
| 8 | 详细 | （形） | xiángxì | in detail, detailed |
| 9 | 音乐 | （名） | yīnyuè | music |
| 10 | 声音 | （名） | shēngyīn | sound |
| 11 | 开(收音机) | （动） | kāi (shōuyīnjī) | to turn on (radio) |
| 12 | 关 | （动） | guān | to turn off, to close |
| 13 | 电视 | （名） | diànshì | television |
| 14 | 报 | （名） | bào | newspaper |
| 15 | 第 | （头） | dì | a prefix indicating the ordinal number |
| | 第一 | | dìyī | No 1 |
| | 第二 | | dì'èr | No 2 |
| 16 | 套 | （量） | tào | a measure word for radio or TV program |
| 17 | 话剧 | （名） | huàjù | play |
| 18 | 频道 | （名） | píndào | channel (of TV broadcast) |
| 19 | 图象 | （名） | túxiàng | picture |
| 20 | 调 | （动） | tiáo | to adjust |
| 21 | 天线 | （名） | tiānxiàn | aerial |

## 专名 Zhuānmíng Proper names

| | | |
|---|---|---|
| 中央台 | Zhōngyāngtái | Central (Radio or T.V.) Station |
| 《广播电视节目报》 | "Guǎngbō Diànshì Jiémù Bào" | *Radio and TV Guide* |
| 《茶馆》 | "Cháguǎnr" | *The Tea House,* a play by the well-known modern Chinese playwright, Lao She（老舍）. It tells about the changes Chinese society had undergone from the last days of the Qing dynasty to the eve of the founding of the People's Republic of China |

## study points • 注释 • zhùshì

1 听不清楚 (tīng bu qīngchu)

Consider the following question and answer pairs:

Q. 你能听清楚吗？(Nǐ néng tīng qīngchu ma?)

A. 我能听清楚。(Wǒ néng tīng qīngchu.)

Q. 你可以听清楚吗？(Nǐ kěyǐ tīng qīngchu ma?)

A. 我可以听清楚。(Wǒ kěyǐ tīng qīngchu.)

There is a more common version for the above patterns.

Q. 你听得清楚吗？(Nǐ tīng de qīngchu ma?)

A. 我听得清楚。(Wǒ tīng de qīngchu.)

The negative is formed by substituting "不" for "得":

我听不清楚。(Wǒ tīng bu qīngchu.)

2 中央台第一套节目是话剧《茶馆》。

(Zhōngyāngtái dìyītào jiémù shì huàjù《Cháguǎnr》.)

A cardinal number preceded by the prefix "第" (dì) becomes an ordinal one.

3 再小一点儿 (zài xiǎo yìdiǎnr)

“再”(zài) here is equivalent to “still + comparative” in English.

## supplementary words • 补充生词 • bǔchōng shēngcí

| | | | |
|---|---|---|---|
| 1 | 柜子 | （名）guìzi | wardrobe |
| 2 | 好吃 | （形）hǎochī | delicious |
| 3 | 举 | （动）jǔ | to hold up |
| 4 | 灯 | （名）dēng | light |
| 5 | 毛病 | （名）máobing | trouble |
| 6 | 音量 | （名）yīnliàng | volume (sound) |
| 7 | 耳塞子 | （名）ěrsāizi | earphones |
| 8 | 插 | （动）chā | to plug |

## • exercises • 练习 • liànxí

***1. Rewrite the following sentences using “得”(de) or “不”(bù):**

Model: 我 能 听 懂。—— 我 听 得 懂。
Wǒ néng tīng dǒng. —— Wǒ tīng de dǒng.

1) 我 能 看 见。
Wǒ néng kàn jiàn.

2) 今天 他 能 写 完 这些 汉字。
Jīntiān tā néng xiě wán zhèxiē Hànzì.

3) 我 想，他 半 小 时 能 讲 完。
Wǒ xiǎng, tā bànxiǎoshí néng jiǎng wán.

4) 我 看 这个 房间 能 坐 下 二十个人。
Wǒ kàn zhège fángjiān néng zuò xià èrshíge rén.

5) 这个 柜子 能 放 下 这些 衣服。
Zhège guìzi néng fàng xià zhèxiē yīfu.

6) 我十分钟不能看完这篇文章。
Wǒ shífēnzhōng bù néng kàn wán zhèpiān wénzhāng.

7) 这么多好吃的东西，我一个人怎么能吃完！
Zhème duō hǎochī de dōngxi, wǒ yíge rén zěnme néng chī wán!

8) 他还是个小孩儿，不能看懂这个电影。
Tā hái shì ge xiǎoháir, bù néng kàn dǒng zhège diànyǐng.

***2. Complete the dialogues after the model:**

Model: A: 你那篇文章今天写得完写不完？
Nǐ nàpiān wénzhāng jīntiān xiě de wán xiě bu wán?

B: 写得完。你呢？
Xiě de wán. Nǐ ne?

A: 我那篇（可能）写不完。
Wǒ nàpiān (kěnéng) xiě bu wán.

1) A: 你那本小说这星期看_________？
Nǐ nàběn xiǎoshuōr zhè xīngqī kàn_________？

B: _________。你呢？
_________. Nǐ ne?

A: 我这本可能_________。
Wǒ zhèběn kěnéng_________.

2) A: 这辆车_________？
Zhèliàng chē_________？

B: 坐得下四个人。那辆呢？
Zuò de xià sìge rén. Nàliàng ne?

A: _________。
_________.

3) A: 你坐在这儿_________？
Nǐ zuò zài zhèr_________？

B: 看得见。你呢？
Kàn de jiàn. Nǐ ne?

A: _________。
_________.

4) A: 声音开小了，你_________？
Shēngyīn kāi xiǎo le, nǐ_________？

B: 我听得清楚。你呢？
Wǒ tīng de qīngchu. Nǐ ne?

A: _________。
_________。

5) A: 他们 家的 门牌 号，你 ______？
Tāmen jiā de ménpái hào, nǐ ______？
B: 我 记得住。你 呢？
Wǒ jì de zhù. Nǐ ne？
A: ______________。
______________.

6) A: 从 你家 到 电影院，二十分钟 ______？
Cóng nǐ jiā dào diànyǐngyuàn, èrshífēnzhōng ______？
B: ______________。从 你 家呢？
______________. Cóng nǐ jiā ne？
A: ______________。
______________.

**3. Make sentences after the model:**

Model: 声音 你 调 小 点儿，再 小 点儿，好 了。
Shēngyīn nǐ tiáo xiǎo diǎnr, zài xiǎo diǎnr, hǎo le.

1) 声音 开 大 点儿。
Shēngyīn kāi dà diǎnr.
2) 车 开 快 点儿。
Chē kāi kuài diǎnr.
3) 手 举 高点儿。
Shǒu jǔ gāo diǎnr.
4) 让 他 站 远 点儿。
Ràng tā zhàn yuǎn diǎnr.
5) 你 走 慢 点儿。
Nǐ zǒu màn diǎnr.
6) 你 过 去 点儿。
Nǐ guò qu diǎnr.

**4. Listen to the dialogues:**

1) 小 李: 天 黑了，看 不 见 了，开 灯 吧!
Xiǎo Lǐ: Tiān hēi le, kàn bu jiàn le, kāi dēng ba!
小 赵: 不 用，还 看 得 见。
Xiǎo Zhào: Bú yòng, hái kàn de jiàn.
小 李: 还 看得见？你 练 眼睛 哪! 报上 的字 那么 小，不开 灯，准 看不 见了。
Xiǎo Lǐ: Hái kàn de jiàn? Nǐ liàn yǎnjing na! Bàoshang de zì nàme xiǎo, bù kāi dēng, zhǔn kàn bu jiàn le.
小 赵: 我 只 看 标题。这 大 字标题，在 你那儿 都
Xiǎo Zhào: Wǒ zhǐ kàn biāotí. Zhè dà zì biāotí, zài nǐ nàr dōu

看 得见。你 看 哪！
kàn de jiàn. Nǐ kàn na!

小 李: 我 看不见！ 快 开 灯 吧！你是不 想
Xiǎo Lǐ: Wǒ kàn bu jiàn! Kuài kāi dēng ba! Nǐ shì bù xiǎng
要 眼睛 了！
yào yǎnjing le!

2) 弟弟: 电视机有 毛病 了。图象 很清楚，可是
dìdi: Diànshìjī yǒu máobing le. Túxiàng hěn qīngchu, kěshì
声音 怎么 一点儿 也 听 不 见？
shēngyīn zěnme yìdiǎnr yě tīng bu jiàn?

哥哥: 是 啊。音量 再 调 大点儿。
gēge: Shì a. Yīnliàng zài tiáo dà diǎnr.

弟弟: 好，再 调 大点儿。现 在 调 到 最大了，还
dìdi: Hǎo, zài tiáo dà diǎnr. Xiànzài tiáo dào zuì dà le, hái
听 不见！
tīng bu jiàn!

哥哥: 你 看看，耳塞子还 插着 呢，哪儿会 听 得 见
gēge: Nǐ kànkan, ěrsāizi hái chāzhe ne, nǎr huì tīng de jiàn
声 音！
shēngyīn!

# 33 I've Been To Xian Before
# 我以前来过西安 wǒ yǐqián láiguo Xī'ān

(Before leaving Xian, Mr. Chen Mingshan tells Zhang Xin his impressions of the city.)

| | | |
|---|---|---|
| 陈：<br>Chén: | 时间过得真快，到西安已经八天了。<br>Shíjiān guò de zhēn kuài, dào Xī'ān yǐjing bātiān le. | How time flies! I've been in Xian for eight days already. |
| 张：<br>Zhāng: | 一切都很好吧？我记得<br>Yíqiè dōu hěn hǎo ba? Wǒ jìde | Is everything O. K.? I remember you telling me |

| | | |
|---|---|---|
| | 你 说过，① 你 以前 来过<br>nǐ shuōguo, nǐ yǐqián láiguo<br>西安。<br>Xī'ān. | that you've been here before. |
| 陈 ：<br>Chén: | 是。一九四〇年 来过一次。②<br>Shì. Yījiǔsìlíngnián láiguo yícì. | Yes, once in 1940. |
| 张 ：<br>Zhāng: | 这次来西安，旧 地 重 游，<br>Zhècì lái Xī'ān, jiù dì chóng yóu,<br>有 什么 感想 呢？<br>yǒu shénme gǎnxiǎng ne? | Well, how do you find it after all these years? |
| 陈 ：<br>Chén: | 四十年 来，西安 的 变化<br>Sìshínián lái, Xī'ān de biànhuà<br>实在 太 大了。城市 比 以<br>shízài tài dà le. Chéngshì bǐ yǐ<br>前 大 多 了，③ 街道 也 跟<br>qián dà duō le, jiēdào yě gēn<br>以前 不 一样 了。<br>yǐqián bù yíyàng le. | Xian has certainly changed a lot in the past 40 years. It's a much bigger city now, and the streets too are different. |
| 张 ：<br>Zhāng: | 比 以前 宽 了。<br>Bǐ yǐqián kuān le. | They are wider now. |
| 陈 ：<br>Chén: | 也 比 以前 干净 了。那 时<br>Yě bǐ yǐqián gānjing le. Nà shí<br>候，街道 两边儿 的 树<br>hour, jiēdào liǎngbiānr de shù<br>很 少，工厂、学校、<br>hěn shǎo, gōngchǎng、xuéxiào、<br>商店、医院 也 没有 现<br>shāngdiàn、yīyuàn yě méiyǒu xiàn<br>在 这样 多。④<br>zài zhèyàng duō. | And cleaner too. There were very few trees on the sidewalks then, and there weren't so many factories, schools, stores and hospitals. |
| 张 ：<br>Zhāng: | 高 楼 大厦 更 少。<br>Gāo lóu dàshà gèng shǎo. | There were even less tall buildings. |
| 陈 ：<br>Chén: | 现在 西安 到处 充满着<br>Xiànzài Xī'ān dàochù chōngmǎnzhe<br>生气，真 是 一个 古老 而<br>shēngqì, zhēn shì yíge gǔlǎo ér<br>又 年轻 的 城市。⑤<br>yòu niánqīng de chéngshì. | Xian is full of vitality now. It is indeed an ancient and youthful city. |

| | | |
|---|---|---|
| 张：<br>Zhāng: | 来 西安 这么 多 天 了，到<br>Lái Xī'ān zhème duō tiān le，dào<br>华清池 洗过 温泉 澡<br>Huáqīngchí xǐguo wēnquán zǎo<br>没有？<br>méiyǒu？ | After all these days in Xian, have you been to the hot springs at Hua Ching Chi for a bath? |
| 陈：<br>Chén: | 到 西安的 第二天就 去了，<br>Dào Xī'ān de dì'èrtiān jiù qù le，<br>后来 艾琳 她们 又 去过<br>hòulái Àilín tāmen yòu qùguo<br>两 次。<br>liǎngcì． | Yes, on the very next day of our arrival. Irene and the children went twice again. |
| 张：<br>Zhāng: | 这 几天 都 参观了 哪些<br>Zhè jǐtiān dōu cānguānle nǎxiē<br>地 方 了？<br>dìfang le？ | Where else have you visited in the last few days? |
| 陈：<br>Chén: | 能 去的 地方 差 不 多<br>Néng qù de dìfang chà bu duō<br>都 去了。历史 博物馆 去<br>dōu qù le．Lìshǐ Bówùguǎn qù<br>过 两次 了，但是 只 看<br>guo liǎngcì le，dànshì zhǐ kàn<br>完 一遍。明天 还 想<br>wán yíbiàn．Míngtiān hái xiǎng<br>再 去一次。我 想 再 详<br>zài qù yícì．Wǒ xiǎng zài xiáng<br>细地 了解 一些 唐 代 中<br>xì de liǎojiě yìxiē Táng dài Zhōng<br>外 文化 交流 的 情<br>wài wénhuà jiāoliú de qíng<br>况 。⑥<br>kuàng。 | I've been to most places that I can possibly go. I've been to the history museum twice, but only had time to go through it once. I intend to go again tomorrow. I want to find out more about the cultural exchange between China and the West during the Tang dynasty. |
| 张：<br>Zhāng: | 这个 题目 很 值得 研究。<br>Zhège tímù hěn zhíde yánjiū．<br>对 了，这 几天 西安 正<br>Duì le，zhè jǐtiān Xī'ān zhèng<br>上演 大型 舞剧《丝路 花<br>shàngyǎn dàxíng wǔjù " Sī Lù Huā | Yes, this is a worth-while research subject. By the way, the dance drama "Tales of the Silk Route" is now being performed in Xi'an. You |

| | | |
|---|---|---|
| | 雨》，你们 看 吗？<br>Yǔ ”， nǐmen kàn ma? | want to see it? |
| 陈 ：<br>Chén: | 上个 月 北京 演 过，我<br>Shàngge yuè Běijīng yǎnguo, wǒ<br>们 在 北京 看过 了。这<br>men zài Běijīng kànguo le . Zhè<br>个 舞剧 很 有 意思，无论<br>ge wǔjù hěn yǒu yìsi , wúlùn<br>音乐 还是 舞蹈 都 很<br>yīnyuè háishi wǔdǎo dōu hěn<br>好。你 看过 了 吗？<br>hǎo. Nǐ kànguo le ma? | We saw it last month when it was performed in Beijing. It is a very interesting performance. Both the music and the dancing are very good. Did you see it? |
| 张 ：<br>Zhāng: | 没有 呢。明 天 看。你<br>Méiyǒu ne . Míngtiān kàn. Nǐ<br>们 还看 吗？⑦<br>men hái kàn ma? | No. We are going to-morrow. Do you want to see it again? |
| 陈 ：<br>Chén: | 不 了。明 天 晚上 得<br>Bù le . Míngtiān wǎnshang děi<br>准 备 准 备，后 天 就 回<br>zhǔnbeizhǔnbei, hòutiān jiù huí<br>去 了。我 有 一个 侄子在<br>qu le . Wǒ yǒu yíge zhízi zài<br>郑州 。回 北京 时 路过<br>Zhèngzhōu. Huí Běijīng shí lùguò<br>郑州 ，我 还得 在 郑<br>Zhèngzhōu, wǒ hái děi zài Zhèng<br>州 呆 两 天。<br>zhōu dāi liǎngtiān . | No, thank you. We have to prepare for our departure tomorrow evening. We'll be leaving the day after tomorrow. I've a nephew in Zheng-zhou and I'll have to stay there for two days before returning to Beijing. |
| 张 ：<br>Zhāng: | 哪天 回 美 国 定 了 吗？<br>Nǎtiān huí Měiguó dìng le ma? | Have you fixed a date for returning to the States? |
| 陈 ：<br>Chén: | 定 了，二十三号。二十六号<br>Dìng le , èrshísānhào. Èrshíliùhào<br>以前 必须 赶 回 美 国。<br>yǐqián bìxū gǎn huí Měiguó.<br>明年 有 机会 我 再 来。<br>Míngnián yǒu jīhui wǒ zài lái . | Yes, the 23rd. I have to get back before the 26th. I'll come again next year if I have a chance. |

| | | |
|---|---|---|
| 张　: Zhāng: | 希望 下次来 能　多呆几 天　。 Xīwàng xiàcì lái néng duō dāi jǐ tiān. | Hope you can stay longer next time you come. |
| 陈　: Chén: | 一定，一定。 Yídìng，yídìng. | Sure, sure. |

## • new words • 生词 • shēngcí

| | | | |
|---|---|---|---|
| 1 | 一切 | （代）yíqiè | all, everything |
| 2 | 过 | （助）guo | a suffix to show a past experience |
| 3 | 以前 | （名）yǐqián | former times, before |
| 4 | 感想 | （名）gǎnxiǎng | reflection, feeling |
| 5 | 城市 | （名）chéngshì | city |
| 6 | 街道 | （名）jiēdào | street |
| 7 | 宽 | （形）kuān | wide |
| 8 | 干净 | （形）gānjìng | clean |
| 9 | 学校 | （名）xuéxiào | school |
| 10 | 商店 | （名）shāngdiàn | shop, store |
| 11 | 大厦 | （名）dàshà | tall building |
| 12 | 更 | （副）gèng | more, still more |
| 13 | 到处 | （名）dàochù | everywhere |
| 14 | 充满 | （动）chōngmǎn | to fill, to be full of |
| 15 | 生气 | （名）shēngqì | vitality, life |
| 16 | 古老 | （形）gǔlǎo | ancient |
| 17 | 而 | （连）ér | a connective, in the text it means "as well as" |
| 18 | 年轻 | （形）niánqīng | young |

| | | | | |
|---|---|---|---|---|
| 19 | 洗澡 | | xǐ zǎo | bath, to take a bath |
| 20 | 温泉 | （名） | wēnquán | hot spring |
| 21 | 后来 | （名） | hòulái | later, after that |
| 22 | 哪些 | （代） | nǎxiē | which (pl.) |
| 23 | 但是 | （连） | dànshì | but |
| 24 | 遍 | （量） | biàn | times (emphasizing the whole process) |
| 25 | 了解 | （动、名） | liǎojiě | to understand, to find out ,understanding, investigation |
| 26 | 交流 | （动） | jiāoliú | to exchange |
| 27 | 题目 | （名） | tímù | topic, subject |
| 28 | 上演 | （动） | shàngyǎn | to perform, to put on a show |
| 29 | 型 | （名） | xíng | scale, model |
| 30 | 舞剧 | （名） | wǔjù | dance drama, ballet |
| 31 | 无论 | （连） | wúlùn | no matter |
| | 无论……还是……都…… | | wúlùn…háishi…dōu… | no matter… or …all |
| 32 | 定 | （动） | dìng | to settle, to fix |
| 33 | 必须 | （助动） | bìxū | must |
| 34 | 赶 | （动） | gǎn | to hurry |
| 35 | 明年 | （名） | míngnián | next year |

## 专名　　Zhuānmíng　　Proper names

| | | |
|---|---|---|
| 华清池 | Huáqīngchí | Huaching Springs, a place in Xian famous for its hot springs. |
| 历史博物馆 | Lìshǐ Bówùguǎn | The Historical Museum |
| 《丝路花雨》 | "Sī Lù Huā Yǔ" | *Tales of the Silk Route* a full-length dance drama about China's early cultural exchanges with Central Asia. |

| | | |
|---|---|---|
| 郑州 | Zhèngzhōu | Zhengzhou capital of Honan province in central China. |

## study points • 注释 • zhùshì

1 我记得你说过。(Wǒ jìde nǐ shuōguo.)

"过" (guò) placed after a verb indicates a past experience or action:

我十年前来过西安。(Wǒ shíniánqián láiguo Xī'ān.)

他看过这个舞剧。(Tā kànguo zhège wǔjù.)

The negative is formed by adding "没有" (méi (yǒu)) before the verb:

他们没有洗过温泉澡。(Tāmen méiyǒu xǐguo wēnquán zǎo.)

昨天老张没有来过这儿。(Zuótiān Lǎo Zhāng méiyǒu láiguo zhèr.)

2 一九四〇年来过一次。(Yījiǔsìlíngnián láiguo yícì.)

Common measure words for verbs are "次" (cì), "遍" (biàn), "回" (huí), "趟" (tàng), etc. "一次" is once, "两次" is twice and so on. "遍" also expresses the idea of "the whole process from the beginning to the end":

历史博物馆我去过两次了，但是还没有看完一遍。

(Lìshǐ Bówùguǎn wǒ qùguo liǎngcì le, dànshì hái méiyǒu kàn wán yíbiàn.)

3 城市比以前大多了。(Chéngshì bǐ yǐqián dà duō le.)

"大多了" is "much bigger", "重多了" is "much heavier", therefore "多" serves to emphasize the degree of difference.

4 工厂、学校、商店、医院也没有现在这样多。

(Gōngchǎng、xuéxiào、shāngdiàn、yīyuàn yě méiyǒu xiànzài zhèyàng duō.)

"没有" can also be used for comparison in Chinese:

他没有你大。(Tā méiyǒu nǐ dà.)

我的车没有你的车新。(Wǒ de chē méiyou nǐ de chē xīn.)

This is paralell to the "not as …as" structure in English.

5 真是一个古老而又年轻的城市。

(Zhēn shì yíge gǔlǎo ér yòu niánqīng de chéngshì.)

"而" (ér) is a cojoining word for adjectives.

The structure of "adjective + 而 (ér) + 又 (yòu) + adjective" indicates two kinds of states or situations that exist at the same time.

6 我想再详细地了解一些唐代中外文化交流的情况。

(Wǒ xiǎng zài xiángxì de liǎojiě yìxiē Táng dài Zhōng wài wénhuà jiāoliú de qíngkuàng.)

中外 (Zhōng wài) is the short term for "China and the foreign countries".

7 你们还看吗? (Nǐmen hái kàn ma?)

"还" here means "again", "once more" or "still".

## supplementary words • 补充生词 • bǔchōng shēngcí

| | | | | |
|---|---|---|---|---|
| 1 | 读 | (动) | dú | to read |
| 2 | 磁带(盘) | (名) | cídài | magnetic tape |
| 3 | 胖 | (形) | pàng | fat |
| 4 | 炒 | (动) | chǎo | to stir and fry |
| 5 | 香 | (形) | xiāng | fragrant or smell deliciously |
| 6 | 好听 | (形) | hǎotīng | pleasant to the ear |
| 7 | 头发 | (名) | tóufa | hair |
| 8 | 爱动 | | ài dòng | active (physically) |
| 9 | 体育 | (名) | tǐyù | physical exercise |
| 10 | 游泳 | (动、名) | yóuyǒng | to swim, swimming |
| 11 | 过去 | (名) | guòqù | the past |
| 12 | 水 | (名) | shuǐ | water |
| 13 | 跑步 | | pǎo bù | jogging, to run |
| | 法国 | | Fǎguó | France |

## • exercises • 练习 • liànxí

1. **Make sentences using "过"(guo):**

1) Model: 听 说 你看过 话剧《茶馆 》, 请你给 我们
Tīng shuō nǐ kànguo huàjù "Cháguǎnr", qǐng nǐ gěi wǒmen
介绍介绍。(话剧《茶 馆》)
jièshaojièshao. (huàjù "Cháguǎnr")

(1) 那个 工厂
nàge gōngchǎng

(2) 颐和园
Yíhéyuán

(3) 这个 电影
zhège diànyǐng

(4) 那个 报告
nàge bàogào

2) Model: 约翰 先生 一九七六年 到过 法国。(一九七六年 ,法国)
Yuēhàn xiānsheng yījiǔqīliùnián dàoguo Fǎguó. (yījiǔqīliùnián, Fǎguó)

(1) 一九七七年, 英 国
yījiǔqīqīnián, Yīngguó

(2) 前 年 ,加拿大
qiánnián, Jiānádà

(3) 去 年, 日本
qùnián, Rìběn

(4) 今年 , 中 国
jīnnián, Zhōngguó

(5) 这 几年, 许多 地方
zhè jǐnián, xǔduō dìfang

*2. **Complete the following dialogues:**

Model:
A: 你 看 没 看过 这个 电影?
Nǐ kàn méi kànguo zhège diànyǐng?
B: 我 没 看过。你 看过 吗?
Wǒ méi kànguo. Nǐ kànguo ma?
A: 我 看过 两次了。(次)
Wǒ kànguo liǎngcì le. (cì)

(1) A: 你 读________ 这本 小说?
Nǐ dú ________ zhèběn xiǎoshuōr?
B: 我 没 读过。你________?
Wǒ méi dúguo. Nǐ ________?

A: ________________。( 遍 )
________________. ( biàn )

(2) A: 他 研究 ________ 这个 问题？
Tā yánjiū ________ zhège wèntí?
B: ________。________？
________. ________？
A: 我 研究了 两个 月 了。
Wǒ yánjiūle liǎngge yuè le.

(3) A: 你 买 ________ 这种 糖？
Nǐ mǎi ________ zhèzhǒng táng?
B: ________。________？
________. ________？
A: 我 ________。( 次 )
Wǒ ________. ( cì )

(4) A: 你 听 ________ 这盘儿 磁带？
Nǐ tīng ________ zhèpánr cídài?
B: ________。________？
________. ________？
A: 我 ________________。( 遍 )
Wǒ ________________. ( biàn )

(5) A: 你 吃 ________ 北京 烤鸭？
Nǐ chī ________ Běijīng kǎoyā?
B: ________。________？
________. ________？
A: ________________。( 回 )
________________. ( huí )

(6) A: 你 见 ______ 这位 先生？
Nǐ jiàn ______ zhèwèi xiānsheng?
B: 我 没 见过。________？
Wǒ méi jiànguo. ________？
A: 我 见过 几次面 。
Wǒ jiànguo jǐcì miàn.

***3. Practice making sentences of comparison:**

1) Model: A: 那 时候，这儿的 树 没有 这么 多。
Nà shíhour, zhèr de shù méiyǒu zhème duō.
B: 可 不，现在 这儿的 树 比 以前 多 多 了。
Kě bù, xiànzài zhèr de shù bǐ yǐqián duō duō le.

(1) A: 前 几天 没有 今天 这么冷。
Qián jǐtiān méiyǒu jīntiān zhème lěng.

B: ______________。
______________.

(2) A: 两年 前，来这儿旅游 的人 没有 这么多。
Liǎngnián qián, lái zhèr lǚyóu de rén méiyǒu zhème duō.

B: ______________。
______________。

(3) A: 两年 以前，他 没有 现在 这么胖。
Liǎngnián yǐqián, tā méiyǒu xiànzài zhème pàng.

B: ______________。
______________.

(4) A: 去年 这种 皮鞋 没有 今年 这么贵。
Qùnián zhèzhǒng píxié méiyǒu jīnnián zhème guì.

B: ______________。
______________.

(5) A: 上次 来这儿的 收获 没有 这次 这么大。
Shàngcì lái zhèr de shōuhuò méiyǒu zhècì zhème dà.

B: ______________。
______________.

2) Model: A: 上 星期 没有 这么热。
Shàng xīngqī méiyǒu zhème rè.

B: 哪儿啊！比现在热 多了。
Nǎr a! Bǐ xiànzài rè duō le.

(1) A: 他 炒 的菜 没有 你炒 的 这么 香。
Tā chǎo de cài méiyǒu nǐ chǎo de zhème xiāng.

B: ______________。
______________.

(2) A: 这种 椅子没有 那种舒服。
Zhèzhǒng yǐzi méiyǒu nàzhǒng shūfu.

B: ______________。
______________.

(3) A: 这个舞剧的 音乐 没有 那个的好听。
Zhège wǔjù de yīnyuè méiyǒu nàge de hǎotīng.

B: ______________。
______________.

(4) A: 他 知道 的情 况 没有 你们 详细。
Tā zhīdao de qíngkuàng méiyǒu nǐmen xiángxì.

B: ______________________。
______________________.

4. **Listen to the dialogue:**

老　钱：　老　关，今天你见　到　王　先生　了 没有？
Lǎo Qián: Lǎo Guān, jīntiān nǐ jiàn dào Wáng xiānsheng le méiyǒu?

老　关：　见　到 了。
Lǎo Guān: Jiàn dào le.

老　钱：　这　是 你 第一次 见　到 他 吧？
Lǎo Qián: Zhè shì nǐ dìyīcì jiàn dào tā ba?

老　关：　哪儿 啊！五年　前，我　招待过　他 一次。他　现在 比　以前 老　多 了，白 头发 也　多　多 了。
Lǎo Guān: Nǎr a! Wǔnián qián, wǒ zhāodàiguo tā yícì. Tā xiànzài bǐ yǐqián lǎo duō le, bái tóufa yě duō duō le.

老　钱：　那　时候　他 没有 这么　胖　吧？
Lǎo Qián: Nà shíhour tā méiyǒu zhème pàng ba?

老　关：　可 不，那　时候　他 比 你　现在　还　瘦　呢。
Lǎo Guān: Kě bù, nà shíhour tā bǐ nǐ xiànzài hái shòu ne.

老　钱：　可　看 起来，王　先生　比 我　身体　好　多 了。
Lǎo Qián: Kě kàn qǐlai, Wáng xiānsheng bǐ wǒ shēntǐ hǎo duō le.

老　关：　是　啊。我　说　老　钱，你　得 注意　身体 呀。　两年　前 你 比 现在 爱　动，差 不 多　每天　都参加　体育　活　动。记得 一年　夏天，咱们　还 一起参加过　几个 大学 的　游　泳　比赛 呢！
Lǎo Guān: Shì a. Wǒ shuō Lǎo Qián, nǐ děi zhùyì shēntǐ ya. Liǎng nián qián nǐ bǐ xiànzài ài dòng, chà bu duō měitiān dōu cānjiā tǐyù huódòng. Jìde yìnián xiàtiān, zánmen hái yìqǐ cānjiāguo jǐge dàxué de yóuyǒng bǐsài ne!

老　钱：　那　是　过去 的　事儿 了！　去年　夏天，我　没　下 过一次　水，一 场　球　也　没　打过。不　行　啊，得改 改。下 个　月　一号，我　开始　跑　步。
Lǎo Qián: Nà shì guòqù de shìr le! Qùnián xiàtiān, wǒ méi xiàguo yícì shuǐ, yìchǎng qiú yě méi dǎguo. Bù xíng a, děi gǎigai. Xiàge yuè yíhào, wǒ kāishǐ pǎo bù.

老　关：　还　等　什么　下个月！　明天　早上，我 来 找你。咱 们　一起 跑　步。
Lǎo Guān: Hái děng shénme xiàge yuè! Míngtiān zǎoshang, wǒ lái zhǎo nǐ. Zánmen yìqǐ pǎo bù.

老钱： 好啊！
Lǎo Qián: Hǎo a !

***5. Translate the following sentences into Chinese:**

1) Lao Zhao has been to the United States.
2) Lao Zhao has gone to the United States.
3) He lived in China for twenty years.
4) He has been living in China for the last twenty years.
5) Lao Chen is not as old as Lao Zhang.

# 34 We'll Be Leaving China Tonight
# 晚 上 我们 就 要 离开 中 国 了
# wǎnshang wǒmen jiù yào líkāi Zhōngguó le

(The Chens are preparing to leave China.)

| | | |
|---|---|---|
| 艾：<br>Ài: | 飞机票 拿 来了 没有？①<br>Fēijīpiào ná lai le méiyǒu? | Have we got the plane tickets? |
| 陈：<br>Chén: | 拿 来了。<br>Ná lai le. | Yes. |
| 伟：<br>Wěi: | 爸爸，给 姑姑和舅舅 的 电<br>Bàba, gěi gūgu hé jiùjiu de diàn | Dad, have you cabled Auntie and Uncle? |

| | | |
|---|---|---|
| | 报 打了吗？②<br>bào dǎ le ma? | |
| 陈：<br>Chén: | 没有 呢，一会儿去 打。艾<br>Méiyǒu ne, yíhuìr qù dǎ. Ài<br>琳，东西 收拾 得 怎么<br>lín, dōngxi shōushi de zěnme<br>样 了。<br>yàng le. | Not yet. I'll do that later. How's the packing, Irene? |
| 艾：<br>Ài: | 差 不 多 了。那 两个<br>Chà bu duō le. Nà liǎngge<br>箱子 托运，别的 东西<br>xiāngzi tuōyùn, biéde dōngxi<br>自己 带.<br>zìjǐ dài. | Nearly done. Those two cases are to be sent by freight. The rest will be hand-carried. |
| 莉：<br>Lì: | 妈妈，早晨 送 去洗 的<br>Māma, zǎochén sòng qu xǐ de<br>衬衫 和裤子 送 来了吗？<br>chènshān hé kùzi sòng lai le ma? | Is the laundry back yet, Mom? I sent in a blouse and a pair of slacks this morning. |
| 艾：<br>Ài: | 送 来了。<br>Sòng lai le. | They are here. |
| 陈：<br>Chén: | 我 昨天 新 买 的 眼镜 和<br>Wǒ zuótiān xīn mǎi de yǎnjìng hé<br>领带 给 我 拿 出 来 了 没<br>lǐngdài gěi wǒ ná chu lai le méi<br>有？<br>yǒu? | Have you gotten out the glasses and tie I bought yesterday? |
| 艾：<br>Ài: | 拿 出 来了。<br>Ná chu lai le. | Yes. |
| 陈：<br>Chén: | 晚上 就要 离开了，你们<br>Wǎnshang jiù yào líkāi le, nǐmen<br>想想，还 有 些 什么<br>xiǎngxiang, hái yǒu xiē shénme<br>事儿 要 办？<br>shìr yào bàn? | Is there anything else you people want to do before we leave this evening? |
| 伟：<br>Wěi: | 我 想 再去 天安门 照<br>Wǒ xiǎng zài qù Tiān'ānmén zhào<br>几 张 照 片，上次 的 照<br>jǐzhāng zhàopiàn, shàngcì de zhào | I want to take a few more pictures of Tian An Men. The ones I took last time didn't |

| | | |
|---|---|---|
| | 片 没有 照 好。<br>piàn méiyǒu zhào hǎo. | come out well. |
| 陈：<br>Chén: | 莉莉，你有 事儿吗？<br>Lìli, nǐ yǒu shìr ma? | How about you, Lily? |
| 莉：<br>Lì: | 我 想 帮助 妈妈 收拾<br>Wǒ xiǎng bāngzhù māma shōushi<br>收拾 东西，可是 大伟 让<br>shōushi dōngxi, kěshì Dàwěi ràng<br>我 跟他 一起去。<br>wǒ gēn tā yìqǐ qù. | Actually I want to help mother with the packing, but David wants me to go with him. |
| 艾：<br>Ài: | 东西 快 收拾 好了。我<br>Dōngxi kuài shōushi hǎo le. Wǒ<br>自己干就行了。你 跟弟弟<br>zìjǐ gàn jiù xíng le. Nǐ gēn dìdi<br>一起去吧。<br>yìqǐ qù ba. | There isn't much more to be done. I'll manage myself. You go with David. |
| 伟：<br>Wěi: | 飞机 几点的？<br>Fēiji jǐdiǎn de? | What time is our plane? |
| 陈：<br>Chén: | 八点 一刻的。<br>Bādiǎn yíkè de. | A quarter after eight. |
| 伟：<br>Wěi: | 咱们 几点 离开 饭店？<br>Zánmen jǐdiǎn líkāi fàndiàn? | When shall we leave here then? |
| 陈：<br>Chén: | 六点半。你们 五点半<br>Liùdiǎnbàn. Nǐmen wǔdiǎnbàn<br>左右 回 来 就 行 了。③<br>zuǒyòu huí lai jiù xíng le. | Six thirty. It'll be all right if you come back around five thirty. |
| 艾：<br>Ài: | 莉莉，你们 照 完 相 以<br>Lìli, nǐmen zhào wán xiàng yǐ<br>后，顺 便 到 王府井<br>hòu, shùnbiàn dào Wángfǔjǐng<br>百 货 大楼 再 买 点儿 小<br>Bǎihuò Dàlóu zài mǎi diǎnr xiǎo<br>礼品吧。早 点儿回 来。<br>lǐpǐn ba. Zǎo diǎnr huí lai. | Lily, after you've finished taking pictures, run to the department store in Wang Fu Jing and buy some more gifts and souvenirs. Hurry back. |
| 莉：<br>Lì: | 好。<br>Hǎo. | All right. |
| 艾：<br>Ài: | 帐 结了吗？<br>Zhàng jié le ma? | Have you checked out yet? |

| | | |
|---|---|---|
| 陈：<br>Chén: | 这 不 忙 。④ 我 现 在 就 去。 帐 结 完 了，我 去 打 电 报。<br>Zhè bù máng. Wǒ xiànzài jiù qù. Zhàng jié wán le, wǒ qù dǎ diànbào. | No hurry. I'm going to do it now. Then I'll send the cable. |
| | （电话铃声） | (The telephone rings) |
| 艾：<br>Ài: | 谁 来的 电话？<br>Shuí lái de diànhuà? | Who was it? |
| 陈：<br>Chén: | 老 李 来的。他们 单位 决 定 让 他 今天 晚上 到 上海 参加 一个 重要 会议，所以 晚上 不 能 来 送 我们。他 表示 抱歉 。他 说 一会儿老 丁 要 来。<br>Lǎo Lǐ lái de. Tāmen dānwèi juédìng ràng tā jīntiān wǎnshang dào Shànghǎi cānjiā yíge zhòngyào huìyì, suǒyǐ wǎnshang bù néng lái sòng wǒmen. Tā biǎoshì bàoqiàn. Tā shuō yíhuìr Lǎo Dīng yào lái. | Lao Li. His unit has decided to send him to Shanghai tonight for an important conference, so he apologizes for not being able to see us off tonight. He said Lao Ding will come in a moment. |
| 艾：<br>Ài: | 没 说 什么 时候 来？<br>Méi shuō shénme shíhour lái? | Did he say what time is she coming? |
| 陈：<br>Chén: | 没有，就 说 一会儿 来。⑤ 我 现在 赶 快 去 结 帐、打 电 报。<br>Méiyou, jiù shuō yíhuìr lái. Wǒ xiànzài gǎnkuài qù jié zhàng、dǎ diànbào. | No, except that she'll be here shortly. So I better go and settle the account and send the cable now. |
| 艾：<br>Ài: | 你 快 去 快 回。<br>Nǐ kuài qù kuài huí. | You'd better hurry and get back soon. |

## • new words • 生词 • shēngcí

| | | | | |
|---|---|---|---|---|
| 1 | 拿 | （动） | ná | to take |
| 2 | 姑姑 | （名） | gūgu | aunt (father's sister) |
| 3 | 舅舅 | （名） | jiùjiu | uncle (mother's brother) |
| 4 | 收拾 | （动） | shōushi | to pack, to tidy up |
| 5 | 箱子 | （名） | xiāngzi | suitcase, trunk |
| 6 | 托运 | （动） | tuōyùn | to check (luggage), to send by freight |
| 7 | 洗 | （动） | xǐ | to wash |
| 8 | 衬衫 | （名） | chènshān | shirt, blouse |
| 9 | 裤子 | （名） | kùzi | trousers |
| 10 | 眼镜 | （名） | yǎnjìngr | glasses, spectacles |
| 11 | 领带 | （名） | lǐngdài | tie |
| 12 | 照 | （动） | zhào | to take (a picture) |
| 13 | 照片 | （名） | zhàopiàn | picture, snapshot |
| 14 | 饭店 | （名） | fàndiàn | hotel, restaurant |
| 15 | 左右 | （名） | zuǒyòu | a noun indicating an approximate number (quantity), around, about |
| 16 | 照相 | | zhào xiàng | to take pictures |
| 17 | 顺便 | （副） | shùnbiàn | on the way, in passing |
| 18 | 礼品 | （名） | lǐpǐn | present, gift |
| 19 | 结帐 | | jié zhàng | to settle account, to check out |
| 20 | 忙 | （形） | máng | busy |
| 21 | 单位 | （名） | dānwèi | unit, organization |
| 22 | 决定 | （动、名） | juédìng | to decide, decision |
| 23 | 参加 | （动） | cānjiā | to attend, to take part in |
| 24 | 会议 | （名） | huìyì | meeting, conference |
| 25 | 所以 | （连） | suǒyǐ | so, therefore |

| | | | |
|---|---|---|---|
| 26 抱歉 | （形）bàoqiàn | to apologize | |

| 专名 | Zhūanmíng | Proper names |
|---|---|---|
| 天安门 | Tiān'ānmén | Tenanmen, main gate of the Imperial Palace, situated in the centre of Beijing |
| 王府井百货大楼 | Wángfǔjǐng Bǎihuò Dàlóu | Wangfujing Department Store, the biggest department store in Beijing |
| 上海 | Shànghǎi | Shanghai, China's biggest and most industrialized city |

## study points • 注释 • zhùshì

1 飞机票拿来了没有？(Fēijīpiào ná lai le méiyǒu?)

In Chinese, passive sentences are usually indicated by the word "被"(bèi) or "给" (gěi).

我被人打了。(Wǒ bèi rén dǎ le.)

村庄给烧了。(Cūnzhuāng gěi shāo le.)

But there is another kind of passive sentences in which no passive indicators are necessary. This kind of sentences is used mostly in spoken Chinese.

东西都收拾好了。(Dōngxi dōu shōushi hǎo le.)

电报打了吗？(Diànbào dǎ le ma?)

2 给姑姑和舅舅的电报打了吗？(Gěi gūgu hé jiùjiu de diànbào dǎ le ma?)

Father's sisters are called "姑姑"(gūgu) ( they can be called "姑妈"(gūmā) or "姑母"(gūmǔ) if they are married). Mother's brothers are called "舅舅" (jiùjiu). Father's elder brothers are called "伯伯"(bóbo), and his younger brothers are called "叔叔"(shūshu). Mother's sisters are called "姨" (yí) (they can be called "姨妈" (yímā) or "姨母" (yímǔ) if they are married).

3 你们五点半左右回来就行了。(Nǐmen wǔdiǎnbàn zuǒyòu huí lai jiù xíng le.)

"左右" literally means "in the neighborhood of"; so it is an expression of approximation.

4 这不忙。(Zhè bù máng.)

This is a colloquial expression for "No hurry".

5 就说一会儿来。(Jiù shuō yíhuìr lái.)

The main uses of the adverb "就" (jiù) are:

1) to show the limit or scope:

就说一会儿来。(Jiù shuō yíhuìr lái.)

就这些。(Jiù zhèxiē.) (Lesson 14)

2) to mean within a short time:

我们很快就要离开北京了。

(Wǒmen hěn kuài jiù yào líkāi Běijīng le.) (Lesson 19)

晚上就上飞机了。(Wǎnshang jiù shàng fēijī le.) (Lesson 20)

3) to show one action closely followed by another:

跟小王谈完就去。(Gēn Xiǎo Wáng tán wán jiù qù.) (Lesson 19)

昨天我们吃了早饭就出去了。

(Zuótiān wǒmen chīle zǎofàn jiù chū qu le.) (Lesson 20)

4) to show the lack of choices under the circumstances:

那就买八号的吧。(Nà jiù mǎi bāhào de ba.) (Lesson 21)

5) to emphasize something that had taken place a very long time ago:

两千多年以前，中国人民就有这样伟大的创造。(Liǎngqiān duō nián yǐqián, Zhōngguó rénmín jiù yǒu zhèyàng wěidà de chuàngzào.) (Lesson 22)

6) to emphasize a fact:

老张就住在钟楼附近。

(Lǎo Zhāng jiù zhù zài Zhōnglóu fùjìn.) (Lesson 24)

## supplementary words • 补充生词 • bǔchōng shēngcí

| | | | | |
|---|---|---|---|---|
| 1 | 岁数 | (名) | suìshu | age |
| 2 | 开会 | | kāi huì | to hold meeting, conference |
| 3 | 里 | (量) | lǐ | Li (equal to half a kilometer) |
| 4 | 斤 | (量) | jīn | Jin (equal to half a kilogram) |
| 5 | 拍 | (动) | pāi | to send (cable) |
| 6 | 租 | (动) | zū | to hire |

| | | | |
|---|---|---|---|
| 7 | 行动 | （动、名）xíngdòng | movement, to take action |
| 8 | 装 | （动）zhuāng | to pack |
| 9 | 任务 | （名）rènwu | task |
| 10 | 罐头 | （名）guàntou | canned food(s) |

## • exercises • 练习 • liànxí

*1. **Fill in the blanks with the right choice:**

1) A: 信 呢？
Xìn ne？

B: ________。
________.

(1) 寄 走信了。
Jì zǒu xìn le.

(2) 信 寄 走了。
Xìn jì zǒu le.

2) A: 你 买 来 什么 了？
Nǐ mǎi lai shénme le？

B: ________。
________.

(1) 面 包、水果 买来了。
Miànbāo、shuǐguǒ mǎi lai le.

(2) 买 来了 面包 、水果。
Mǎi lai le miànbāo、shuǐguǒ.

3) A: 图象 调 好了吧？
Túxiàng tiáo hǎo le ba？

B: ________。
________.

(1) 图象 调 好了。
Túxiàng tiáo hǎo le.

(2) 调 好 图象 了。
Tiáo hǎo túxiàng le.

4) A: 啤酒拿来了 没有？
Píjiǔ ná lai le méiyǒu?

B: ____________。
____________.

(1) 拿 来啤酒了。
Ná lai píjiǔ le .

(2) 啤酒拿来了。
Píjiǔ ná lai le .

5) A: 门 打开 了吧？
Mén dǎ kāi le ba?

B: ____________。
____________.

(1) 打开 门 了。
Dǎ kāi mén le .

(2) 门 打开 了。
Mén dǎ kāi le .

6) A: 给 朋友 的礼品 买 好 了吗？
Gěi péngyou de lǐpǐn mǎi hǎo le ma?

B: ____________。
____________.

(1) 给 朋友 的礼品 买 好了。
Gěi péngyou de lǐpǐn mǎi hǎo le .

(2) 买 好了给 朋友 的礼品。
Mǎi hǎo le gěi péngyou de lǐpǐn .

***2. Answer the questions using "*左右*" (zuǒyòu):**

Model: A: 那个 人 多 大 岁数？
Nàge rén duō dà suìshu?

B: 三 十 岁 左右。（二十九岁）
Sānshísuì zuǒyòu. ( èrshíjiǔsuì )

1) A: 会 几点 能 开 完？
Huì jǐdiǎn néng kāi wán?

B: ____________。（四点二十五）
____________. ( sìdiǎn èrshíwǔ )

2) A: 那儿大概 有 多 少 书？
Nàr dàgài yǒu duōshao shū?

B: ____________。（四十九本）
____________. ( sìshíjiǔběn )

3) A: 你看他年纪有多大?
Nǐ kàn tā niánjì yǒu duō dà?
B: ＿＿＿＿＿＿。(四十一岁)
＿＿＿＿＿＿. ( sìshíyīsuì )

4) A: 从你们家到汽车站有多远?
Cóng nǐmen jiā dào qìchēzhàn yǒu duō yuǎn?
B: ＿＿＿＿＿＿。(半里多点儿)
＿＿＿＿＿＿. ( bànlǐ duō diǎnr )

5) A: 你说他有多高?
Nǐ shuō tā yǒu duō gāo?
B: ＿＿＿＿＿＿。(一米零三)
＿＿＿＿＿＿. ( yìmǐ líng sān )

6) A: 这个箱子有多重?
Zhège xiāngzi yǒu duō zhòng?
B: ＿＿＿＿＿＿。(十九斤多)
＿＿＿＿＿＿. ( shíjiǔjīn duō )

*3. **Make sentences with** "……了，就……" (…le, jiù…):

Model: 相照完了，就早点儿回来。
Xiàng zhào wán le, jiù zǎo diǎnr huí lai.

1) 买，礼物，吃饭
mǎi, lǐwù, chī fàn

2) 收拾，东西，托运
shōushi, dōngxi, tuōyùn

3) 取，飞机票，拍，电报
qǔ, fēijīpiào, pāi, diànbào

4) 结，帐，离开，饭店
jié, zhàng, líkāi, fàndiàn

5) 穿，衣服，散步
chuān, yīfu, sàn bù

6) 写，信，寄
xiě, xìn, jì

4. **Listen to the dialogue:**

张: 今天天气真好！走，出去玩儿玩儿，照几张相。
Zhāng: Jīntiān tiānqi zhēn hǎo! Zǒu, chū qu wánrwanr, zhào jǐzhāng xiàng.

李: 应该，应该。我找小王去。
Lǐ: Yīnggāi, yīnggāi. Wǒ zhǎo Xiǎo Wáng qu.

张　：小王的电话刚打完，他知道了。
Zhāng: Xiǎo Wáng de diànhuà gāng dǎ wán, tā zhīdao le.

李：吃的东西……
Lǐ: Chī de dōngxi…

张　：吃的东西他准备。
Zhāng: Chī de dōngxi tā zhǔnbèi.

李：汽车租了吗？
Lǐ: Qìchē zū le ma?

张　：汽车租好了。
Zhāng: Qìchē zū hǎo le.

李：你行动够快的！我去收拾一下儿东西。
Lǐ: Nǐ xíngdòng gòu kuài de! Wǒ qù shōushi yíxiàr dōngxi.

张　：东西都装好了。你的任务是等小王，小王来了咱们就走。我去看看汽车来了没有。
Zhāng: Dōngxi dōu zhuāng hǎo le. Nǐ de rènwu shì děng Xiǎo Wáng, Xiǎo Wáng láile zánmen jiù zǒu. Wǒ qù kànkan qìchē lái le méiyǒu.

李：好吧，你快去快回。
Lǐ: Hǎo ba, nǐ kuài qù kuài huí.

张　：我不回来了。小王来了你们就下楼。
Zhāng: Wǒ bù huí lai le. Xiǎo Wáng láile nǐmen jiù xià lóu.

（小张走了。一会儿小王来了。）
(Xiǎo Zhāng zǒu le. Yíhuìr Xiǎo Wáng lái le.)

李：小王，你来了。吃的东西准备得怎么样了？
Lǐ: Xiǎo Wáng, nǐ lái le. Chī de dōngxi zhǔnbèi de zěnmeyàng le?

王　：吃的都准备好了。看，面包、水果、罐头、啤酒、糖，都买来了。
Wáng: Chī de dōu zhǔnbèi hǎo le. Kàn, miànbāo、shuǐguǒ、guàntou、píjiǔ、táng, dōu mǎi lai le.

李：走吧。
Lǐ: Zǒu ba.

王　：小张呢？
Wáng: Xiǎo Zhāng ne?

李：他在楼下等汽车呢。他不回来了。
Lǐ: Tā zài lóuxià děng qìchē ne. Tā bù huí lai le.

王　：那我们快下去吧。
Wáng: Nà wǒmen kuài xià qu ba.

张　：小　王！小　李！
Zhāng: Xiǎo Wáng! Xiǎo Lǐ!

李：小　张，车　还　没　来？
Lǐ: Xiǎo Zhāng, chē hái méi lái?

张　：车　来　了。
Zhāng: Chē lái le.

王　：你　回　来　有　事儿？
Wáng: Nǐ huí lai yǒu shìr?

张　：胶卷　用　完　了，没　取　出　来，新　胶卷　还　没　装　上　呢。
Zhāng: Jiāojuǎnr yòng wán le, méi qǔ chu lai, xīn jiāojuǎnr hái méi zhuāng shang ne.

王　：那　就　赶　快　装　吧。
Wáng: Nà jiù gǎnkuài zhuāng ba.

张　：新　胶卷　还　没　买　来　呢！
Zhāng: Xīn jiāojuǎnr hái méi mǎi lai ne!

王　：糟糕！
Wáng: Zāogāo!

***5. Translate the sentences into Chinese:**

1) Has the letter to your grandparents been written or not?
2) Have the two suitcases been checked?
3) The address of the addressee should be written at the top of the envelope.
4) How should the affairs be handled?
5) It is not difficult to learn Chinese.

# 35 Wish You A Pleasant Trip
## 祝你们一路平安 zhù nǐmen yílù píng'ān

(The Chens are leaving China. Wang Fang sees them off at the airport.)

| | | |
|---|---|---|
| 王 ：<br>Wáng: | 陈　先生，您不是多<br>Chén xiānsheng, nín bú shì duō<br>两件　行李吗？咱们　去<br>liǎngjiàn xíngli ma? Zánmen qù<br>托运　吧。<br>tuōyùn ba. | Mr. Chen, did you say you had two pieces of excess luggage? Shall we go and get them checked? |

| | | |
|---|---|---|
| 陈：<br>Chén: | 好。在哪儿？<br>Hǎo. Zài nǎr? | Where? |
| 王：<br>Wáng: | 在二层大厅。<br>Zài èrcéng dàtīng. | In the lounge of the second floor. |
| 工作人员：<br>gōngzuò rényuán: | 请您把行李放在这儿，①我称一下儿。<br>Qǐng nín bǎ xíngli fàng zài zhèr, wǒ chēng yíxiàr. | Please take them over here to be weighed. |
| 陈：<br>Chén: | 多少公斤？<br>Duōshao gōngjīn? | How many kilos? |
| 工作人员：<br>gōngzuò rényuán: | 三十二公斤。这是行李托运单，您把这张单子填一下儿。填好以后，到对面交钱。<br>Sānshí'èrgōngjīn. Zhè shì xíngli tuōyùndān, nín bǎ zhèzhāng dānzi tián yíxiàr. Tián hǎo yǐhòu, dào duìmiàn jiāo qián. | Thirty-two. This is the luggage consignment form for you to fill in. After you've finished, pay at the counter opposite. |
| 王：<br>Wáng: | 好了，我们到海关办手续吧。<br>Hǎo le, wǒmen dào hǎiguān bàn shǒuxù ba. | All right. Let's go to the customs. |
| 工作人员：<br>gōngzuò rényuán: | 请把（飞）机票和护照给我看一下儿。<br>Qǐng bǎ (fēi) jīpiào hé hù zhào gěi wǒ kàn yíxiàr. | Please show me your tickets and passports. |
| 陈：<br>Chén: | 好。<br>Hǎo. | Here you are. |
| 王：<br>Wáng: | 来，咱们把行李拿这边儿来。<br>Lái, zánmen bǎ xíngli ná zhèbianr lai. | Come, let's bring the luggage over here. |
| 工作人员：<br>gōngzuò rényuán: | 一共几件？<br>Yígòng jǐjiàn? | How many pieces altogether? |
| 陈：<br>Chén: | 四件。<br>Sìjiàn. | Four. |
| 工作人员：<br>gōngzuò rényuán: | 这是行李牌儿，请收好。<br>Zhè shì xínglipáir, qǐng shōu hǎo. | Here are your tags. |

| | | |
|---|---|---|
| 王：<br>Wáng: | 手续都办完了。<br>Shǒuxù dōu bàn wán le. | Well, that's it. |
| 陈：<br>Chén: | 艾琳，你把（飞）机票和<br>Àilín, nǐ bǎ (fēi) jīpiào hé<br>护照都放在手提包里。<br>hùzhào dōu fàng zài shǒutíbāoli.<br>小王，这次回国得到<br>Xiǎo Wáng, zhècì huí guó dédào<br>你很多帮助，我们<br>nǐ hěn duō bāngzhù, wǒmen<br>全家向你表示衷<br>quán jiā xiàng nǐ biǎoshì zhōng<br>心的感谢。<br>xīn de gǎnxiè. | Irene, put the tickets and passports inside the handbag. Xiao Wang, you've been a great help to us throughout our visit. We must all thank you for it. |
| 王：<br>Wáng: | 别客气。有做得不够<br>Bié kèqi. Yǒu zuò de bú gòu<br>的地方，请原谅。希<br>de dìfang, qǐng yuánliàng. Xī<br>望您对我们的工作<br>wàng nín duì wǒmen de gōngzuò<br>提出意见，帮助我们<br>tí chū yìjiàn, bāngzhù wǒmen<br>以后改进。<br>yǐhòu gǎijìn. | Don't say that. You must excuse me for any inadequacies on my part. I hope you'll give your opinion on our work so as to help us improve in future. |
| 陈：<br>Chén: | 你们的工作做得很<br>Nǐmen de gōngzuò zuò de hěn<br>好，没什么意见，② 真<br>hǎo, méi shénme yìjiàn, zhēn<br>的。离开祖国四十年了，<br>de. Líkāi zǔguó sìshínián le,<br>这次有机会回来，实现了<br>zhècì yǒu jīhui huí lai, shíxiànle<br>多年的愿望，③ 心里<br>duō nián de yuànwàng, xīnli<br>真有说不出的高<br>zhēn yǒu shuō bu chū de gāo<br>兴。<br>xìng. | You've done excellent work, we have no complaint to make. To be able to come back after an absence of fourty years is the realization of a long cherished dream. I just can't describe how happy I am. |

| | | |
|---|---|---|
| 王：<br>Wáng: | 欢迎 你们 随时 回 来<br>Huānyíng nǐmen suíshí huí lai<br>参观 游览。<br>cānguān yóulǎn. | You're welcome any time. |
| 陈：<br>Chén: | 希望 以后 还 有 机会 见<br>Xīwàng yǐhòu hái yǒu jīhui jiàn<br>面。小 王，我们 就 要<br>miàn. Xiǎo Wáng, wǒmen jiù yào<br>分别 了，在 这儿 照 张<br>fēnbié le, zài zhèr zhào zhāng<br>相 作 个 纪念 吧。④莉莉，<br>xiàng zuò ge jìniàn ba. Lìli,<br>把 照相机 拿 过 来。<br>bǎ zhàoxiàngjī ná guo lai.<br>(After Mr. Chen has taken the pictures). | Hope to see you again. Xiao Wang, let's take a picture together to commemorate the occasion. Give me the camera, Lily. |
| 王：<br>Wáng: | 时 间 到 了，你们 进 去<br>Shíjiān dào le, nǐmen jìn qu<br>吧。祝 你们 一路 平安！<br>ba. Zhù nǐmen yílù píng'ān! | It's time for you to go. Wish you a pleasant trip back. |

## • new words • 生词 • shēngcí

| | | | |
|---|---|---|---|
| 1 | 大厅 | （名）dàtīng | lounge, hall |
| 2 | 把 | （介）bǎ | (a preposition whose object is the receiver of the action) |
| 3 | 公斤 | （量）gōngjīn | kilogram |
| 4 | 对面 | （名）duìmiàn | opposite side |
| 5 | 多 | （形）duō | many, much |
| 6 | 海关 | （名）hǎiguān | customs |
| 7 | 手续 | （名）shǒuxù | procedure, formalities |
| | 办手续 | bàn shǒuxù | to go through the procedure (for- |

| | | | |
|---|---|---|---|
| | | | malities) |
| 8 行李牌儿 | （名） | xínglipáir | luggage tag |
| 9 得到 | （动） | dédào | to have got |
| 10 衷心 | （形） | zhōngxīn | heartfelt |
| 11 不够 | | bú gòu | not enough, inadequate |
| 12 原谅 | （动） | yuánliàng | to excuse, to forgive |
| 13 提 | （动） | tí | to lift, to raise |
| 提出 | | tí chū | to raise, to put forward |
| 14 意见 | （名） | yìjiàn | opinion |
| 提意见 | | tí yìjiàn | to criticize, to raise an opinion |
| 15 改进 | （动） | gǎijìn | to improve, to innovate |
| 16 真的 | （副） | zhēnde | really |
| 17 祖国 | （名） | zǔguó | motherland |
| 18 实现 | （动） | shíxiàn | to realize |
| 19 愿望 | （名） | yuànwàng | wish |
| 20 心里 | （名） | xīnli | heart, bottom of the heart |
| 21 随时 | （副） | shuíshí | anytime |
| 22 照相机 | （名） | zhàoxiàngjī | camera |
| 23 过来 | | guò lai | this way (used after a verb to show direction) |
| 24 纪念 | （名、动） | jìniàn | souvenir, to commemorate |

## study points • 注释 • zhùshì

1 请你把行李放在这儿。(Qǐng nǐ bǎ xíngli fàng zài zhèr.)
To emphasize what is being done to the object of a sentence, the preposition "把" (bǎ) is usually used to bring the object before the verb. Thus the pattern for this kind of sentences is as follows:
subject+"把"+object+verb+other elements.

你把这单子填一下儿。(Nǐ bǎ zhè dānzi tián yíxiàr.)
咱们把行李放在这儿。(Zánmen bǎ xíngli fàng zài zhèr.)
我把东西收拾收拾。(Wǒ bǎ dōngxi shōushishōushi.)
他昨天把信写完了。(Tā zuótiān bǎ xìn xiě wán le.)

Note:

1) Since the verb takes an object, it must be transitive. But verbs like "喜欢" (xǐhuan), "觉得" (juéde), "看见" (kàn jiàn), "知道" (zhīdao), "欢迎" (huānyíng), etc. cannot be used in these "把" sentences.
2) There must be other elements, usually adverbial in nature, to follow the verb.
3) Negative adverbs, adverbs of time and auxilliary verbs must be placed before the word "把".
4) The objects of these sentences must be specific.

2 没什么意见。(Méi shénme yìjiàn.)
This can either mean "no opinion" or "no complaint"!

3 实现了多年的愿望。(Shíxiànle duō nián de yuànwàng.)
"多年" (duō nián) means "very many years".

4 在这儿照张相作个纪念吧。(Zài zhèr zhào zhāng xiàng zuò ge jìniàn ba.)
The verb "作" (zuò) can take the verb "纪念" (jìniàn) as its object. "作个纪念" (zuò ge jìniàn) means the same as "作纪念" but is more informal.

## supplementary words • 补充生词 • bǔchōng shēngcí

| | | | | |
|---|---|---|---|---|
| 1 | 脏 | (形) | zāng | dirty |
| 2 | 窗户 | (名) | chuānghu | window |
| 3 | 挂 | (动) | guà | to hang |
| 4 | 它 | (代) | tā | it |
| 5 | 起飞 | (动) | qǐfēi | to take off |
| 6 | 安全带 | (名) | ānquándài | safty belt |
| 7 | 系 | (动) | jì | to tie |
| 8 | 俗话 | (名) | súhuà | common saying |
| 9 | 秧 | (名) | yāng | seedling |

| | | | | |
|---|---|---|---|---|
| 10 | 谷 | （名） | gǔ | grain |
| 11 | 妻 | （名） | qī | wife |
| 12 | 福 | （名） | fú | happiness, luck |
| 13 | 心细 | | xīn xì | careful |
| 14 | 特点 | （名） | tèdiǎn | characteristic |
| 15 | 闲不住 | | xián bu zhù | always keep oneself busy |

## • exercises • 练习 • liànxí

*1. **Complete the sentences using "把" (bǎ):**

Model: 他病了，把他送到医院去吧。
Tā bìng le, bǎ tā sòng dào yīyuàn qu ba.
（送，医院）
（sòng, yīyuàn）

1) 这件衣服脏了，__________。（洗，一下儿）
Zhèjiàn yīfu zāng le, __________. （xǐ, yíxiàr）

2) 刮风了，__________。（门，窗户，关）
Guā fēng le, __________. （mén, chuānghu, guān）

3) 我眼睛不好，__________。（给，念，信）
Wǒ yǎnjing bù hǎo, __________. （gěi, niàn, xìn）

4) 咱们去公园玩儿玩儿，__________。
Zánmen qù gōngyuánr wánrwanr, __________.
（带，水果，照相机）
（dài, shuǐguǒ, zhàoxiàngjī）

5) 现在收拾东西吧，__________。
Xiànzài shōushi dōngxī ba, __________.
（毛衣，衬衫，大衣，放，挂，箱子，柜子）
（máoyī, chènshān, dàyī, fàng, guà, xiāngzi, guìzi）

6) 该吃饭了，__________。
Gāi chī fàn le, __________.
（黄油，面包，鸡蛋汤，菜，拿，端）
（huángyóu, miànbāo, jīdàntāng, cài, ná, duān）

**∗2. Make dialogues after the model:**

Model: A: 托运 几件？
Tuōyùn jǐjiàn？

B: 就 这 两个 箱子。
Jiù zhè liǎngge xiāngzi.

A: 来，把 它们 拿 这儿来。
Lái, bǎ tāmen ná zhèr lai.

1) A: 你 买了 几本？
Nǐ mǎile jǐběn？

B: ________ 三本。
________ sānběn.

A: ______，______ 给 我 看看。
______，______ gěi wǒ kànkan.

2) A: 你 写了 几封 信？
Nǐ xiěle jǐfēng xìn？

B: ________ 两 封。
________ liǎngfēng.

A: ______，______ 寄 走吧。
______，______ jì zǒu ba.

3) A: 你 看了 很 长 时间 电视 了吧？
Nǐ kànle hěn cháng shíjiān diànshì le ba？

B: ________ 一个 小 时。
________ yíge xiǎoshí.

A: ______，__________ 关 上 吧。
______，__________ guān shang ba.

4) A: 你 兑换 多少 美元？
Nǐ duìhuàn duōshao Měiyuán?

B: ________ 二百 美元。
________ èrbǎi Měiyuán.

A: ______，______ 点一点。
______，______ diǎnyídiǎn.

5) A: 你们 有 几件 行李？
Nǐmen yǒu jǐjiàn xínglǐ?

B: ________ 两 件。
________ liǎngjiàn.

A: ________，__________ 放 这儿 吧。
________，__________ fàng zhèr ba.

6) A: 还 有不少 啤酒吧 ?
Hái yǒu bù shǎo píjiǔ ba?

B: ________ 六瓶 了。
________ liùpíng le.

A: ________, __________ 都 拿 来。
________, __________ dōu ná lai.

**3.. Listen to the dialogue:**

( 在 飞机上 )
( Zài fēijīshang )

飞机服务员: 朋友们 ,飞机快 要 起飞了,您 坐 好以后,请 赶快把 安全带 系好。
fēijī fúwùyuán: Péngyoumen, fēijī kuài yào qǐfēi le, nín zuò hǎo yǐhòu, qǐng gǎnkuài bǎ ānquándài jì hǎo.

大伟: 爸爸,您 快 系 安全带 吧。
Dàwěi: Bàba, nín kuài jì ānquándài ba.

陈 明 山: 来,把 这个 小 皮箱 放 到 你那儿去。
Chén Míngshān: Lái, bǎ zhège xiǎo píxiāng fàng dào nǐ nàr qu.

大伟: 您 休息吧,我 把它提 过去。
Dàwěi: Nín xiūxi ba, wǒ bǎ tā tí guo qu.

陈 明 山: 好 吧。艾琳,把 那个 红 皮箱 给 我。
Chén Míngshān: Hǎo ba. Àilín, bǎ nàge hóng píxiāng gěi wǒ.

艾琳: 怎 么? 把 红 箱子 也 放 到 那儿 去? 不用 吧。
Àilín: Zěnme? Bǎ hóng xiāngzi yě fàng dào nàr qu? Bú yòng ba.

陈 明 山: 这 我 知道。你 看,起飞 后 我 得 看 书 啊。
Chén Míngshān: Zhè wǒ zhīdao. Nǐ kàn, qǐfēi hòu wǒ děi kàn shū a.

艾琳: 你 是 要 书啊。
Àilín: Nǐ shì yào shū a.

陈 明 山: 对 了,把 那 几本 书 给 我。
Chén Míngshān: Duì le, bǎ nà jǐběn shū gěi wǒ.

艾琳: 莉莉,把 书 给 爸爸.
Àilín: Lìli, bǎ shū gěi bàba.

莉莉: 给 您。
Lìli: Gěi nín.

陈 明 山: 啊,都 在 这儿了?
Chén Míngshān: À, dōu zài zhèr le?

艾琳：对了，你要的书都在这儿了。
Àilín: Duì le, nǐ yào de shū dōu zài zhèr le.

陈明山：西安买的那本书，把它收到大箱子里了吧？
Chén Míngshān: Xī'ān mǎi de nàběn shū, bǎ tā shōu dào dà xiāngzili le ba?

艾琳：你再看看，最下边儿的那本是不是？
Àilín: Nǐ zài kànkan, zuì xiàbianr de nàběn shì bu shì?

陈明山：啊，正是它。
Chén Míngshān: À, zhèng shì tā.

艾琳：我知道你没看完，收拾东西的时候，特意把它留在外边儿了。
Àilín:: Wǒ zhīdao nǐ méi kàn wán, shōushi dōngxi de shíhour, tèyì bǎ tā liú zài wàibianr le.

陈明山：俗话说："秧好一半谷，妻好一半福"，我可真有福啊。
Chén Míngshān: Súhuà shuō: "Yāng hǎo yíbàn gǔ, qī hǎo yíbàn fú", wǒ kě zhēn yǒu fú a.

艾琳：你呀，什么"谷"啊，"福"啊，快看书吧！
Àilín: Nǐ ya, shénme "gǔ" a, "fú" a, kuài kàn shū ba!

# 复习 (7) Revision (7) fùxí (7)

*1. **Fill in the blanks with "了" (le) or "过" (guo):**

1) 我 去_______那个 商店，我 在 那儿 买_________东西。
Wǒ qù_______nàge shāngdiàn, wǒ zài nàr mǎi_________dōngxi.

2) 以前 我 没 进_______这家 饭馆。
Yǐqián wǒ méi jìn_______zhèjiā fànguǎnr.

3) 怎么，准备_______这么 长 时间，还 没 准备 好？
Zěnme, zhǔnbèi_______zhème cháng shíjiān, hái méi zhǔnbèi hǎo?

4) 他 认识_______一个 老 医生，请 这位 老 先生 给 看看 吧。
Tā rènshi_______yíge lǎo yīshēng, qǐng zhèwèi lǎo xiānsheng gěi kànkan ba.

5) 我们 听_______一会儿 音乐，就 把 收音机 关 了。
Wǒmen tīng_______yíhuìr yīnyuè, jiù bǎ shōuyīnjī guān le.

6) 你 不 是 没 吃_______饺子吗？ 你 尝尝，好吃 不 好吃？
Nǐ bú shì méi chī_______jiǎozi ma? Nǐ chángchang, hǎochī bu hǎochī?

*2. **Rewrite the following sentences after the model:**

Model: 我 前年 大学 毕业 以后 就 开始 工作 了。
Wǒ qiánnián dàxué bì yè yǐhòu jiù kāishǐ gōngzuò le.
我 大学 毕业 以后 工作了 两 年 了。
Wǒ dàxué bì yè yǐhòu gōngzuòle liǎngnián le.

1) 他 从 一九五〇年 到 现在 一直 教 中国 历史。
Tā cóng yījiǔwǔlíngnián dào xiànzài yìzhí jiāo Zhōngguó lìshǐ.

2) 昨天 晚上，从 八点 到 十点 四十分，我 在 家 看 电视 了。
Zuótiān wǎnshang, cóng bādiǎn dào shídiǎn sìshífēn, wǒ zài jiā kàn diànshì le.

3) 他们 九月 十五日 到 二十八日 呆 在 西安。
Tāmen jiǔyuè shíwǔrì dào èrshíbārì dāi zài Xī'ān.

4) 这个 大型 舞剧是 六点半 开始的，九点半才 演完。
Zhège dàxíng wǔjù shì liùdiǎnbàn kāishǐ de, jiǔdiǎnbàn cái yǎn wán.

5) 那个 包裹 老 王 十三号 寄 出 的，他朋 友二十一号 才 收 到。
Nàge bāoguǒ Lǎo Wáng shísānhào jì chū de, tā péngyou èrshíyīhào cái shōu dào.

6) 我们 六点 二十 从 家里 出来，差十分 七点 走 到了 剧 院。
Wǒmen liùdiǎn èrshí cóng jiāli chū lai, chà shífēn qīdiǎn zǒu dàole jùyuàn.

7) 老 刘 前天 就去 上海 出 差了。
Lǎo Liú qiántiān jiù qù Shànghǎi chūchāi le.

8) 从 五岁 到 三十五岁 他 一直 生活 在 北京。
Cóng wǔsuì dào sānshíwǔsuì tā yìzhí shēnghuó zài Běijīng.

*3. **See if "的"(de)、"地"(de)、"得"(de) are correctly used in the following sentences and correct the wrong parts:**

1) 历史 博物馆 地 同志 详 细 得 给 他们 作了 介绍。
Lìshǐ Bówùguǎn de tóngzhì xiángxì de gěi tāmen zuòle jièshào.

2) 到 北京 得 第二天下午，他们 就去 故宫 了。
Dào Běijīng de dì'èrtiān xiàwǔ, tāmen jiù qù Gùgōng le.

3) 时 间 过 地 真 快，我 离家 已经 一个 月 了。
Shíjiān guò de zhēn kuài, wǒ lí jiā yǐjīng yíge yuè le.

4) 小 地 箱子 我 拿 的 动，大 地 箱子 我 拿 不 动。
Xiǎo de xiāngzi wǒ ná de dòng, dà de xiāngzi wǒ ná bu dòng.

5) 他 亲切 得 对 我 说："在 这儿遇见 你，我 太 高兴 了！"
Tā qīnqiè de duì wǒ shuō: "Zài zhèr yùjiàn nǐ, wǒ tài gāoxìng le!"

6) 小 陈 他们在 北海 玩儿 地 很 高兴。
Xiǎo Chén tāmen zài Běihǎi wánr de hěn gāoxìng.

7) 他 们 都 是 从 美 国 回 来探亲 地 华 侨。
Tāmen dōu shì cóng Měiguó huí lai tànqīn de huáqiáo.

8) 老 王 高兴 得 说："你 地 英 语 说 的 太 好 了！"
Lǎo Wáng gāoxìng de shuō: "Nǐ de Yīngyǔ shuō de tài hǎo le!"

# Appendix I

## 词汇表 cíhuì biǎo Vocabulary

### A

| | | | | | Lesson |
|---|---|---|---|---|---|
| ā | 阿姨 | （名） | āyí | aunt (what children call young women) | 25 |
| à | 啊 | （叹） | à | an interjection like "ah" | 2 |
| a | 啊 | （助） | a | ah, oh | 10 |
| āi | 哎呀 | （叹） | āiyā | Oh, dear! (surprise or annoyance | 9 |
| | 哎哟 | （叹） | āiyō | an interjection expressing surprise, pain, etc. | 20 |
| ài | 爱人 | （名） | àiren | wife, husband, fiancée, fiancé | 27 |
| àn | 按时 | （副） | ànshí | on time. | 15 |

### B

| | | | | | |
|---|---|---|---|---|---|
| bā | 八 | （数） | bā | eight | 3 |
| bǎ | 把 | （介） | bǎ | (a preposition whose object is the receiver of the action) | 35 |
| bà | 爸爸 | （名） | bàba | father, dad | 5 |
| ba | 吧 | （助） | ba | modal particle | 5 |
| bǎi | 百 | （数） | bǎi | hundred | 7 |
| | 百闻不如一见 | | bǎi wén bù rú yí jiàn | Seeing is believing. (Hearing a hundred times is not as good as seeing once.) | 22 |
| bàn | 半 | （数） | bàn | half | 9 |
| | 办 | （动） | bàn | to do, to handle, to carry out | 21 |
| bāng | 帮 | （动） | bāng | to help, to aid | 13 |

| | | | | |
|---|---|---|---|---|
| | 帮忙 | bāng máng | to help, help | 24 |
| | 帮助 | （动、名）bāngzhù | to help, help | 22 |
| bāo | 包裹 | （名）bāoguǒ | parcel | 22 |
| bào | 报 | （名）bào | newspaper | 32 |
| bào | 抱歉 | （形）bàoqiàn | to apologize | 34 |
| bēi | 杯 | （量）bēi | cup, glass | 23 |
| běi | 北 | （名）běi | north | 26 |
| | 北边儿 | （名）běibianr | to the north, in the north | 26 |
| bèi | 背 | （动）bèi | to recite, to learn by heart | 28 |
| | 背面 | （名）bèimiàn | back | 30 |
| běn | 本 | （量）běn | a measure word (copy) | 5 |
| | 本子 | （名）běnzi | notebook | 11 |
| bí | 鼻子 | （名）bízi | nose | 26 |
| bǐ | 比 | （介、动、名）bǐ | than, to compare, comparison | 25 |
| | 比较 | （副、动）bǐjiào | comparatively, relatively, to compare, to contrast. | 12 |
| bì | 必须 | （助动）bìxū | must | 33 |
| | 毕业 | （名）bì yè | to graduate | 27 |
| biàn | 遍 | （量）biàn | times (emphasizing the whole process) | 33 |
| | 变化 | （名）biànhuà | change | 20 |
| bianr | ……边儿 | （名）…bianr | (used after words of location to show direction, location, etc.) | 12 |
| biāo | 标题 | （名）biāotí | title, headline. | 32 |
| biǎo | 表 | （名）biǎo | watch | 9 |
| | 表示 | （动）biǎoshì | to show, to express | 24 |
| bié | 别 | （副）bié | do not | 22 |
| | 别的 | （代）biéde | other, else | 4 |
| bǐng | 丙 | （名）bǐng | C | 26 |
| bìng | 病 | （动、名）bìng | to be sick, illness, disease | 15 |
| bō | 播送 | （动）bōsòng | to broadcast | 32 |
| bó | 伯伯 | （名）bóbo | uncle (father's elder brother); also a respectful form of addressing men about the age | |

| | | | | | |
|---|---|---|---|---|---|
| | | | | of one's father | 2 |
| | 伯母 | （名） | bómǔ | aunt | 16 |
| | 博物馆 | （名） | bówùguǎn | museum | 31 |
| | 脖子 | （名） | bózi | neck | 29 |
| bú | 不错 | （形） | búcuò | good, fair, not bad | 12 |
| | 不到长城非好汉 | | bú dào Cháng chéng fēi hǎohàn | We are no true heroes if we do not reach the Great Wall. | 22 |
| | 不够 | | búgòu | not enough, inadequate | 35 |
| | 不过 | （连） | búguò | yet, however | 18 |
| | 不谢 | | bú xiè | You are welcome. Don't mention it. | 3 |
| | 不用 | | bú yòng | not necessary | 7 |
| bù | 不 | （副） | bù | no, not | 1 |
| | 不如 | （动） | bùrú | not as good as, not as well as | 31 |
| | 不行 | （形） | bùxíng | not so good, not so well | 17 |

## C

| | | | | | |
|---|---|---|---|---|---|
| cái | 才 | （副） | cái | only then | 30 |
| cài | 菜 | （名） | cài | dish, vegetable | 14 |
| cān | 参观 | （动） | cānguān | to visit (usually a place) | 4 |
| | 参加 | （动） | cānjiā | to attend, to take part in | 34 |
| céng | 层 | （量） | céng | floor, storey, layer | 3 |
| chā | 叉子 | （名） | chāzi | fork | 23 |
| chá | 茶 | （名） | chá | tea | 2 |
| cha | 差 | （动） | chà | to be short of, to differ from, not up to standard | 9 |
| | 差不多 | | chà bu duō | nearly, more or less | 25 |
| cháng | 长 | （形） | cháng | long | 12 |
| | 尝 | （动） | cháng | to taste, to sample | 23 |
| | 常 | （形、副） | cháng | regular, frequent, often | 25 |
| | 常常 | （副） | chángcháng | often, frequently | 16 |
| chǎng | 场 | （量） | chǎng | show | 9 |
| chāo | 超重 | | chāo zhòng | overweight | 6 |

| | | | | | |
|---|---|---|---|---|---|
| chē | 车 | （名） | chē | vehicle | 18 |
| | 车站 | （名） | chēzhàn | station | 24 |
| chèn | 衬衫 | （名） | chènshān | shirt, blouse | 34 |
| chēng | 称 | （动） | chēng | to weigh | 6 |
| | 称呼 | （名、动） | chēnghu | a form of address, to address, to call | 25 |
| chéng | 成 | （动） | chéng | to become | 27 |
| | 成就 | （名） | chéngjiù | achievement | 31 |
| | 城市 | （名） | chéngshì | city | 33 |
| chī | 吃 | （动） | chī | to eat | 11 |
| chōng | 充满 | （动） | chōngmǎn | to fill, to be full of | 33 |
| chōu | 抽烟 | | chōu yān | to smoke a cigarette (a pipe or cigar) | 2 |
| chū | 出来 | | chū lai | to come out | 16 |
| | 出去 | | chū qu | to go out | 20 |
| | 出租 | （动） | chūzū | to rent out | 13 |
| chú | 橱窗 | （名） | chúchuāng | show window | 29 |
| | 除了 | （介） | chúle | besides, except | 28 |
| chuān | 穿 | （动） | chuān | to put on, to wear | 12 |
| chuáng | 床 | （名） | chuáng | bed | 27 |
| chuàng | 创造 | （名、动） | chuàngzào | create, to creation | 22 |
| chūn | 春天 | （名） | chūntiān | spring | 16 |
| cí | 词典 | （名） | cídiǎn | dictionary | 21 |
| | 辞行 | | cí xíng | to say good-bye, to take leave | 20 |
| cì | 次 | （量） | cì | time | 18 |
| cōng | 聪明 | （形） | cōngming | intelligent, bright, clever | 29 |
| cóng | 从 | （介） | cóng | since, from | 18 |
| | 从……到…… | | cóng…dào… | from…to… | 18 |
| | 从……起 | | cóng…qǐ | from, starting from | 28 |
| cù | 醋 | （名） | cù | vinegar | 14 |
| cūn | 村 | （名） | cūn | village | 30 |

## D

| | | | | | |
|---|---|---|---|---|---|
| dǎ | 打 | (动) | dǎ | to make (a telephone call), to beat, to strike | 10 |
| | 打 | (动) | dǎ | to have (injection) | 15 |
| | 打算 | (动) | dǎsuàn | to intend, to plan | 21 |
| dà | 大 | (形) | dà | big, large, loud, old | 11 |
| | 大后天 | (名) | dàhòutiān | two days from today | 18 |
| | 大家 | (代) | dàjiā | everybody, all | 23 |
| | 大厦 | (名) | dàshà | tall building | 33 |
| | 大使馆 | (名) | dàshǐguǎn | embassy | 4 |
| | 大厅 | (名) | dàtīng | lounge, hall | 35 |
| | 大学 | (名) | dàxué | university | 27 |
| | 大衣 | (名) | dàyī | overcoat | 12 |
| dāi | 呆 | (动) | dāi | to stay | 24 |
| dài | 带 | (动) | dài | to take, to bring | 17 |
| | 代 | (动) | dài | to do something on someone's behalf | 24 |
| | 代 | (名) | dài | dynasty, generation | 31 |
| | 戴 | (动) | dài | to wear (hats, gloves and glasses, etc.) | 29 |
| | 大夫 | (名) | dàifu | doctor | 15 |
| dān | 单位 | (名) | dānwèi | unit, organization | 34 |
| | 单子 | (名) | dānzi | form, list | 7 |
| | 耽误 | (动) | dānwu | to hold up, to delay | 28 |
| dàn | 但 | (连) | dàn | but, however | 16 |
| | 但是 | (连) | dànshì | but | 33 |
| | 蛋糕 | (名) | dàngāo | cake | 8 |
| dāng | 当时 | (名) | dāngshí | at the time | 31 |
| dāo | 刀子 | (名) | dāozi | knife | 23 |
| dào | 到 | (动) | dào | to arrive, to reach, to get to | 13 |
| | 到处 | (名) | dàochù | everywhere | 33 |
| | 到底 | (副) | dàodǐ | after all, in the final analysis, how on earth | 25 |
| dé | 得到 | (动) | dédào | to have got | 35 |
| de | 的 | (助) | de | a structural particle | 1 |
| | 的 | (助) | de | a particle indicating affir- | |

| | | | | |
|---|---|---|---|---|
| | | | mation | 20 |
| | 得 | （助）de | (used before complement to indicate degree or possibility) | 18 |
| | 地 | （助）de | a particle added to adjectives as adverbial | 25 |
| děi | 得 | （助动、动）děi | must, should, to have to, to need | 23 |
| děng | 等 | （动）děng | to wait | 10 |
| dì | 第 | （头）dì | a prefix indicating the ordinal number | 32 |
| | 弟弟 | （名）dìdi | younger brother | 8 |
| | 地点 | （名）dìdiǎn | place, locality, address | 30 |
| | 地方 | （名）dìfāng | place | 20 |
| | 地名 | （名）dìmíng | name of a place | 30 |
| | 地址 | （名）dìzhǐ | address | 24 |
| diǎn | 点 | （动）diǎn | to count | 7 |
| | 点 | （量）diǎn | o'clock | 9 |
| | 点 | （量）diǎn | point | 30 |
| diàn | 电报 | （名）diànbào | telegram, cable | 20 |
| | 电话 | （名）diànhuà | telephone | 10 |
| | 电视 | （名）diànshì | television | 32 |
| | 电梯 | （名）diàntī | lift, elevator | 22 |
| | 电影 | （名）diànyǐng | motion picture, movie, film | 9 |
| dìng | 定 | （动）dìng | to settle, to fix | 33 |
| dōng | 东 | （名）dōng | east | 26 |
| | 东边儿 | （名）dōngbianr | to the east, in the east | 26 |
| | 东西 | （名）dōngxi | thing, things | 4 |
| | 冬天 | （名）dōngtiān | winter | 16 |
| dǒng | 懂 | （动）dǒng | understand | 13 |
| dōu | 都 | （副）dōu | all, already | 10 |
| dòu | 豆腐 | （名）dòufu | bean-curd | 14 |
| dù | 度 | （量）dù | degree | 15 |
| duǎn | 短 | （形）duǎn | short | 12 |
| duì | 对 | （形）duì | yes, right, correct. | 1 |

| | | | | | |
|---|---|---|---|---|---|
| | 对 | （介） | duì | for | 22 |
| | 对 | （量） | duì | pair | 29 |
| | 对不起 | | duì bu qǐ | I am sorry. Excuse me | 1 |
| | 对方 | （名） | duìfāng | the other party (side) | 25 |
| | 对了 | | duì le | by the way | 11 |
| | 对象 | （名） | duìxiàng | fiancée, fiance, object | 27 |
| | 兑换 | （动） | duìhuàn | to change (currencies) | 7 |
| duō | 多 | （副、形） | duō | much, many | 15 |
| | 多少 | （代） | duōshao | how many, how much | 5 |

## E

| | | | | | |
|---|---|---|---|---|---|
| ér | 而 | （连） | ér | a connective, in the text it means "as well as" | 33 |
| | 儿子 | （名） | érzi | son | 2 |
| èr | 二 | （数） | èr | two | 3 |

## F

| | | | | | |
|---|---|---|---|---|---|
| fā | 发烧 | | fā shāo | to have a fever | 15 |
| fǎ | 法语 | （名） | Fǎyǔ | the French language | 28 |
| fàn | 饭 | （名） | fàn | meal | 11 |
| | 饭店 | （名） | fàndiàn | hotel, restaurant | 34 |
| | 饭馆 | （名） | fànguǎnr | restaurant | 14 |
| fāng | 方面 | （名） | fāngmiàn | aspect, side | 21 |
| fáng | 房间 | （名） | fángjiān | room | 3 |
| fǎng | 访问 | （动、名） | fǎngwèn | to visit, visit | 23 |
| fàng | 放 | （动） | fàng | to put | 24 |
| | 放心 | （动） | fàngxīn | to rest assured, to be at ease | 24 |
| fēi | 飞机 | （名） | fēijī | airplane, aircraft | 20 |
| fēn | 分 | （量） | fēn | the lowest denomination of Chinese currency | 5 |
| | 分 | （量） | fēn | minute | 9 |
| | 分别 | （动） | fēnbié | to part, to separate | 27 |
| | 分钟 | （量） | fēnzhōng | minute | 24 |

| | | | | |
|---|---|---|---|---|
| fēng | 封 | （量）fēng | a measure word for letters | 5 |
| | 风 | （名）fēng | wind | 16 |
| | 风景 | （名）fēngjǐng | scenery | 18 |
| | 疯 | （形）fēng | mad, crazy | 29 |
| | 疯子 | （名）fēngzi | madman | 29 |
| fú | 服务员 | （名）fúwùyuán | receptionist, waiter | 3 |
| fù | 附近 | （名）fùjìn | vicinity | 24 |
| | 父亲 | （名）fùqin | father | 25 |
| | 复杂 | （形）fùzá | complicated | 25 |

## G

| | | | | |
|---|---|---|---|---|
| gāi | 该 | （助动）gāi | should, ought to | 9 |
| gǎi | 改进 | （动）gǎijìn | to improve, to innovate | 35 |
| gān | 干杯 | gān bēi | bottoms up, cheers | 23 |
| | 干净 | （形）gānjing | clean | 33 |
| gǎn | 赶 | （动）gǎn | to hurry | 33 |
| | 赶快 | （副）gǎnkuài | as quickly as possible, quickly | 20 |
| | 感冒 | （动、名）gǎnmào | to have a cold, cold, influenza | 15 |
| | 感想 | （名）gǎnxiǎng | reflection, feeling | 33 |
| | 感谢 | （动）gǎnxiè | to thank | 22 |
| gàn | 干 | （动）gàn | to do, to be engaged in | 4 |
| gāng | 刚 | （副）gāng | just, barely | 21 |
| | 刚才 | （名）gāngcái | just now, a moment ago | 19 |
| | 钢笔 | （名）gāngbǐ | pen, fountain-pen | 11 |
| gāo | 高兴 | （形）gāoxìng | happy | 23 |
| gǎo | 搞 | （动）gǎo | to do, to carry on, to be engaged in | 31 |
| gào | 告诉 | （动）gàosu | to tell | 27 |
| gē | 哥哥 | （名）gēge | elder brother | 21 |
| gè | 个 | （量）gè | a measure word | 3 |
| gěi | 给 | （介）gěi | for, to | 5 |
| | 给 | （动）gěi | to give | 6 |

| | | | | | |
|---|---|---|---|---|---|
| gēn | 跟 | （介、连） | gēn | with, and | 19 |
| gèng | 更 | （副） | gèng | more, still more | 33 |
| gōng | 工厂 | （名） | gōngchǎng | factory | 27 |
| | 工程师 | （名） | gōngchéngshī | engineer | 27 |
| | 工作 | （动、名） | gōngzuò | to work, work, job | 7 |
| | 公斤 | （量） | gōngjīn | kilogram | 35 |
| | 公共 | （形） | gōnggòng | public | 27 |
| | 公园 | （名） | gōngyuán | park | 17 |
| gòu | 够 | （形） | gòu | enough, adequate | 18 |
| gū | 姑姑 | （名） | gūgu | aunt (father's sister) | 34 |
| gǔ | 古代 | （名） | gǔdài | ancient times | 21 |
| | 古老 | （形） | gǔlǎo | ancient | 33 |
| | 古玩 | （名） | gǔwán | antique | 20 |
| guā | 刮（风） | （动） | guā (fēng) | to blow (wind) | 16 |
| guà | 挂号 | | guà hào | register,registered | 6 |
| guǎi | 拐 | （动） | guǎi | to turn | 26 |
| guài | 怪不得 | | guài bu de | no wonder | 17 |
| guān | 关 | （动） | guān | to turn off, to close | 32 |
| | 关于 | （介） | guānyú | about, on | 32 |
| guǎn | 管 | （介、动） | guǎn | as, (to call)…as | 25 |
| guàng | 逛 | （动） | guàng | to saunter, to go (shopping) | 21 |
| guī | 规律 | （名） | guīlǜ | law | 27 |
| guì | 贵 | （形） | guì | dear, expensive | 12 |
| | 贵姓 | | guì xìng | the polite way of asking someone's family name | 31 |
| guó | 国 | （名） | guó | country, nation | 3 |
| | 国际 | （名） | guójì | international (community) | 32 |
| | 国庆 | （名） | guóqìng | National Day | 27 |
| guò | 过 | （动） | guò | to pass, to spend | 19 |
| | 过奖 | （动） | guòjiǎng | overpraise, flatter | 28 |
| guò | 过 | （助） | guo | a suffix to show past experience | 33 |
| | 过来 | | guò lai | this way (used after a verb to show direction) | 35 |

## H

| | | | | | |
|---|---|---|---|---|---|
| hā | 哈 | （象声） | hā | ha | 19 |
| hái | 还 | （副） | hái | also, as well, in addition, still | 6 |
| | 还是 | （连、副） | háishi | or. (not used in an declarative sentence) still | 14 |
| | 孩子 | （名） | háizi | child, children, son(s) and daughter(s) | 17 |
| hǎi | 海关 | （名） | hǎiguān | customs | 35 |
| hàn | 汉语 | （名） | Hànyǔ | the Chinese language | 28 |
| | 汉字 | （名） | Hànzì | Chinese character | 28 |
| hǎo | 好 | （形） | hǎo | good, all right | 1 |
| | 好 | （副） | hǎo | well, quite | 25 |
| | 好好 | （副） | hǎohāor | well, sufficiently | 18 |
| | 好了 | | hǎole | enough (used to wind up a remark and introduce the next one) | 18 |
| hào | 号〔日〕 | （名） | hào (rì) | colloquial form for date | 8 |
| | 号 | （量） | hào | number | 26 |
| | 号码儿 | （名） | hàomǎr | number | 22 |
| hē | 喝 | （动） | hē | to drink | 2 |
| hé | 和 | （连、介） | hé | and, with | 6 |
| | 合适 | （形） | héshì | fit, proper, suitable | 12 |
| | 合同 | （名） | hétóng | contract | 20 |
| hěn | 很 | （副） | hěn | very, very much (usually not stressed; stressed only when emphasis is needed) | 12 |
| hóng | 红 | （形） | hóng | red | 16 |
| | 红烧 | | hóngshāo | to stew with red sauce (soya bean sauce) | 14 |
| hòu | 后 | （名） | hòu | back | 26 |
| | 后 | （副） | hòu | then, later | 30 |
| | 后边儿 | （名） | hòubianr | behind | 26 |

| | | | | | |
|---|---|---|---|---|---|
| | 后来 | （名） | hòulái | later, after that | 33 |
| | 后天 | （名） | hòutiān | the day after tomorrow | 10 |
| hū | 呼吸 | （动） | hūxī | to breathe | 15 |
| hú | 糊涂 | （形） | hútu | confused | 25 |
| hù | 互相 | （副） | hùxiāng | each other | 25 |
| | 护照 | （名） | hùzhào | passport | 24 |
| huá | 华侨 | （名） | huáqiáo | overseas Chinese | 1 |
| huà | 话剧 | （名） | huàjù | play | 32 |
| | 话务员 | （名） | huàwùyuán | telephone operator | 10 |
| huān | 欢迎 | （动） | huānyíng | to welcome, to meet | 1 |
| huàn | 换 | （动） | huàn | to change | 12 |
| huáng | 黄油 | （名） | huángyóu | butter | 27 |
| huí | 回 | （动） | huí | to come back, to return | 20 |
| | 回 | （量） | huí | a measure word for time, round | 25 |
| | 回来 | | huí lai | to come back, to return | 9 |
| | 回去 | | huí qu | to go back, to return | 15 |
| | 回信 | | huí xìn | reply | 30 |
| huì | 会 | (助动、动) | huì | can, will, to know how to | 2 |
| | 会议 | （名） | huìyì | meeting, conference | 34 |
| huó | 活动 | (名、动) | huódòng | activity, to move | 4 |
| huǒ | 火车 | （名） | huǒchē | train | 21 |
| huò | 或 | （连） | huò | or | 30 |
| | 或者 | （连） | huòzhě | or | 18 |

## J

| | | | | | |
|---|---|---|---|---|---|
| jī | 鸡 | （名） | jī | chicken | 14 |
| | 鸡蛋 | （名） | jīdàn | egg | 14 |
| | 机场 | （名） | jīchǎng | airport | 13 |
| | 机会 | （名） | jīhuì | opportunity | 23 |
| jí | 极 | (形、副、名) | jí | utmost, extremely, pole | 22 |
| | 急 | （形） | jí | urgent, hurried, impatient | 20 |
| jǐ | 几 | （代） | jǐ | some, several | 5 |
| jì | 寄 | （动） | jì | to post, to mail | 5 |

| | | | | |
|---|---|---|---|---|
| | 记得 | （动）jìde | to remember | 27 |
| | 季节 | （名）jìjié | season | 16 |
| | 纪念 | （名、动）jìniàn | souvenir, to commemorate | 35 |
| jiā | 家 | （名）jiā | family, home | 10 |
| | 家庭 | （名）jiātíng | family | 27 |
| jiǎ | 甲 | （名）jiǎ | A | 26 |
| jiǎn | 简单 | （形）jiǎndān | simple | 25 |
| | 简直 | （副）jiǎnzhí | simply (for emphasis) | 31 |
| | 捡到 | jiǎn dào | to find, to pick up by chance | 11 |
| jiàn | 件 | （量）jiàn | a measure word for overcoats, coats, as well as for things or matters, etc. | 12 |
| | 见 | （动）jiàn | to see, to meet | 18 |
| | 见面 | jiàn miàn | to meet | 24 |
| | 健康 | （名、形）jiànkāng | health, healthy | 23 |
| jiǎng | 讲 | （动）jiǎng | to explain, to say, to talk | 25 |
| jiāo | 教 | （动）jiāo | to teach | 28 |
| | 交流 | （动）jiāoliú | to exchange | 33 |
| jiǎo | 角 | （量）jiǎo | *jiao*, a unit of Chinese currency, equal to 1／10 *yuan* | 6 |
| | 角 | （名）jiǎo | corner | 30 |
| | 脚 | （名）jiǎo | foot | 29 |
| jiào | 叫 | （动）jiào | to call, to be called, one's name is… | 1 |
| | 叫 | （动）jiào | to call, to order | 13 |
| | 叫 | （动）jiào | to call, to address | 25 |
| jiē | 接 | （动）jiē | to receive, to take, to connect | 27 |
| | 街 | （名）jiē | street | 30 |
| | 街道 | （名）jiēdào | street | 33 |
| jié | 结合 | （动、名）jiéhé | to combine, combination | 23 |
| | 结婚 | jié hūn | to marry | 27 |
| | 结帐 | jié zhàng | to settle account, to check out | 34 |
| | 结束 | （动）jiéshù | to finish, to be over | 20 |

| | | | | | |
|---|---|---|---|---|---|
| | 节目 | （名） | jiémù | program | 32 |
| jiě | 姐姐 | （名） | jiějie | elder sister | 9 |
| jiè | 介绍 | （动、名） | jièshào | to introduce | 2 |
| jīn | 今后 | （名） | jīnhòu | future | 21 |
| | 今天 | （名） | jīntiān | today | 7 |
| jìn | 进 | （动） | jìn | to come in, to enter | 2 |
| | 进来 | | jìn lai | to come in | 13 |
| | 进去 | | jìn qu | to go in, to enter | 22 |
| | 近 | （形） | jìn | near, close | 27 |
| | 经常 | （形） | jīngcháng | often | 23 |
| jīng | 经济 | （名） | jīngjì | economy, economics | 31 |
| | 京剧 | （名） | jīngjù | Beijing opera | 10 |
| jìng | 净 | （副） | jìng | only | 23 |
| | 敬 | （动） | jìng | to toast,to respect | 23 |
| jiǔ | 九 | （数） | jiǔ | nine | 7 |
| | 酒 | （名） | jiǔ | alcoholic drinks | 14 |
| | 酒逢知己千杯少 | | jiǔ féng zhījǐ qiānbēi shǎo | Even a thousand cups are not enough when good friends meet. | 23 |
| jiù | 旧 | （形） | jiù | old, out-dated | 11 |
| | 旧地重游 | | jiù dì chóng yóu | to revisit a place that one used to know well | 18 |
| | 就 | （副） | jiù | just, only, (as soon) as, etc., also used in clauses of result | 14 |
| | 舅舅 | （名） | jiùjiu | uncle (mother's brother) | 34 |
| jù | 剧院 | （名） | jùyuàn | theater | 26 |
| jué | 觉得 | （动） | juéde | to feel, to think | 28 |
| | 决定 | （动、名） | juédìng | to decide, decision | 34 |

## K

| | | | | | |
|---|---|---|---|---|---|
| kā | 咖啡 | （名） | kāfēi | coffee | 11 |
| kāi | 开 | （动） | kāi | to start, to drive | 24 |
| | 开 | （动） | kāi | to open | 31 |
| | 开（收音机） | （动） | kāi (shōuyīnjī) | to turn on (radio) | 32 |

| | | | | |
|---|---|---|---|---|
| | 开门 | kāi mén | to open the door, open to the public | 31 |
| | 开始 | （动）kāishǐ | to begin, to start | 28 |
| | 开水 | （名）kāishuǐ | boiled water | 15 |
| kàn | 看 | （动）kàn | to see, to look at | 4 |
| | 看病 | kàn bìng | to see a doctor, doctor examining patient | 15 |
| | 看见 | kànjiàn | to see | 29 |
| | 看望 | （动）kànwàng | to visit, to see | 20 |
| kǎo | 烤 | （动）kǎo | to roast | 23 |
| ké | 咳嗽 | （动）késou | to cough | 15 |
| kě | 可 | （副）kě | (for emphasis) | 28 |
| | 可不是 | kě bu shì | isn't it | 27 |
| | 可能 | （助动、形）kěnéng | possible, may | 18 |
| | 可是 | （连）kěshì | but, however | 25 |
| | 可惜 | （形）kěxī | unfortunate, the pity is | 31 |
| | 可以 | （助动、形）kěyǐ | can, may, will do, good enough | 13 |
| kè | 刻 | （量）kè | quarter (of an hour) | 9 |
| | 客气 | （形）kèqi | polite, courteous | 22 |
| kòngr | 空儿 | （名）kòngr | free time, spare time | 21 |
| kǒu | 口 | （名）kǒu | mouth | 25 |
| kù | 裤子 | （名）kùzi | trousers | 34 |
| kuài | 块〔元〕 | （量）kuài (yuán) | colloquial form for *"yuan"* | 6 |
| | 快 | （副、形）kuài | soon, quick, fast | 19 |
| | 快车 | （名）kuàichē | express train | 21 |
| | 筷子 | （名）kuàizi | chopsticks | 23 |
| kuān | 宽 | （形）kuān | wide | 33 |
| kuǎn | 款待 | （动、名）kuǎndài | to entertain, hospitality | 24 |

## L

| | | | | |
|---|---|---|---|---|
| là | 辣子 | （名）làzi | hot pepper | 14 |
| la | 啦 | （助）la | a modal particle | 26 |
| lái | 来 | （动）lái | to come | 2 |

| | | | | | |
|---|---|---|---|---|---|
| | ……来 | (名) | …lái | since | 22 |
| | 来 | (助) | lái | approximately | 17 |
| láo | 劳驾 | | láo jià | a polite way to ask someone to do something or to make way. | 12 |
| lǎo | 老 | (头、形) | lǎo | old, elderly | 2 |
| | 老大 | (名) | lǎodà | the eldest (son, daughter) | 27 |
| | 老家 | (名) | lǎojiā | home town, birthplace | 17 |
| | 老人 | (名) | lǎorén | old man(woman),old people | 17 |
| | 老头儿 | (名) | lǎotóur | old man | 27 |
| | 老先生 | (名) | lǎoxiānsheng | elderly gentleman | 17 |
| | 老爷 | (名) | lǎoye | maternal grandfather | 30 |
| | 老友重逢 | | lǎo yǒu chóng féng | reunion of old friends | 27 |
| le | 了 | (助) | le | a particle | 9 |
| lèi | 累 | (形) | lèi | tired, weary | 18 |
| lěng | 冷 | (形) | lěng | cold, chilly | 16 |
| lí | 离 | (介、动) | lí | from, to leave | 24 |
| | 离开 | (动) | líkāi | to leave | 19 |
| lǐ | 里 | (名) | lǐ | a particle used to indicate "within certain time, space or scope | 14 |
| | 里边儿 | (名) | lǐbianr | inside | 14 |
| | 礼品 | (名) | lǐpǐn | present, gift | 34 |
| | 礼物 | (名) | lǐwù | present, gift | 8 |
| lì | 历史 | (名) | lìshǐ | history | 21 |
| li | ……里 | (名) | …lǐ | (used after nouns meaning within a certain limit of time or space) | 16 |
| liàn | 练习 | (动、名) | liànxí | to practise, practice | 28 |
| liáng | 量 | (动) | liáng | to measure, to take measurement | 15 |
| liǎng | 两 | (数) | liǎng | two | 6 |
| liàng | 辆 | (量) | liàng | a measure word for vehicles | 13 |
| liáo | 聊 | (动) | liáo | to chat | 27 |

| | | | | | |
|---|---|---|---|---|---|
| liǎo | 了不起 | (形) | liǎobuqǐ | great (in praise of…) | 22 |
| | 了解 | (动、名) | liǎojiě | to understand, to find out, understanding, investigation | 33 |
| líng | 零 | (数) | líng | zero, nil | 7 |
| | 零下 | | líng xià | below zero | 16 |
| | 0 | (数) | líng | zero, nil | 27 |
| lǐng | 领带 | (名) | lǐngdài | tie | 34 |
| liú | 留 | (动) | liú | to leave behind | 22 |
| | 留学生 | (名) | liúxuéshēng | foreign students, students studying abroad | 28 |
| | 流利 | (形) | liúlì | fluent | 28 |
| liù | 六 | (数) | liù | six | 7 |
| lóu | 楼 | (名) | lóu | building | 26 |
| lou | 喽 | (助) | lou | a particle meaning nat-urally | 31 |
| lù | 路 | (名) | lù | road, street, way | 26 |
| | 路过 | (动) | lùguò | to pass | 21 |
| | 路口 | (名) | lùkǒu | end of a road (street) | 26 |
| | 路人 | (名) | lùrén | passerby | 26 |
| | 路上 | (名) | lùshang | (on the) road, (on the) way | 27 |
| | 录音 | (名) | lùyīn | recording | 28 |
| lǚ | 旅途 | (名) | lǚtú | journey, trip | 22 |
| | 旅游 | (动) | lǚyóu | to visit as tourist | 23 |

## M

| | | | | | |
|---|---|---|---|---|---|
| mā | 妈妈 | (名) | māma | mother, mom | 5 |
| má | 麻烦 | (动、名、形) | máfan | to trouble, trouble, trouble-some | 10 |
| mǎ | 马上 | (副) | mǎshàng | immediately, right away | 11 |
| ma | 吗 | (助) | ma | a particle used at the end of a sentence to turn it into a question | 1 |
| | 嘛 | (助) | ma | an interjection to give em- | |

| | | | | | |
|---|---|---|---|---|---|
| | | | | phasis | 16 |
| mǎi | 买 | (动) | mǎi | to buy, to purchase | 4 |
| mán | 馒头 | (名) | mántou | steamed bread in the shape of a half ball | 14 |
| mǎn | 满意 | (动、形) | mǎnyì | to satisfy, satisfactory | 20 |
| màn | 慢 | (形) | màn | slow | 10 |
| máng | 忙 | (形) | máng | busy | 34 |
| máo | 毛〔角〕 | (量) | máo (jiǎo) | colloquial form for "*jiao*" | 6 |
| | 毛 | (名) | máo | wool | 29 |
| | 毛衣 | (名) | máoyī | sweater, jumper, pull-over | 29 |
| mào | 贸易 | (动、名) | màoyì | to trade, trade | 20 |
| | 帽子 | (名) | màozi | hat, cap, head-gear | 29 |
| méi | 没 | (动、副) | méi | to have not, there is (are) not, no, not | 13 |
| | 没关系 | | méi guānxi | That is all right. It does not matter. | 1 |
| | 没想到 | | méi xiǎng dào | unexpected, out of expectation | 21 |
| | 没(有) | (副) | méi(yǒu) | (to have) not, (there is (are)) not, no | 4 |
| měi | 每 | (代) | měi | every, each | 16 |
| | 美 | (形) | měi | pretty, beautiful | 16 |
| | 美德之家 | | měidé zhī jiā | home of the virtuous | 23 |
| | 美元 | (名) | Měiyuán | American dollar | 7 |
| mèi | 妹妹 | (名) | mèimei | younger sister | 21 |
| mén | 门 | (名) | mén | door, gate | 31 |
| | 门牌 | (名) | ménpái | number (of a house) | 30 |
| men | 们 | (尾) | men | a suffix added to nouns or pronouns to make them plural | 2 |
| mǐ | 米饭 | (名) | mǐfàn | cooked rice | 14 |
| miàn | 面包 | (名) | miànbāo | bread | 27 |
| míng | 明年 | (名) | míngnián | next year | 33 |
| | 明天 | (名) | míngtiān | tomorrow | 4 |
| | 明信片 | (名) | míngxìnpiàn | post-card | 6 |

| | | | | |
|---|---|---|---|---|
| | 名不虚传 | míng bù xū chuán | to live up to it name | 23 |
| | 名字 | （名）míngzi | name | 15 |
| mǒu | 某 | （代）mǒu | certain | 25 |
| mǔ | 母亲 | （名）mǔqin | mother | 25 |

## N

| | | | | |
|---|---|---|---|---|
| ná | 拿 | （动）ná | to take | 34 |
| nǎ | 哪 | （代）nǎ | which | 3 |
| | 哪里 | （代）nǎlǐ | not at all, where | 17 |
| | 哪些 | （代）nǎxiē | which (pl.) | 33 |
| nà | 那 | （代）nà | that | 2 |
| | 那不 | nà bù | an expression to direct people's attention to something obvious | 29 |
| | 那(么) | （连）nà(me) | then | 11 |
| | 那些 | （代）nàxiē | those | 25 |
| nǎi | 奶奶 | （名）nǎinai | grandma | 17 |
| nán | 难 | （形）nán | difficult | 28 |
| | 男 | （名）nán | man, male | 29 |
| | 南 | （名）nán | south | 26 |
| | 南边儿 | （名）nánbianr | to the south, in the south | 26 |
| nǎr | 哪儿 | （代）nǎr | where | 3 |
| nàr | 那儿 | （代）nàr | there | 21 |
| ne | 呢 | （助）ne | a particle | 4 |
| nèi | 内 | （名）nèi | inside (usually used in written language) | 20 |
| | 内容 | （名）nèiróng | content, body | 30 |
| néng | 能 | （助动）néng | can, to be able to | 13 |
| ǹg | 嗯 | （叹）ǹg | an interjection to express appreciation or consent | 12 |
| nǐ | 你 | （代）nǐ | you (sing.) | 2 |
| | 你们 | （代）nǐmen | you (pl.) | 2 |
| nián | 年 | （名）nián | year | 16 |

| | | | | | |
|---|---|---|---|---|---|
| | 年级 | （名） | niánjí | grade, year | 17 |
| | 年纪 | （名） | niánjì | age | 17 |
| | 年龄 | （名） | niánlíng | age | 17 |
| | 年轻 | （形） | niánqīng | young | 33 |
| niàn | 念 | （动） | niàn | to read | 28 |
| | 念书 | | niàn shū | to study, to read a book, to go to school | 18 |
| nín | 您 | （代） | nín | you (a respectful form of address for the second person singular) | 1 |
| nǚ | 女 | （名） | nǚ | woman, female | 29 |
| | 女儿 | （名） | nǚ'ér | daughter | 2 |
| nuǎn | 暖和 | （形） | nuǎnhuo | warm | 16 |

## O

| | | | | | |
|---|---|---|---|---|---|
| ó | 哦 | （叹） | ó | an interjection indicating surprise or doubt | 4 |
| ò | 哦 | （叹） | ò | an interjection like "oh" | 10 |

## P

| | | | | | |
|---|---|---|---|---|---|
| pá | 爬 | （动） | pá | to climb, to crawl | 22 |
| pái | 牌价 | （名） | páijià | exchange rate | 7 |
| péng | 朋友 | （名） | péngyou | friend | 4 |
| pí | 皮 | （名） | pí | fur, hide, skin | 29 |
| | 啤酒 | （名） | píjiǔ | beer | 14 |
| piào | 票 | （名） | piào | ticket, coupon | 9 |
| pín | 频道 | （名） | píndào | channel (of TV broadcast) | 32 |
| píng | 瓶 | （量） | píng | bottle | 14 |
| | 平安 | （形） | píng'ān | safe, free from dangers | 20 |
| pǔ | 普通 | （形） | pǔtōng | ordinary, common | 25 |
| | 普通话 | （名） | pǔtōnghuà | common speech (standard modern spoken Chinese) | 17 |

## Q

| | | | | | |
|---|---|---|---|---|---|
| qī | 七 | （数） | qī | seven | 7 |
| qǐ | 起 | （动） | qǐ | to rise | 28 |
| | 起床 | | qǐ chuáng | to get out of bed, to get up | 28 |
| | 起来 | （动） | …qǐ lai | an expression indicating that an action is in progress | 25 |
| qì | 汽车 | （名） | qìchē | car, automobile | 13 |
| | 气温 | （名） | qìwēn | temperature (weather) | 16 |
| qiān | 千 | （数） | qiān | thousand | 7 |
| | 签订 | （动） | qiāndìng | to sign | 20 |
| qián | 钱 | （名） | qián | money | 6 |
| | 前 | （名） | qián | front | 26 |
| | 前边儿 | （名） | qiánbianr | in front, ahead | 26 |
| | 前年 | （名） | qiánnián | the year before last | 31 |
| | 前天 | （名） | qiántiān | day before yesterday | 24 |
| qīn | 亲戚 | （名） | qīnqi | relative , kin | 20 |
| | 亲切 | （形） | qīnqiè | friendly, warm | 25 |
| qīng | 清楚 | （形） | qīngchu | clear | 25 |
| | 青年 | （名） | qīngnián | youth, young man (men) | 31 |
| qíng | 晴 | （形） | qíng | fine (weather) | 16 |
| | 情况 | （名） | qíngkuàng | situation | 25 |
| | 情景 | （名） | qíngjǐng | situation, scene | 27 |
| qǐng | 请 | （动） | qǐng | to please, to invite | 2 |
| | 请问 | | qǐng wèn | Excuse me, but…? May I ask…? | 1 |
| qiū | 秋天 | （名） | qiūtiān | autumn, fall | 16 |
| qū | 区 | （名） | qū | district | 30 |
| qǔ | 取 | （动） | qǔ | to fetch, to get | 15 |
| qù | 去 | （动） | qù | to go | 4 |
| quán | 全 | （形） | quán | all, whole | 10 |
| què | 确实 | （形） | quèshí | really, truly | 23 |

## R

| | | | | | |
|---|---|---|---|---|---|
| ràng | 让 | （动） | ràng | to ask, to let, to give up | 25 |
| rè | 热 | （形） | rè | hot | 16 |
| | 热情 | （形、名） | rèqíng | warm, warm-heartedness | 24 |
| rén | 人 | （名） | rén | person, people | 3 |
| | 人民 | （名） | rénmín | people | 22 |
| | 人民币 | （名） | Rénmínbì | Renminbi (Chinese currency) | 7 |
| | 人员 | （名） | rényuán | personnel, staff | 7 |
| rèn | 认识 | （动、名） | rènshi | to know, understanding | 25 |
| rì | 日 | （名） | rì | written form for date | 8 |
| | 日期 | （名） | rìqī | date | 30 |
| | 日语 | （名） | Rìyǔ | the Japanese language | 28 |
| ròu | 肉 | （名） | ròu | meat | 14 |
| rú | 如果 | （连） | rúguǒ | if | 30 |

## S

| | | | | | |
|---|---|---|---|---|---|
| sān | 三 | （数） | sān | three | 3 |
| | 三句话不离本行 | | sānjù huà bù lí běnháng | talking shop | 28 |
| shā | 沙发 | （名） | shāfā | sofa | 27 |
| shǎ | 傻子 | （名） | shǎzi | fool, idiot | 29 |
| shāng | 商店 | （名） | shāngdiàn | shop, store | 33 |
| shàng | 上 | （动） | shàng | to be in (with grade or year in school and university) | 17 |
| | 上 | （名） | shàng | last, previous, above, on top of, on the surface of | 18 |
| | 上 | （动） | shàng | to go, to get on, to board | 19 |
| | 上边儿 | （名） | shàngbianr | upper part | 30 |
| | 上去 | | shàng qù | to go up | 22 |
| | 上午 | （名） | shàngwǔ | morning | 9 |
| | 上学 | | shàng xué | to go to school | 17 |
| | 上演 | （动） | shàngyǎn | to perform, to put on a show | 33 |
| shang | ……上 | （名） | …shang | (used after nouns corre- | |

| | | | | |
|---|---|---|---|---|
| | | | sponding to "on" or "above") | 11 |
| shǎo | 少 | (形) shǎo | less, little, few | 24 |
| shēn | 深 | (形) shēn | deep, profound | 15 |
| | 身边儿 | (名) shēnbiān | one's side | 27 |
| | 身上 | (名) shēnshang | on the body | 29 |
| | 身体 | (名) shēntǐ | physical health, body | 17 |
| shén | 什么 | (代) shénme | what | 4 |
| shēng | 声调 | (名) shēngdiào | tone | 28 |
| | 声音 | (名) shēngyīn | sound | 32 |
| | 生活 | (动、名) shēnghuó | to live, life | 28 |
| | 生气 | (名) shēngqì | vitality, life | 33 |
| | 生日 | (名) shēngrì | birthday | 8 |
| shěng | 省 | (名) shěng | province | 30 |
| shí | 十 | (数) shí | ten | 5 |
| | ……时 | (名) …shí | time | 18 |
| | 时候 | (名) shíhour | time | 8 |
| | 时间 | (名) shíjiān | time | 18 |
| | 实现 | (动) shíxiàn | to realize | 35 |
| | 实在 | (副、形) shízài | really, so real, honest, substantial | 20 |
| shǐ | ……史 | (名) …shǐ | history | 31 |
| shì | 是 | (动) shì | to be (is, are…) | 1 |
| | 事儿 | (名) shìr | business, work, engagement | 4 |
| | 事情 | (名) shìqing | matter, business | 20 |
| | 试 | (动) shì | to try on, to try | 12 |
| | ……室 | (名) …shì | room, section | 15 |
| | 市 | (名) shì | city, municipality | 30 |
| shōu | 收 | (动) shōu | to accept, to keep | 28 |
| | 收获 | (名、动) shōuhuò | results, yield, to harvest | 20 |
| | 收拾 | (动) shōushi | to pack, to tidy up | 34 |
| | 收音机 | (名) shōuyīnjī | radio | 19 |
| shǒu | 手 | (名) shǒu | hand | 29 |
| | 手套 | (名) shǒutàor | gloves, mittens | 29 |
| | 手提包 | (名) shǒutíbāo | handbag | 24 |
| | 手续 | (名) shǒuxù | procedures, formalities | 35 |

| | | | | |
|---|---|---|---|---|
| | 手艺 | （名）shǒuyì | skill | 27 |
| | 首先 | （副、名）shǒuxiān | first beginning | 30 |
| shòu | 售货员 | （名）shòuhuòyuán | shop assistant | 11 |
| shū | 书 | （名）shū | book | 19 |
| | 书店 | （名）shūdiàn | book store | 21 |
| | 舒服 | （形）shūfu | well, comfortable | 15 |
| | 叔叔 | （名）shūshu | uncle | 25 |
| shú | 熟悉 | （形）shúxi | familiar | 25 |
| | 熟练 | （形）shúliàn | skilled, skilful | 23 |
| shù | 树 | （名）shù | tree | 16 |
| shuāng | 双方 | （名）shuāngfāng | both sides | 20 |
| shuí | 谁 | （代）shuí, shéi | who, whom | 3 |
| shuì | 睡 | （动）shuì | to go to bed, to sleep | 28 |
| shùn | 顺 | （介）shùn | along | 26 |
| | 顺便 | （副）shùnbiàn | on the way, in passing | 34 |
| shuō | 说 | （动）shuō | to speak | 10 |
| | 说不定 | shuō bu dìng | perhaps, probably | 29 |
| | 说话 | shuō huà | to talk | 23 |
| | 说曹操，曹操就到 | shuō Cáo Cāo, Cáo Cāo jiù dào | Talking of the devil and the devil comes. | 19 |
| sī | 司机 | （名）sījī | driver | 13 |
| sì | 四 | （数）sì | four | 7 |
| sòng | 送 | （动）sòng | to send, to take, to present, to see off. | 10 |
| | 送行 | sòng xíng | to see (somebody)…off | 24 |
| suí | 随时 | （副）suíshí | anytime | 35 |
| suì | 岁 | （名）suì | year (of age) | 17 |
| sūn | 孙子 | （名）sūnzi | grandson | 17 |
| suǒ | 所以 | （连）suǒyǐ | so, therefore | 34 |

T

| | | | | |
|---|---|---|---|---|
| tā | 他 | （代）tā | he, him | 3 |
| | 他们 | （代）tāmen | they, them | 18 |
| | 她 | （代）tā | she, her | 4 |

| | | | | | |
|---|---|---|---|---|---|
| | 她们 | （代） | tāmen | they, them (female) | 21 |
| tài | 太 | （副） | tài | too, too much | 12 |
| | 太太 | （名） | tàitai | wife, Mrs, madam | 2 |
| | 太阳 | （名） | tàiyang | sun | 16 |
| tán | 谈 | （动） | tán | to talk | 19 |
| | 谈话 | | tán huà | to talk, to speak | 19 |
| | 谈判 | （动） | tánpàn | to negotiate | 20 |
| tàn | 探亲 | | tàn qīn | to visit relatives | 25 |
| tāng | 汤 | （名） | tāng | soup | 14 |
| táng | 糖 | （名） | táng | sugar, sweets, candies | 14 |
| tào | 套 | （量） | tào | a measure word for radio or TV program | 32 |
| tè | 特快 | （名） | tèkuài | special express train | 21 |
| | 特意 | （副） | tèyì | specially | 27 |
| téng | 疼 | （动） | téng | to ache, to have a pain | 15 |
| tí | 提 | （动） | tí | to lift, to raise | 35 |
| | 题目 | （名） | tímù | subject | 33 |
| tǐ | 体温 | （名） | tǐwēn | body temperature | 15 |
| tiān | 天 | （名） | tiān | day, sky | 8 |
| | 天气 | （名） | tiānqì | weather | 16 |
| | 天线 | （名） | tiānxiàn | aerial | 32 |
| | 添 | （动） | tiān | to add | 24 |
| tián | 填 | （动） | tián | to fill (in) | 7 |
| tiáo | 条 | （量） | tiáo | a measure word for something elongated in shape | 26 |
| | 调 | （动） | tiáo | to adjust | 32 |
| tiáo | 调皮鬼 | （名） | tiáopíguǐ | naughty or mischievous person | 29 |
| tīng | 听 | （动） | tīng | to listen, to hear | 13 |
| | 听说 | | tīng shuō | to hear, to be told | 14 |
| | 听见 | | tīng jiàn | to hear | 25 |
| tíng | 停 | （动） | tíng | to stop | 9 |
| tōng | 通 | （动） | tōng | to be through, to lead to | 25 |
| tóng | 同行 | （名） | tóngháng | someone of the same trade or profession | 31 |

| | | | | | |
|---|---|---|---|---|---|
| | 同志 | （名） | tóngzhì | comrade | 3 |
| tǒng | 筒 | （量） | tǒng | can, tin | 11 |
| tóu | 头 | （名） | tóu | head | 15 |
| tú | 图象 | （名） | túxiàng | picture | 32 |
| tuō | 托运 | （动） | tuōyùn | to check luggage, to send by freight | 34 |

W

| | | | | | |
|---|---|---|---|---|---|
| wài | 外 | （名） | wài | outside | 19 |
| | 外币 | （名） | wàibì | foreign currency | 7 |
| | 外边儿 | （名） | wàibianr | open air, outside, outdoors | 19 |
| | 外国 | （名） | wàiguó | foreign country | 11 |
| wán | 完 | （动） | wán | to finish, to end | 19 |
| wǎn | 晚 | （形） | wǎn | late | 9 |
| | 晚上 | （名） | wǎnshang | evening, night | 4 |
| | 碗 | （名、量） | wǎn | bowl | 14 |
| wǎng | 往 | （动） | wǎng | to go | 22 |
| wàng | 往 | （介） | wàng | toward | 26 |
| | 忘 | （动） | wàng | to forget | 27 |
| wánr | 玩儿 | （动） | wánr | to play, to enjoy oneself | 17 |
| wéi | 围 | （动） | wéi | to wrap, to surround | 29 |
| | 围巾 | （名） | wéijīn | scarf, muffler | 29 |
| wěi | 伟大 | （形） | wěidà | great | 22 |
| wèi | 喂 | （叹） | wèi | hello | 10 |
| | 位 | （量） | wèi | a measure word used respectfully for people | 11 |
| | 为 | （介） | wèi | for | 21 |
| | 为什么 | | wèi shénme | why | 25 |
| | 味道 | （名） | wèidào | taste, flavor | 23 |
| wēn | 温泉 | （名） | wēnquán | hot spring | 33 |
| wén | 文化 | （名） | wénhuà | culture | 31 |
| wèn | 问 | （动） | wèn | to ask, to inquire into | 11 |
| | 问好 | | wèn hǎo | to send regards, to ask after | 24 |
| | 问题 | （名） | wèntí | problem, question | 13 |

| | | | | |
|---|---|---|---|---|
| wǒ | 我 | （代）wǒ | I, me | 1 |
| | 我们 | （代）wǒmen | we, us | 8 |
| wú | 无论 | （连）wúlùn | no matter | 33 |
| wǔ | 五 | （数）wǔ | five | 5 |
| | 舞蹈 | （名）wǔdǎo | dance | 27 |
| | 舞剧 | （名）wǔjù | dance drama, ballet | 33 |

## X

| | | | | |
|---|---|---|---|---|
| xī | 希望 | （动）xīwàng | to wish, to hope | 24 |
| xǐ | 洗 | （动）xǐ | to wash | 34 |
| | 洗澡 | xí zǎo | to bathe, to take a bath | 33 |
| | 喜欢 | （动）xǐhuan | to like | 23 |
| xì | 系 | （名）xì | department | 31 |
| xiā | 虾 | （名）xiā | prawn, shrimp | 14 |
| xià | 下 | （名）xià | next, lower, below, under | 8 |
| | 下（雨、雪） | （动）xià (yǔ, xuě) | to fall (rain, snow) | 16 |
| | 下 | （动）xià | to get off, to disembark | 18 |
| | 下班 | xià bān | to come or go off work | 27 |
| | 下边儿 | （名）xiàbianr | below | 26 |
| | 下来 | xià lai | to come down | 22 |
| | 下去 | xià qu | to go down | 22 |
| | 下午 | （名）xiàwǔ | afternoon | 8 |
| | 夏天 | （名）xiàtiān | summer | 16 |
| xiān | 先 | （副）xiān | firstly, before hand | 15 |
| | 先生 | （名）xiānsheng | Mr., sir, gentleman | 1 |
| xiàn | 县 | （名）xiàn | county | 30 |
| | 现在 | （名）xiànzài | present, now | 9 |
| xiāng | 相会 | （动）xiānghuì | to meet, to come together | 23 |
| | 相见时难别亦难 | xiāngjiàn shí nán bié yì nán | difficult to meet, difficult to part | 24 |
| | 相信 | （动）xiāngxìn | to believe | 29 |
| | 相遇 | （动）xiāngyù | to meet | 21 |
| | 箱子 | （名）xiāngzi | suitcase, trunk | 34 |
| xiáng | 详细 | （形）xiángxì | in detail, detailed | 32 |

| | | | | |
|---|---|---|---|---|
| xiǎng | 想 | (助动、动) xiǎng | to want, to intend, to think | 14 |
| xiàng | 象 | (动) xiàng | to look like, to resemble | 17 |
| | 向 | (介) xiàng | to, towards | 20 |
| xiāo | 消息 | (名) xiāoxi | news | 32 |
| xiǎo | 小 | (头、形) xiǎo | little, small, young (used before family names of young people one knows well) | 11 |
| | 小姐 | (名) xiǎojie | miss | 1 |
| | 小卖部 | (名) xiǎomàibù | small shops at railway stations or hotels, as different to regular shops | 11 |
| | 小朋友 | (名) xiǎopéngyou | little friend, children (a polite way to address a child or children one does not know) | 17 |
| | 小时 | (名) xiǎoshí | hour | 13 |
| | 小学 | (名) xiǎoxué | elementary school | 17 |
| xiào | 笑 | (动) xiào | to laugh, to smile | 29 |
| xiē | 些 | (量) xiē | some, a little (indicating a certain quantity or degree) | 14 |
| xiě | 写 | (动) xiě | to write | 8 |
| | 写法 | (名) xiěfǎ | the way to write | 30 |
| xiè | 谢谢 | (动) xièxie | to thank | 1 |
| xīn | 新 | (形) xīn | new, recent | 11 |
| | 新闻 | (名) xīnwén | news | 32 |
| | 心里 | (名) xīnli | heart, bottom of the heart | 35 |
| xìn | 信 | (名) xìn | letter | 5 |
| | 信封 | (名) xìnfēng | envelope | 5 |
| xīng | 星期 | (名) xīngqī | week | 8 |
| | 星期天〔星期日〕 | (名) xīngqītiān (xīngqī rì) | Sunday | 8 |
| xíng | 行 | (形) xíng | all right, O. K., capable | 11 |
| | 行李 | (名) xíngli | luggage, baggage | 24 |
| | 行李牌儿 | (名) xínglipáir | luggage tag | 35 |
| | 型 | (名) xíng | scale, model | 33 |
| xìng | 姓 | (动、名) xìng | one's family name is…, family | |

| | | | | |
|---|---|---|---|---|
| | | | name | 31 |
| | 姓名 | （名）xìngmíng | full name | 25 |
| | 幸福 | （形）xìngfú | happy | 27 |
| | 兴趣 | （名）xìngqù | interest | 31 |
| xióng | 雄伟 | （形）xióngwěi | magnificent | 22 |
| xiū | 休息 | （动）xiūxi | to rest | 15 |
| xū | 需要 | （动、名）xūyào | to need, need | 24 |
| xǔ | 许多 | （形）xǔduō | many, a lot of | 20 |
| xuē | 靴子 | （名）xuēzi | boots | 29 |
| xué | 学 | （动）xué | to learn | 28 |
| | 学生 | （名）xuésheng | student, pupil | 28 |
| | 学习 | （动、名）xuéxí | to learn, study | 28 |
| | 学校 | （名）xuéxiào | school | 33 |
| xuě | 雪 | （名）xuě | snow | 16 |

Y

| | | | | |
|---|---|---|---|---|
| yā | 鸭（子） | yā (zi) | duck | 23 |
| yán | 研究 | （动、名）yánjiū | to study, research | 21 |
| | 颜色 | （名）yánsè | color | 12 |
| yǎn | 演 | （动）yǎn | to perform, to put on a show | 10 |
| | 演员 | （名）yǎnyuán | actor, actress | 27 |
| | 眼镜 | （名）yǎnjìngr | glasses, spectacles | 34 |
| | 眼睛 | （名）yǎnjing | eye | 29 |
| yàn | 宴请 | （动）yànqǐng | to host a dinner party, to give a banquet | 23 |
| yàng | 样子 | （名）yàngzi | style, look, model | 12 |
| yào | 要 | （动）yào | to want, to need, to ask | 6 |
| | 要 | （助动）yào | will, would | 8 |
| | 要……了 | yào…le | to be going to (an adverb to indicate sth. about to happen) | 19 |
| | 要 | （动）yào | to ask sb. to do sth. | 20 |
| | 药 | （名）yào | medicine | 15 |

| | | | | | |
|---|---|---|---|---|---|
| | 药方 | (名) | yàofāngr | prescription | 15 |
| | 药房 | (名) | yàofáng | dispensary, pharmacy, drugstore | 15 |
| yé | 爷爷 | (名) | yéye | grandpa | 17 |
| yě | 也 | (副) | yě | too, also | 4 |
| | 也就是说 | | yě jiù shì shuō | that is to say | 30 |
| yèr | 叶儿 | (名) | yèr | leaf | 16 |
| yī | 一 | (数) | yī | one | 3 |
| | 衣服 | (名) | yīfu | clothes, clothing | 19 |
| | 衣柜 | (名) | yīguì | wardrobe | 27 |
| | 医生 | (名) | yīshēng | doctor | 15 |
| | 医学 | (名) | yīxué | medical science | 19 |
| | 医院 | (名) | yīyuàn | hospital | 27 |
| yí | 一定 | (副、形) | yídìng | surely, definitely, sure, definite | 16 |
| | 一共 | (副) | yígòng | altogether, in all | 6 |
| | 一会儿 | (名) | yíhuìr | a moment, a little bit later | 11 |
| | 一路 | (名) | yílù | the whole journey, all the way | 20 |
| | 一路顺风 | | yílù shùn fēng | bon voyage, a pleasant trip | 24 |
| | 一切 | (代) | yíqiè | all, everything | 33 |
| | 一下儿 | (量) | yíxiàr | a measure word for verbs, also used to indicate the action as being short or informal | 2 |
| | 一样 | (形) | yíyàng | same | 30 |
| yǐ | 乙 | (名) | yǐ | B | 26 |
| | 以后 | (名) | yǐhòu | after | 13 |
| | 以前 | (名) | yǐqián | former times, before | 33 |
| | 以外 | (名) | yǐwài | apart from | 28 |
| | 已经 | (副) | yǐjīng | already | 19 |
| | 椅子 | (名) | yǐzi | chair | 27 |
| yì | 一边……一边…… | | yìbiān…yìbiān | at the same time, …while… | 23 |
| | 一点儿 | (量) | yìdiǎnr | a bit, a little | 4 |
| | 一家 | (名) | yìjiā | family | 23 |
| | 一起 | (副、名) | yìqǐ | together, being together | 21 |

| | | | | | |
|---|---|---|---|---|---|
| | 一些 | （量） | yìxiē | some, several | 21 |
| | 一直 | （副） | yìzhí | ever, all along | 18 |
| | 意见 | （名） | yìjiàn | opinion | 35 |
| | 意思 | （名） | yìsi | meaning | 23 |
| yīn | 阴 | （形） | yīn | cloudy, overcast | 16 |
| | 因为 | （连） | yīnwei | because | 25 |
| | 音乐 | （名） | yīnyuè | music | 32 |
| yīng | 英镑 | （名） | Yīngbàng | English pound | 7 |
| | 英文 | （名） | Yīngwén | English | 30 |
| | 英语 | （名） | Yīngyǔ | the English language | 28 |
| | 应该 | （助动） | yīnggāi | should, to ought | 22 |
| yíng | 营业员 | （名） | yíngyèyuán | clerk | 6 |
| yòng | 用 | （动） | yòng | to use | 23 |
| | 用来 | | yòng lái | to be used purposely | 25 |
| yóu | 邮局 | （名） | yóujú | post office | 5 |
| | 邮票 | （名） | yóupiào | stamp | 5 |
| | 游览 | （动） | yóulǎn | to tour, to go sightseeing | 16 |
| yǒu | 有 | （动） | yǒu | to have, there is (are) | 4 |
| | 有的 | （代） | yǒude | some | 25 |
| | 有点儿 | | yǒudiǎnr | somewhat, a little bit | 15 |
| | 有时候 | | yǒu shíhour | sometimes | 16 |
| | 有意思 | | yǒu yìsi | interesting, meaningful | 18 |
| | 友谊 | （名） | yǒuyì | friendship | 23 |
| yòu | 又 | （副） | yòu | again | 24 |
| | 右 | （名） | yòu | right | 26 |
| yú | 鱼 | （名） | yú | fish | 14 |
| | 愉快 | （形） | yúkuài | happy, enjoyable | 22 |
| yǔ | 雨 | （名） | yǔ | rain | 16 |
| | 语调 | （名） | yǔdiào | intonation | 28 |
| | 语法 | （名） | yǔfǎ | grammar | 28 |
| | 语言 | （名） | yǔyán | language | 28 |
| | 语音 | （名） | yǔyīn | pronunciation, phonetics | 28 |
| yù | 预报 | （名、动） | yùbào | forecast | 16 |
| | 遇见 | | yù jiàn | to meet, to come upon | 21 |
| yuán | 元 | （量） | yuán | *yuan*, a unit of Chinese cur- | |

| | | | | | |
|---|---|---|---|---|---|
| | | | | rency | 6 |
| | 元旦 | （名） | yuándàn | New Year's Day | 27 |
| | 原谅 | （动） | yuánliàng | to excuse, to forgive | 35 |
| yuǎn | 远 | （形） | yuǎn | far, distant | 24 |
| | 远在天边，近在眼前 | | yuǎn zài tiān biān, jìn zài yǎn qián | If you look far it is ten thousand miles away, and if you look near, it is right in front of you. | 29 |
| yuàn | 愿望 | （名） | yuànwàng | wish | 35 |
| | 愿意 | （助动） | yuànyì | to be willing | 28 |
| yuè | 月 | （名） | yuè | month | 8 |

## Z

| | | | | | |
|---|---|---|---|---|---|
| zá | 杂技 | （名） | zájì | acrobatics | 4 |
| | 杂志 | （名） | zázhì | magazine, journal | 19 |
| zài | 在 | （动） | zài | to be (is, are…), to be situated | 3 |
| | 在 | （介） | zài | at, in | 10 |
| | 在 | （副） | zài | an adverb indicating sth. is in progress | 19 |
| | 再 | （副） | zài | too, also, in addition to | 5 |
| | 再见 | | zàijiàn | good-bye, see you again | 1 |
| zán | 咱们 | （代） | zánmen | we, us (inclusive first person) | 8 |
| zāo | 糟糕 | （形） | zāogāo | awful, too bad | 9 |
| zǎo | 早 | （形） | zǎo | early | 24 |
| | 早晨 | （名） | zǎochén | morning | 11 |
| | 早饭 | （名） | zǎofàn | breakfast | 20 |
| | 早上 | （名） | zǎoshang | morning | 28 |
| zěn | 怎么 | （代） | zěnme | why, how, what | 21 |
| | 怎么办 | | zěnme bàn | how to do, what to do | 21 |
| | 怎么了 | | zěnme le | What is wrong? What is the matter? | 29 |
| | 怎么样 | （代） | zěnmeyàng | how | 12 |
| | 怎样 | （代） | zěnyàng | how | 30 |

| | | | | | |
|---|---|---|---|---|---|
| zhá | 炸 | （动） | zhá | to fry | 14 |
| zhàn | 站 | （名） | zhàn | station, stop | 27 |
| | 站 | （动） | zhàn | to stand | 29 |
| zhāng | 张 | （量） | zhāng | a measure word(piece,sheet) | 5 |
| | 张开 | | zhāngkāi | to open | 15 |
| zhǎng | 长 | （动） | zhǎng | to grow | 29 |
| zhāo | 招 | （动） | zhāo | to attract | 28 |
| | 招待 | （动） | zhāodài | to entertain | 27 |
| | 招手 | | zhāo shǒu | to wave | 29 |
| zhǎo | 找 | （动） | zhǎo | to look for, to look up | 3 |
| | 找 | （动） | zhǎo | to give change | 6 |
| zhào | 照 | （动） | zhào | to take (a picture) | 34 |
| | 照片 | （名） | zhàopiàn | picture, snapshot | 34 |
| | 照相 | | zhào xiàng | to take pictures | 34 |
| | 照相机 | （名） | zhàoxiàngjī | camera | 35 |
| zhè | 这 | （代） | zhè | this | 2 |
| | 这不 | | zhè bù | (used to call attention to something that is obvious) | 19 |
| | 这么 | （代） | zhème | so, such | 20 |
| | 这些 | （代） | zhèxiē | these | 14 |
| | 这样 | （代） | zhèyàng | this, such | 11 |
| zhe | 着 | （助） | zhe | (a paritcle placed after verbs to show continuation of action or state) | 29 |
| zhēn | 针 | （名） | zhēn | syringe, needle | 15 |
| | 真 | （形） | zhēn | true, real | 16 |
| | 真的 | （副） | zhēnde | really | 35 |
| zhēng | 争取 | （动） | zhēngqǔ | to try, to manage | 24 |
| zhèng | 正 | （副） | zhèng | just, exactly (indicating an action in progress) | 18 |
| | 正面 | （名） | zhèngmiàn | front | 30 |
| | 正在 | （副） | zhèngzài | in the process of, in the middle of | 19 |
| | 政治 | （名） | zhèngzhì | politics | 31 |
| zhèr | 这儿 | （代） | zhèr | here | 11 |

| | | | | | |
|---|---|---|---|---|---|
| zhī | 支 | （量） | zhī | a measure word for cylindrical objects or songs or army units | 11 |
| | 知道 | （动） | zhīdào | to know | 23 |
| | ……之间 | | …zhījiān | between, among | 25 |
| zhí | 值得 | （动） | zhíde | to be worth | 23 |
| | 直接 | （形） | zhíjiē | direct, straight | 24 |
| | 侄子 | （名） | zhízi | nephew | 21 |
| zhǐ | 只 | （副） | zhǐ | only | 24 |
| | 只要 | （连） | zhǐyào | if only, so long as | 24 |
| zhōng | 中国话 | （名） | Zhōngguóhuà | spoken Chinese | 13 |
| | 中间儿 | （名） | zhōngjiànr | middle | 30 |
| | 中文 | （名） | Zhōngwén | Chinese | 30 |
| | 中午 | （名） | zhōngwǔ | noon | 27 |
| | 中心 | （名） | zhōngxīn | center | 31 |
| | 中学 | （名） | zhōngxué | high school | 27 |
| | 衷心 | （形） | zhōngxīn | heartfelt | 35 |
| zhǒng | 种 | （量） | zhǒng | kind, sort | 11 |
| zhòng | 重要 | （形） | zhòngyào | important | 20 |
| zhǔ | 主要 | （形） | zhǔyào | main | 25 |
| zhù | 住 | （动） | zhù | to live, to stay | 3 |
| | 祝 | （动） | zhù | to wish, to congratulate | 20 |
| | 助教 | （名） | zhùjiào | teaching assistant | 31 |
| | 注射 | （动） | zhùshè | to inject | 15 |
| | 注意 | （动） | zhùyì | to note, to be sure of, to heed | 15 |
| zhuǎn | 转 | （动） | zhuǎn | to turn, to change | 16 |
| zhǔn | 准 | （形） | zhǔn | sure, certain | 29 |
| | 准备 | （动、名） | zhǔnbèi | to prepare, to get ready, preparation | 20 |
| zhuō | 桌子 | （名） | zhuōzi | table | 11 |
| zì | 自己 | （代） | zìjǐ | self | 28 |
| | 自然 | （形、名、副） | zìrán | natural, nature, naturally | 27 |
| zǒu | 走 | （动） | zǒu | to go, to leave, to walk | 9 |
| | 走路 | | zǒu lù | to walk | 26 |
| zǔ | 祖国 | （名） | zǔguó | motherland | 35 |

| | | | | |
|---|---|---|---|---|
| zuǐ | 嘴 | （名）zuǐ | mouth | 15 |
| zuì | 最 | （副）zuì | most | 16 |
| | 最后 | （名）zuìhòu | last | 30 |
| zuó | 昨天 | （名）zuótiān | yesterday | 11 |
| zuǒ | 左 | （名）zuǒ | left | 30 |
| | 左右 | （名）zuǒyòu | a noun indicating an approximate number, (quantity), around, about | 34 |
| zuò | 坐 | （动）zuò | to sit | 2 |
| | 作 | （动）zuò | to do, to work | 21 |
| | 做 | （动）zuò | to do, to make | 22 |

## 专名 ZHUĀNMÍNG PROPER NAMES

### A

| | | | | |
|---|---|---|---|---|
| ài | 艾琳 | Àilín | Irene | 2 |

### B

| | | | | |
|---|---|---|---|---|
| běi | 北海 | Běihǎi | a park in Beijing | 18 |
| | 北京 | Běijīng | Beijing (Peking) | 16 |
| | 北京饭店 | Běijīng Fàndiàn | Beijing Hotel | 10 |
| bǐ | 比利·威尔逊 | Bǐlì Wēi'ěrxùn | Bailey Wilson | 11 |

### C

| | | | | |
|---|---|---|---|---|
| chá | 《茶馆》 | Cháguǎnr | *Tea House* (a play by Lao She, a major contemporary Chinese play-wright) | 32 |
| cháng | 长城 | Chángchéng | the Great Wall | 4 |
| chén | 陈 | Chén | a common Chinese family name | 1 |
| | 陈明山 | Chén Míngshān | a name | 1 |

D

| | | | | |
|---|---|---|---|---|
| dà | 《大闹天宫》 | Dà Nào Tiāngōng | The Monkey King Creates Havoc in Heaven | 10 |
| | 大伟 | Dàwěi | David | 2 |
| dīng | 丁淑琴 | Dīng Shūqín | a name | 16 |

G

| | | | | |
|---|---|---|---|---|
| gù | 故宫 | Gùgōng | the Imperial Palace (the Forbidden City or the Palace Museum) | 4 |
| guǎng | 《广播电视节目报》 | Guǎngbō Diànshì Jiémù Bào | *Radio and TV Guide* | 32 |
| guō | 郭 | Guō | a common Chinese family name | 28 |
| | 郭玉珍 | Guō Yùzhēn | a name | 28 |
| guó | 国际机场 | Guójì Jīchǎng | International Airport | 13 |

H

| | | | | |
|---|---|---|---|---|
| hàn | 《汉英词典》 | Hàn Yīng Cídiǎn | *The Chinese-English Dictionary* | 21 |
| hé | 和平新村 | Hépíng Xīn Cūn | New Peace Village (an area in Xian) | 26 |
| hēng | 亨利 | Hēnglì | Henry | 4 |
| huá | 华清池 | Huáqīngchí | Huaqing Spring, a place in Xian famous for its hot springs | 33 |

K

| | | | | |
|---|---|---|---|---|
| kūn | 昆明 | Kūnmíng | Kunming, capital of Yunnan Province in the south- | |

| | | | | |
|---|---|---|---|---|
| | | | west of China | 27 |

L

| | | | | |
|---|---|---|---|---|
| lǐ | 李 | Lǐ | a common Chinese family name | 2 |
| | 《李时珍》 | 《Lǐ Shízhēn》 | title of a film after the name of an ancient Chinese pharmacist | 9 |
| | 李文汉 | Lǐ Wénhàn | a name | 2 |
| lì | 莉莉 | Lìlì | Lily | 2 |
| | 历史博物馆 | Lìshǐ Bówùguǎn | the Historical Museum | 33 |
| lín | 林 | Lín | a common Chinese family name | 31 |
| | 林小东 | Lín Xiǎodōng | a name | 31 |
| liú | 刘 | Liú | a common Chinese family name | 11 |
| | 琉璃厂 | Liúlíchǎng | a famous street in Beijing for selling Chinese paintings, calligraphy, stationaries and antiques. | 20 |
| lǚ | 旅游局 | lǚyóujú | The Tourist Bureau | 1 |

M

| | | | | |
|---|---|---|---|---|
| měi | 美国 | Měiguó | the United States | 3 |

Q

| | | | | |
|---|---|---|---|---|
| qián | 乾陵博物馆 | Qián Líng Bówùguǎn | Qian Ling Museum (one of the museums in Xian) | 31 |
| quán | 全聚德烤鸭店 | Quánjùdé Kǎoyā Diàn | Quan Ju De Roast Duck Restaurant (the best known Beijing Duck restaurant in Beijing) | 23 |

R

| | | | | |
|---|---|---|---|---|
| rén | 人民剧场 | Rénmín Jùchǎng | People's Theater | 10 |

S

| | | | | |
|---|---|---|---|---|
| shàng | 上海 | Shànghǎi | Shanghai | 34 |
| sī | 《丝路花雨》 | Sī Lù Huā Yǔ | *Tales of the Silk Route* | 33 |

T

| | | | | |
|---|---|---|---|---|
| táng | 唐 | Táng | Tang, an early dynasty in the history of China, between 618 and 907 | 31 |
| | 唐代绘画展览 | Tángdài Huìhuà Zhǎnlǎn | Exhibition of Paintings of the Tang Dynasty | 20 |
| tiān | 天安门 | Tiān'ānmén | Tiananmen, the main gate of the Imperial Palace, situated in the centre of Beijing | 34 |
| | 天坛 | Tiāntán | the Temple of Heaven, a park in Beijing | 18 |

W

| | | | | |
|---|---|---|---|---|
| wáng | 王 | Wáng | a common Chinese family name | 1 |
| | 王芳 | Wáng Fāng | a woman's name | 1 |
| | 王府井百货大楼 | Wángfǔjǐng Bǎihuò Dàlóu | Wangfujing Department store, the biggest department store in Beijing | 34 |

X

| | | | | |
|---|---|---|---|---|
| xī | 西安 | Xī'ān | Xian, capital of Shaanxi Province in the north-west | |

| | | | | |
|---|---|---|---|---|
| | | | of China. | 8 |
| | 西安大学 | Xī'ān Dàxué | Xian University | 31 |
| | 西方 | Xīfāng | the West | 23 |
| xiāng | 香山 | Xiāngshān | Fragrant Hills (one of Beijing's scenic spots, known for its crimson maple leaves in autumn) | 16 |
| xiǎo | 小江 | Xiǎojiāng | a given name | 17 |

Y

| | | | | |
|---|---|---|---|---|
| yān | 燕山中学 | Yānshān Zhōngxué | name of a middle school | 18 |
| yí | 颐和园 | Yíhéyuán | the Summer Palace, a park in Beijing | 18 |
| yīng | "英雄" | "Yīngxióng" | Hero (here, a brand name of Chinese pens) | 11 |
| yǒu | 友谊商店 | Yǒuyì Shāngdiàn | Friendship Store, a store for foreigners and overseas Chinese | 19 |
| yù | 玉珍 | Yùzhēn | a name | 27 |
| yuē | 约翰·史密斯 | Yuēhàn Shǐmìsī | John Smith | 3 |

Z

| | | | | |
|---|---|---|---|---|
| zhāng | 张 | Zhāng | a common Chinese family name | 27 |
| | 张新 | Zhāng Xīn | a name | 27 |
| zhèng | 郑州 | Zhèngzhōu | Zhengzhou,capital of Henan Province in central China | 33 |
| zhōng | 中国 | Zhōngguó | China | 9 |
| | 《中国画报》 | 《Zhōngguó Huàbào》 | *China Pictorial* | 5 |
| | 中华人民共和国 | Zhōnghuá Rénmín Gònghéguó | the People's Republic of China | 30 |
| | 中山公园 | Zhōngshān Gōngyuán | a park named after Dr. Sun Yat-sen in Beijing | 18 |

| | | | |
|---|---|---|---|
| 中央台 | Zhōngyāngtái | Central (Radio or T. V.) Station | 32 |
| 钟楼 | Zhōnglóu | the Bell Tower | 24 |

# 补充词汇表 bǔchōng cíhuì biǎo Supplementary Vocabulary

| | | | | | Lesson |
|---|---|---|---|---|---|
| | | | **A** | | |
| ā | 阿姨 | （名） | āyí | auntie | 17 |
| á | 啊 | （叹） | á | exclamation of doubt | 2 |
| a | 啊 | （助） | a | ah, oh | 2 |
| ài | 爱动 | | ài dòng | physically active | 33 |
| ān | 安排 | （动） | ānpái | to arrange | 4 |
| | 安全带 | （名） | ānquándài | safety belt | 35 |
| àn | 岸 | （名） | àn | shore | 31 |
| | | | **B** | | |
| bǎ | 把 | （量） | bǎ | a measure word | 5 |
| bái | 白 | （形） | bái | white | 29 |
| | 白酒 | （名） | báijiǔ | spirits (alcohol) | 14 |
| | 白天 | （名） | báitiān | day (time) | 16 |
| | 白血球 | （名） | báixuèqiú | white blood cell | 15 |
| bān | 班门弄斧 | | Bān mén nòng fǔ | to display one's slight skill before an expert. | 25 |
| bàn | 办 | （动） | bàn | to go through | 24 |
| bāo | 包裹单 | （名） | bāoguǒdān | parcel invoice | 6 |
| bǎo | 保险 | （形、名） | bǎoxiǎn | safe, security | 24 |
| bào | 报 | （名） | bào | newspaper | 5 |
| | 报告 | （动、名） | bàogào | to report, report | 19 |
| bēi | 杯 | （量） | bēi | cup, glass | 5 |
| bǐ | 比赛 | （动、名） | bǐsài | to compete, match | 19 |
| biàn | 变 | （动） | biàn | to change | 16 |
| bù | 布 | （名） | bù | cloth | 12 |

| | | | | | |
|---|---|---|---|---|---|
| | 不敢当 | | bù gǎndāng | not at all (literally, I don't deserve it.) | 25 |
| | 不如 | （动） | bùrú | not as good as, not as well as | 23 |

C

| | | | | | |
|---|---|---|---|---|---|
| chā | 插 | （动） | chā | to plug | 32 |
| chǎn | 刬 | （动） | chǎn | to lift | 23 |
| cháng | 长短 | （名） | chángduǎnr | length | 12 |
| | 长途 | （名） | chángtú | long distance | 22 |
| chǎo | 炒 | （动） | chǎo | to stir and fry | 33 |
| chī | 吃 | （动） | chī | to eat | 9 |
| chǐ | 尺 | （量） | chǐ | a measure word | 12 |
| chū | 出差 | | chū chāi | to be sent out on business | 28 |
| | 出发 | （动） | chūfā | to start off | 21 |
| chǔ | 处理 | （动） | chǔlǐ | to handle | 11 |
| chuán | 船 | （名） | chuán | boat | 31 |
| chuāng | 窗户 | （名） | chuānghu | window | 35 |
| chuáng | 床 | （名） | chuáng | bed | 5 |
| cí | 磁带〔盘〕 | （名） | cídài〔pán〕 | magnetic tape | 33 |
| cōng | 聪明 | （形） | cōngming | intelligent, clever | 17 |
| cún | 存 | （动） | cún | to deposit | 7 |
| | 存折 | （名） | cúnzhé | bank-book | 7 |
| cuò | 错 | （形） | cuò | wrong | 26 |

D

| | | | | | |
|---|---|---|---|---|---|
| dǎ | 打开 | | dǎ kāi | to open | 30 |
| | 打球 | | dǎ qiú | to play ball games | 9 |
| | 打伞 | | dǎ sǎn | to hold an umbrella | 29 |
| | 打听 | （动） | dǎtīng | to ask, to find out | 26 |
| dà | 大概 | （副） | dàgài | about | 6 |
| | 大人 | （名） | dàren | grown-up | 22 |
| | 大小 | （名） | dàxiǎor | size | 12 |

| | | | | |
|---|---|---|---|---|
| dān | 耽误 | （动）dānwu | to take up (one's time) | 25 |
| dāng | 当然 | （形、副）dāngrán | certain, certainly | 13 |
| dé | 得 | （动）dé | to be ready | 12 |
| dēng | 灯 | （名）dēng | light | 32 |
| dì | 地铁 | （名）dìtiě | underground railway, subway | 23 |
| diǎn | 点（菜） | （动）diǎn (cài) | to order (dishes) | 20 |
| diàn | 电报 | （名）diànbào | telegram, cable | 10 |
| | 电报纸 | （名）diànbàozhǐ | telegram form | 10 |
| diào | 掉 | （动）diào | to fall | 16 |
| dīng | 盯 | （动）dīng | to stare | 29 |
| dìng | 定期 | （名）dìngqī | time (deposit), fixed (deposit) | 7 |
| diū | 丢 | （动）diū | to lose | 24 |
| dú | 读 | （动）dú | to read | 33 |
| dù | 肚子 | （名）dùzi | stomach | 15 |
| duān | 端 | （动）duān | to take, to hold | 23 |
| duì | 对面 | （名）duìmiàn | opposite side | 26 |

E

| | | | | |
|---|---|---|---|---|
| ér | 儿媳妇 | （名）érxífu | daughter-in-law (son's wife) | 22 |
| ěr | 耳塞子 | （名）ěrsāizi | earphones | 32 |

F

| | | | | |
|---|---|---|---|---|
| fǎ | 法郎 | （名）Fǎláng | Franc | 7 |
| fān | 翻译 | （动、名）fānyì | to translate, translation | 21 |
| fǎn | 反 | （形）fǎn | the other way round | 26 |
| fàn | 饭店 | （名）fàndiàn | restaurant, hotel | 3 |
| fāng | 方便 | （形）fāngbiàn | convenient | 23 |
| | 方向 | （名）fāngxiàng | direction | 26 |
| fáng | 房租 | （名）fángzū | rent | 22 |
| féi | 肥 | （形）féi | loose | 12 |
| | 肥瘦儿 | （名）féishòur | width | 12 |
| fēn | 分钟 | （名）fēnzhōng | minute | 19 |
| fú | 幅 | （量）fú | a measure word for pic- | |

| | | | | | |
|---|---|---|---|---|---|
| | | | | tures and paintings | 30 |
| | 福 | （名） | fú | happiness, luck | 35 |
| fù | 副 | （量） | fù | a measure word (pair) | 11 |

G

| | | | | | |
|---|---|---|---|---|---|
| gǎi | 改 | （动） | gǎi | to make changes | 30 |
| gāng | 刚 | （副） | gāng | just | 19 |
| gāo | 高 | （形） | gāo | high | 15 |
| | 高尔夫球 | （名） | gāo'ěrfūqiú | golf | 28 |
| gào | 告别 | （动） | gàobié | to say good-bye | 19 |
| gē | 歌剧 | （名） | gējù | opera | 10 |
| gè | 各 | （代） | gè | every | 27 |
| | 个子 | （名） | gèzi | height | 28 |
| gēn | 跟 | （介） | gēn | with | 13 |
| gōng | 工资 | （名） | gōngzī | wage, pay | 22 |
| | 公费医疗 | | gōngfèi yīliáo | free medical care | 22 |
| | 恭敬不如从命 | | gōngjìng bùrú cóng mìng | The best way to show respect is to obey. | 27 |
| gǒu | 狗 | （名） | gǒu | dog | 18 |
| gòu | 够 | （形） | gòu | enough | 12 |
| | 够用 | | gòu yòng | enough (for a purpose) | 22 |
| gǔ | 谷 | （名） | gǔ | grain | 35 |
| gù | 顾客 | （名） | gùkè | customer | 6 |
| guà | 挂 | （动） | guà | to hang | 35 |
| guāi | 乖 | （形） | guāi | well-behaved | 17 |
| guàn | 罐头 | （名） | guàntou | canned food(s) | 34 |
| guǎng | 广播 | （动、名） | guǎngbō | to broadcast, broadcast | 19 |
| guì | 柜子 | （名） | guìzi | wardrobe | 32 |
| guó | 国家 | （名） | guójiā | country, nation | 16 |
| guò | 过去 | （名） | guòqù | the past | 33 |

H

| | | | | | |
|---|---|---|---|---|---|
| hā | 哈 | （象声） | hā | ha (laughing sound) | 2 |

| | | | | | |
|---|---|---|---|---|---|
| hǎn | 喊 | （动） | hǎn | to shout | 29 |
| hàn | 汉语 | （名） | Hànyǔ | Chinese | 23 |
| hǎo | 好吃 | （形） | hǎochī | delicious | 32 |
| | 好听 | （形） | hǎotīng | pleasant to the ear | 33 |
| | 好玩儿 | （形） | hǎowánr | enjoyable | 18 |
| hēi | 黑 | （形） | hēi | black | 30 |
| hóng | 红 | （形） | hóng | red | 11 |
| hòu | 后天 | （名） | hòutiān | day after tomorrow | 8 |
| huā | 花生米 | （名） | huāshēngmǐ | peanut | 14 |
| huá | 划（船） | （动） | huá (chuán) | to row | 31 |
| huà | 画 | （动） | huà | to draw, to paint | 30 |
| | 话剧 | （名） | huàjù | play | 10 |
| | 画儿 | （名） | huàr | drawing, painting | 30 |
| | 画展 | （名） | huàzhǎn | exhibition of paintings | 4 |
| huáng | 黄瓜 | （名） | huángguā | cucumber | 14 |
| huí | 回 | （动） | huí | to come back, to return | 8 |
| huó | 活期 | （名） | huóqī | demand (deposit) | 7 |
| huǒ | 火车 | （名） | huǒchē | train | 20 |

J

| | | | | | |
|---|---|---|---|---|---|
| jì | 系 | （动） | jì | to tie | 35 |
| | 记性 | （名） | jìxing | memory | 17 |
| jiā | 夹 | （动） | jiā | to pick up | 23 |
| | 家乡 | （名） | jiāxiāng | native place | 16 |
| jiàng | 酱肉 | （名） | jiàngròu | cooked meat seasoned in soy sauce | 14 |
| jiāo | 教书 | | jiāo shū | to teach | 31 |
| | 交流 | （动） | jiāoliú | to exchange | 25 |
| | 胶卷 | （名） | jiāojuǎnr | film | 20 |
| jiǎo | 饺子 | （名） | jiǎozi | dumpling | 14 |
| jiào | 教育 | （名、动） | jiàoyù | education, to educate | 31 |
| jiē | 接 | （动） | jiē | to take, to receive | 21 |
| jié | 节目 | （名） | jiémù | program | 18 |
| jiě | 解答 | （动） | jiědá | to answer | 25 |

| | | | | | |
|---|---|---|---|---|---|
| jiè | 借 | （动） | jiè | to borrow, to lend | 20 |
| jīn | 金 | （名） | jīn | gold | 30 |
| | 斤 | （量） | jīn | jin (equal to half a kilo) | 34 |
| | 金笔 | （名） | jīnbǐ | gold-tipped pen | 11 |
| | 今年 | （名） | jīnnián | this year | 17 |
| jìn | 进行 | （动） | jìnxíng | to proceed | 25 |
| jiǔ | 酒 | （名） | jiǔ | alcoholic drink | 13 |
| jǔ | 举 | （动） | jǔ | to hold up | 32 |
| jù | 句 | （名、量） | jù | sentence, a measure word | 17 |

K

| | | | | | |
|---|---|---|---|---|---|
| kā | 咖啡 | （名） | kāfēi | coffee | 2 |
| kāi | 开（车） | （动） | kāi (chē) | (a vehicle) to start | 19 |
| | 开会 | | kāi huì | to hold a meeting or conference | 34 |
| | 开球 | | kāi qiú | to serve the ball | 19 |
| | 开始 | （动） | kāishǐ | to begin | 15 |
| | 开玩笑 | | kāi wánxiào | to make jokes | 21 |
| kàn | 看够 | | kàn gòu | to see enough of | 18 |
| kě | 可不是 | | kěbushì | exactly, indeed | 16 |
| kè | 客人 | （名） | kèrén | guest | 19 |
| kōng | 空气 | （名） | kōngqì | air | 17 |
| kòng | 空儿 | （名） | kòngr | spare time | 28 |
| kǒu | 口 | （量） | kǒu | a measure word | 22 |
| | 口袋 | （名） | kǒudài | pocket | 24 |
| | 口音 | （名） | kǒuyīn | accent | 17 |
| kù | 裤子 | （名） | kùzi | trousers | 12 |
| kuài | 块 | （量） | kuài | a measure word (lump, piece, etc.) | 11 |
| kuǎn | 款 | （名） | kuǎn | deposit | 7 |

L

| | | | | | |
|---|---|---|---|---|---|
| lā | 拉 | （动） | lā | to pull | 29 |

| | | | | |
|---|---|---|---|---|
| lán | 篮球 | （名）lánqiú | basketball | 28 |
| lǎo | 老大爷 | （名）lǎodàye | grandpa (polite way to address elderly men) | 17 |
| lǐ | 里 | （量）lǐ | li (equal to half a kilometre) | 34 |
| lì | 历史学家 | （名）lìshǐxuéjiā | historian | 25 |
| liǎ | 俩 | （数量）liǎ | two | 29 |
| liàn | 练 | （动）liàn | to practice | 27 |
| liè | 列车 | （名）lièchē | train | 19 |
| lǚ | 旅客 | （名）lǚkè | passenger | 19 |
| | 旅行 | （动、名）lǚxíng | to travel, travel | 24 |
| lù | 路 | （量）lù | a measure word | 26 |

M

| | | | | |
|---|---|---|---|---|
| mǎ | 马克 | （名）Mǎkè | Mark | 7 |
| | 马路 | （名）mǎlù | street, road | 26 |
| | 马戏 | （名）mǎxì | circus | 18 |
| mài | 卖 | （动）mài | to sell | 6 |
| mǎn | 满 | （形）mǎn | full | 27 |
| máng | 忙 | （形）máng | busy | 20 |
| máo | 毛病 | （名）máobing | trouble | 32 |
| méi | 没错儿 | méi cuòr | exactly | 7 |
| | 没什么 | méi shénme | You are welcome. Don't mention it. | 7 |
| mén | 门口儿 | （名）ménkǒur | doorway | 29 |
| mǐ | 米 | （量）mǐ | metre | 28 |
| miàn | 面包 | （名）miànbāo | bread | 14 |
| | 面前 | （名）miànqián | before, in front of | 25 |
| | 面条 | （名）miàntiáor | noodles | 14 |
| míng | 名贵 | （形）míngguì | valuable | 27 |

N

| | | | | |
|---|---|---|---|---|
| ná | 拿 | （动）ná | to bring | 22 |
| nà | 那么 | （连）nàme | then | 1 |

| | | | | |
|---|---|---|---|---|
| | 那儿 | （代）nàr | there | 4 |
| nǎi | 奶奶 | （名）nǎinai | grandma | 2 |
| nán | 难得 | （形）nándé | rare | 27 |
| | 难看 | （形）nánkàn | ugly | 30 |
| néng | 能力 | （名）nénglì | ability | 31 |
| niú | 牛奶 | （名）niúnǎi | milk | 14 |
| | 牛肉 | （名）niúròu | beef | 14 |
| nǚ | 女士 | （名）nǚshì | lady | 23 |

## P

| | | | | |
|---|---|---|---|---|
| pá | 扒 | （动）pá | to gather up, to rake up | 23 |
| pāi | 拍 | （动）pāi | to send (cable) | 34 |
| pái | 牌儿 | （名）páir | brand | 11 |
| pán | 盘儿 | （量）pánr | a measure word (dish, plate) | 14 |
| pàng | 胖 | （形）pàng | fat | 33 |
| pǎo | 跑 | （动）pǎo | to run | 26 |
| | 跑步 | pǎo bù | jogging, to run | 33 |
| péi | 陪 | （动）péi | to accompany | 20 |
| pí | 啤酒 | （名）píjiǔ | beer | 2 |
| | 脾气 | （名）píqi | temper | 15 |
| | 皮鞋 | （名）píxié | leather shoes | 12 |
| pīn | 拼盘 | （名）pīnpánr | mixed cold dish, hors d'oeuvre | 14 |
| píng | 凭 | （动）píng | to use (as evidence) | 7 |
| | 瓶 | （量）píng | bottle | 5 |

## Q

| | | | | |
|---|---|---|---|---|
| qī | 妻 | （名）qī | wife | 35 |
| qǐ | 起床 | qǐ chuáng | to get up, to get out of bed | 9 |
| | 起飞 | （动）qǐfēi | to take off | 35 |
| qì | 气象台 | （名）qìxiàngtái | weather station | 16 |
| qián | 前天 | （名）qiántiān | day before yesterday | 8 |
| qiú | 球迷 | （名）qiúmí | fans (ball games) | 28 |

| | | | | |
|---|---|---|---|---|
| qǔ | 取（款） | （动）qǔ (kuǎn) | to draw (money) | 7 |
| quān | 圈 | （名、量）quānr | circle, round | 28 |

R

| | | | | |
|---|---|---|---|---|
| rén | 人数 | rén shù | number of people | 30 |
| rèn | 任务 | （名）rènwu | task | 34 |
| rì | 日元 | （名）Rìyuán | (Japanese) yen | 7 |
| róng | 容易 | （形）róngyì | easy | 23 |

S

| | | | | |
|---|---|---|---|---|
| sàn | 散步 | sàn bù | to go for a walk | 9 |
| sǎng | 嗓子 | （名）sǎngzi | throat | 15 |
| shàn | 扇子 | （名）shànzi | fan | 30 |
| shàng | 上楼 | shàng lóu | to go upstairs | 19 |
| shēn | 身体 | （名）shēntǐ | body | 15 |
| shēng | 声 | （名）shēng | voice, sound | 30 |
| | 生活 | （动、名）shēnghuó | to live, life | 23 |
| shī | 失散 | （动）shīsàn | to lose | 27 |
| shí | 石头 | （名）shítou | stone | 30 |
| shōu | 收 | （动）shōu | to receive, to keep | 24 |
| shǒu | 首都 | （名）shǒudū | capital | 16 |
| | 手绢 | （名）shǒujuànr | handkerchief | 11 |
| | 手套 | （名）shǒutàor | gloves | 11 |
| | 手续 | （名）shǒuxù | procedure | 24 |
| shòu | 瘦 | （形）shòu | tight, thin | 12 |
| | 售票员 | （名）shòupiàoyuán | conductor | 26 |
| shū | 叔叔 | （名）shūshu | uncle | 2 |
| shuāng | 双 | （量）shuāng | a measure word (pair) | 12 |
| shuǐ | 水 | （名）shuǐ | water | 33 |
| | 水电费 | （名）shuǐdiànfèi | payment for water and electricity | 22 |
| | 水果 | （名）shuǐguǒ | fruit | 19 |
| shuì | 睡觉 | shuì jiào | to sleep | 9 |

| | | | | | |
|---|---|---|---|---|---|
| sú | 俗话 | （名） | súhuà | saying | 35 |
| suàn | 算术 | （名） | suànshù | arithmetic | 18 |
| suì | 岁数 | （名） | suìshu | age | 34 |
| sūn | 孙女 | （名） | sūnnür | granddaughter | 17 |

T

| | | | | | |
|---|---|---|---|---|---|
| tā | 它 | （代） | tā | it | 35 |
| tái | 台 | （名） | tái | station | 22 |
| | 抬 | （动） | tái | to carry (on shoulder) | 29 |
| | 台球 | （名） | táiqiú | billiards | 28 |
| tǎo | 讨论 | （动） | tǎolùn | to discuss | 24 |
| tè | 特产 | （名） | tèchǎn | special produce | 27 |
| | 特点 | （名） | tèdiǎn | characteristic | 35 |
| tǐ | 体育 | （名） | tǐyù | physical exercises | 33 |
| tiáo | 条 | （量） | tiáo | a measure word | 12 |
| tiào | 跳 | （动） | tiào | to jump | 29 |
| | 跳高 | （名） | tiàogāo | high jump | 28 |
| tóng | 同学 | （名） | tóngxué | school-mate | 21 |
| | 同志 | （名） | tóngzhì | comrade | 1 |
| tǒng | 统筹医疗费 | （名） | tǒngchóu yī liáofèi | payment for a co-operative medical care | 22 |
| tóu | 头发 | （名） | tóufa | hair | 33 |
| tuì | 退休金 | （名） | tuìxiūjīn | retire pension | 22 |
| tuō | 托儿费 | （名） | tuō'érfèi | payment for child care | 22 |
| | 托儿所 | （名） | tuō'érsuǒ | nursery | 22 |

W

| | | | | | |
|---|---|---|---|---|---|
| wài | 外地 | （名） | wàidì | other places | 20 |
| wǎn | 晚饭 | （名） | wǎnfàn | supper, dinner | 9 |
| wàn | 万 | （数） | wàn | ten thousand | 7 |
| wǎng | 网球 | （名） | wǎngqiú | tennis | 28 |
| wàng | 忘 | （动） | wàng | to forget | 24 |
| wèi | 位 | （量） | wèi | a measure word for people | 10 |

| | | | | |
|---|---|---|---|---|
| wén | 文化宫 | （名）wénhuàgōng | cultural palace | 4 |
| | 文章 | （名）wénzhāng | article, composition | 30 |
| wǔ | 午饭 | （名）wǔfàn | lunch | 9 |
| wù | 雾 | （名）wù | fog | 16 |

## X

| | | | | |
|---|---|---|---|---|
| xī | 西餐 | （名）xīcān | western food | 23 |
| | 西服 | （名）xīfú | suit | 24 |
| | 西药 | （名）xīyào | western medicine | 15 |
| xí | 席 | （名）xí | banquet, table | 27 |
| xǐ | 洗（照片） | （动）xǐ (zhàopiàn) | to develop (photos) | 21 |
| | 洗尘 | （动）xǐchén | to celebrate someone's home-coming | 27 |
| | 喜欢 | （动）xǐhuan | to like | 14 |
| xià | 下午 | （名）xiàwǔ | afternoon | 4 |
| xián | 闲不住 | xián bu zhù | always keep oneself busy | 35 |
| xiāng | 香 | （形）xiāng | fragrant or smell deliciously | 33 |
| | 箱子 | （名）xiāngzi | suitcase, trunk | 29 |
| xiǎo | 小说 | （名）xiǎoshuōr | novel | 31 |
| xīn | 心细 | xīn xì | careful | 35 |
| xíng | 行动 | （动、名）xíngdòng | movement, to take action | 34 |
| | 行李架 | （名）xínglijià | luggage rack | 24 |
| xìng | 幸福 | （形、名）xìngfú | happy, happiness | 23 |
| xué | 学术 | （名）xuéshù | scholarship, academic sub-jects | 25 |
| | 学校 | （名）xuéxiào | school | 5 |
| xuè | 血压 | （名）xuèyā | blood pressure | 15 |

## Y

| | | | | |
|---|---|---|---|---|
| yá | 牙 | （名）yá | tooth | 15 |
| ya | 呀 | （助）ya | a modal particle | 28 |
| yǎn | 眼 | （名、量）yǎn | eye, look | 31 |
| | 眼镜盒 | （名）yǎnjìnghér | case (for keeping glasses) | 24 |

| | | | | | |
|---|---|---|---|---|---|
| yāng | 秧 | （名） | yāng | seedling | 35 |
| yáng | 羊肉 | （名） | yángròu | mutton | 14 |
| | 羊肉泡馍 | | yángròu pào mó | a popular dish in the north-west of China | 27 |
| | 洋娃娃 | （名） | yángwáwa | doll | 21 |
| yàng | 样 | （名、量） | yàngr | appearance, kind; a measure word | 11 |
| yào | 钥匙 | （名） | yàoshi | key | 11 |
| yé | 爷爷 | （名） | yéye | grandpa | 2 |
| yī | 衣帽钩 | （名） | yīmàogōur | pegs for coats and hats | 24 |
| | 铱金 | （名） | yījīn | iridium | 11 |
| | 医院 | （名） | yīyuàn | hospital | 15 |
| yí | 一定 | （形、副） | yídìng | definite, definitely, must | 1 |
| yǐ | 椅子 | （名） | yǐzi | chair | 5 |
| yì | 一起 | （名、副） | yìqǐ | together | 13 |
| yīn | 音量 | （名） | yīnliàng | volume (sound) | 32 |
| yīng | 英语 | （名） | Yīngyǔ | English | 17 |
| yóu | 游泳 | （动、名） | yóuyǒng | to swim, swimming | 33 |
| yú | 鱼翅 | （名） | yúchì | shark's fin | 27 |
| yǔ | 雨衣 | （名） | yǔyī | raincoat | 29 |
| yún | 云 | （名） | yún | cloud | 16 |
| yùn | 运动 | （动、名） | yùndòng | to do exercises, sports | 28 |

## Z

| | | | | | |
|---|---|---|---|---|---|
| zāng | 脏 | （形） | zāng | dirty | 35 |
| zǎo | 早 | （形） | zǎo | early | 12 |
| | 早饭 | （名） | zǎofàn | breakfast | 9 |
| zěn | 怎么 | （代） | zěnme | how | 6 |
| zhàn | 占线 | | zhàn xiàn | the line is busy | 10 |
| zhào | 照 | （动） | zhào | to take (photos) | 21 |
| | 照片 | （名） | zhàopiàn | photo | 21 |
| | 罩衫 | （名） | zhàoshān | a kind of jacket | 12 |
| | 照相馆 | （名） | zhàoxiàngguǎn | photo studio | 21 |
| zhè | 这么 | （代） | zhème | so | 13 |

| | | | | |
|---|---|---|---|---|
| zhēn | 真是的 | zhēnshide | a mild disapproval | 31 |
| zhèn | 阵雨 | (名) zhènyǔ | shower | 16 |
| zhèng | 正好 | (形、副) zhènghǎo | precise, precisely, no more, no less | 7 |
| zhī | 只 | (量) zhī | a measure word | 11 |
| zhǐ | 指 | (动) zhǐ | to point | 29 |
| | 指正 | (动) zhǐzhèng | to criticize | 25 |
| zhōng | 中锋 | (名) zhōngfēng | centre(a position in ball games) | 28 |
| | 中式 | (名) Zhōngshì | Chinese style | 12 |
| | 中药 | (名) zhōngyào | Chinese medicine | 15 |
| | 钟头 | (名) zhōngtóu | hour | 31 |
| | 衷心 | (形) zhōngxīn | heartfelt | 25 |
| zhòng | 重 | (形) zhòng | heavy | 15 |
| zhū | 猪肉 | (名) zhūròu | pork | 14 |
| zhǔ | 主持人 | (名) zhǔchírén | chairperson | 25 |
| zhuāng | 装 | (动) zhuāng | to pack | 34 |
| zhuō | 桌子 | (名) zhuōzi | table | 5 |
| zì | 字 | (名) zì | character | 10 |
| | 自己 | (代) zìjǐ | self | 23 |
| zū | 租 | (动) zū | to hire | 34 |
| zuó | 昨天 | (名) zuótiān | yesterday | 8 |
| zuǒ | 左边儿 | (名) zuǒbianr | left side | 26 |
| zuò | 作 | (动) zuò | to do | 18 |
| | 做 | (动) zuò | to make | 12 |
| | 座谈 | (动) zuòtán | to discuss (informally) | 25 |

## 专名 ZHUĀNMÍNG PROPER NAMES

B

| | | | |
|---|---|---|---|
| 北京 | Běijīng | Beijing (Peking) | 3 |
| 北京饭店 | Běijīng Fàndiàn | Beijing Hotel (Peking Hotel) | 3 |

C

| | | | |
|---|---|---|---|
| 《茶馆》 | "Cháguǎnr" | "The Tea House" | 10 |

D

| | | | |
|---|---|---|---|
| 地下宫殿 | Dìxià Gōngdiàn | Underground Palace | 20 |

F

| | | | |
|---|---|---|---|
| 法国 | Fǎguó | France | 33 |

G

| | | | |
|---|---|---|---|
| 广州 | Guǎngzhōu | Guangzhou (Canton), capital of Guangdong Province in south China | 16 |

H

| | | | |
|---|---|---|---|
| 华侨大厦 | Huáqiáo Dàshà | Overseas Chinese Hotel | 10 |

J

| | | | |
|---|---|---|---|
| 加拿大 | Jiānádà | Canada | 3 |

L

| | | | |
|---|---|---|---|
| 李 | Lǐ | a common Chinese family name | 1 |
| 李小兰 | Lǐ Xiǎolán | name of a girl | 17 |

M

| | | | |
|---|---|---|---|
| 民族饭店 | Mínzú Fàndiàn | Nationalities Hotel | 13 |

Q

| | | | |
|---|---|---|---|
| 青岛 | Qīngdǎo | a major coastal city in Shandong Province) | 14 |

R

| | | | |
|---|---|---|---|
| 日本 | Rìběn | Japan | 3 |

S

| | | | |
|---|---|---|---|
| 上海 | Shànghǎi | Shanghai | 10 |
| 首都剧场 | Shǒudū Jùchǎng | Capital Theater | 10 |

T

| | | | |
|---|---|---|---|
| 唐人街 | Tángrénjiē | Chinatown | 23 |

W

| | | | |
|---|---|---|---|
| 王大娘 | Wáng dàniáng | Auntie Wang | 22 |
| 王力 | Wáng Lì | a well-known professor Chinese linguistics | 28 |

X

| | | | |
|---|---|---|---|
| 西单 | Xīdān | name of a commercial centre in the west of Beijing | 4 |
| 西德 | Xīdé | West Germany | 7 |
| 小同 | Xiǎotóng | name of a girl | 19 |

Y

| | | | |
|---|---|---|---|
| 颐和园 | Yíhéyuán | the Summer Palace | 8 |
| 英国 | Yīngguó | Britain; England | 3 |

## Z

| | | | |
|---|---|---|---|
| 张 | Zhāng | a common Chinese family name | 1 |
| 张大中 | Zhāng Dàzhōng | name of a man | 1 |
| 张文汉 | Zhāng Wénhàn | name of a man | 1 |
| 赵 | Zhào | a common Chinese family name | 1 |
| 中国 | Zhōngguó | China | 3 |
| 中国书店 | Zhōngguó Shūdiàn | China Book store | 26 |
| 中国银行 | Zhōngguó Yínháng | China Bank | 7 |

# Appendix II

## 练习答案 liànxí dá'àn Key To Exercises

### 语音 Yǔyīn KEY TO PHONETIC EXERCISES

2\. 2)

(1) ~~b~~/p (2) b/~~p~~ (3) ~~d~~/t (4) d/~~t~~ (5) ~~zh~~/ch
(6) zh/~~ch~~ (7) ~~j~~/q (8) j/~~q~~ (9) c/~~s~~ (10 ~~c~~/s
(11) ~~ch~~/sh (12) ch/~~sh~~ (13) ~~q~~/x (14) q/~~x~~ (15) zh/~~j~~
(16) ~~zh~~/j (17) ch/~~q~~ (18) ~~ch~~/q (19) g/~~k~~ (20) ~~g~~/k
(21) ~~z~~/c (22) z/~~c~~ (23) sh/~~x~~ (24) ~~sh~~/x (25) ~~z~~/j
(26) z/~~j~~ (27) c/~~q~~ (28) ~~c~~/q (29) ~~s~~/x (30) s/~~x~~
(31) z/~~zh~~ (32) ~~z~~/zh (33) c/~~ch~~ (34) ~~c~~/ch (35) s/~~sh~~
(36) ~~s~~/sh

3)

(1) + (2) (3) + (4) (5) (6) +
(7) (8) + (9) (10) + (11) (12) +

4)

(1) z, j (2 ) z, zh (3) j, zh (4) c, ch (5) c, q (6) q, ch
(7) x, sh (8) s, sh (9) s,x (10) d,t (11) ch, zh (12) q, j

3\. 2)

(1) a/~~e~~ (2) ~~a~~/e (3) ~~an~~/en (4) an/~~en~~ (5) ~~ang~~/eng
(6) ang/~~eng~~ (7) ~~ai~~/ei (8) ai/~~ei~~ (9) ~~ao~~/ou (10) ao/~~ou~~
(11) ~~ou~~/uo (12) ou/~~uo~~ (13) ia/~~ie~~ (14) ~~ia~~/ie (15) iao/~~iu~~
(16) ~~iao~~/iu (17) ua/~~uo~~ (18) ~~ua~~/uo (19) ~~u~~/ü (20) ~~u~~/ü
(21) ~~u~~/iu (22) u/~~iu~~ (23) ~~uo~~/üe (24) uo/~~üe~~ (25) ~~an~~/ang
(26) an/~~ang~~ (27) en/~~eng~~ (28) ~~en~~/eng (29) ~~in~~/ing (30) in/~~ing~~
(31) ian/~~iang~~ (32) ~~ian~~/iang (33) ~~uan~~/uang (34) uan/~~uang~~ (35) ~~un~~/ong
(36) un/~~ong~~

3)

(1) (2) + (3) (4) + (5) (6) +
(7) + (8) (9) + (10) (11) (12) +

4)

(1) ù,ǔ (2) ù, ǔ (3) uè, uò (4) uē, üè (5) án, áng

(6) éng, èn (7) īn, íng (8) iǎng, ǎn (9) uān, uǎng (10) ūn, óng
(11) iē, ià (12) iāo, iú

4. 1) B

(1) bái/bǎi (2) cháng/chǎng (3) qǐng/qǐng (4) jí/jǐ
(5) lǎi/lǎo (6) méi/měi (7) liáng/liǎng (8) guó/guǒ

C

(1) wán (2) wǎn (3) zuǒ (4) zuó
(5) mǎi (6) mái (7) lán (8) lǎn

2) B

(1) bāo/bào (2) fāng/fàng (3) qiān/qiàn (4) jīn/jìn
(5) shū/shù (6) wēn/wèn (7) mō/mò (8) yē/yè

C

(1) dài (2) dāi (3) shōu (4) shòu
(5) jī (6) jì (7) jiāng (8) jiàng

5. 1)

(1) yóulǎn (2) yóujú (3) gōngchǎng (4) gōngyuánr
(5) máoyī (6) màoyì (7) láo jià (8) lǎojiā

2)

(1) shōushi (2) xiūxi (3) xiāngcài (4) xiànzài
(5) kuāngguǎng (6) qǐng jìn (7) qiú duì (8) nǚxu

## KEY TO EXERCISES IN THE 35 LESSONS

### 第一课 dìyīkè Lesson 1

2. 1) 请 问, 您 是 张 大中 先生 吗?
Qǐng wèn, nín shì Zhāng Dàzhōng xiānsheng ma?

2) 请 问, 您 是 王 同志 吗?
Qǐng wèn, nín shì Wáng tóngzhì ma?

3) 请 问, 您 是 李 小姐 吗?
Qǐng wèn, nín shì Lǐ xiǎojie ma?

4) 请 问, 您 是 赵 先 生 吗?
Qǐng wèn, nín shì Zhào xiānsheng ma?

6. 1) 您 好!
Nín hǎo!

2) 请 问, 您 是 赵 小姐 吗?
Qǐng wèn, nín shì Zhào xiǎojie ma?

3) 欢 迎 您, 张 同志!
Huānyíng nín, Zhāng tóngzhì!

4) 我 不是 王 芳。
Wǒ bú shì Wáng Fāng.

5) 我 叫 张 大中。
Wǒ jiào Zhāng Dàzhōng.

## 第二课 dì'èrkè Lesson 2

3. 1) 请 进。
Qǐng jìn.

2) 请 坐。
Qǐng zuò.

3) 请 喝茶。
Qǐng hē chá.

4) 请 抽 烟。
Qǐng chōu yān.

5) 请 喝啤酒。
Qǐng hē píjiǔ.

6) 请 喝咖啡。
Qǐng hē kāfēi.

4. 1) 介绍
jièshào

2) 介 绍，是，是
jièshào, shì, shì

3) 是，介绍，是，是，是
shì, jièshào, shì, shì, shì

## 第三课 dìsānkè Lesson 3

3. 1) 爷爷，奶奶，叔叔
yéye, nǎinai, shūshu

2) 太太，女儿，儿子
tàitai, nǚ'ér, érzi

4. 1) 这 是 谁？
Zhè shì shuí?

2) 谁 叫 张 大 中？
Shuí jiào Zhāng Dàzhōng?

3) 他们 是 哪 国 人？
Tāmen shì nǎ guó rén?

4) 他们 住 哪儿？
Tāmen zhù nǎr?

5) 谁 找 陈 明 山 先 生？
Shuí zhǎo Chén Míngshān xiānsheng?

6) 他 爷爷 住 哪个 房间？
Tā yéye zhù nǎge fángjiān?

7) 老 赵 找 谁？
Lǎo Zhào zhǎo shuí?

8) 八一三二 房间 在哪儿？
Bāyāosān'èr fángjiān zài nǎr?

9) 他 爷爷 住 哪个 饭店？
Tā yéye zhù nǎge fàndiàn?

5. 1) 他 是 谁？他 是 谁 儿子？谁 是 你 儿子？
Tā shì shuí? Tā shì shuí érzi? Shuí shì nǐ érzi?

2) 李 叔叔 找 谁？谁 找 你 爷爷？李 叔叔 找 谁 爷爷？
Lǐ shūshu zhǎo shuí? Shuí zhǎo nǐ yéye? Lǐ shūshu zhǎo shuí yéye?

7. 1) 他 是 谁？
Tā shì shuí?

2) 他 是 哪 国 人？
Tā shì nǎ guó rén?

3) 他 住 哪儿?
Tā zhù nǎr ?

4) 他 住 哪个 房间?
Tā zhù nǎge fángjiān?

5) 你 找 谁?
Nǐ zhǎo shuí?

## 第四课 dìsìkè Lesson 4

3. 1) (1) 我不去。我去故宫。
Wǒ bú qù. Wǒ qù Gùgōng.

(2) 我不去。我去看朋友。
Wǒ bú qù. Wǒ qù kàn péngyou.

(3) 我不去。我去长城。
Wǒ bú qù. Wǒ qù Chángchéng.

(4) 我不去。我去买东西。
Wǒ bú qù. Wǒ qù mǎi dōngxi.

2) (1) A: 你们下午有活动吗?
Nǐmen xiàwǔ yǒu huódòng ma?
B: 没有。你呢?
Méiyǒu. Nǐ ne?

(2) A: 你们晚上有事儿吗?
Nǐmen wǎnshang yǒu shìr ma?
B: 没有。你呢?
Méiyǒu. Nǐ ne?

(3) A: 你们明天有安排吗?
Nǐmen míngtiān yǒu ānpái ma?
B: 没有。你呢?
Méiyǒu. Nǐ ne?

4. 1) b 2) c 3) c 4) b 5) c 6) b

## 第五课 dìwǔkè Lesson 5

3. 1) 几 jǐ 2) 多少 duōshao 3) 多少 duōshao 4) 几 jǐ 5) 几 jǐ

5. 1) 一个朋友
yíge péngyou

2) 一封信
yìfēng xìn

3) 几张邮票
jǐzhāng yóupiào

4) 一本《中国画报》
yìběn "Zhōngguó Huàbào"

5) 五个信封
wǔge xìnfēng

6) 八把椅子
bābǎ yǐzi

7) 十张桌子
shízhāng zhuōzi

8) 三张床
sānzhāng chuáng

## 复习 (1) fùxí (1) Review (1)

2. 1) 不 bù 2) 不 bù 3) 没 méi 4) 不 bù 5) 不 bù 6) 不 bù 7) 没 méi 8) 不 bù 9) 不 bù
10) 没 méi

## 第六课 dìliùkè Lesson 6

3. 1) 明 信 片五分 一 张。
Míngxìnpiàn wǔfēn yìzhāng.

2) 信 封 一分 一个。
Xìnfēng yìfēn yígè.

3) 《中 国 画 报》 一块 三 一本。
"Zhōngguó Huàbào" yíkuài sān yìběn.

4) 桌 子 十 五 块 一 张。
Zhuōzi shíwǔkuài yìzhāng.

5) 信 封 一毛 钱 十个。
Xìnfēng yìmáo qián shígè.

6) 椅子八 块 五 一把。
Yǐzi bākuài wǔ yìbǎ.

4. 1) 一 张 八分 邮 票。三 张 明 信 片。 两 毛 三。
Yìzhāng bāfēn yóupiào. Sānzhāng míngxìnpiàn. Liǎngmáo sān.

2) 多 少? 多 少 钱? 两 毛。 多 少 钱 一本? 两 块 八。
Duōshao? Duōshao qián? Liǎngmáo. Duōshao qián yìběn? Liǎngkuài bā.
两 毛。
Liǎngmáo.

## 第七课 dìqīkè Lesson 7

3. 1) 什 么 外币?
Shénme wàibì?

2) 兑 换 外币吗? 是 多 少? 兑 换 人民币 六百 八十五元 二毛 三 分。
Duìhuàn wàibì ma? Shì duōshao? Duìhuàn Rénmínbì liùbǎi bāshíwǔyuán èrmáo sānfēn.

3) 多 少? 五百 英 镑。 五百 英 镑 兑 换 人民币 一千 六百 四十二元 一毛 五分。
Duōshao? Wǔbǎi Yīngbàng. Wǔbǎi Yīngbàng duìhuàn Rénmínbì yìqiān liùbǎi sìshí'èryuán yìmáo wǔfēn.

4) 一 千 二百。 一千 二百 马克 兑 换 人民 币 一千 零 一十六元 一 毛 六分。
Yìqiān èrbǎi. Yìqiān èrbǎi Mǎkè duìhuàn Rénmínbì yìqiān líng yīshíliùyuán yì máo liùfēn.

## 第八课 dìbākè Lesson 8

3. 1) 几号
jǐhào

2) 星期几
xīngqījǐ

3) 什 么 时候
shénme shíhour

4) 下 星期几
xià xīngqījǐ

5) 什 么 时候
shénme shíhour

## 第九课 dìjiǔkè Lesson 9

2. 1) 现在两点零五。
Xiànzài liǎngdiǎn líng wǔ.
2) 现在三点一刻了。
Xiànzài sāndiǎn yíkè le.
3) 四点半了。
Sìdiǎnbàn le.
4) 我的表十一点五十了。
Wǒ de biǎo shíyīdiǎn wǔshí le.

## 第十课 dìshíkè Lesson 10

3. 1) (1) 是不是话剧？
shì bu shì huàjù?
(2) 是不是张大中同志
shì bu shì Zhāng Dàzhōng tóngzhì
(3) 是不是艾琳？
shì bu shì Àilín?
2) (1) 演《茶馆》，您看不看？
yǎn "Cháguǎnr", nín kàn bu kàn?
(2) 演《李时珍》，您看不看？
yǎn "Lǐ Shízhēn", nín kàn bu kàn?
(3) 演歌剧，您看不看？
yǎn gējù, nín kàn bu kàn?
3) (1) 有没有昨天的报？
yǒu méiyǒu zuótiān de bào?
(2) 有没有后天的电影票？
yǒu méiyǒu hòutiān de diànyǐngpiào?
(3) 有没有《中国画报》？
yǒu méiyǒu "Zhōngguó Huàbào"?
4) (1) 去不去西安？
qù bu qù Xī'ān?
(2) 去不去故宫？
qù bu qù Gùgōng?
(3) 去不去华侨大厦？
qù bu qù Huáqiáo Dàshà?

4. 1) 抽不抽
chōu bu chōu
2) 喝不喝
hē bu hē
3) 买不买
mǎi bu mǎi
4) 送不送
sòng bu sòng
5) 演不演
yǎn bu yǎn

## 复习 (2) fùxí (2) Review (2)

3. 1) 星期一，星期二，星期三，星期四，星期五，星期六，星期日
xīngqīyī, xīngqī'èr, xīngqīsān, xīngqīsì, xīngqīwǔ, xīngqīliù, xīngqīrì
2) 一月，三月，五月，七月，八月，十月，十二月有三十一天。
Yīyuè, sānyuè, wǔyuè, qīyuè, bāyuè, shíyuè, shí'èryuè yǒu sānshíyītiān.
四月，六月，九月，十一月有三十天。
Sìyuè, liùyuè, jiǔyuè, shíyīyuè yǒu sānshítiān.
二月有二十八天或者二十九天。
Èryuè yǒu èrshíbātiān huòzhě èrshíjiǔtiān.

## 第十一课 dìshíyīkè Lesson 11

2. 1) (1) 这块手绢是谁的?
Zhèkuài shǒujuànr shì shuí de?
(2) 这把钥匙是哪位的?
Zhèbǎ yàoshi shì nǎwèi de?
(3) 这副手套是哪个同志的?
Zhèfù shǒutàor shì nǎge tóngzhì de?

2) (1) 这副手套是你的吗?
Zhèfù shǒutàor shì nǐ de ma?
(2) 这把钥匙是你的吗?
Zhèbǎ yàoshi shì nǐ de ma?
(3) 这块手绢是你的吗?
Zhèkuài shǒujuànr shì nǐ de ma?

3) (1) 是不是陈先生的?
shì bu shì Chén xiānsheng de?
(2) 是不是大伟的?
shì bu shì Dàwěi de?
(3) 是不是史密斯太太的?
shì bu shì Shǐmìsī tàitai de?

3. 1) 不是我的,是我弟弟的。
Bú shì wǒ de, shì wǒ dìdi de.

2) 不是我姐姐的,是她朋友的。
Bú shì wǒ jiějie de, shì tā péngyou de.

3) 不是我们家的,是我们学校的。
Bú shì wǒmen jiā de, shì wǒmen xuéxiào de.

4) 不是小刘的,是老张的。
Bú shì Xiǎo Liù de, shì Lǎo Zhāng de.

## 第十二课 dìshí'èrkè Lesson 12

2. 小,旧,短,颜色不好,样子不好,长短不合适,肥瘦儿不合适,大小儿不合适
xiǎo, jiù, duǎn, yánsè bù hǎo, yàngzi bù hǎo, chángduǎn bù héshì, féishòur bù héshì, dàxiǎor bù héshì

3. 1) 顾客: 太小。有大点儿的吗?
gùkè: Tài xiǎo. Yǒu dà diǎnr de ma?
顾客: 这件大小儿合适。
gùkè: Zhèjiàn dàxiǎor héshì.

2) 顾客: 太长。有短点儿的吗?
gùkè: Tài cháng. Yǒu duǎn diǎnr de ma?
顾客: 这件长短合适。
gùkè: Zhèjiàn chángduǎn héshì.

3) 顾客: 太瘦。有肥点儿的吗?
gùkè: Tài shòu. Yǒu féi diǎnr de ma?
顾客: 这双肥瘦儿、大小儿都合适。
gùkè: Zhèshuāng féishòur、dàxiǎor dōu héshì.

5. 1) 这个剧场很大。
Zhège jùchǎng hěn dà.
2) 这条鱼不贵。
Zhètiáo yú bú guì.

3) 那件上衣样子很好。
Nàjiàn shàngyī yàngzi hěn hǎo.

4) 颜色不太好。
Yánsè bú tài hǎo.

5) 这件大衣很合适。
Zhèjiàn dàyī hěn héshì.

## 第十三课 dìshísānkè Lesson 13

2. 1) 会，会
huì, huì

2) 能，能
néng, néng

3) 会，会
huì, huì

4) 能，能
néng, néng

## 第十四课 dìshísìkè Lesson 14

2. 1) (1) 服务员同志，有没有面包？
Fúwùyuán tóngzhì, yǒu méiyǒu miànbāo?

(2) 请问，有没有牛奶？
Qǐng wèn, yǒu méiyǒu niúnǎi?

(3) 今天晚上有没有电影？
Jīntiān wǎnshang yǒu méiyǒu diànyǐng?

2) (1) 你要什么酒，啤酒还是白酒？
Nǐ yào shénme jiǔ, píjiǔ háishi báijiǔ?

(2) 你去北京饭店还是民族饭店？
Nǐ qù Běijīng Fàndiàn háishi Mínzú Fàndiàn?

(3) 你们星期六还是星期天去颐和园？
Nǐmen xīngqīliù háishi xīngqītiān qù Yíhéyuán?

(4) 他还是你？
Tā háishi nǐ ?

3. 1) 来个拼盘。大拼盘。
Lái ge pīnpánr. Dà pīnpánr.

2) 来个汤。黄瓜汤。
Lái ge tāng. Huángguatāng.

3) 来碗面条。小碗的。
Lái wǎn miàntiáor. Xiǎo wǎn de.

## 第十五课 dìshíwǔkè Lesson 15

2. 1) 我头疼。
Wǒ tóu téng.

2) 我牙疼。
Wǒ yá téng.

3) 我肚子疼。
Wǒ dùzi téng.

3. 1) (1) 这个人身体很好。
Zhège rén shēntǐ hěn hǎo.

(2) 这个人脾气很好。
Zhège rén píqì hěn hǎo.

(3) 这个人中国话很好。
Zhège rén Zhōngguóhuà hěn hǎo.

2) (1) 你体温很高。
Nǐ tǐwēn hěn gāo.

(2) 他嗓子很红。
Tā sǎngzi hěn hóng.

(3) 我头很疼。
Wǒ tóu hěn téng.

(4) 他妈妈病很重。
Tā māma bìng hěn zhòng.

(5) 他 弟弟 白血球 很 高。
Tā dìdi báixuèqiú hěn gāo.

4. 1) (1) 有 点儿
yǒu diǎnr
(2) 点儿
diǎnr
(3) 有 点儿
yǒu diǎnr
(4) 一点儿
yìdiǎnr
(5) 有 点儿
yǒu diǎnr
(6) 有 点儿
yǒu diǎnr

2) (1) 还
hái
(2) 再
zài
(3) 还
hái
(4) 再
zài
(5) 再
zài
(6) 再
zài
(7) 还
hái

## 复习 (3) fùxí (3) Review 3

2. 1) 那个 面包 很 大。
Nàge miànbāo hěn dà.
那个 面包 是 大 的。
Nàge miànbāo shì dà de.

2) 小 王 的裤子 很 长。
Xiǎo Wáng de kùzi hěn cháng.
小 王 的裤子 是 长 的。
Xiǎo Wáng de kùzi shì cháng de.

3) 这 种 蛋糕 很 贵。
Zhèzhǒng dàngāo hěn guì.
这 种 蛋糕 是 贵 的。
Zhèzhǒng dàngāo shì guì de.

4) 那 张 桌子 很 高。
Nàzhāng zhuōzi hěn gāo.
那 张 桌子 是 高 的。
Nàzhāng zhuōzi shì gāo de.

5) 她 衣服 很 红。
Tā yīfu hěn hóng.
她 衣服 是 红 的。
Tā yīfu shì hóng de.

3. 1) 你 能 不 能 给 我 一个 信 封?
Nǐ néng bu néng gěi wǒ yíge xìnfēng?

2) 他 想 不 想 吃 糖醋鱼?
Tā xiǎng bu xiǎng chī tángcùyú?

3) 你 会 不 会 抽 烟?
Nǐ huì bu huì chōu yān?

4) 他 们 有 事儿 不 能 来 了。
Tāmen yǒu shìr bù néng lái le.

5) 一个 小 时 以后, 他会 不 会 去 文 化 宫? 一个 小 时 以后, 他会 去 文 化 宫 吗?
Yíge xiǎoshí yǐhòu, tā huì bu huì qù wénhuàgōng? Yíge xiǎoshí yǐhòu, tā huì qù wénhuàgōng ma?

6) 请 问, 半个 小 时 能 不 能 到 学 校? 请 问, 半个 小 时 能 到 学 校 吗?
Qǐng wèn, bànge xiǎoshí néng bu néng dào xuéxiào? Qǐng wèn, bànge xiǎoshí néng dào xuéxiào ma?

## 第十六课 dìshíliùkè Lesson 16

4. 1) 太阳 出 来了。 Tàiyang chū lai le.
2) 春 天 到 了。 Chūntiān dào le.
3) 他 上 哪儿了? Tā shàng nǎr le?
4) 我 的 表 停 了。 Wǒ de biǎo tíng le.
5) 我 老 了。 Wǒ lǎo le.

## 第十七课 dìshíqīkè Lesson 17

1. 1) 几岁了? Jǐsuì le?
2) 多 大 年纪 了? Duō dà niánjì le?
3) 多 大 了? Duō dà le?

2. 1) 几号 了? Jǐhào le?
2) 几点 了? Jǐdiǎn le?
3) 几 年级 了? Jǐ niánjí le?

3. 1) A: 您 的 普通话 真 不错 啊! Nín de pǔtōnghuà zhēn búcuò a! B: 不 行 啊。 Bùxíng a.
2) A: 您 的 英语 真 不错 啊! Nín de Yīngyǔ zhēn búcuò a! B: 不 行 啊。 Bùxíng a.
3) A: 您 的 记性 真 不错 啊! Nín de jìxing zhēn búcuò a! B: 不 行 啊。 Bùxíng a.

6. 1) 现 在 几点了? Xiànzài jǐdiǎn le?
2) 今 天 几号? Jīntiān jǐhào?
3) 今天 星期几? Jīntiān xīngqījǐ?
4) 大 伟 多 大 了? Dàwěi duō dà le?
5) 你 上 几 年级 了? Nǐ shàng jǐ niánjí le?
6) 小 江 几岁了? Xiǎo Jiāng jǐsuì le?
7) 老大爷，您 多 大 年纪 了? Lǎodàye, nín duō dà niánjì le?
8) 你 是 哪儿 人? Nǐ shì nǎr rén?

## 第十八课 dìshíbākè Lesson 18

2. 1) A: 学 校 都 xuéxiào dōu B: 没 都 去 méi dōu qù
2) A: 老 朋 友 都 lǎo péngyou dōu B: 没 都 去 méi dōu qù
3) A: 电 影 都 diànyǐng dōu B: 没 都 看 méi dōu kàn

4. 1) 你 今天 晚 上 去 哪儿了? Nǐ jīntiān wǎnshang qù nǎr le?
2) 他们 昨天 去 颐和园 了。 Tāmen zuótiān qù Yíhéyuán le.
3) 前 天 晚 上 你 作 什么 了? Qiántiān wǎnshang nǐ zuò shénme le?
4) 昨 天 你 去 故 宫 了 吗? Zuótiān nǐ qù Gùgōng le ma?
5) 他 前 天 没 来。 Tā qiántiān méi lái.

## 第十九课 dìshíjiǔkè Lesson 19

1. 1) 正 zhèng
2) 就 要 jiù yào
3) 正 zhèng

4) 就 要， 正
jiù yào, zhèng

5) 正
zhèng

2. 1) 看 报 呢
kàn bào ne

2) 在 写 信 呢
zài xiě xìn ne

3) 在 打 电话 呢
zài dǎ diànhuà ne

4. 1) 我 快 五十 了。
Wǒ kuài wǔshí le .

2) 他 们 快 要 离开 北京 了。
Tāmen kuài yào líkāi Běijīng le .

3) 我 们 正 说 王 先 生， 他 就 来 了。
Wǒmen zhèng shuō Wáng xiānsheng, tā jiù lái le .

4) 你 要 干 什 么?
Nǐ yào gàn shénme?

5) 他 们 没 在 谈 话。
Tāmen méi zài tán huà.

6) 我 进 去 的 时候， 他 正 在 写 信。
Wǒ jìn qu de shíhour, tā zhèng zài xiě xìn.

## 第二十课 dìèrshíkè Lesson 20

1. 1) 买， 看， 写， 寄， 借
mǎi, kàn, xiě, jì , jiè

2) 参 观， 看， 说， 看 望， 买， 喝， 吃， 叫
cānguān, kàn, shuō, kànwàng, mǎi, hē , chī, jiào

2. 1) 咖啡， 菜， 大衣， 啤酒， 饭， 茶， 信， 书， 单子， 外币
kāfēi , cài, dàyī , píjiǔ , fàn, chá, xìn, shū, dānzi, wàibì

2) 一 场 电 影， 一本 书， 几个 朋 友， 两 张 报
yìchǎng diànyǐng, yìběn shū, jǐge péngyou, liǎngzhāng bào

3. 1) 昨 天 我 出 去 看了 一个 亲戚。
Zuótiān wǒ chū qu kànle yíge qīnqi.

2) 他 下午 去 机场 了。
Tā xiàwǔ qù jīchǎng le .

3) 她 没 吃 晚饭 就 睡 了。
Tā méi chī wǎnfàn jiù shuì le .

4) 他 们 吃 饭 了。
Tāmen chī fàn le .

4. 1) 我 买了 一个 胶 卷。
Wǒ mǎile yíge jiāojuǎnr.

2) 我 买了 两 斤 大 虾。
Wǒ mǎile liǎngjīn dà xiā.

3) 我 买了 两 本 杂志。
Wǒ mǎile liǎngběn zázhì.

5. 1) 吃了 饭
chīle fàn

2) 看了 电 影
kànle diànyǐng

3) 游览 了 长 城
yóulǎn le Chángchéng

4) 买了 古玩
mǎile gǔwán

7. 1) 莉莉 买了 一本 杂志。
Lìli mǎile yìběn zázhì.

2) 我 们 昨 天 参观了 一个 学 校。
Wǒmen zuótiān cānguānle yíge xuéxiào.

3) 他 吃了 晚饭 就 出 去 了。
Tā chīle wǎnfàn jiù chū qu le .

4) 他 来了, 我们 就去 颐和园。
Tā láile, wǒmen jiù qù Yíhéyuán.

5) 上星期 他 每天 去 看 电影。
Shàngxīngqī tā měitiān qù kàn diànyǐng.

## 复习 (4) fùxí (4) Review 4

1. 1) 这些 古玩 是 赵 先 生 的? 这些 古玩 是 赵 先 生 的吗?
Zhèxiē gǔwán shì Zhào xiānsheng de? Zhèxiē gǔwán shì Zhào xiānsheng de ma?
这 些 古玩 是 谁 的? 这些 古玩 是 不是 赵 先 生 的?
Zhèxiē gǔwán shì shuí de? Zhèxiē gǔwán shì bu shì Zhào xiānsheng de?
这 些 古玩 是 赵 先 生 的 还是 张 先 生 的?
Zhèxiē gǔwán shì Zhào xiānsheng de háishi Zhāng xiānsheng de?

2) 他 们 有 一辆 新 汽车? 他们 有 一辆 新 汽车 吗?
Tāmen yǒu yíliàng xīn qìchē? Tāmen yǒu yíliàng xīn qìchē ma?
他 们 有 几辆 新 汽车? 他们 有 一辆 新 汽车 还是 旧 汽车?
Tāmen yǒu jǐliàng xīn qìchē? Tāmen yǒu yíliàng xīn qìchē háishi jiù qìchē?

3) 她 的 休息 时间 多? 她 的 休息 时间 多 吗?
Tā de xiūxi shíjiān duō? Tā de xiūxi shíjiān duō ma?
谁 的 休息 时间 多? 她 的 休 息 时间 多 不 多?
Shuí de xiūxi shíjiān duō? Tā de xiūxi shíjiān duō bu duō?
她 的 休息 时间 多 还是 少?
Tā de xiūxi shíjiān duō háishi shǎo?

4) 他 买了 两瓶 啤酒? 他 买了 两 瓶 啤酒 吗?
Tā mǎile liǎngpíng píjiǔ? Tā mǎile liǎngpíng píjiǔ ma?
他 买了 什么? 他 买 没 买 啤酒? 他 买了 两 瓶 还是 三瓶 啤酒?
Tā mǎile shénme? Tā mǎi méi mǎi píjiǔ? Tā mǎile liǎngpíng háishi sānpíng píjiǔ?

5) 他们 昨天 去 看 画展 了? 他们 昨 天 去 看 画展 了吗?
Tāmen zuótiān qù kàn huàzhǎn le? Tāmen zuótiān qù kàn huàzhǎn le ma?
他 们 昨 天 干 什么 了? 他们 昨 天 去 没 去 看 画展?
Tāmen zuótiān gàn shénme le? Tāmen zuótiān qù mei qù kàn huàzhǎn?
他 们 昨 天 去 看 画展 了 还是 去 看 电 影 了?
Tāmen zuótiān qù kàn huàzhǎn le háishi qù kàn diànyǐng le?

2. 1) 没 méi　2) 没，不 méi, bù　3) 不 bù　4) 不 bù
5) 没 méi　6) 没 méi　7) 没，不 méi, bù　8) 没 méi

3. 1) 昨 天 下午 没 签订 合同。
Zuótiān xiàwǔ méi qiāndìng hétóng.

2) 他上午写了信就出去了。
Tā shàngwǔ xiěle xìn jiù chū qu le.

3) 明天我看望了老朋友，就去琉璃厂。
Míngtiān wǒ kànwàngle lǎo péngyou, jiù qù Liúlíchǎng.

4) 昨天的电视我看了，真好！
Zuótiān de diànshì wǒ kàn le, zhēn hǎo!

5) 上星期你们参观故宫没有？
Shàng xīngqī nǐmen cānguān Gùgōng méiyǒu?

6) 王先生说他给买飞机票。
Wáng xiānsheng shuō tā gěi mǎi fēijīpiào.

## 第二十一课 dìèrshíyīkè Lesson 21

1. 1) (1) 他从他妹妹那儿来。
Tā cóng tā mèimei nàr lái.

(2) 我们从张大中同志那儿来。
Wǒmen cóng Zhāng Dàzhōng tóngzhì nàr lái.

2) (1) 我们到陈伯伯那儿去。
Wǒmen dào Chén bóbo nàr qù.

(2) 陈小姐到她朋友那儿去了。
Chén xiǎojie dào tā péngyou nàr qù le.

2. 1) 在家呢，在家，给谁
zài jiā ne, zài jiā, gěi shuí

2) 跟我，跟你，给我，给你，跟你。
gēn wǒ, gēn nǐ, gěi wǒ, gěi nǐ, gēn nǐ.

3. 1) 他们从日本来。
Tāmen cóng Rìběn lái.

2) 你到哪儿去？
Nǐ dào nǎr qù?

3) 他跟同学一起去打球。
Tā gēn tóngxué yìqǐ qù dǎ qiú.

4) 老刘要跟小陈说一件事儿。
Lǎo Liú yào gēn Xiǎo Chén shuō yíjiàn shìr.

5) 我给你们介绍一下儿。
Wǒ gěi nǐmen jièshào yíxiàr.

4. 1) (1) 没想到你来看我了。
méi xiǎng dào nǐ lái kàn wǒ le.

(2) 我正打算到你那儿去取票。
Wǒ zhèng dǎsuàn dào nǐ nàr qù qǔ piào.

(3) 没想到你已经买来了。
méi xiǎng dào nǐ yǐjīng mǎi lai le.

2) (1) 买六点五十的吧。
Mǎi liùdiǎn wǔshí de ba.

(2) 等一会儿吧。
Děng yíhuìr ba.

(3) 以后 再去吧。
Yǐhòu zài qù ba.

6. 1) 你从哪儿来?
Nǐ cóng nǎr lái?

2) 我到英国去。
Wǒ dào Yīngguó qù.

3) 王先生给孩子买了几本书。
Wáng xiānsheng gěi háizi mǎile jǐběn shū.

4) 你下午给我打电话吧。
Nǐ xiàwǔ gěi wǒ dǎ diànhuà ba.

5) 他跟你谈什么了?
Tā gēn nǐ tán shénme le?

6) 赵先生请老刘跟他们一起去香山。
Zhào xiānsheng qǐng Lǎo Liú gēn tāmen yìqǐ qù Xiāngshān.

## 第二十二课 dìèrshí'èrkè Lesson 22

1. 1) 我上邮局打长途电话去。
Wǒ shàng yóujú dǎ chángtú diànhuà qu.

2) 我上银行兑换外币去。
Wǒ shàng yínháng duìhuàn wàibì qu.

3) 我找小陈去。
Wǒ zhǎo Xiǎo Chén qu.

4) 我们到故宫去了。
Wǒmen dào Gùgōng qu le.

5) 他到这儿给赵先生送书来了。
Tā dào zhèr gěi Zhào xiānsheng sòng shū lai le.

6) 他打算晚上到老刘那儿送火车票去。
Tā dǎsuàn wǎnshang dào Lǎo Liú nàr sòng huǒchēpiào qu

2. 1) 下来 xià lai 2) 上去 shàng qu 3) 回来 huí lai 4) 进去 jìn qu

3. 1) 他们现在不回英国去。
Tāmen xiànzài bù huí Yīngguó qu.

2) 老刘要上楼去。
Lǎo Liú yào shàng lóu qu.

3) 请进屋来吧。
Qǐng jìn wū lai ba.

4) 莉莉,拿茶来呀!
Lìli, ná chá lai ya!

5) 上午张先生送来了一本《汉英词典》。
Shàngwǔ Zhāng xiānsheng sòng laile yìběn "Hàn Yīng Cídiǎn"。

4. 1) (1) 对不起
Duì bu qǐ
(2) 请等一会儿
Qǐng děng yíhuìr

(3) 对不起，请等一会儿。
Duì bu qǐ, qǐng děng yíhuìr.

2) (1) 怎么样？美
zěnmeyàng? měi

(2) 怎么样？热
zěnmeyàng? rè

(3) 怎么样？多
zěnmeyàng? duō

5. 1) 别客气。
Bié kèqi.

2) 这是我应该做的。
Zhè shì wǒ yīnggāi zuò de.

3) 这是我应该做的。
Zhè shì wǒ yīnggāi zuò de.

7. 1) come up 2) go up 3) come down 4) go down 5) come in
6) go in 7) come out 8) go out 9) come back 10) go back

## 第二十三课 dì'èrshísānkè Lesson 23

1. 1) (1) 西方人用刀子、叉子吃饭。
Xīfāngrén yòng dāozi, chāzi chī fàn.

(2) 电报纸用钢笔写。
Diànbàozhǐ yòng gāngbǐ xiě.

(3) 我们两个用汉语谈话。
Wǒmen liǎngge yòng Hàngyǔ tán huà.

2) (1) 他坐出租汽车去国际机场。
Tā zuò chūzū qìchē qù Guójì Jīchǎng.

(2) 约翰先生坐火车去上海。
Yuēhàn xiānsheng zuò huǒchē qù Shànghǎi.

(3) 他们一家坐飞机回英国。
Tāmen yìjiā zuò fēijī huí Yīngguó.

3. 1) 她一边走一边看。
Tā yìbiān zǒu yìbiān kàn.

2) 他们一边参观一边谈话。
Tāmen yìbiān cānguān yìbiān tán huà.

3) 很多人一边工作一边上学。
Hěn duō rén yìbiān gōngzuò yìbiān shàng xué.

6. 1) 中国人用筷子吃饭。
Zhōngguórén yòng kuàizi chī fàn.

2) 来北京游览的外国朋友都要到长城看一看。
Lái Běijīng yóulǎn de wàiguó péngyou dōu yào dào Chángchéng kàn yi kàn.

3) 来，为我们的友谊干一杯！
Lái, wèi wǒmen de yǒuyì gān yìbēi!

4) 我们得回去了。
Wǒmen děi huí qu le.

## 第二十四课 dì'èrshísìkè Lesson 24

1. 1) (1) 他住在人民剧场附近。
Tā zhù zài Rénmín Jùchǎng fùjìn.

(2) 他住在四层。
Tā zhù zài sìcéng.

(3) 票放在手提包里了。
Piào fàng zài shǒutíbāoli le.

(4) 手提包放在行李架上了。
Shǒutíbāo fàng zài xínglijiàshang le.

2) (1) 准备好了。 (2) 收好了。 (3) 办好了。
Zhǔnbèi hǎo le. Shōu hǎo le. Bàn hǎo le.

3) (1) 没借到。 (2) 没借到。 (3) 没收到。
Méi jiè dào Méi jiè dào. Méi shōu dào.

2. 1) 还有什么问题需要讨论的吗?
Hái yǒu shénme wèntí xūyào tǎolùn de ma?

2) 还有什么手续需要办的吗?
Hái yǒu shénme shǒuxù xūyào bàn de ma?

3) 还有什么工作需要研究的吗?
Hái yǒu shénme gōngzuò xūyào yánjiū de ma?

## 第二十五课 dì'èrshíwǔkè Lesson 25

1. 1) 谁 shuí 2) 哪天 nǎtiān 3) 哪儿 nǎr 4) 几点 jǐdiǎn 5) 什么 shénme

2. 1) 北京饭店比民族饭店高。
Běijīng Fàndiàn bǐ Mínzú Fàndiàn gāo.

2) 莉莉比大伟大三岁。
Lìli bǐ Dàwěi dà sānsuì.

3) 老丁比陈太太瘦一点儿。
Lǎo Dīng bǐ Chén tàitai shòu yīdiǎnr.

4) 这件上衣比那件样子好。
Zhèjiàn shàngyī bǐ nàjiàn yàngzi hǎo.

5) 这个国家跟那个国家差不多大。
Zhège guójiā gēn nàge guójiā chà bu duō dà.

6) 他年纪跟她差不多大。
Tā niánjì gēn tā chà bu duō dà.

5. 1) 你叫什么名字?
Nǐ jiào shénme míngzi?

2) 大伟管王大中叫叔叔。
Dàwěi guǎn Wáng Dàzhōng jiào shūshu.

3) 她叫陈先生讲中国人的称呼。
Tā jiào Chén xiānsheng jiǎng Zhōngguórén de chēnghu.

4) 请进来!
Qǐng jìn lai!

5) 请问，小张同志住哪儿？
Qǐng wèn, Xiǎo Zhāng tóngzhì zhù nǎr?

6) 老陈请小李一家去他家。
Lǎo Chén qǐng Xiǎo Lǐ yìjiā qù tā jiā.

## 复习 (5) fùxí (5) Review 5

1.

| | | |
|---|---|---|
| 长——短<br>cháng —— duǎn | 大——小<br>dà —— xiǎo | 冷——热<br>lěng —— rè |
| 对——错<br>duì —— cuò | 多——少<br>duō —— shǎo | 快——慢<br>kuài —— màn |
| 早——晚<br>zǎo —— wǎn | 新——旧<br>xīn —— jiù | 肥——瘦<br>féi —— shòu |
| 复杂——简单<br>fùzá —— jiǎndān | 上——下<br>shàng —— xià | 里——外<br>lǐ —— wài |
| 这——那<br>zhè —— nà | 以前——以后<br>yǐqián —— yǐhòu | 买——卖<br>mǎi —— mài |
| 来——去<br>lái —— qù | 进——出<br>jìn —— chū | 开始——结束<br>kāishǐ —— jiéshù |
| 出国——回国<br>chū guó —— huí guó | 国内——国外<br>guónèi —— guówài | |

2.

| | | | | |
|---|---|---|---|---|
| 1) 从<br>cóng | 2) 为<br>wèi | 3) 在<br>zài | 4) 让<br>ràng | 5) 跟<br>gēn |
| 6) 对<br>duì | 7) 在，跟<br>zài, gēn | 8) 让，在<br>ràng, zài | 9) 给，往<br>gěi, wàng | 10) 管，管<br>guǎn, guǎn |

3.
1) 他刚从小赵家来。
Tā gāng cóng Xiǎo Zhào jiā lái.

2) 我们明天下午去看小刘。
Wǒmen míngtiān xiàwǔ qù kàn Xiǎo Liú.

3) 晚上他们从中国回英国。
Wǎnshang tāmen cóng Zhōngguó huí Yīngguó.

4) 陈先生在那个书店买了一些历史方面的书。
Chén xiānsheng zài nàge shūdiàn mǎile yìxiē lìshǐ fāngmiàn de shū.

5) 后天晚上演杂技，王小姐给她朋友一张票。
Hòutiān wǎnshang yǎn zájì, Wáng xiǎojie gěi tā péngyou yìzhāng piào.

6) 小张跟大伟他们一起游览长城。
Xiǎo Zhāng gēn Dàwěi tāmen yìqǐ yóulǎn Chángchéng.

7) 他从他哥哥那儿回学校。
Tā cóng tā gēge nàr huí xuéxiào.

8) 前天我问了，今天上午我又问了。
Qiántiān wǒ wèn le, jīntiān shàngwǔ wǒ yòu wèn le.

9) 你们什么时候去广州？
Nǐmen shénme shíhòur qù Guǎngzhōu?

10) 时间 这么 晚 了，他们 一定 不 回来 了。
Shíjiān zhème wǎn le, tāmen yídìng bù huí lai le.

## 第二十六课 dì'èrshíliùkè Lesson 26

1. 1) 东边儿 dōngbianr 2) 北边儿 běibianr 3) 前边儿 qiánbianr 4) 后边儿 hòubianr

2. 1) 怎么 去？ zěnme qù? 2) 怎么 走？ zěnme zǒu? 3) 在 哪儿？ zài nǎr? 4) 哪儿是 nǎr shì

4. 1) 钟 楼 上边儿有 什 么？
Zhōnglóu shàngbianr yǒu shénme?

2) 剧 场 东边儿 是 烤 鸭 店。
Jùchǎng dōngbianr shì kǎoyādiàn.

3) 莉莉 坐 在 丁 伯母 右边儿。
Lìli zuò zài Dīng bómǔ yòubianr.

4) 前 边 儿 是 不 是 和平 新村？
Qiánbianr shì bu shì Hépíng Xīncūn?

5) 请 问，去 中 国 书店 怎么 走？
Qǐng wèn, qù Zhōngguó Shūdiàn zěnme zǒu?

6) 顺 这条 路 往 前 走，见了 路口 向 右 拐，就 到 了。
Shùn zhètiáo lù wàng qián zǒu, jiànle lùkǒu xiàng yòu guǎi, jiù dào le.

## 第二十七课 dì'èrshíqīkè Lesson 27

1. 1) 他 们一家 是 坐 火车 去 上 海 的。
Tāmen yìjiā shì zuò huǒchē qù Shànghǎi de.

2) 他 们 是 九月 五日 下午 到 北京 的。
Tāmen shì jiǔyuè wǔrì xiàwǔ dào Běijīng de.

3) 我 家 老大 是 去年 结 的 婚。
Wǒ jiā lǎodà shì qùnián jié de hūn.

4) 他 们 是 在 汽车站 分别 的。
Tāmen shì zài qìchēzhàn fēnbié de.

5) 我 是 在 中 学 学 的 汉语。
Wǒ shì zài zhōngxué xué de Hànyǔ.

2. 1) 我 很 高兴。 Wǒ hěn gāoxìng. 2) 我 高 兴 极 了。 Wǒ gāoxìng jí le. 3) 我 太 高 兴 了。 Wǒ tài gāoxìng le.

5. 1) 我 是 一九五二年 四月 回 到 国内 的。
Wǒ shì yījiǔwǔ'èrnián sìyuè huí dào guónèi de.

我 一九五二年 四月 回 到 了 国内。
Wǒ yījiǔwǔ'èrnián sìyuè huí dào le guónèi.

2) 老 张 是 在 美国 认识 老 刘 的。
Lǎo Zhāng shì zài Měiguó rènshi Lǎo Liú de.

老 张 在 美国 认识了 老 刘。
Lǎo Zhāng zài Měiguó rènshile Lǎo Liú.

3) 他是跟他爸爸一起去英国的。
Tā shì gēn tā bàba yìqǐ qù Yīngguó de.
他跟他爸爸一起去了英国。
Tā gēn tā bàba yìqǐ qù le Yīngguó.

## 第二十八课 dì'èrshíbākè Lesson 28

1. 2) (1) 雨下得很大。 Yǔ xià de hěn dà. (2) 车开得很快。 Chē kāi de hěn kuài. (3) 他回答得很对。 Tā huídá de hěn duì.

2. 1) 写得很好！您过奖了。 xiě de hěn hǎo! Nín guòjiǎng le.
2) 打得真好！ dǎ de zhēn hǎo!
3) 演得真好！ yǎn de zhēn hǎo!

3. 1) 怪不得他汉语说得这么好。 Guài bu de tā Hànyǔ shuō de zhème hǎo.
2) 怪不得我这么不舒服。 Guài bu de wǒ zhème bù shūfu.
3) 怪不得我没见到他。 Guài bu de wǒ méi jiàn dào tā.

4. 1) (1) 有时间没有 yǒu shíjiān méiyǒu
(2) 有别的活动没有 yǒu biéde huódòng méiyǒu
(3) 有事儿没有 yǒu shìr méiyǒu

## 第二十九课 dì'èrshíjiǔkè Lesson 29

1. 1) 穿着，戴着，端着，拿着
chuānzhe, dàizhe, duānzhe, názhe
2) 抽着，看着，念着，站着，拿着，写着
chōuzhe, kànzhe, niànzhe, zhànzhe, názhe, xiězhe
3) 坐着，长着，围着，穿着，笑着
zuòzhe, zhǎngzhe, wéizhe, chuānzhe, xiàozhe

2. 1) 站着 zhànzhe
2) 写着呢吗 xiězhe ne ma
3) 注意看着呢吗 zhùyì kànzhe ne ma
4) 写着 xiězhe

5. 1) 那个小孩儿身上穿着一件红毛衣。
Nàge xiǎoháir shēnshang chuānzhe yíjiàn hóng máoyī.
2) 外边儿下着大雨。
Wàibianr xiàzhe dà yǔ.
3) 今天的报在桌子上放着呢。
Jīntiān de bào zài zhuōzishang fàngzhe ne.
4) 他笑着对我招了招手。
Tā xiàozhe duì wǒ zhāole zhāo shóu.

## 第三十课 dìsānshíkè Lesson 30

1\. 1) 完 wán 2) 到 dào 3) 完 wán 4) 好 hǎo
5) 在 zài 6) 到 dào 7) 到 dào 8) 完 wán
9) 见 jiàn

## 复习 (6) fùxí (6) Review 6

1 1) 四号 楼 在 三号 楼 后边儿。
Sìhào lóu zài sānhào lóu hòubianr.
2) 汽车站 在 剧场 南边儿。
Qìchēzhàn zài jùchǎng nánbianr.
3) 我 的 房间 在他 的 房间 的 左边儿。
Wǒ de fángjiān zài tā de fángjiān de zuǒbianr.
4) 陈 先生 坐 在 张 先生 的右边儿。
Chén xiānsheng zuò zài Zhāng xiānsheng de yòubianr.
5) 她们 三个人 这样 站着：刘 小姐 在中间儿， 王 小姐 在 她 左边儿， 赵 小姐 在她 右边儿 。
Tāmen sānge rén zhèyàng zhànzhe: Liú xiǎojie zài zhōngjiànr, Wáng xiǎojie zài tā zuǒbianr, Zhào xiǎojie zài tā yòubianr.
6) 小 汽车 在 前边儿，大汽车 在 后边儿 。
Xiǎo qìchē zài qiánbianr, dà qìchē zài hòubianr.

2\. 1) 他俩 是 走着 去友谊 商店 的。
Tā liǎ shì zǒuzhe qù Yǒuyì Shāngdiàn de.
2) 上 星期 他 是 跟 王 伯伯 一起 参观 画展 的。
Shàng xīngqī tā shì gēn Wáng bóbo yìqǐ cānguān huàzhǎn de.
3) 他 是 中午 十二点 回 到 家 里 的。
Tā shì zhōngwǔ shí'èrdiǎn huí dào jiā li de.
4) 他 是 去年 国庆节 结 的 婚。
Tā shì qùnián guóqìngjié jié de hūn.
5) 你 是 跟他 在 哪儿 见 的 面？
Nǐ shì gēn tā zài nǎr jiàn de miàn?
6) 我 们 是 十年 前 的 秋天 分别 的。
Wǒmen shì shínián qián de qiūtiān fēnbié de.
7) 那些 书 是 九月 六号 借来的。
Nàxiē shū shì jiǔyuè/liùhào jiè lai de.
8) 他是在那个 大 商 店 买 的 电视机。
Tā shì zài nàge dà shāngdiàn mǎi de diànshìjī.

3\. 1) 的 de 2) 得 de 3) 的 de 4) 的，得 de, de

5) 得，得 de，de　6) 的，得 de，de　7) 的，得 de，de　8) 的，的，得 de，de，de

## 第三十一课　dìsānshíyīkè　Lesson 31

1. 1) 他 大学 毕业 几年 了？他 大学 毕业 多 长 时间 了？
Tā dàxué bìyè jǐnián le？Tā dàxué bìyè duō cháng shíjiān le？

2) 他 俩 认识 几个 月 了？他 俩 认识 多 长 时间 了？
Tā liǎ rènshi jǐge yuè le？Tā liǎ rènshi duō cháng shíjiān le？

3) 他 们 聊了 几个 小 时 了？ 他们 聊了 多 长 时间 了？
Tāmen liáole jǐge xiǎoshí le？Tāmen liáole duō cháng shíjiān le？

4) 他 出 去 几个 星期 了？他 出 去 多 长 时间 了？
Tā chū qu jǐge xīngqī le？Tā chū qu duō cháng shíjiān le？

5) 你 们 分别 几年 了？ 你们 分别 多 长 时间 了？
Nǐmen fēnbié jǐnián le？Nǐmen fēnbié duō cháng shíjiān le？

6) 你 们 等 他 几天 了？ 你们 等 他 多 长 时间 了？
Nǐmen děng tā jǐtiān le？Nǐmen děng tā duō cháng shíjiān le？

3. 1) 你 听了 多 长 时间 广播？ 听了 半个 钟头 的 广 播。
Nǐ tīngle duō cháng shíjiān guǎngbō？ Tīngle bànge zhōngtóu de guǎngbō.

2) 你 学了 多 长 时间 历史？ 学了 三年 半 的 历史。
Nǐ xuéle duō cháng shíjiān lìshǐ？Xuéle sānniánbàn de lìshǐ.

3) 你 研究了 多 长 时间 中 文？研究了 二十 多 年 的 中 文。
Nǐ yánjiūle duō cháng shíjiān Zhōngwén？Yánjiūle èrshí duō nián de Zhōngwén.

4) 你 坐了 多 长 时间 飞机？ 坐了 三个 小时 的 飞机。
Nǐ zuòle duō cháng shíjiān fēijī？ Zuòle sānge xiǎoshí de fēijī.

5) 你 画了 多 长 时间 画儿？ 画了 半天 的 画儿。
Nǐ huàle duō cháng shíjiān huàr？Huàle bàntiān de huàr.

## 第三十二课　dìsānshí'èrkè　Lesson 32

1. 1) 我 看 得 见。
Wǒ kàn de jiàn.

2) 今天 他 写 得 完 这些 汉字。
Jīntiān tā xiě de wán zhèxiē Hànzì.

3) 我 想，他 半 小时 讲 得 完。
Wǒ xiǎng，tā bàn xiǎoshí jiǎng de wán.

4) 我 看 这个 房间 坐 得 下 二十个 人。
Wǒ kàn zhège fángjiān zuò de xià èrshíge rén.

5) 这个 柜子 放 得 下 这些 衣服。
Zhège guìzi fàng de xià zhèxiē yīfu.

6) 我 十分钟 看 不 完 这篇 文 章。
Wǒ shífēnzhōng kàn bu wán zhèpiān wénzhāng.

7) 这 么 多 好吃 的 东西，我 一个 人 怎么 吃 得 完！
Zhème duō hǎochī de dōngxi，wǒ yíge rén zěnme chī de wán！

8) 他 还 是 个 小孩儿，看 不 懂 这个 电影 。
Tā hái shì ge xiǎoháir，kàn bu dǒng zhège diànyǐng.

2. 1) 看 得 完 看 不 完？ 看 得 完。看 不 完。
Kàn de wán kàn bu wán? Kàn de wán. Kàn bu wán.

2) 坐 得下 坐 不 下 四个人？ 那辆 可能 坐 不 下。
zuò de xià zuò bu xià sìge rén? Nàliàng kěnéng zuò bu xià.

3) 看 得见 看 不见？ 我 看 不见。
kàn de jiàn kàn bu jiàn? Wǒ kàn bu jiàn.

4) 听 得清楚 听 不清 楚？我 听 不清楚 。
tīng de qīngchu tīng bu qīng chu? Wǒ tīng bu qīngchu.

5) 记得 住 记 不住？ 我 记 不住 。
jì de zhù jì bu zhù? Wǒ jì bu zhù.

6) 到 得了 到 不 了？ 到 得 了。到 不 了。
dào de liǎo dào bu liǎo? Dào de liǎo. Dào bu liǎo.

## 第三十三课 dìsānshísānkè Lesson 33

2. 1) 没 读过。读过。我 读过 两 遍 了。
méi dúguo. dúguo. Wǒ dúguo liǎngbiàn le.

2) 没 研究过 。我 没 研究过 。你 研究过 吗？
méi yánjiūguo. Wǒ méi yánjiūguo. Nǐ yánjiūguo ma?

3) 没 买过。我 没 买过。你 买过 吗？买过 两次 了。
méi mǎiguo. Wǒ méi mǎiguo. Nǐ mǎiguo ma?mǎiguo liǎngcì le.

4) 没 听过 。我 没 听过。你 听过 吗？ 听过 两次 了。
méi tīngguo. Wǒ méi tīngguo. Nǐ tīngguo ma? tīngguo liǎngcì le.

5) 没 吃过。我 没 吃过。你 吃过 吗？ 我 吃过 两回 了。
méi chīguo. Wǒ méi chīguo. Nǐ chīguo ma? Wǒ chīguo liǎnghuí le.

6) 没 见过 。你 见过 吗？
méi jiànguo. Nǐ jiànguo ma?

3. 1) (1) 可不，今天 比 前 几天 冷 多 了。
Kě bù，jīntiān bǐ qián jǐtiān lěng duō le.

(2) 可 不，现 在 来 这儿旅游 的 人 比 两 年 前 多 多 了。
Kě bù, xiànzài lái zhèr lǚyóu de rén bǐ liǎngnián qián duō duō le.

(3) 可 不，他 现在 比 两年 以前 胖 多 了。
Kě bù，tā xiànzài bǐ liǎngnián yǐqián pàng duō le.

(4) 可 不，今年 这 种 皮鞋 比 去年 贵 多 了。
Kě bù, jīnnián zhèzhǒng píxié bǐ qùnián guì duō le.

(5) 可不，这次 来 这儿 的 收获 比 上次 大 多 了。
Kě bù，zhècì lái zhèr de shōuhuò bǐ shàngcì dà duō le.

2) (1) 哪儿啊！ 比 我 炒 的 香 多 了。
Nǎr a！ Bǐ wǒ chǎo de xiāng duō le.

(2) 哪儿啊！ 比 那 种 椅子 舒服 多 了。
Nǎr a！ Bǐ nàzhǒng yǐzi shūfu duō le.

(3) 哪儿啊! 比 那个 舞剧 的 音乐 好听 多 了。
Nǎr a ! Bǐ nàge wǔjù de yīnyuè hǎotīng duō le .

(4) 哪儿啊! 比 我们 知道 的 详细 多 了。
Nǎr a ! Bǐ wǒmen zhīdao de xiángxì duō le .

5. 1) 老 赵 去过 美国。
Lǎo Zhào qùguo Měiguó .

2) 老 赵 去 美国 了。
Lǎo Zhào qù Měiguó le .

3) 他 在 中国 住过 二十年。
Tā zài Zhōngguó zhùguo èrshínián .

4) 他 在 中 国 住了 二十年 了。
Tā zài Zhōngguó zhùle èrshínián le .

5) 老 陈 没有 老 张 大。
Lǎo Chén méiyǒu Lǎo Zhāng dà .

## 第三十四课 dìsānshísìkè Lesson 34

1. 1) (2); 2) (2); 3) (1); 4) (2); 5) (2); 6) (1)

2. 1) 四点半 左右
sìdiǎnbàn zuǒyòu

2) 五十本 左右
wǔshíběn zuǒyòu

3) 四十岁 左右
sìshísuì zuǒyòu

4) 半里 左右
bànlǐ zuǒyòu

5) 一米 左右
yìmǐ zuǒyòu

6) 二十斤 左右
èrshíjīn zuǒyòu

3. 1) 礼物 买 好 了 就 吃 饭。
Lǐwù mǎi hǎo le jiù chī fàn .

2) 东 西 收 拾 好 了 就 托 运。
Dōngxi shōushi hǎo le jiù tuōyùn .

3) 飞机票 取 来 了 就 拍 电报。
Fēijīpiào qǔ lai le jiù pāi diànbào .

4) 帐 结了 就 离开 饭店。
Zhàng jiéle jiù líkāi fàndiàn .

5) 衣服 穿 好 了 就 散步。
Yīfu chuān hǎo le jiù sànbù .

6) 信 写 完 了 就 寄。
Xìn xiě wán le jiù jì .

5. 1) 给 爷爷 奶奶 的 信 写 好 了 没有?
Gěi yéye nǎinai de xìn xiě hǎo le méiyǒu?

2) 那 两个 箱子 托运 了 吗?
Nà liǎngge xiāngzi tuōyùn le ma?

3) 收信人 的 地址 写 在 信封 上边儿。
Shōuxìnrén de dìzhǐ xiě zài xìnfēng shàngbianr .

4) 这 事儿怎么 办 呢?
Zhè shìr zěnme bàn ne?

5) 汉语 不 难 学。
Hànyǔ bù nán xué.

## 第三十五课 dìsānshíwǔkè Lesson 35

1. 1) 把 它 洗一下儿吧。
bǎ tā xǐ yíxiàr ba.

2) 把 门 和 窗 户 关 上 吧。
bǎ mén hé chuānghu guān shang ba.

3) 给 我 把 信 念念 吧。
gěi wǒ bǎ xìn niànnian ba.

4) 把 水果 、照相机 带 上 吧。
bǎ shuǐguǒ、zhàoxiàngjī dài shang ba.

5) 把 大衣 挂 在 柜子里,把 毛衣、衬 衫 放 在 箱子里 吧。
bǎ dàyī guà zài guìzili, bǎ máoyī、chènshān fàng zài xiāngzili ba.

6) 把 黄 油、面 包 拿来,把 菜、鸡蛋汤 端 来 吧。
bǎ huángyóu、miànbāo ná lai, bǎ cài、jīdàntāng duān lai ba.

2. 1) 就 这。来,把 它们
jiù zhè. lái, bǎ tāmen

2) 就 这。来,把 它们
jiù zhè. lái, bǎ tāmen

3) 就。来,把 电视
jiù. lái, bǎ diànshì

4) 就。来,把 它们
jiù. lái, bǎ tāmen

5) 就。来,把 它们
jiù. lái, bǎ tāmen

6) 就。来,把 它们
jiù. lái, bǎ tāmen

## 复习 (7) fùxí (7) Review 7

1. 1) 过,过
guo, guo

2) 过
guo

3) 了
le

4) 了
le

5) 了
le

6) 过
guo

2. 1) 他 教 中国 历史 教 了 三十 多 年 了。
Tā jiāo Zhōngguó lìshǐ jiāo le sānshí duō nián le.

2) 昨 天 晚 上,我 在 家 看 电视 看了 两 小时 四十分钟。
Zuótiān wǎnshang, wǒ zài jiā kàn diànshì kànle liǎng xiǎoshí sìshífēnzhōng.

3) 他 们 在 西安 呆了 十 三 天。
Tāmen zài Xī'ān dāile shísāntiān.

4) 这个 大型 舞剧 演了 三个 钟 头。
Zhège dàxíng wǔjù yǎnle sānge zhōngtóu.

5) 那个 包 裹 寄 了 一个 星期。
Nàge bāoguǒ jìle yíge xīngqī.

6) 我 们 去 剧院 走了 半个 钟 头。
Wǒmen qù jùyuàn zǒule bànge zhōngtóu.

7) 老 刘 去 上 海 出差，去了 两天 了。
Lǎo liú qù Shànghǎi chūchāi, qùle liǎngtiān le.

8) 他 在 北京 生活了 三十年 。
Tā zài Běijīng shēnghuóle sānshínián.

3. 1) 的，地 de, de　2) 的 de　3) 得 de　4) 的，得，的 de, de, de
5) 地 de　6) 得 de　7) 的 de　8) 地，的，得 de, de, de